Teaching Teens with ADD, ADHD & Executive Function Deficits

Second Edition

Best Wishes for
academic success &
Chris

Teaching Teens with ADD, ADHD & Executive Function Deficits

Second Edition

A Quick Reference Guide for Teachers and Parents

Chris A. Zeigler Dendy, M.S.

Woodbine House   2011

All rights reserved. Published in the United States of America by Woodbine House, Inc., 6510 Bells Mill Road, Bethesda, MD 20817. 800-843-7323. www.woodbinehouse.com

This book is a revised and expanded edition of *Teaching Teens with ADD and ADHD: A Quick Reference Guide for Teachers and Parents* (Woodbine House, 2000).

Photos on pages xiii, 1, 35, and 235 © 2000 Clark Hill.

Library of Congress Cataloging-in-Publication Data

Zeigler Dendy, Chris A.
  Teaching teens with ADD, ADHD & executive function deficits : a quick reference guide for teachers and parents / by Chris A. Zeigler Dendy. -- 2nd ed., Rev. and expanded.
        p. cm.
  Rev. ed. of: Teaching teens with ADD and ADHD / Chris A. Zeigler Dendy. 2000.
  Includes bibliographical references and index.
  ISBN 978-1-60613-016-2
  1. Attention-deficit-disordered youth--Education (Secondary)--Handbooks, manuals, etc. 2. Attention-deficit hyperactivity disorder--Handbooks, manuals, etc. I. Zeigler Dendy, Chris A. Teaching teens with ADD and ADHD. II. Title.
  LC4713.2.Z453 2011
  371.94--dc22
                                                           2011006833

Manufactured in the United States of America

10 9 8 7 6 5 4 3 2 1

Dedication

This book is dedicated to three special people:

- Our extraordinary son, **Alex Zeigler**, whose intellectual giftedness in combination with his baffling academic struggles inspired our twenty-year search for answers. It is our hope that by sharing lessons we learned the hard way that other families with children struggling with attention deficit disorders may enjoy a happier future. Thanks to my creative partnership with Alex and his technological genius, we have developed some wonderful resources together: our books, the ADD/ADHD Iceberg, our website, and last but not least, *Real Life ADHD!*, our new ground-breaking DVD.

- My partner on our "ADD/ADHD mission," **Tommy Dendy**, my perfect mate whose behind-the-scenes encouragement and unconditional support have allowed me to pursue the development of first-class materials related to attention deficits.

- My sister, **Dr. Billie Abney**, a retired chiropractor and adult with ADHD, who is now an award-winning classroom teacher. She has generously shared her innovative, exciting teaching strategies that could only come from her creative "ADD/ADHD brain." An amazingly tenacious person, she is completing her second doctorate soon.

A Word about Terminology

In this book, the abbreviation **ADD/ADHD** and the term **attention deficit disorder** are used when referring to both the hyperactive and inattentive types of attention deficit/ hyperactivity disorder. The abbreviation **ADHD** is used when information is specific to the hyperactive form of the disorder alone, and **ADD** is used for information specific to the inattentive form. (This is consistent with federal IDEA regulations, which contain the abbreviations ADD/ADHD, ADD, and ADHD. This is perhaps because they seem to more accurately convey the difference between the two conditions than AD/HD, the term used by the American Psychiatric Association for both forms of attention deficit disorder.)

I also chose to use the masculine pronoun "he" in some sections of the book and the feminine pronoun "she" in other sections so as not to imply that all teenagers with ADD or ADHD are either male or female.

Table of Contents

Acknowledgments

Special thanks go to my editor and seven incredible friends, my partners who have given unselfishly of their time and wisdom to help make this book better. I think one of the things that made my first book, *Teenagers with ADD and ADHD*, so successful is that I was smart enough to know that I didn't know all the answers. So, I called upon some very wise and talented colleagues to help make certain the second edition of this book was the absolute best we could make it.

Susan Stokes, M.F.A., an amazingly talented editor. Having worked together since 1993, Susan and I have developed a wonderfully comfortable working relationship. She has a phenomenal gift for spotting the rough spots in my writing and making them sound so much better. The comments I made about her in my first edition are still very true: she has taught me the beauty of writing with simplicity and clarity. My writing is greatly enriched by her gifted editorial touch.

Joan Helbing, M.S., a generous and talented educator and expert on ADHD. Joan is a psychometrist and expert on ADHD who consults directly with classroom teachers and provides frequent training sessions for regional educators in Wisconsin. She and I shared the exciting experience of being two of the three co-creators of the CHADD's Teacher to Teacher Training modules. Joan unselfishly shared mountains of teaching strategies and materials, never asking for personal credit.

Linda Sorensen, Ed.D. & **Linda Smith**, M.S., an amazing team of educators and advocates for students with ADHD. Both Lindas—who are Utah residents—have been extremely generous in sharing the innovative teaching strategies they have identified.

Sandra Dendy, B.S., a veteran middle school teacher who happens to be my daughter-in-law. As the mother of three children with ADHD and an outstanding teacher, she has generously shared favorite teaching strategies that she has found effective.

Mary Durheim, B.S., knows all things related to federal law governing education of students with ADHD. I absolutely could not have written Section Four on the federal laws without her. A Texan, Mary is always generous with her time, and was especially helpful in researching and sending specific legal citations regarding my questions.

Billie Abney, D.C., Ed.S. (ABD), my baby sister, an inspirational master teacher in Georgia (also an award-winning science teacher). Many of my most innovative teaching ideas have come from her nonconventional, energetic approach to teaching. As an adult with ADHD, her high energy and engaging teaching style have created student waiting lists for her classes.

Selena Latham Conley, Ed.S., an energetic dedicated special education teacher in Georgia. Selena, too, has been very generous in sharing her favorite innovative teaching strategies.

Thanks to earlier contributors: From the foundation that was laid in my first edition I will always be grateful to several contributors:

- Claudia Dickerson, Ph.D., veteran Georgia school psychologist;
- Kathy Hubbard Weeks, ADD/504 Consultant, Wisconsin;
- Pam Esser, Executive Director and educator, ADDA-SR, Texas.

A Special Thank You to Contributors

I am deeply indebted to so many wonderful, dedicated educators, mental health professionals, physicians, and parents who helped me greatly enrich the quality of both the first and second editions of this book. Many people went above and beyond the call of duty, spending significant time talking with me and sending me great materials. Special thanks to everyone who contributed.

Sections 1–3

- Billie Abney. High school science teacher, Sonoraville High School, Sonoraville, GA.
- Kathleen Allen, licensed counselor, Pediatric Center, Stone Mountain, GA.
- Virginia Brickman, former director of support services, DeKalb County Schools, Decatur, GA.
- Sara Clark, veteran teacher and horticulturist, Sonoraville High School, Georgia.
- Selena Conley, special education teacher, Trion, GA
- Don and Penny Dieckman, former Gwinnett CHADD officers, Leesburg, FL.
- Evelyn Green, former president of National CHADD, Chicago Public Schools, Chicago, IL.
- Opal Harris, teacher, Mesquite Independent School District (ISD); Past President ADDA-SR, Houston, TX.
- Joan Helbing, EEN diagnostician/trainer (ADD Consultant), Appleton Area School District, Appleton, WI.
- Susan Bible Jessup, former math teacher, Gainesville Middle School, Gainesville, GA.
- Carol Jordan, former teacher and reading coordinator, Lawrenceville, GA.
- Claudia Jordan, former remedial and developmental language arts teacher, including English as a second language (ESOL), Central Gwinnett High School, Lawrenceville, GA.
- Harold R. Meyer, Director, The ADD Resource Center, veteran ADHD advocate, New York, NY.
- Debra Moore, counselor, educational consultant, Carrollton, TX.
- Sherry Pruitt, clinical director, Parkaire Consultants, Alpharetta, GA.
- Susan Putman, former math teacher, Coppell Middle School North, Coppell, TX.
- Carol Robertson, former instructor, special education, WA.
- Linda Smith, educator, co-creator of CHADD Parent to Parent Training, Utah.
- Susie Smith, former middle school language arts teacher, Lullwater School, Decatur, GA.
- Linda Sorensen, secondary mentor leader, staff development department, Davis County School District, Bountiful, UT.
- Joan Teach, educational consultant, Decatur, GA.
- Ivan Vance, senior consultant (retired), Special Education Department, Region 10 ESC, Richardson, TX.
- Mary Kay Wells, former chairman, math department, Lincoln High School, Tallahassee, FL.
- Marcy Winograd, former chairman, English department, Paul Revere Middle School, Los Angeles, CA.

Sections 4-6

- Ann Abramowitz, ADHD researcher, Emory University, Decatur, GA.
- Judy Bandy, nurse, and Holly West Jones, ADHD coach and educator, co-creators of the innovative and successful Learning Lab Program, Eden Prarie, MN.
- William Buzogany, M.D., Medical Director of Lad Lakes Residential and Community Treatment Program; Consulting Psychiatrist, Ethan Allen School; Associate Professor of Psychiatry, University of Wisconsin, Madison, WI.
- Dee Doochin, Professional Certified Coach, and Holly Hamilton, Master Certified ADHD coach, ADD-UP, Nashville, TN.
- Dick Downey, former director of special education, Gwinnett County Public Schools, Lawrenceville, GA.
- Mary Durheim, educational consultant, Section 504 hearing officer, and mediator.
- Michael Epstein, professor of special education, University of Nebraska, Lincoln.
- Edward Gotlieb, M.D., director, Pediatric Center, Stone Mountain, GA.
- Peter Jensen, M.D., lead investigator, NIMH Multimodal Treatment Study of Children with ADHD (MTA); The REACH Institute, New York, NY.
- Dixie Jordan, coordinator, Project for Parents of Children with Emotional or Behavioral Disorders, PACER Center, Minneapolis, MN.
- Theodore Mandelkorn, M.D., director, ADHD Clinic, Mercer Island, WA.
- Ottie Manis, former guidance counselor, Ridgeland High School, Ft. Oglethorpe, GA.
- Nancy McDougall and Janet Roper, guidance counselors, Oakmeadow Elementary School, San Antonio, TX; coauthors of *Creative Coaching*.
- Jane Moser, former vice principal, Meadowcreek High School, Norcross, GA.
- Hill Walker, associate dean, Division of Special Education and Rehabilitation, Institute on Violence and Destructive Behavior, University of Oregon, Eugene, OR.
- Kathy Hubbard Weeks, former ADD Consultant/ Section 504 Coordinator, WI.
- Sharon K. Weiss, author and innovative behavioral consultant in private practice specializing in the challenging behaviors of middle and high school students; McLean, VA.
- Debbie Wilkes, former transition specialist, Richardson Independent School District, Richardson, TX.

Introduction

"Children do well if they can!"

—Ross Greene, Ph.D.
The Explosive Child & Lost in School

Over the years, as I have studied and come to understand the complexities of educating students with ADD and ADHD, I've come to the conclusion that our children really do want to do well in school. In essence, Dr. Greene has succinctly captured my beliefs in this one simple statement.

However, in spite of their best efforts, academic success often eludes students with ADD or ADHD, especially once they reach middle school or high school. Since 90 percent of them will face academic challenges at some point in their school career, it is our responsibility to play detective and figure out why they struggle. This book explains the reasons these students struggle, plus provides the guidance you need to take the next steps and implement a strategy to address their problems.

This inspiring guidance for teachers from Dr. Haim Ginott still holds true today, forty-five years after he first wrote this paragraph.

> *"I've come to the frightening conclusion that I am the decisive element in the classroom. It's my personal approach that creates the climate. It's my daily mood that makes the weather. As a teacher, I possess a tremendous power to make a child's life miserable or joyous. I can be a tool of torture or an instrument of inspiration. I can humiliate or humor, hurt, or heal. In all situations, it is my response that decides whether a crisis will be escalated or deescalated and a child humanized or dehumanized."*

—Haim G. Ginott
From *Teacher and Child: A Book for Parents and Teachers*

81 Concise Summaries. This book offers concise summaries of eighty-one key issues related to helping teenagers with ADD or ADHD succeed in school. Each of these summaries was written specifically with teachers and parents of middle and high school students in mind. The summaries address characteristics of ADD, ADHD, and executive function deficits and their impact on a teenager's school performance and behavior. Specific intervention strategies are provided for common behaviors and symptoms that interfere with academic success.

New Material. New to this second edition are essays on gifted students who also have attention deficits, tips for strengthening social skills, homework tips specifically for parents, plus an update on the latest brain research related to ADHD, learning, and behavior. In addition, I have significantly expanded several sections by incorporating the latest information regarding the profound impact executive function deficits have on both a student's academic performance and behavior. Although I first discussed the link between ADD, ADHD, executive function deficits, and school performance twelve years ago, the research proving the connection has only been available since the publication of the first edition of my book. This new edition will provide the guidance that both parents and teachers need to understand this major shift in conceptualizing the challenges linked to attention deficits.

Teacher and Parent-Friendly Information. As a former teacher, I understand the time-consuming extra demands that often interfere with the teacher's primary job of teaching students. Consequently, I have made this material as easy to use as possible. Teachers may wish to use these summaries as a quick reference when dealing with a specific aspect of ADD, ADHD, or executive function deficits. If needed, more general information on a broad variety of topics is available in my first book, *Teenagers with ADD & ADHD: A Guide for Parents and Professionals,* second edition (Woodbine House, 2006).

Clear Guidance for Both Parents and Professionals. Teachers, guidance counselors, school psychologists and social workers, administrators, and parents should find this material helpful. Educators may use these summaries to educate themselves, or they may elect to give them to parents who need more information on ADD, ADHD, and executive function deficits. Parents may also find the information helpful for their own teenager or extended family members, or they may decide to share selected summaries with interested teachers.

A Personal Message to Teachers from the Author

Interestingly enough, after spending half of my forty-year professional career in education and the other half working in the children's mental health field, I have come to believe that:

> *Succeeding in school is one of the most therapeutic things that can happen to a teenager. In fact, school successes may often be more helpful for students struggling with ADD or ADHD than an hour of counseling a week. In my opinion, teachers are often the critical factor determining the success or failure for students with this condition!*

Attention deficit disorder *can* be baffling and frustrating even for someone like me, a former teacher, school psychologist, and mental health counselor. Although some might consider me a parenting and teaching "expert," I must tell you that raising and educating a teenager with an attention deficit was the most difficult and humbling challenge of my life.

Fascinating New Research on ADHD. Research on the brain, ADHD, and executive functions in the last few years has offered wonderful insights into why students with ADHD struggle academically. The most astounding new research for me was the discovery that children with ADHD have a three-year delay in brain maturation. Bet you didn't know that. Here's another fact that may be news to you: these students have fewer chemicals known as neurotransmitters in the section of the brain that controls the ability to pay attention to boring school work. Now you know why a student can pay attention to video games but has trouble getting his homework done. The majority of our students with ADHD also have problems with executive functions that control their ability to be organized, get started and finish school work, and remember assignments. The impact of executive functions has a profound, but often unrecognized, impact on the schoolwork of students with ADHD: in fact, deficits in these key cognitive skills were the primary reasons for our younger son's school problems, not his ADHD symptoms.

Having ADD, ADHD, and executive function deficits puts students at risk for serious problems in school. According to the landmark National Institute of Mental Health study on ADHD, ***two-thirds of***

children with ADHD have at least one other coexisting problem. The more complex the attention deficit disorder, the greater the risk for a multitude of problems:

- learning disabilities,

- failing a grade,

- skipping school,

- suspension,

- expulsion, and, ultimately,

- dropping out of school and not going to college.

Consequently, the school years for these students are often the most difficult and challenging of their whole lives.

Teachers play a pivotal role in the ultimate success or failure of these teenagers in adulthood. When adults were asked how they coped successfully with an attention deficit disorder, they said, *"Someone believed in me."* **Teachers,** next to parents, ***were named as the most influential person*** who had helped them succeed. Clearly, teachers have a powerful impact on shaping each student's life! Remember, a teenager's self-esteem is often built upon the messages that adults give him.

Teachers are the mirrors by which students measure their self-worth and ability. When a teacher conveys the message that a teenager is capable and worthwhile, the teen believes the message. Unfortunately, the converse is also true: negative messages can quickly cause serious harm. Researchers tell us that a struggling child's self-esteem can be damaged as early as second grade. Successful adults who did poorly in school still recall painful memories and self-doubts about their school failures.

Our Family's Struggles. Sadly enough, both of our sons struggled in school even though they were very bright. During their early school years, it was obvious to me that both sons wanted to do well but couldn't sustain their good intentions. As a former teacher, it was painful for me to watch them struggle in school and yet not know the best way to help them.

Today, both our sons are college graduates and are doing well. Our older son is married, a father, and, every parent's dream, gainfully employed in a job he loves. Our younger son has just finished filming, editing, and producing our new DVD, *Real Life ADHD!*, which features 30 young people ranging in age from 12-22 from states all across the country. However, looking back, my husband and I were not so optimistic during our sons' high school years. We worried a lot and, at times, were very frightened for our teenagers.

How Can Teachers and Parents Help? Across the nation, thousands of families of teenagers with ADD or ADHD are wrestling with the same concerns that my husband and I faced: What does the future hold? Will our child be able to graduate from high school, let alone go to college or even hold down a job? The answer to these questions is an enthusiastic "yes"—if ***informed educators and parents intervene by providing extra supports and accommodations to help students succeed in school.*** My family has been lucky. Many extraordinary teachers, counselors, school psychologists, and administrators believed in our teenagers and helped them succeed.

I firmly believe that ***teachers want these students to succeed,*** but may not always fully understand the complexities of ADD, ADHD, and executive function deficits and the problems that often accompany these conditions, or know the most effective intervention strategies. My purpose in writing this book is to give teachers this information and make their jobs a little easier, in the process making school a more positive experience for students with attention deficits.

I believe that each teenager should have the opportunity to love learning and school, just as I did. So, as the humble parent of two sons and a daughter with ADD/ADHD, I want to share with you what I have learned about helping these teenagers succeed in school. Hopefully, these materials, developed during my forty-year professional career as a teacher, school psychologist, and mental health counselor, will help *you* be the inspirational teacher who makes a positive difference in the lives of teenagers with attention deficit disorders!

Sincere best wishes,
Chris Abney Zeigler Dendy

P.S. Please e-mail me and tell me which strategies in the book were particularly helpful, as well as those that did not work very well. I also welcome suggestions of new ideas or ways of improving these strategies. I look forward to hearing from you at chris@chrisdendy.com. To find out more about my family and me, you may visit our website at www.chrisdendy.com.

SECTION 1

The Basics

By understanding the basics about ADD and ADHD, teachers will be able to teach teenagers more effectively. Most teachers already know that attention deficit disorders are much more than just a case of simple hyperactivity. What often makes an attention deficit so complex is that two-thirds of students with the disorder have at least one other coexisting condition such as a learning disability, anxiety, or depression. Recent scientific findings also offer important insights into the academic performance of students with attention deficit disorders. For example, within the last few years, researchers found that deficits in executive functions cause major academic challenges for the majority of children with ADD/ADHD. In addition, experts also reported that key areas of the brain mature three or four years more slowly in people with ADD/ADHD than in children without attention deficits.

Because of the potential negative impact of untreated ADD and ADHD, the national focus on these disorders has expanded tremendously within the past few years. A brief overview of these initiatives will explain the profound impact these studies will have on how we teach and treat these students. Hopefully, this section will answer an important question for any remaining doubting educators: *"Does ADD/ADHD really exist or is it an excuse for a lazy student"*? I believe this section makes it clear that for some students **an attention deficit disorder is truly a disability.**

KEY STRATEGY: Be aware of the complexities of attention deficit disorders, especially coexisting conditions that can affect school performance:
- Address deficits in executive functions (disorganization, working memory deficits, and difficulty getting started).
- Address common learning challenges (memorization, writing essays and reports, and completing complex math problems).
- Teach skills and compensatory strategies.
- Talk with parents to determine whether the ADHD and any other coexisting conditions are being treated.

What Every Teacher Must Know about ADD and ADHD!

1. **ADD/ADHD occurs in nearly 10 percent of all children, according to a survey conducted by the Centers for Disease Control and Prevention (CDC).** However, rates of attention deficit disorder vary around the globe and in the United States. Within the U.S., reported rates vary from nearly 5 percent in Colorado to above 10 percent in several states, including Alabama, Kentucky, and West Virginia. Rates reported internationally include: 11.2 percent in India, 16.6 percent in the United Kingdom, 9.5 percent in Puerto Rico, 19.8 percent in Ukraine, and 15.5 percent in Saudi Arabia. Boys diagnosed with ADD or ADHD outnumber girls approximately two to one. The primary difference between girls and boys with attention deficits is that the boys are usually more aggressive and oppositional. Although comparable rates of attention deficit disorders are reported across all ethnic groups, African-American and Hispanic students are less likely to be diagnosed.

2. **ADD/ADHD is a complex neurobiological disorder.** Researchers believe that people with ADD/ADHD have a few structures within the brain that are smaller and that their *neurotransmitters,* the chemical messengers of the brain, do not work properly. The neurotransmitters norepinephrine and dopamine are thought to work inefficiently. Recent research has found that the critical frontal circuits in the ADHD brain mature three years later than in the non-ADHD brain. In addition, key executive skills located in the prefrontal area of the brain are deficient in many students with ADHD. Although experts don't agree upon the prevalence of executive function (EF) deficits, in 2010, Dr. Russell Barkley reported that executive function deficits occur in 89-98 percent of people with ADHD. Barkley states that the data from rating scales are a better indicator of real world functioning of executive skills than traditional tests for deficits in these areas. Fortunately, a new rating scale is now available to assess these deficits in adults: *The Barkley Deficits in Executive Functioning Scale.*

   In 2009, another major discovery was made regarding brain functioning and ADHD. Researchers found a reduced number of dopamine receptors and transporters in the nucleus accumbens (the "reward center" of the brain). This helps explain a common complaint from parents; students with ADHD have difficulty focusing on routine tasks like homework yet can play video games or text for hours. See Summary 2 for more details.

3. **There are two distinctly different types of attention deficit disorders.** Federal education law refers to those with hyperactivity and impulsivity as having ADHD (attention deficit hyperactivity disorder) and those who are predominately inattentive as having ADD (attention deficit disorder). However, AD/HD (attention-deficit/hyperactivity disorder) is the technically correct diagnostic label for both types of ADHD as established by the American Psychiatric Association. See Summary 5.

4. **All children with ADD/ADHD are not alike.** Symptoms of attention deficits may be mild, moderate, or severe, or may be combined with other conditions. This means adults will see variability in skills and maturity levels in these students.

5. **ADD/ADHD often occurs with other conditions.** According to information from a major study at the National Institute of Mental Health (NIMH), over two-thirds of children with ADHD have at least one other coexisting condition. See Figure 1. These conditions are often undiagnosed and untreated, yet may have a significant impact on academic performance.

   Most research has been done on *children* with attention deficits rather than adolescents. However, when information is gathered on teenagers, the occurrence of these coexisting conditions tends to be higher. When symptoms are severe and other conditions are present, both ADD and ADHD are much more challenging to the child, family, and school to diagnose and treat effectively.

Figure 1. Conditions That Occur with ADD/ADHD		
	Prevalence According to NIMH/ CDC, Biederman, Barkley	**Miscellaneous Studies on ADHD Teens**
Learning Disabilities	25% – [50%]	--
Tourette Syndrome	11%	--
Anxiety	34%	37%
Depression	(16%)	28%
Bipolar Disorder (BPD)	4%	12%
Substance Abuse	(5%)	40% (ADHD with CD only)
Oppositional Defiant Disorder	(40%)	59%
Conduct Disorder (CD)	14%	43%

(Percentages given above in parenthesis are from studies by Joseph Biederman, M.D., and Tim Wilens, M.D. CDC percentages are noted in [brackets]. All other percentages in the second column are found in Dr. Russell Barkley's book, Attention-Deficit Hyperactivity Disorder, third edition.)

6. **Students with ADHD have a three-year delay in brain development.** In 2007, experts reported that the ADHD brain is three years less mature than the non-ADHD brains. In addition, researcher Russell Barkley has reported that teenagers may have a ***30 percent delay in age-appropriate developmental skills*** needed in the real world. Developmental delays are reflected in poor organizational skills, weak self-help abilities, poor personal hygiene (bathing, brushing teeth), delayed motor skills, less independence, and problems keeping friends. Consequently, these students may seem less mature and responsible than their peers. The skill levels of a sixteen-year-old with ADHD may be more like those of an eleven-year-old.

7. **Several behaviors linked to brain functioning and development often accompany ADD/ADHD,** causing problems at home and school. Students with ADD or ADHD may experience problems with some, but usually not all, of these behaviors:

   - **Executive functioning difficulties:** Executive skills are critical for success in school, yet are lacking in many students with attention deficits. (See Section 3: Summary 31.) Working memory is one of the most important executive skills, yet one study found that some teens with ADHD have the working memory of seven-year-olds. Practical implications of deficits in executive skills include difficulty completing school work, writing essays, solving complex math problems, being organized, managing and being on time, and planning ahead. Students who have deficits in executive skills require more support and supervision than their peers. These deficits should be identified and accommodated, and, if appropriate, included in the IEP/504 Plan. Deficits in specific executive skills that interfere with the ability to do well academically may include:
     - **working memory and recall**: briefly holding facts in your head and manipulating them, sequencing information, and finally getting it organized and down on paper; memorizing facts;
     - **activation, arousal, and effort**: getting started, staying alert, and finishing work;
     - **complex problem solving**: taking the whole apart, analyzing it, and putting it back together;

- **control of emotions:** low frustration tolerance, emotional blow-ups;
- **internalizing language:** using "self-talk" to guide behavior.

■ **Forgetfulness and disorganization:** These problems interfere with completion of school work (forgetting to do or turn in homework and tests, forgetting due dates for projects, forgetting to stay after school or for detention). Since forgetfulness and disorganization are signs of executive function deficits and are also among the diagnostic criteria for ADD/ADHD, instructional strategies or accommodations may be required for both. See Summaries 32 and 33.

■ **Variability in school work** from day to day and class to class: This is often baffling to teachers and parents. Some days a student can do the work completely and accurately, but most days he can't. Without medication, the student's ability to force himself to continually refocus on school work is impaired. Researchers have linked difficulties focusing on routine school work to deficits in dopamine transporters and receptors. See Summary 2.

■ **Not learning from punishment and rewards** as easily as other children: This characteristic makes teaching and disciplining them more difficult. Misbehavior may be repeated. They don't seem to learn from their mistakes, prompting Dr. Sam Goldstein to observe that they "know what to do but don't always do what they know."

■ **An impaired sense of time:** Students with attention deficits may be tardy, have difficulty estimating time requirements, not allow adequate time for homework, school projects, and travel to school, and have difficulty planning ahead, especially for assignments and long-term projects. See Summaries 34-37.

■ **Sleep disturbances:** Over 50 percent of these students have trouble falling asleep and/or waking up. Furthermore, half do not get restful sleep and are still tired even after eight hours of sleep. Good sleep is critical for school success. For example, consolidation of important information in the brain occurs during sleep. Consequently, students may have difficulty memorizing information, plus be sleep deprived and sleep in class.

■ **Levels of alertness:** These students not only have trouble regulating levels of waking and sleeping, but also levels of alertness. They may have difficulty staying alert enough to listen and take class notes. Although fidgeting may be distracting to others, it can actually help teens with ADD or ADHD keep their brains alert.

■ **Difficulties with transitions and changes in routine:** Changing classes or schools, going to and returning from lunch or recess, having a substitute teacher, or riding the bus home after school are often high-risk times for misbehavior.

8. **ADD/ADHD runs in families.** Over 50 percent of children with attention deficits have at least one parent, and roughly 30 percent have a sibling, with the condition.

9. **Effective Treatment: both medication and exercise help.** Researchers advise us that medication works effectively for most children (75–92 percent). When medication works properly, schoolwork and behavior will improve significantly. Unfortunately, only 32 percent of people with ADHD take medication. However, with regard to key executive skills deficits—disorganization, forgetfulness, and an impaired sense of time—medication helps but doesn't correct all these problems. Medications do have other limitations: when the medicine wears off, inattention and lack of concentration are problematic. Shorter-acting stimulant medication often wears off during two crucial transition times: lunchtime and the bus ride home after school. Longer-acting medications often wear off during the all-important homework hours. See Summaries 54-59.

In his book *Spark*, John Ratey, psychiatrist and popular author, shows that exercise optimizes learning by increasing the neurotransmitters dopamine, serotonin, norepinephrine, and neurotrophins BDNF (brain-derived neurotropic factor). Ratey describes BDNF as MiracleGro for the brain. Neurotrophins are essential to the survival, growth, and differentiation of neurons. Although the benefit of exercise is not as significant as medication, exercise does improve learning, memory, executive skills, and growth of new brain cells. See Summary 3.

10. **Teenagers don't outgrow ADD/ADHD.** Symptoms of attention deficits often present lifelong challenges. The primary observable difference in teenagers is that they may become less hyperactive than they were as children. However, the hyperactivity is often replaced by restlessness. Roughly 65 percent will face some challenges at work, with family, and relationships due to continuing symptoms of attention deficits. A lucky 10-20 percent of adults have no ADD/ADHD symptoms and are indistinguishable from adults without the disorder. Unfortunately, the remaining group of adults face more serious challenges, including possible drug involvement, legal problems such as failing to file income taxes or forgetting to pay speeding tickets, bills, or child support, or serious brushes with law enforcement (arrests for DUI, impulsive check forgery, or fraudulent use of a credit card).

Adults often find a career that is compatible with their personality, so symptoms don't present problems for most adults with ADD or ADHD in the workplace. In addition, the brain matures and symptoms become less severe with age, and the adult learns new skills or learns to compensate. For some adults, but not all, continuing to take medication will be a necessity.

ADD and ADHD Are Neurobiological Disorders

Scientists have made great progress in research on attention deficit disorders in the last ten years. However, research is still in its infancy. Although researchers still do not know exactly what causes this condition, they do know that it is often inherited. A couple of tests—the PET Scan (positron emission tomography) and the MRI (magnetic resonance imaging)—offer scientific evidence that ADHD is a neurobiological disorder that results in significant maturational delays in attention and key executive skills. (Most of this research has been conducted on ADHD, rather than ADD.) During the next few years, researchers should discover even more information about this challenging condition. Here is what researchers have learned so far:

- **Cerebral blood flow is reduced** in some parts near the front of the brain. These areas of the brain control several functions: 1) attention, 2) impulsivity—the ability to "stop and think" before acting, 3) sensitivity to rewards and punishment, 4) emotions, and 5) memory.

- **There is underactivity in the brain.** Problems with neurotransmitters such as dopamine and norepinephrine may cause underactivity in the brain, according to studies performed in the early 1990s at the National Institute of Mental Health (NIMH). (Neurotransmitters are chemicals in the brain that help messages travel from one brain cell to the next. See Summary 3.) NIMH researcher Dr. Alan Zametkin used a PET scan to study adults and teenaged girls with ADHD while they were involved in thinking tasks. He found reduced blood flow and lower metabolism, or absorption, of glucose in the frontal areas of the central nervous system of the

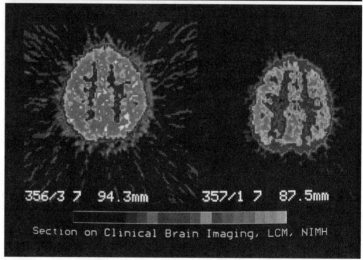

Figure 2. PET Scan of Cerebral Glucose Metabolism in Adults with ADHD

Photo courtesy of Alan J. Zametkin, M.D., National Institutes of Health.

brain. Figure 2 shows the reduced brain activity in an adult with ADHD. In the original color picture, the non-ADHD brain had larger areas of red and green indicating increased activity in the brain during a thinking task. In contrast, the ADHD brain had reduced brain activity as indicated by the two enlarged dark areas near the center of the brain. When people with ADHD take stimulant medications such as Ritalin, Concerta, or Adderall, PET scans show an increase of activity in these areas of the brain.

- **Several genes that are linked to ADD/ADHD have been identified.** Out of thirteen or so genes that have been linked to attention deficits, three are of primary interest to researchers: two dopamine receptor genes—DRD2 and DRD4—and a dopamine transporter gene—DAT1. The receptors and transporters control the level of dopamine in each neuron. (Dopamine is a brain chemical that plays a major role in regulating attention, concentration, movement, behavior, response to punishment and reward, working memory, learning, analysis of problem and assignments, problem solving, and the ability to store information in long-term memory.)

A Harvard researcher found that people with attention deficits have 70 percent higher levels of dopamine transporters in the spaces between the ends (synapses) of individual neurons. Because these receptors and transporters are not working properly, the right levels of dopamine are not available in the neurons. Researchers have shown that inefficient levels of dopamine interfere with attention, learning, and proper behavior. For a more detailed, yet easy-to-read explanation, see Appendix 8, *A Bird's-Eye View of Life with ADD and ADHD (Dendy and Zeigler, 2007).*

- **Three sections of the brain are smaller** in people with ADHD, according to results of magnetic resonance imaging (MRI) studies: the cerebellum, caudate nucleus, and corpus callosum. No brain damage was found to these sections; they were simply smaller. The reduced volume was primarily attributed to smaller areas of white matter, which contain the connections between the nerve cell bodies located in the brain's gray matter. Gray matter is associated with intellectual and motor tasks; white matter might be compared to telephone lines that carry messages between telephones (neurons). Researchers report that these sections of the brain affect: 1) alertness, 2) executive function, 3) the ability to control shifts from one task to another, and 4) the ability to assist with the transfer of information between neurons.

- **There is a three-year delay in the maturity of ADHD brains.** In 2007, Dr. Phillip Shaw and other researchers at the National Institute of Health (NIH) found a significant delay in the development of critical frontal areas in the ADHD brain in children ages seven to ten. This part of the brain controls thinking, language, and impulse control. On average, brain development of children with ADHD was three years behind their peers who did not have ADHD.

- **There is a 30 percent delay in the development of executive skills.** According to Dr. Russell Barkley, the development of critical executive functions (EF) are delayed by approximately 30 percent in many students with ADHD. This means that a 16-year-old may behave more like an 11-year-old. According to Dr. Barkley, EF delays occur in an estimated 89-98 percent of people with ADHD.

- **There are deficits in the "brain's reward system" that are linked to the inattention and reduced motivation associated with ADHD.** Through the use of a PET scan, Dr. Nora Volkow, Jim Swanson, and colleagues at NIDA found that people with ADHD had reduced dopamine receptors and transporters in the two areas of the brain that are involved in reward and motivation—the nucleus accumbens and the caudate nucleus. These deficits help explain why students have difficulty sustaining interest in boring school work, yet are riveted by video games or other high-interest tasks. The take-home message for teachers is that high-interest teaching strategies for school work are critical for improving academic performance.

- **Three frontal lobe circuits of the brain mature at a slower pace.** According to Dr. Martha Denckla, a leading neuroscientist, three major fontal lobe circuits show weakness in the ADHD brain. Simply put, the controls in these circuits are synonymous with executive functions. Consequently, the delays in these areas significantly affect the development of executive skills in students with ADHD. The three areas and the approximate maturational timelines for people **who do not have** ADHD are as follows:

  1. Motor control—age 15: Three parts of the brain that have the greatest impact on ADHD are also the areas that control motor activities. Consequently many of these students may have poor motor coordination. Furthermore they may have difficulty starting, maintaining, stopping, and inhibiting movement when instructed to do so. For example, some students can't sit still in class or in a test-taking situation; they may mash the wrong button even though they were instructed to inhibit their response.

     Tips: Aerobic exercise, strengthening, and stretching can be very helpful by priming the "executive pump." Specific activities suggested by Dr. Denckla include martial arts, yoga, dance, swimming, and drumming.

  2. Cognitive control—age 25: Cognitive control refers to a student's ability to selectively pay attention to important information and use key executive skills including

working memory, shifting from one task to another, and planning, sequencing, and organizing information. Before anything can be learned, the brain must selectively shift from an old task and pay attention to a new task. For example, a student must shift from listening to a teacher and then start working on algebra problems. First, however, the brain must prepare to shift (this is known as "response preparation"). This action sounds so easy, but students with ADHD have a delayed response preparation time and have difficulty actually getting started on the required task.

Tips: Denckla suggests providing more structure to the student, giving proactive support, and "engineering his environment for success." In addition, Barkley reminds us that these students need reminders that are external, either something they can see or hear.

3. Combined emotional and cognitive control—age 32: Simply put, by this age most people without ADHD have a brain that is fully mature in all areas of their lives. Most adults in their thirties are therefore better able to process information on an emotional level and use that knowledge to respond appropriately to social, family, and work situations in a flexible and adaptive manner. According to Denckla, maturation in this area of the brain enables the adult to control expression of his emotions while being fully aware of experiencing the emotion. For adults with ADHD, life is much better at this age, but there may still be struggles with executive skills such as getting started, finishing tasks, planning ahead for the future, and controlling emotions.

Tips: Establishing external reminders is critically important; for example: setting phone or computer alarms as a prompt to pay bills or pick up children. Changing the environment is also helpful; set up automatic bill pay so bills are not forgotten. Practice strategies for handling emotional situations: count to ten or remove yourself from the situation.

It is critically important for adults and students to reframe this information as positively as we can: the brains of children with ADHD will continue to mature well into the thirties. Hang in there! Things will get better in the future—just not soon enough to suit most parents and teachers.

Resources

Barkley, Russell A. *Attention-Deficit Hyperactivity Disorder: A Handbook for Diagnosis and Treatment.* Third edition. New York, NY: Guilford Press, 2006.

Barkley, Russell A. Week-long ADHD Workshop. 26th Annual Cape Cod Summer Symposia. Cape Cod, MA, 2004.

Denckla, Martha B. "The Syndrome Called ADHD and the Symptom 'Attention Deficit' Overlap Only Partially." Presented at the 26th Annual Learning and the Brain Conference. Washington, DC, 2010.

Dendy, Chris A.Z. and Zeigler, Alex. *A Bird's-Eye View of Life with ADD and ADHD.* Cedar Bluff, AL: Cherish the Children, 2007.

Prince, Jefferson B. "An Update on the Neurobiology of Attention Deficit Hyperactivity Disorders." Presented at ADHD: Collaborating4Success! conference. University of Alabama, Tuscaloosa, AL, 2010.

Ratey, John. "A User's Guide to the Brain: Through the Lens of Attention." Presented at ADDA Conference. Atlanta, Georgia, 2000.

Ratey, John. *Spark: The Revolutionary New Science of Exercise and the Brain.* New York, NY: Little, Brown and Company, 2008.

Shaw, Philip, et al. "Attention-Deficit/Hyperactivity Disorder Is Characterized by a Delay in Cortical Maturation." *Proceedings of the National Academy of Sciences,* Dec. 11, 2007, Vol.104, No. 50:19663-4.

Swanson, James, et al. "Cognitive Neuroscience of Attention Deficit Hyperactivity Disorder and Hyperkinetic Disorder." *Current Opinion-in–Neurobiology*, April 1998, Vol. 8, No. 2: 263-71.

Volkow, N.D., Swanson, J.M., et al. "Evaluating Dopamine Reward Pathway in ADHD: Clinical Implications." *Journal of the American Medical Association,* Sept. 9, 2009, Vol. 302, No. 10:1084-91.

SUMMARY 3

Neurotransmitters Can Make or Break a Good School Day!

For better or worse, why do teenagers behave as they do? Do students with attention deficits get up each morning and maliciously say, "Today my goal is to ruin Mrs. Smith's day"? Of course not, but after a tough day at school, teachers may sometimes wonder.

Although you probably haven't thought much about neurotransmitters, they play a major role in determining whether you, the teacher, have a good day at school. Researchers have found that neurotransmitters have a profound impact on shaping our day-to-day behavior, including our mood, ability to pay attention, memory, sociability, and sleep habits.

When brain neurotransmitters are working properly, students:
- pay attention,
- start working promptly,
- stick with routine assignments and complete work,
- remember and comply with teacher requests, and
- are well behaved.

When neurotransmitters are too low or inefficient and don't work properly (as in students with attention deficits), teachers may observe that students:
- don't listen,
- have difficulty getting started on tasks,
- don't maintain focus and complete routine class work,
- are irritable and argumentative,
- sleep in class due to lack of restful sleep at night.

Academically, students:
- have great difficulty maintaining focus on routine school work,
- have difficulty comprehending what they read,
- can't memorize isolated facts such as multiplication tables,
- have trouble organizing their thoughts to write an essay,
- have difficulty holding facts in their heads while working a complex math problem, or quickly retrieving information from stored memory.

How Do Neurotransmitters Work?

Since deficits in neurotransmitters are thought to contribute to symptoms of ADD and ADHD, let's look at how neurotransmitters are *supposed* to work.

The human nervous system has trillions of nerve cells or *neurons* that carry messages throughout the body. These messages may tell a teenager to listen, pay attention when the teacher is talking, remember the assignment, and stick with the task until it is finished.

Technically speaking, the nerve cells carry *impulses* (nerve signals) from one end of the cell to the other—from the dendrite to the axon. There is a space between neurons, known as a *synaptic cleft*. Since the axon and dendrites of adjacent neurons do not touch, messages must cross this synaptic space. Neurotransmitters, the chemical messengers of the brain, are released at the synapse to help the message move across to the *receptor sites* on the neighboring neuron.

Children with ADHD start out life with less white brain matter (connective tissues that carry messages) than their peers. Reduced white matter makes it more difficult for the brain to send and receive internal messages to pay attention, get started, and complete work. When an attention deficit is present, researchers believe that messages move down the neuron, but stop and don't always cross the synapse to the next neuron. This disruption is most likely caused by *a reduced amount of white matter and a chemical inefficiency in neurotransmitters,* which interrupts the normal flow of messages throughout the body. Researchers explain that ADHD brains have 70 percent more dopamine transporters that whisk the dopamine away from the synapse before it can trigger the receptor site to open and accept the message. Consequently, the message cannot cross to the next neuron.

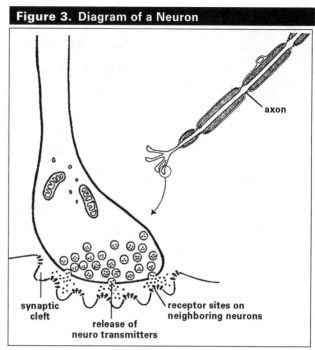

Figure 3. Diagram of a Neuron

axon

synaptic cleft

release of neuro transmitters

receptor sites on neighboring neurons

From Know Your Brain, NIH Publication No. 92-3440-a.

Neurotransmitters That Affect ADD and ADHD

Three neurotransmitters are thought to have a strong impact on behaviors considered typical of attention deficit disorders: norepinephrine, dopamine, and, to a lesser degree, serotonin.

- *Dopamine:* Research has shown that when the neurotransmitter dopamine is **too low,** a teenager is inattentive and distractible, has difficulty sticking with routine tasks and completing the job, thinking ahead, and delaying a response, or may be cognitively impulsive. But there can also be problems when dopamine is **too high;** in this case, a teenager may have *obsessive compulsive disorder (OCD)* and attend to and repeat behavior too often. (Researchers suspect that super-sensitivity to dopamine may be an underlying cause of both OCD and Tourette syndrome, discussed in Summary 78.)

- *Norepinephrine:* When norepinephrine is **too low,** a teenager may be indifferent, depressed, or aggressive. If it is **too high,** the teenager may tend to be a thrill seeker or be impulsively aggressive.

- *Serotonin:* Serotonin gives us a sense of well-being. When serotonin is **too low,** a person is more irritable and aggressive. In fact, when serotonin was lowered intentionally in a research study, normally tranquil people became more aggressive. Serotonin also affects a child's ability to fall asleep and achieve a deep, restful, restorative sleep.

The Impact of ADHD Medications and Exercise on Neurotransmitters

Stimulant medications such as Ritalin, Concerta, and Adderall are so called because they stimulate activity in the central nervous system, often increasing the level of neurotransmitter activity and blood flow in the brain. These medications are known to promote the efficient use of dopamine and norepinephrine—the very neurotransmitters that appear to be involved in attention deficits. Strattera, a nonstimulant medication, enhances the effectiveness of norepinephrine.

Dr. John Ratey has spearheaded the movement to educate us about the role that exercise plays in enhancing brain functioning. Dr. Ratey explains that exercise improves learning, memory, and executive skills, plus stimulates growth of new brain cells. Specifically, exercise increases the neurotransmitters serotonin, dopamine, and the neurotrophin BDNF (brain-derived neurotropic factor). (Neurotrophins are proteins that encourage the growth and survival of neurons.) Ratey refers to BDNF as MiracleGro for brain cells. Exercise is a great adjunct to medication; however, medication remains the most effective treatment for improving attention and concentration.

The ADD/ADHD Iceberg

The characteristics of ADD and ADHD may be compared with an iceberg: *only the tip of the problem is visible!* Typically, teachers and parents see the obvious "tip" first: the behavior problems, such as failing to complete homework, talking back, arguing, and other impulsive misbehavior. Yet for so many teenagers, an attention deficit is much more complex than just these obvious behaviors. School is often incredibly challenging because of their inattention, disorganization, executive function deficits, and other serious learning problems. Remember, *over two-thirds of students with an attention deficit disorder have a least one other diagnosable condition* that often has a significant impact on school performance.

Conditions that commonly accompany ADD or ADHD, including specific learning disabilities, deficits in executive functions, depression, anxiety, bipolar disorder, and sleep disturbances, often are overlooked by treatment professionals and may *never* be treated. These coexisting conditions are discussed in detail in Summary 78, "When Teens Continue to Struggle in School."

When you think of attention deficit disorder, visualize this iceberg with only one-eighth of its mass visible above the water line. As is true of icebergs, often the most challenging aspects of ADD and ADHD are hidden beneath the surface.

Teachers may find the blank ADD/ADHD Iceberg (Appendix A1) helpful in identifying areas of concern for the student. In preparing for teacher-parent staff meetings, several groups such as CHADD's Parent to Parent Training ask teachers and parents to fill in a similar blank ADD/ADHD Iceberg to help them better understand the child's ADHD.

Figure 4. The ADD/ADHD Iceberg

THE ADD/ADHD ICEBERG
Only 1/8 of an iceberg is visible!!
Most of it is hidden beneath the surface!!

THE TIP OF THE ICEBERG:
The Obvious ADD/ADHD Behaviors

IMPULSIVITY
Lacks self-control   Difficulty awaiting turn
Blurts out   Interrupts
Tells untruths   Intrudes
Talks back   Loses temper

HYPERACTIVITY
Restless   Talks a lot
Fidgets   Can't sit still
Runs or climbs a lot   Always on the go

INATTENTION
Disorganized   Doesn't follow through
Doesn't pay attention   Is forgetful
Doesn't seem to listen   Distractible
Makes careless mistakes   Loses things
Doesn't do school work

HIDDEN BENEATH THE SURFACE:
The Not So Obvious Behaviors!!

NEUROTRANSMITTER DEFICITS IMPACT BEHAVIOR
Inefficient levels of neurotransmitters,
dopamine, norepinephrine, & serotonin,
result in reduced brain activity
on thinking tasks.

WEAK EXECUTIVE FUNCTIONING
Working Memory and Recall
Activation, Alertness, and Effort
Internalizing language
Controlling emotions
Complex Problem Solving

IMPAIRED SENSE OF TIME
Doesn't judge passage of time accurately
Loses track of time
Often late
Doesn't have skills to plan ahead
Forgets long-term projects or is late
Difficulty estimating time required for tasks
Difficulty planning for future
Impatient
Hates waiting
Time creeps
Homework takes forever
Avoids doing homework

SLEEP DISTURBANCE (56%)
Doesn't get restful sleep
Can't fall asleep
Can't wake up
Late for school
Sleeps in class
Sleep deprived
Irritable
Morning battles with parents

THREE YEAR DELAY IN BRAIN MATURATION
30% developmental delay
Less mature
Less responsible
18 yr. old acts like 12

NOT LEARNING EASILY FROM REWARDS AND PUNISHMENT
Repeats misbehavior
May be difficult to discipline
Less likely to follow rules
Difficulty managing his own behavior
Doesn't study past behavior
Doesn't learn from past behavior
Acts without sense of hindsight
Must have immediate rewards
Long-term rewards don't work
Doesn't examine his own behavior
Difficulty changing his behavior

COEXISTING CONDITIONS
2/3 have at least one other condition
Anxiety (34%)   Depression (29%)
Bipolar (12%)   Substance Abuse (5-40%)
Tourette Disorder (11%)
Obsessive Compulsive Disorder (4%)
Oppositional Defiant Disorder (54-67%)
Conduct Disorder (22-43%)

SERIOUS LEARNING PROBLEMS (90%)
Specific Learning Disability (25-50%)
Poor working memory   Can't memorize easily
Forgets teacher and parent requests
Slow math calculation (26%)
Spelling Problems (24%)
Poor written expression (65%)
Difficulty writing essays
Slow retrieval of information
Poor listening and reading comprehension
Difficulty describing the world in words
Difficulty rapidly putting words together
Disorganization
Slow cognitive processing speed
Poor fine motor coordination
Poor handwriting
Inattention   Impulsive learning style

LOW FRUSTRATION TOLERANCE
Difficulty Controlling Emotions
Short fuse   Emotionally reactive
Loses temper easily
May give up more easily
Doesn't stick with things
Speaks or acts before thinking
Concerned with own feelings
Difficulty seeing others' perspective
May be self-centered
May be selfish

**** ***********

ADD/ADHD is often more complex than most people realize!
Like icebergs, many problems related to ADD/ADHD are not visible. ADD/ADHD may be mild, moderate, or severe,
is likely to coexist with other conditions, and may be a disability for some students.

Reprinted from A Bird's-Eye View of Life with ADD & ADHD

1

SUMMARY 5 — Official Diagnostic Criteria for AD/HD: The DSM

The official criteria for diagnosing attention deficit disorders are contained in the DSM *(The Diagnostic and Statistical Manual of Mental Disorders)* of the American Psychiatric Association. The DSM criteria are updated periodically to reflect increased knowledge in the field. Although the fourth edition of the DSM (DSM-IV TR) contains the currently recognized criteria, DSM-V is due to be published in 2013. The criteria published in the DSM are the same criteria that all physicians and licensed treatment professionals use to diagnose ADD and ADHD.

To be technically correct, *four official diagnoses for AD/HD were established* in 1994:
1. Attention-Deficit/Hyperactivity Disorder, Predominately **Inattentive** Type
2. Attention-Deficit/Hyperactivity Disorder, Predominately **Hyperactive-Impulsive** Type
3. Attention-Deficit/Hyperactivity Disorder, **Combined Type** (1 & 2)
4. Attention-Deficit/Hyperactivity Disorder **Not Otherwise Specified** (NOS)

To be diagnosed as having AD/HD, a student must have six of nine characteristics in either section *(1) Inattentive* or *(2) Hyperactive-Impulsive* (see below). If he has six (or more) characteristics in the Inattentive section, he is diagnosed with **AD/HD, Predominately Inattentive Type.** If he has six (or more) characteristics in the Hyperactive-Impulsive section, he is diagnosed with **AD/HD, Predominately Hyperactive-Impulsive Type. AD/HD, Combined Type,** is diagnosed if an individual has at least six characteristics under *both* ADD/inattentive *and* ADHD/hyperactive-impulsive, for a total of twelve or more characteristics.

For these diagnoses to be given, some impairment must be present in two or more settings (such as at school and at home).

Obviously, many of the characteristics under hyperactive-impulsive may no longer be present in teenagers. However, the characteristics may have been observed during elementary school and perhaps recorded in school records.

Proposed DSM-V Changes. Committees are currently meeting to develop the new **DSM-V.** Dr. Xavier Castellanos gave a report from the workgroup in April of 2009. The committee was seeking public feedback on their recommended changes related to diagnosing individuals who have the disorder. For example:

1. **Terminology:** Consider using the terms ADD & ADHD, or ADHD only but differentiate between the two subtypes

2. **ADHD Hyperactive/Impulsive:** retain current ADHD predominately hyperactive/impulsive diagnostic criteria or add four new impulsivity criteria:
   - often acts without thinking
   - is often impatient
   - often rushes through activities or tasks, is fast paced,
   - often has difficulty resisting immediate temptations or appealing opportunities, while disregarding negative consequences

3. **Age of onset:** Leave the diagnostically required age of onset at no later than 7 years of age or raise it to 12, since age 7 was established arbitrarily without any basis in research.

4. **Adults' criteria:** reduce the number of criteria required for diagnosis in adults from 6 to 3, since symptoms of ADHD decline with age.

Decisions will be made on the issues based upon data that are currently being collected.

Diagnostic Criteria for Attention-Deficit/Hyperactivity Disorder

Blanks have been added in front of each of the DSM-IV criteria so teachers may place a checkmark by those behaviors exhibited by the student. These criteria were established based upon the behaviors of children ages 14 and under, so they may not accurately describe older teens.

1. Inattention

_____ often fails to give close attention to details or makes careless mistakes in schoolwork, work, or other activities

_____ often has difficulty sustaining attention in tasks or play activities

_____ often does not seem to listen when spoken to directly

_____ often does not follow through on instructions and fails to finish schoolwork, chores, or duties in the work place (not due to oppositional behavior or failure to understand directions)

_____ often has difficulty organizing tasks and activities

_____ often avoids, dislikes, or is reluctant to engage in tasks that require sustained mental effort (such as schoolwork, or homework)

_____ often loses things necessary for tasks or activities at school, home, or the work place, (e.g., toys, school assignments, pencils, books, or tools)

_____ is often easily distracted by extraneous stimuli

_____ is often forgetful in daily activities

2. Hyperactivity [Did the teenager exhibit these behaviors in elementary school?]

_____ often fidgets with hands or feet or squirms in seat

_____ often leaves seat in classroom or in other situations in which remaining seated is expected

_____ often runs about or climbs excessively in situations where it is inappropriate (in adolescents or adults, may be limited to subjective feelings of restlessness)

_____ often has difficulty playing or engaging in leisure activities quietly

_____ is often "on the go" or often acts as if "driven by motor"

_____ often talks excessively

Impulsivity

_____ often blurts out answers before questions have been completed

_____ often has difficulty awaiting turn

_____ often interrupts or intrudes on others (e.g., butts into conversations or games)

(Reprinted with permission from the Diagnostic and Statistical Manual of Mental Disorders, *Fourth Edition, Text Revision (Copyright 2000). Washington, DC: American Psychiatric Association, 1994.)*

Implications for Teachers

■ *ADD/ADHD is more difficult to diagnose in teenagers.*

The hyperactive/impulsive characteristics are more common in younger children and may no longer be present in teenagers. If in doubt about the presence of hyperactivity, ask parents to describe the teenager's behavior when he was younger or review the cumulative folder for information about elementary school years. Hyperactivity is often replaced by restlessness in adolescence. See Summary 6.

■ *Several groups of students who have ADD/ADHD may be overlooked.*

1. **Students with the Inattentive Type:** Some people still believe the myth that a child must be hyperactive to be diagnosed as having an attention deficit disorder. So, some middle and high school students who have the inattentive type may not be diagnosed in elementary school.

2. **Girls:** Since girls with ADD or ADHD typically are not as aggressive as boys, they may not meet all the criteria to be diagnosed. Some experts argue that girls with attention deficit disorders may meet fewer than six criteria. See Summary 9 for more information on girls.

3. **Gifted Students:** Gifted students are often able to compensate for difficulties with attention, hyperactivity, or impulsivity until middle or high school, when demands for executive skills increase dramatically. Conflicts may arise as a result of the mismatch between increased academic demands and the student's delayed maturity and deficits in executive skills that impair key academic skills. See Summaries 10 and 15.

4. **African-American and Hispanic Students:** Students who are nonwhite may also be overlooked. For example, researchers found that only 5 percent of African-American and 2 percent of Hispanic youth with ADHD were diagnosed, compared to 8 percent of Caucasian children. This important issue is discussed in more detail in the *CHADD Educators' Manual on ADHD.*

5. **Students in Special Education:** Some children diagnosed in earlier years as having a specific learning disability (SLD) or emotional or behavioral disorder (EBD) may also have ADD or ADHD. So, take another look at students in special education classes to see if they also have symptoms of inattention or hyperactivity. If they do, effective treatment may help them be more successful in school.

References

Bauermeister, Jose. Medication Treatment of ADHD in Latino/Hispanic Children. *Child and Adolescent Psychopharmacology News,* 2005, Vol. 10, No. 5, 7-11.

Bussing, Regina, Zima, B.T., Perwien, A.R., Belin, T. & Widawski, M. "Children in Special Education Programs: Attention Deficit Hyperactivity Disorder, Use of Services and Unmet Needs." *American Journal of Public Health,* 1998, Vol. 88, 880-86.

Dendy, Chris A.Z , Teeter Ellison, Anne & Durheim, Mary. *CHADD Educator's Manual on ADHD.* Landover, MD: CHADD, 2006.

Diagnostic and Statistical Manual of Mental Disorders, Fourth Edition, Text Revision (Copyright 2000). Washington, DC: American Psychiatric Association, 2000.

Milich, Richard, Balentine, M.A. & Lynam, D.R. "The Predominately Inattentive Subtype—Not a Subtype of ADHD." *The ADHD Reports*, 2002, Vol. 10, No. 1, 1-5.

Diagnosis of ADD or ADHD in Adolescence

At school, *classroom teachers are the people most likely to first suspect that a student has an attention deficit disorder.* Even if the attention deficit isn't obvious, teachers recognize when students are struggling in class. If a teenager is suspected of having ADD or ADHD, a qualified professional such as a school psychologist, private psychologist, or doctor may then confirm the teacher's suspicions or determine that another problem exists. Obviously, a medical doctor must be involved if medication is needed.

Most experienced teachers are already pretty good at recognizing students who may have ADD and ADHD. This overview of procedures for diagnosing an attention deficit may help teachers correctly identify teenagers with this condition and refer them for formal evaluation.

Recognizing an attention deficit can be confusing at times because *all of us may have* some *symptoms of ADD/ADHD.* However, what sets these teens apart is the number and severity of the symptoms. Unlike pregnancy, attention deficit is not an "either you are or you aren't" diagnosis. Symptoms of the disorder may be mild, moderate, or severe. To be diagnosed as having an attention deficit, a student must exhibit six of nine official criteria to a degree that interferes with her ability to function successfully at school and at home. Official diagnostic criteria are listed in Summary 5.

Many children with ADD or ADHD, particularly those who are hyperactive, are diagnosed in early childhood or elementary school. By the time they reach adolescence, they have usually been receiving treatment for several years. However, *it is not unusual for teenagers to reach adolescence or even adulthood without having the disorder diagnosed!*

There are a variety of reasons that the diagnosis of attention deficit may be delayed until adolescence or later. Very bright students with an attention deficit often compensate in elementary school and can get by without being detected. Deficits in executive skills are present in elementary school, but teachers provide the structure and guidance children with ADD/ADHD are unable to provide themselves. However, teachers in higher grades expect independent work completion on more complex assignments; thus demands for executive skills increase during these years. This explains why problems may not surface until students enter middle and high school, when they must cope with more classes and teachers, as well as increased academic demands. Girls with ADD or ADHD are often overlooked, because they are not aggressive nor do they typically have behavior problems. See Summary 9.

Important Points to Know about Diagnosing ADD/ADHD

- There is *no test for ADD/ADHD.*

- *Underachievement* in school should be a red flag signaling teachers and parents to evaluate for ADD or ADHD or other learning problems.

- *The best indicators* of an attention deficit are the diagnostic criteria contained in the DSM (Summary 5). How many characteristics does the student exhibit? If she has six of nine characteristics, chances are good that she has an attention deficit.

How a Diagnosis Is Confirmed

The treatment professional, school social worker, or school psychologist might collect information from the following sources to confirm a diagnosis of ADD or ADHD:

■ *DSM diagnostic criteria* (meets 6 of 9 criteria in Summary 5)

■ A *childhood/family history* from the parents (history of ADD or ADHD or ADD/ADHD behaviors in the family; hyperactivity may or may not be observed)

■ *Description of school performance* by parents and the student (of average or higher intelligence but is underachieving; gets by in elementary school, but struggles in middle and high school)

■ *School report cards.* Grades may be low. Teacher comments on report cards may include: "Not working up to potential. Doesn't listen. Fails to use time wisely. Doesn't complete work. Doesn't turn work in on time. Makes too many zeros." For hyperactive students, teachers may find: "Talks too much. Can't stay in seat. Fidgets. Has difficulty sitting still." Or for students with the inattentive type: "Daydreams or stares into space."

■ *Classroom observations.* The student may not listen, may have trouble getting started, may be off-task, or may not complete work. Observations should be conducted during routine class situations rather than novel, high-interest activities such as games.

■ *Official school records,* including standardized academic achievement tests that may have been developed by individual states, for example the WKCE (Wisconsin Knowledge and Concepts Evaluation); national achievement tests such as the *IOWA Test of Basic Skills*; Individualized Education Programs (IEP); Section 504 Plan, school psychological evaluations. Group achievement tests such as the *IOWA* are reviewed for patterns that are indicative of learning problems.
  ● Group tests: Certain subtests of the *IOWA*, such as math computation, spelling, or capitalization, may be low.
  ● Psychological evaluations: Scale scores on the Wechsler Intelligence Scale for Children (*WISC-IV*) may be low on what is known as the *Working Memory or Processing Speed Indices* [Arithmetic, Coding, and Digit Span]. However, students with ADD/ADHD do not *always* make low scores on these subtests.

Other Helpful Indicators of ADD/ADHD

Student support staff, such as a school counselor, social worker, or psychologist, may ask teachers to complete a behavior rating scale, or the school psychologist may administer other formal tests. Evaluators select the appropriate tests based upon a student's challenges. Obviously not all tests will be administered.

1. **Intellectual Assessment:** Typically, a school psychologist administers an intelligence test such as the Wechsler Intelligence Scale for Children-IV (WISC-IV) or Wechsler Intelligence Scale for Adults (if the student is 16 or older).

2. **Academic Achievement Tests:** These tests help identify academic strengths and learning problems.
  ● Iowa Test of Basic Skills (*IOWA)*
  ● Curriculum based assessment; in other words, review of current class- and homework.
  ● Woodcock Johnson Psychoeducational Battery—Revised
  ● Wechsler Individual Achievement Test (WIAT)
  ● Stanford Achievement Test
  ● Kaufman Test of Educational Achievement
  ● Peabody Individual Achievement Test (PIAT)
  ● Tool of Written Language (TOWL)

3. **Behavior Rating Scales:** Several checklists include typical behaviors common in children and teens with ADD and ADHD and may be helpful. The SNAP-IV (Swanson, Nolan, and Pelham) is one of the most commonly used rating scales.
  ● Behavioral Assessment System for Children (BASC)

- Brown Attention Deficit Disorder Scales for children and adolescents
- *CBCL*-Child Behavior Checklists/Auchenbach (parent, teacher, and youth versions)
- Conners Rating Scale—Revised: Long Version (CTRS-R:L and CPRS-R:L)
- SNAP-IV (teacher and parent rating scales with18 questions;
- The Vanderbilt Scales (both the parent and teacher scales are free online: www. psychiatry24x7.com/bgdisplay.jhtml?itemname=adhd_toolkit)
- Behavioral & Emotional Rating Scales (BERS), one of the few strength-based assessment tools.

4. **Executive Function Rating Scales:**
    - BRIEF—Behavior Rating Inventory of Executive Functions (86 items; 15 minutes to complete)
    - *The Barkley Deficits in Executive Functioning Scale*—A new rating scale to assess executive function deficits in adults.The Scale includes two forms—one long (15-20 minutes to complete) and one short (4-5 minutes)—that assess skills in these areas: time management; organization and problem solving; self-restraint; self-motivation; and self-regulation of emotions.

5. **Other tests** such as the Developmental Test of Visual Motor Integration (VMI) may be given to identify related problems.

6. A thorough ***physical examination*** should be conducted to rule out other disorders.

Coexisting problems such as *learning disabilities, sleep disturbances, anxiety, depression, defiance, or aggression* are found in over two-thirds of students with ADD or ADHD and must be identified and treated. Typically, treatment of attention deficit disorder in isolation is not enough to ensure that a teenager will be successful in school and life. See Summary 78 for a discussion of coexisting conditions.

For more detailed information about diagnosing ADD and ADHD, refer to Chapter 2 in *Teenagers with ADD and ADHD,* 2nd edition (Dendy, 2007).

Words of Caution and Concern

> *"Our daughter believed that if her son had ADHD the school would have told her. When he was diagnosed, she was shocked to learn that teachers are told specifically never to say to a parent that a child might have ADHD."*

Obviously, teachers cannot officially diagnose ADD or ADHD, nor is it appropriate for teachers to tell parents that they think a teenager has an attention deficit disorder. Educators don't want to unnecessarily alarm parents. It may be wise to ***talk about the behaviors of concern*** rather than giving a diagnostic label:

> *"Your son has trouble paying attention. Frequently, he doesn't complete his homework and turn it in on time. I know you are also concerned about his school work. I would like to ask the school psychologist to observe him and review his records. Perhaps she will have some suggestions about appropriate next steps to help him succeed in school."*

Next steps typically include referring the child for a school evaluation or suggesting the parent talk with the family doctor. Keep in mind, also, the problem the teenager is experiencing may not be an attention deficit, but may be another disorder such as a specific learning disability, depression, or anxiety.

Common Myths about ADD and ADHD: Fact vs. Fiction

Several common myths may interfere with diagnosis and treatment of teenagers with ADD or ADHD:

Myth I: All children/teenagers with ADD or ADHD are hyperactive.

Some teachers and parents still mistakenly believe that a child or teenager with ADD or ADHD must be hyperactive. They may be unaware that by the teenage years, hyperactivity is usually no longer present and has been replaced by restlessness. In addition, children with milder cases of ADHD may not seem excessively hyperactive. Students who have ADD may actually seem more like couch potatoes who lack energy. Consequently, teenagers with ADHD who are restless, but not hyperactive, or who have ADD inattentive may be overlooked.

> *"Very few ADHD children are hyperactive in the true sense. I see maybe one or two a year, referred in by kindergarten or first grade teachers. Most ADHD children and teenagers are fidgety, playing with something in their hand, standing by their desk, but are not overtly hyperactive or antisocial."*
>
> —Dr. Theodore Mandlekorn, M.D., Director, Puget Sound Behavioral Medicine, Mercer Island, WA

> *"When I call teachers and mention that 'John' has ADD/ADHD, frequently the teacher says, 'That can't be true. John isn't hyperactive.'"*
>
> —Pediatric Center Staff, Decatur, GA

Myth II: Hyperactive children/teenagers with ADHD can't sit still for ten minutes.

By the teenage years, students *can* sit still in class, although sometimes they may daydream or sleep. They can also stay focused for most of an evaluation and can maintain a conversation with the school psychologist or other school administrator during a half-hour interview. Most teenagers with ADHD concentrate and focus better in one-to-one and novel situations.

Myth III: ADD and ADHD disappear in adolescence and adulthood.

One reason it was originally believed that youngsters outgrow ADHD is because their hyperactivity decreases as they reach adolescence. However, the attention problems often persist in adulthood. Instead of hyperactivity, restlessness, inattentiveness, or sleeping in class may be observed. Sometimes teachers will see physical signs of restlessness such as tapping a pencil, swinging a foot, or doodling. Experts report that students with ADHD often fidget in order to keep their brain alert for more difficult school tasks. The teenager with ADHD who feels "hyper" knows it isn't acceptable to get up and walk around in class, so instead he may tune out mentally or sleep. Some teenagers say they feel as if their brain is still hyperactive, jumping from one topic to another.

Myth IV: ADHD medications like Ritalin no longer work in adolescents.

Research has shown that stimulant medications like Ritalin, Concerta, or Adderall and nonstimulants like Strattera are effective for children, teenagers, and even adults with attention deficits. When medication is working properly, students will show a decrease in hyperactivity, impulsivity, negative behaviors, and verbal hostility, while their attention, concentration, compliance, and completion of school work will improve significantly. See Summaries 56-61.

Myth V: ADD and ADHD will always be diagnosed in early childhood.

The age of diagnosis may vary depending on the severity and type of ADD/ADHD. Children who are extremely hyperactive are usually diagnosed early. Children with milder cases of ADHD or those who have ADD inattentive may not be diagnosed until middle or high school or later. Some teenagers with an attention deficit may even continue into adulthood without detection. Unfortunately, some parents and high school personnel may not consider an attention deficit as a potential culprit underlying student underachievement! They incorrectly assume that if ADD or ADHD were present, it would have been diagnosed in elementary school.

Myth VI: ADD and ADHD are over-diagnosed.

Researchers have established that attention deficit disorders occur in roughly 10 percent of children in the United States. Although 4.4 million children meet criteria, only 32-56 percent of them are being treated for the condition. African-Americans and Hispanics experience even lower treatment rates— only 20 percent. In their survey of actual prescriptions written for treating ADHD, the Center for Mental Health Services reported that 7 percent of children ages 5 to 14 and 1.2 percent of students ages 15 to 19 received ADHD medications. The appallingly reduced treatment rate in high school could be linked to the old myth that our children outgrow attention deficit disorders. Obviously, media headlines touting over-diagnosis of attention-deficit disorders often are not based upon scientific facts. Most informed professionals and parents are worried more about the *under*-diagnosis and treatment of ADD/ADHD.

Part of the speculation about over-diagnosis results from an increase in the number of ADHD prescriptions being written. Let's look at some possible reasons why prescriptions have increased. Obviously, now that more students are being treated, the number of students on medication has increased.

- *ADD/ADHD has been under-diagnosed for years.* Some researchers speculate that we "are finally playing catch-up" to the predicted 10 percent prevalence rate. Many researchers believe this is the primary reason for increases in the number of students being diagnosed.

- *ADD/ADHD may be increasing because of environmental trauma.* Although ADD and ADHD are often inherited, trauma or toxins in the environment may also cause attention deficits. For example, exposure to lead, or having a mother who drinks or smokes during pregnancy, may cause children to exhibit symptoms of this condition.

- *The criteria for the inattentive type of ADD were not included in the DSM until 1994.* Some educators are still focusing on the stereotypical hyperactivity as the defining behavior for diagnosis of ADHD. Consequently, well-behaved, daydreaming teenagers with the inattentive type ADD may slide below their radar.

- *Children and teenagers with borderline ADD/ADHD may be receiving treatment now.* Perhaps children and teenagers who have a borderline attention deficit (with 5 but not 6 characteristics of the DSM criteria) are being identified and referred for treatment by parents who are desperate to find help for their struggling child.

SUMMARY 8 — Differences between Students with ADD and ADHD

Although students with ADHD and ADD share some basic characteristics, they are different in several areas.

Teenagers who have ADHD tend to be:

- hyperactive,
- energetic,
- talkative, and
- outgoing.

In contrast, ***teenagers with ADD*** tend to be:

- less energetic,
- somewhat introverted,
- less likely to talk in class, and
- daydreamers.

A Few Additional Thoughts about Inattentive Type ADD

Dr. Richard Milich, a University of Kentucky professor, found that 28 percent of young people with the inattentive type have what he refers to as "sluggish cognitive tempo" (SCT). This means that these students process information more slowly than their peers. For example, they read, write, comprehend, and recall information more slowly. Practically speaking, they take longer to read assignments, complete class work and homework, retrieve information for written assignments and tests, and respond to questions in class. The remaining 72 percent of those with the inattentive type of ADD seem to be sub-threshold ADHD, hyperactive/impulsive. In other words, they may not quite meet the six required eligibility criteria for combined type ADHD.

The chart below gives a quick summary of the similarities and differences between these two major types of attention deficit disorders. Remember, any given student with ADD/ADHD will have some, but probably not all of, the characteristics in any given column.

Similarities: Students with ADD and ADHD may share these characteristics:

inattention	positive response to stimulant medications
trouble getting started on schoolwork or home-work	short-term memory problems
poor sustained attention (persistence on tasks)	working memory problems
problems with written expression, complex math, reading comprehension	risk-taking behavior
poor handwriting (fine motor skills)	

Differences: Students with ADHD and ADD also have very distinct differences. However, students with combined type ADHD will have symptoms from both columns.

ADHD (hyperactive-impulsive type) *(Behaviors more likely in elementary students)*	ADD (inattentive type)
hyperactive	has low energy, not hyperactive
impulsive	less impulsive
Positive response to medication	Less positive response to medication
talkative	quieter, less talkative
blurts out answers	some have slow processing speed (may seem confused at times)
talks and acts before thinking	sometimes, slow to respond in class sometimes, slow retrieval of information sometimes, slow perceptual-motor speed sometimes, slow writing, reading, recall, verbal responses
class clown	quieter, socially distant
difficulty making and keeping friends	gets along better with peers; some are shy & withdrawn
misses social cues	difficulty making decisions

Less Common Characteristics: The following behaviors are not present in all students with ADD or ADHD, but when present, they are more likely to be associated with the type of attention deficit noted.

ADHD	ADD
aggression	anxiety (may reduce impulsivity)
oppositional behavior	less oppositional behavior
defiance	less defiance
conduct disorder	

Girls with ADD or ADHD

ADD/ADHD in girls is overlooked by many professionals, including doctors. For example, David Rabiner, Ph.D., a researcher at Duke, noted that "pediatricians were significantly more likely to diagnose boys with ADHD than girls, even when the problems described by parents were quite comparable." With regard to educators, given that boys are more hyperactive, aggressive, and defiant, teachers are more likely to recognize their problems. Often, only girls with obvious behavior problems and more severe cases of ADD/ADHD are easily diagnosed. Although both untreated boys and girls are at high risk for poor outcomes, girls are still more likely to "fly under the radar" and remain undiagnosed.

Hopefully as teachers become aware of this oversight, they will identify girls who exhibit symptoms of ADD or ADHD more easily. Teachers should pay particular attention to the "daydreamers" and to students with executive skills deficits such as disorganization and difficulty getting started and finishing work that are described in Sections 2 and 3.

Research on Girls with ADHD

Since most ADHD research has been conducted on boys, few studies on girls with ADHD are available. Current research places the ratio of boys to girls with ADHD at 2 to 1. However, some experts argue it is more likely 1 to 1 since girls with ADHD are more frequently overlooked. Fortunately, two leading researchers, Russell Barkley and Joseph Biederman, M.D., have made it a point to study ADHD in girls.

Biederman's research is of particular significance because it is the largest and most comprehensive study to date on girls. The study has followed a group of 187 girls, including 96 with ADHD, for eleven years now. The most important finding of Biederman's study is that girls are at high risk of having the same coexisting conditions as boys. For example, both boys and girls experience comparable deficits in executive functions and academic impairment. However, when girls with ADHD are compared with girls who don't have ADHD, they show far more impairment than their non-ADHD peers. Clearly, aggressive diagnosis and treatment of both girls and boys is critical.

- **Types of ADHD:** According to Biederman, 59 percent of the girls in his study had the combined type ADHD (hyperactive and inattentive), 27% had ADHD predominantly inattentive type, and only 7% had the hyperactive only type.

- **Risk of Academic Problems:** Although no more impaired than boys with ADHD, girls with ADHD had greater academic challenges than girls *without ADHD*: they are 2.5 times more likely to have a learning disability, 16 times more likely to have repeated a grade, and 10 times as likely to be in special education classes. Interestingly, their IQ scores and academic achievement test scores are not that much lower than those of their non-ADHD peers, which underscores the frustration these students must experience as a result of their underachievement. David Rabiner, Ph.D. speculates that students with ADHD do well on these individually administered tests of intelligence and achievement but are unable to meet real world day-to-day academic demands in the classroom.

- **Risk of Coexisting Conditions:** 45 percent of the girls were diagnosed with other coexisting conditions. Although the rates of most coexisting conditions were comparable for boys and girls, there was one notable exception; substance use was higher in girls. For instance, girls were four times as likely to smoke as boys. However, they were less likely to be diagnosed with oppositional defiant and conduct disorders. Specifically, researchers found that girls with ADHD were at greater risk than girls *without ADHD* for being diagnosed with these six conditions: mood disorders such as depression or bipolar, anxiety, antisocial disorders, behavioral disorders, substance abuse, and eating disorders.

- **Depression:** Dr. Biederman summarized the rates of depression in girls with and without ADHD after five years of his study were completed. He found that females with ADHD were 5.4 times more likely to develop major depression than their peers. The average age for onset of depression was 17 and it lasted 3 years on average, twice as long as for females without ADHD. Females with ADHD tend to internalize criticism more than boys and are likely to engage in "self-blame and shame."

- **ODD, CD, and Anxiety:** Girls with ADHD have behavior disorders such as Oppositional Defiant Disorder or Conduct Disorder at half the rate of boys with ADHD. However, boys and girls have comparable rates of anxiety and mood disorders such as depression. When anxiety is high, a student may be less likely to act or speak impulsively. Students who are anxious may also be more likely to follow school rules and complete school work on time.

- **Eating Disorders:** According to Biederman's study, 16 percent of girls with ADHD may have an eating disorder, a rate that is 3.6 times greater than for girls who do not have ADHD.

Additional Observations from Experts

Observations from Biederman and Barkley, as well as Pat Quinn, M.D. and Kathleen Nadeau, Ph.D., who are noted authorities on girls with ADHD, are summarized in this section.

- **General observations:** A national debate is growing over whether or not girls with ADD or ADHD should be judged by slightly different criteria than boys. The official criteria used to diagnose attention deficits were based primarily on research into the more active and aggressive behavior of boys. Girls with milder cases of attention deficit disorders may not meet all six symptoms required for a diagnosis by DSM IV. See Summary 5.

- **Diagnosis:** Pediatricians are more likely to overlook ADHD in girls than in boys.

- **Family Life:** Parents of girls with ADHD describe their family life as less cohesive and as having higher rates of conflict than in non-ADHD families.

- **Academic Performance:** According to Quinn, the girls least likely to be diagnosed are those who are very bright and who must expend tremendous energy compensating for their ADHD. They may seem "driven, or anxious, or over-focused on their studies."

- **Hyperactivity:** Hyperactivity in girls is more likely to manifest itself verbally instead of physically. Girls often talk a lot and tend to be more emotionally reactive, according to Dr. Nadeau.

- **Puberty:** Nadeau also reports that during puberty, boy's symptoms get better but girl's worsen.

- **Sexual activity:** Early sexual activities for both boys and girls are of concern. These girls become sexually active at an earlier age, have more sexual partners, and are more likely to get pregnant than their non-ADHD peers.

- **Peer rejection:** Girls with ADHD experience more peer rejection than boys do. According to Quinn, one key reason may be that girls socialize and verbalize differently from boys. Girls, more than boys, must live in a highly verbal, socially interactive manner that they are ill equipped to handle. Additionally, cooperation and sensitivity to others are required for successful interactions; again skills are required that are deficient in students with ADHD. Difficulties with verbal expression and verbal control contribute to their problems making and keeping friends.

Differences Reported by Parents

To add to the information available from the small number of studies on females with attention deficit disorders, I sought information from women who have attention deficits disorders or who have daughters with this condition. The ADHD and ADD behaviors both girls and boys exhibit are similar, according to these women. However, mothers noted these major differences:

- *Societal expectations for girls and boys are distinctly different.* Society expects "boys to be boys," but those same behaviors from girls are viewed as much worse. Even mothers treat their sons and daughters with attention deficits differently. Dr. Russell Barkley found that mothers give more praise and direction to their sons, even though the boys are less compliant than girls. Treatment professionals are not immune to this bias either. In another study, clinicians missed the diagnosis of attention-deficit disorder in girls 50 percent of the time.

- *Girls with ADD or ADHD feel the sting of social rejection* much more intensely than boys do, according to their mothers. Both girls and boys with attention deficits may miss social cues, alienate classmates, and have few friends, but girls seem to be more bothered by their social delays.

  Suggestion: Finding ways to strengthen social skills is important but extremely difficult. For girls, school is often viewed as the center of their social life. Researchers report that girls value friendliness; if you don't speak, you're considered "stuck up." Being clean and dressing fashionably is also important. To gain greater peer acceptance, girls must smile, make eye contact, and greet other girls in social situations.

- *Anxiety may be a major problem*. One mother talked about her daughter's anxiety: *"She worries about things I haven't even thought up yet. When she worries, she just can't let it go. School is a major source of anxiety for her. She wants to do so well, often thinks she's doing well, and then is completely shocked to find out otherwise. In addition, she sets unrealistically high standards for herself. She'd like to be perfect, and anything less than that sets her up for anxiety."*

  Suggestions: Encourage the student to exercise on a regular basis; this will help reduce anxiety. Meditation, using positive visual imagery, or using self-calming activities like listening to music or taking a walk also may be helpful. Consider talking with a physician about treating the anxiety.

- *Girls may compensate for their anxiety with compulsive behavior.* Informally, parents tell us that some girls resort to compulsive list making because they are so anxious about forgetting their school work. One mother reported that when her older daughter with ADD was 17 or 18, she started making lists because she was involved in so many activities that she was afraid she would forget something. This daughter could also lose track of time, or hyper-focus for three hours or more on a project she really loved. Her younger daughter, who also has ADD, is more laid-back and doesn't seem to be particularly anxious.

Differences Reported by Teachers

Boys with ADD or ADHD tend to be more oppositional and aggressive than girls and thus are more of a discipline problem at school. While 67 percent of boys with ADHD are diagnosed as having oppositional defiant disorder (ODD), only 33 percent of girls qualify. Twenty-five percent of boys with ADHD have conduct disorders (CD), while only 10 percent of girls meet the same criteria. So, girls who are struggling more quietly may not come to the teacher's attention as having any major problems. The characteristics of ODD and CD are listed in Summary 78.

Resources

Biederman, Joseph et al. "Adult Psychiatric Outcomes of Girls with Attention Deficit Hyperactivity Disorder: 11-Year Follow-up in a Longitudinal Case-control Study." *American Journal of Psychiatry,* April 2010, Vol. 167, No. 4:409-17.

Biederman, Joseph et al. "Are Girls with ADHD at Risk for Eating Disorders? Results from a Controlled, Five-Year Prospective Study." *Journal of Developmental and Behavioral Pediatrics,* Aug. 2007, Vol. 28, No. 4:302-7.

Biederman, Joseph et al. "Clinical Correlates of ADHD in Females: Findings from a Large Group of Girls Ascertained from Pediatric and Psychiatric Referral Sources." *Journal of the American Academy of Child and Adolescent Psychiatry,* Vol. 38, Issue 8:966-75.

Dendy, Chris A.Z , Teeter Ellison, Anne & Durheim, Mary. *CHADD Educator's Manual on ADHD.* Landover, MD: CHADD, 2006.

Gaub, Mianda & Carlson, Caryn. "Gender Differences in ADHD: A Meta-analysis and Critical Review." *Journal of The Academy of Child and Adolescent Psychiatry,* 1997, Vol. 36:1036-45.

Nadeau, Kathleen & Quinn, Pat. *Understanding Girls with AD/HD.* Silver Spring, MD: Advantage Books, 2000.

Rabiner, David. "ADHD/ADD in Girls." 2009. Article available at www.helpforadd.com.

Solden, Sari, Hallowell, Ed & Ratey, John. *Women with Attention Deficit Disorder.* Second edition. Grass Valley, CA: Underwood Books, 2005.

Gifted Students with ADD or ADHD

According to federal guidelines in the Individuals with Disabilities Education Act (IDEA), gifted and talented students with disabilities are described as:

> Students *"who give evidence of high achievement capability in areas such as intellectual, creative, artistic, or leadership capacity, or in specific academic fields, and who need services or activities not ordinarily provided by the school in order to fully develop those capabilities." [20 U.S.C. Section 7801(22)]*

Researchers at the National Research Center on the Gifted and Talented have found that gifted students with ADHD face two particularly challenging issues: 1) they are often more impaired than other children diagnosed with ADHD, so gifted students with milder ADHD may be overlooked, and 2) higher intellectual ability may mask ADHD, resulting in delayed diagnosis. They may also show uneven scores on IQ and achievement tests, with scores ranging from low average to high, according to Deirdre V. Lovecky, Ph.D., a psychologist and Director of the Gifted Resource Center of New England. As with all young people with ADHD, delayed maturity is also evident in organizational skills, social relationships, and emotional control, but is even more confusing when contrasted with their high intellectual ability and "potential."

Several factors contribute to the delayed diagnosis of gifted students. Due to their inattention and other ADHD symptoms, these students may make lower scores on the tests used to determine eligibility for programs for the gifted. Thus, their true abilities and their performance may not be recognized because their giftedness is masked by their ADHD symptoms. Additionally, teachers are less likely to notice the ADHD if students are not disruptive in class. Likewise, parents are more likely to be skeptical of an ADHD diagnosis when they know their child is so bright. However, parents should remember, *a high IQ alone is not enough to be successful in school*. In fact, researchers tell us that working memory, a key executive skill, is a better predictor of school success than IQ. Working memory deficits are often a cause of great frustration among gifted students with ADHD. Theodore Mandelkorn, M.D., voices this frustration in our video, *Real Life ADHD* (Zeigler, Dendy, & Dendy, 2011) by relaying what he told his teacher when he was failing the fifth grade: "Don't tell me how smart I am until you can tell me how to make my brain work right."

Teaching Gifted Students with ADD/ADHD

According to Linda C. Neumann, editor of the *2e:Twice-exceptional Newsletter*, the concept of *dual differentiation* is critically important in the education of children who have both intellectual gifts and learning challenges. As the National Association of Gifted Children (NAGC) outlined in one of their position papers: "Students who have both gifts and learning disabilities require a dually differentiated program: one that nurtures their gifts and talents while accommodating for learning weaknesses." Furthermore, Susan Baum, educator, researcher, and author of *To Be Gifted and Learning Disabled*, explains the need for strength-based programs that individualize instruction to meet students' gifts *and* accommodate their deficits. Baum explains that this approach applies to curriculum and instruction, and includes modifications as well as accommodations.

A dually differentiated curriculum offers options in:
- what students learn,
- how they learn it,
- how they demonstrate their learning, and
- where they learn best (environment).

Dr. Lovecky gives this helpful advice in a *2e Newsletter* article: "Gifted children with AD/HD show great strengths and weaknesses, both of which need to be addressed. Strengths must be developed both to enhance the child and to help him/her compensate for weaker areas. Weaknesses must be addressed by remediation and use of compensatory mechanisms so that the child can learn to work efficiently and with less frustration. Gifted children with AD/HD need to be educated with gifted peers. However, in accelerating them or giving them extra work, one must be certain they have the support skills to manage the tasks, to compensate for weaker executive function skills."

Besides a dually differentiated curriculum, one other key to student success is realistic teacher expectations. Because these students are so smart, teachers may have unrealistic expectations that they will be capable of working independently and taking greater responsibility for completion of their schoolwork. Many gifted students with ADD/ADHD struggle enough with ordinary academic challenges without being expected to handle the great amounts and complexity of school work that typically developing gifted students often tackle. In addition, gifted students with ADD/ADHD are often unable to muster the independent work habits and organizational skills (with minimal supervision) that teachers usually expect of gifted students.

The summaries in Sections 2 and 3 lay out specific intervention strategies for learning challenges that are common in many students with ADHD: difficulties in reading, math, reading comprehension, handwriting, written expression, complex math, and organizational skills. Using external visual and auditory cues plus organizational structure is critical. Since gifted and nongifted students with ADHD share many of the same challenges, interventions from these sections should be helpful.

Coexisting Learning Challenges

As explained in Summaries 42 & 46, gifted students with ADD or ADHD may be eligible for IDEA services in certain circumstances under the category of Other Health Impairment (OHI) or Specific Learning Disability (SLD). Evaluators should also consider other disabilities since researchers indicate that roughly one-sixth of gifted students have a disability. According to a position paper of the National Association of Gifted Children, to identify gifts, schools should analyze individual subtest scores and patterns on tests as well as actual performance in multiple areas of intelligence via a student's products, auditions, and interviews ("smarts" in music, art, people, numbers, and words).

Classes for Gifted Students

Gifted students who have ADHD experience many of the same challenges associated with the three-year delay in ADHD brain maturity and deficits in executive skills—for example, they often behave similarly to younger children. Consequently, placing them with other gifted students of the same age may present major challenges. Other gifted students may have little patience with their lack of organizational skills, weak "work habits," and social immaturity, yet these students benefit from the stimulation of this peer group. This creates a major dilemma that unfortunately has no right or wrong answer.

Parents and teachers must gather the evidence and make a decision about the best placement for a particular student on a case-by-case basis. On the surface, participation in classes for gifted students sounds great. However if the gifted classes just "pile it higher and deeper" (result mostly in more written and busy work), these classes are probably not the best choice for many students with ADD or ADHD.

Recommendations from the National Research Center on Gifted and Talented Students

1. Be aware that ADD or ADHD and giftedness can coexist.

2. Explore multiple perspectives in your pursuit of information about ADD/ADHD. (Read the scientific research—don't listen to just anyone's opinion; some self-proclaimed "experts" ignore the science).

3. Remember that the most important criterion for diagnosing ADD/ADHD is the degree of impairment experienced by the child in two or more settings, typically home and school.

4. Use a multidisciplinary team to arrive at diagnoses and to develop comprehensive treatment plans.

5. Become familiar with a variety of educational and behavioral strategies to determine which combinations might be effective for the individual student.

6. Be cautious about promises of "quick-fixes"—whether behavioral, educational, or medical.

7. Be aware that individuals with ADD/ADHD have their greatest difficulties in the "output" stage of cognitive processing (completing written school work, writing essays, and concise verbal expression).

8. Determine whether "shifting attention" is a point of vulnerability for the student. (Does the child hyper-focus, "get stuck" on an activity, and have trouble shifting gears to a new event?)

9. Model and support the process of "knowing thyself." (Educate the student about her ADD/ADHD.)

10. Advocate for and support systematic research into ADD/ADHD within the gifted population.

Intervention Strategies

1. If a teen is diagnosed with ADD/ADHD, evaluators should consider reevaluation for giftedness. Hints of a student's giftedness may be reflected in uneven high and low subtest scale scores and indices from previous intelligence tests. See analysis of test score discrepancies within the WISC intelligence test in *Teenagers with ADD & ADHD,* 2nd ed. (Dendy, 2006).

2. Tailor interventions to the student's strengths and needs.

3. Focus on talent development, rather than on remediation of deficits, according to Maureen Neihart, a psychologist who has studied ADD/ADHD and giftedness.

4. Address intellectual, organizational, social, and behavioral needs and use the intervention strategies provided in Section 2 of this book.

5. Maintain classroom stimulation; don't create a sterile, unstimulating environment.

6. Don't "water down" assignments; gifted children prefer complexity. However, do consider pros and cons of shorter or simplified assignments. Students with slow processing speed will require shorter assignments or extended time.

Resources

Baum, Susan. *To Be Gifted and Learning Disabled*: *Strategies for Helping Bright Students with LD, ADHD and More.* Rev. ed., Mansfield Center, CT: Creative Learning Press, 2004.

Dendy, Chris A. Zeigler. *Teenagers with ADD and ADHD.* 2nd ed. Bethesda, MD: Woodbine House, 2006.

Dendy, Chris & Alex Zeigler. *Real Life ADHD! A DVD.* Cedar Bluff, AL: Chris A. Z. Dendy Consulting LLC, 2011.

Kaufmann, F., Kalbfleisch, M. L., & Castellanos, F. X. (2000). *Attention Deficit Disorders and Gifted Students: What Do We Really Know?* Storrs, CT: The National Research Center on the Gifted and Talented, University of Connecticut, 2000.

Lovecky, Deirdre. *Different Minds: Gifted Children with AD/HD, Asperger Syndrome, and Other Learning Deficits.* Philadelphia, PA: Jessica Kingsley Publishers, 2004.

Lovecky, Deirdre. "Gifted Children with AD/HD." *2e:Twice-exceptional Newsletter,* April 2004. (www.2eNewsletter.com)

National Association of Gifted Children. GAGC Position Paper: "Students with Concomitant Gifts and "Learning Disabilities." Washington, DC: NAGC, 1998.

Neihart, M. "Gifted Children with Attention Deficit Hyperactivity Disorder (ADHD)." Reston, VA: Council for Exceptional Children, 2004.

Neumann, Linda (Editor, *2e: Twice-exceptional Newsletter*). Personal correspondence, 2010.

SUMMARY 11

Increased National Attention Focused on ADD and ADHD

When I was just starting out as a teacher, I thought that students with attention deficit disorders were simply not trying hard enough or were not disciplined enough to do well in school. Other teachers have undoubtedly felt the same way. Eventually, most teachers realize that it is not just laziness. However, very few realize just how complex and devastating an attention deficit disorder can be in a student's life, especially if it is untreated. It's important for teachers to remember Dr. Ross Green's wise advice: students with ADD/ADHD "will do well if they can."

Fortunately, in recent years many of the leading organizations in the U.S. have begun to recognize what a profound impact this condition may have on a student's life. Recent breakthroughs in research on the brain have riveted national attention on this important condition and co-occurring deficits in executive functions. There are several important ongoing studies. Key activities that have occurred within the last decade are briefly listed below.

NIMH ADD/ADHD Study

The National Institute of Mental Health (NIMH) conducted a landmark study involving almost 600 students with attention deficits aged seven to ten at six sites around the country. The fact that this research, known as the MTA study, is the largest ever instituted by NIMH on any topic for any age group makes a strong statement regarding the profound influence of ADD/ADHD in the lives of children and their families. This study will have a significant impact on educational and health care policies regarding these young people. Preliminary results for the three-year study were released in December 1999; additional follow-up findings were published in 2007. Key findings include:

- Over two-thirds of the children in the study had at least one other disorder such as depression, anxiety, or learning disabilities.
- Medication alone was more effective than behavioral interventions alone.
- Medication alone was almost as effective as the combined treatment of medication plus behavioral interventions.
- Many students may be receiving medication doses that are too low for maximum improvement in school work and behavior.

2007 Eight-Year Follow-up Report

- The study and planned interventions ended in 1999 after three years. After that time, no planned interventions were provided to study participants; treatment the students received in the community was not monitored. By 2007, the students in both primary treatment groups had changed interventions—some who had been on medications dropped them, and some who had been on behavioral interventions only began taking meds. As a result, the status of the children in both groups was similar, so no conclusions can be reached about long-term effectiveness of medication versus behavioral treatments.

- Peter Jensen, M.D., the lead researcher, emphasized the key role parents play in providing consistent support and guidance for their children. Children who had socially and economically stable homes fared better.

- In summary, combined behavioral and medication interventions are still considered the best treatment strategies—if either one is stopped, many of the benefits are lost. Dr. Russell Barkley recommends that interventions be started earlier, be sustained, and target more than just school because 65 to 86 percent of children have symptoms that persist into adulthood. Long-term effects persist for:
    Occupation and finances,
    Educational impairments,
    Health concerns,
    Driving impairments, and
    Intimate personal relationships.

Implications for Teachers to Consider

- Students with ADD or ADHD who continue to struggle after receiving treatment and classroom accommodations may have a coexisting condition that is not being treated.

- For many students, behavioral strategies alone will not change their behavior or ability to complete school work. Academic deficits must be identified and addressed.

- Medication is a key part of treatment.

- Reports from teachers on how well medication is working are critical in helping doctors know when medication doses should be adjusted. (See Summary 59.)

AAP Offers Clinical Guidelines on Assessment and Treatment of ADHD

On May 1, 2000, the American Academy of Pediatrics (AAP) released new recommendations for primary care physicians, including pediatricians, to use when assessing school-age children for ADD or ADHD. Separate treatment guidelines were issued in 2001. They are available online at www.aap.org/qualityimprovement/quiin/ADHDToolkit.html.

Surgeon General's Report on Mental Health

The first ever Surgeon General's Report on Mental Health was released in 1999. Attention deficit disorder was one of the few conditions that was discussed in some detail. Over the years, the Surgeon General's Reports have had a profound impact on shaping public policy and the health of the nation. Reports on these issues are disseminated to state governments, community mental health centers, and mental health professionals. Although the material in the report is dated now, it served its primary purpose of making mental health professionals more aware of the long-term impact of ADD/ADHD on the mental health of adults.

CDC/DOE Sponsored Conference on ADHD: Ongoing ADHD Research

The Atlanta-based Center for Disease Control and Prevention and the U.S. Department of Education, Office of Special Education Programs, jointly sponsored a conference in September 1999 on *"ADHD: A Public Health Perspective."* The CDC and DOE are concerned about the public health implications of ADD and ADHD on the behavior of our young people, including their increased risk for school failure, dropping out of school, risk-taking behavior, and, for some, substance abuse or involvement with the juvenile justice system.

Currently the CDC is conducting the largest ever epidemiological study on ADHD—studying children in the general population, not those being treated in clinics. *PLAY*, or Project to Learn about ADHD in Youth, will look at short- and long-term outcomes, prevalence rates, coexisting conditions, and treatment strategies. The most recent (2010) ADHD data published by the CDC shows a new prevalence rate of 10 percent.

Revisions to the Individuals with Disabilities Education Act (IDEA)

Until 1997, it was rare for students with ADD or ADHD to qualify for special education services unless they had another "qualifying" diagnosis such as a specific learning disability. After hearings were held around the U.S. regarding needed revisions to the Individuals with Disabilities Education Act (IDEA) in 1997, ADD and ADHD were added to the list of specific disabilities that could potentially qualify a student for special education services. A more detailed discussion of the impact of these revisions and the related regulations that were released in 1999 are provided in Section Four, Summaries 43-46. IDEA was reauthorized in 2004 and final regulations published in 2005. Again, ADD and ADHD were listed as disabilities that could qualify a student for special education under the category of "other health impairment."

Resources

American Academy of Pediatrics (AAP). "Guidelines for Diagnosing ADHD" and "Guidelines for Treating ADHD." www.aap.org (search for AAP ADHD Guidelines for Treating ADHD or AAP Guidelines for ADHD). These tools are intended primarily for physicians.

Barkley, Russell, et al. *ADHD in Adults: What the Science Says*. New York, NY: The Guilford Press, 2008.

Barkley, Russell. Week-long ADHD Workshop. 26th Annual Cape Cod Summer Symposia. Cape Cod, MA, 2004.

Center for Disease Control and Prevention. Numerous articles on ADHD, including some in Spanish. www.cdc.gov (at website click "Search"; "ADHD home page").

Department of Education/IDEA:
ww.ed.gov/offices/osers/idea (click on "The Law").
www.lrp.com/ed (click on "IDEA Full Text").

Jensen, Peter. "Implications of the Multimodal Treatment Study (MTA) Study for Parents and Professionals." CHADD Conference presentation. Washington, DC, 1999.

Jensen, Peter. "Good News and Bad News from the NIMH/MTA study: Outcomes after 8 Years." ADDA-SR Annual conference. Dallas, TX, 2008.

National Institute of Mental Health (NIMH). http://archpsyc.ama (click "Past Issues," December 1999).

Office of the Surgeon General. www.surgeongeneral.gov (click on "Mental Health Report").

SECTION 2

The Link Between ADD/ADHD, Executive Function Deficits, and Academic Performance:

Written Expression, Complex Math, Memorization, Reading Comprehension

Teachers and parents are often puzzled when bright students with attention deficits don't do well in school. During the last decade, leading researchers on attention deficit disorders have determined that these academic struggles can be traced, at least in large part, to deficits in *executive functions (EF).* In fact, deficiencies in executive skills are often responsible for the phenomenon that parents refer to as "hitting the brick wall" in middle school. Ironically, students may have significant deficits in executive functions even though they earn normal scores on standardized tests. Clearly, these students are learning in spite of their poor grades, disorganization, and failure to complete assignments in a timely manner. Drs. Martha Denckla and Russell Barkley were the first researchers to identify the profound impact of executive function deficits on students with attention deficit disorders.

An Overview of Executive Function

Executive function may be described as the brain's ability to manage learning activities and behavior, or, in other words, the *"brain's C.E.O."* Educators and parents should note that difficulties with executive functions are not just limited to students with ADD/ADHD. Students with learning disabilities and a variety of other neurological challenges including Asperger syndrome, autism, Tourette syndrome, obsessive compulsive disorder (OCD), and bipolar disorder may also experience these challenges.

Currently, experts don't agree on the prevalence of deficits in executive function (EF). Rates vary depending upon how EF deficits are assessed. Barkley reports that when more formal EF tests are used, 35 to 50 percent of individuals with ADD or ADHD are considered impaired. However, the rate is 89 to 98 percent when EF rating scales such as the *Behavior Rating Inventory of Executive Function* (BRIEF) or *The Barkley Deficits in Executive Functioning Scale* are used. Barkley has found that rating scales are the most accurate predictor of real world functioning.

If executive function deficits and related learning problems are untreated and medicine is not correct, students with an attention deficit disorder are more likely than their peers to fail a subject, be retained, be suspended, drop out of high school, or never graduate from college. Ninety percent experience some difficulty during their school years.

Components of Executive Function

These key components of executive function and their impact on school performance are reviewed in Summary 12:

- working memory and recall,
- impulsivity and inhibiting behavior,
- activation, arousal, and effort,
- internalizing language,
- complex problem solving (analysis and synthesis),
- controlling emotions,
- shifting,
- planning/organizing academic work and oneself,
- organizing materials,
- monitoring oneself and evaluating thoughts and actions.

Forgetfulness, disorganization, and an impaired sense of time also contribute to problems with traditional ***time management skills.***

When Are Executive Skills Needed?

Dr. Gerard Gioia and his associates have shown that the less familiar or more complex a task, the greater the demand for executive functions. According to Steven Guy, Ph.D., coauthor along with Gioia of the BRIEF—an assessment tool for executive function deficits—executive functions are needed in several situations:

- when information in tasks is new,
- in stressful situations,
- when planning ahead for the future,
- when tasks are complex and require multiple steps,
- when working memory demands are greater.

Impact of Executive Skills on Learning and Behavior

Belatedly, educators have learned that an average or above average IQ alone is *not* enough to do well in school. Students must also have strong executive function skills. Practically speaking, I've found it helpful to view the impact of executive function deficits in two general categories:

1. specific *academic challenges* such as writing essays, remembering what is read (comprehension), memorizing information, and completing complex math; and

2. *essential related skills* such as organization, getting started on and finishing work, remembering tasks and due dates, completing homework and long-term projects

in a timely manner, processing information in an efficient and timely manner, having good time awareness and management, using self-talk to direct behavior, using weekly reports, and planning ahead for the future. See Section 3 for strategies to address these issues.

As will be explained later, teachers typically recognize and accommodate academic challenges but are more likely to punish deficits in related skills such as difficulty getting started and finishing work—because these problems can look like laziness.

Additional Challenges to Address

In addition to EF deficits, three additional major problems may interfere with school success for students with ADD or ADHD:

1. **learning problems** (written expression, math computation, reading comprehension, slow processing speed);

2. **coexisting conditions** (untreated anxiety, depression, Tourette syndrome, or bipolar disorder);

3. **medication** (student not receiving medication or taking wrong medicine; doses too low).

Does Medication Help Students Academically?

As is explained in Section 5, Students with ADD or ADHD who are on medication show improved grades and academic performance. However, medication doesn't "fix" all deficits in executive skills. Because these skills are linked to differences in brain chemistry, a combination of medical, behavioral, and academic interventions offers the most effective intervention strategy.

The Role of Effective Teaching Strategies and Technology

During the last ten years, there have been two developments that are extremely beneficial to students with ADD/ADHD:

1. the increased use of brain-based teaching strategies to maximize our children's ability to learn; and

2. the increased use of technology to help our children compensate for weak memory and organizational skills.

Specific suggestions are provided in this section to help teachers strengthen instructional strategies in several key areas:
- modifying teaching methods and resources,
- modifying assignments,
- modifying testing and grading,
- modifying the level of supervision,
- utilizing technology.

The Importance of Accommodations

Because of deficits in executive skills as well as the challenges presented by the attention deficit itself, many students with attention deficit disorders need *accommodations* to succeed in class. Under federal law, schools are mandated to make changes in the classroom (accommodations) to help students with disabilities compensate for academic problems. For example, students who can't memorize multiplication tables may be allowed to use a calculator, or students who have slow processing skills may be given shorter assignments or extended time on tests.

Although not all students with attention deficits meet eligibility requirements for special education accommodations, many do. This section of the book provides an overview of accommodations that are helpful for teenagers with and without coexisting conditions. Federal laws are discussed in Section Four.

KEY STRATEGIES

Use a comprehensive approach:

- Educate students, parents, and teachers about the impact of ADD/ADHD and executive function deficits on learning and behavior.
- Provide classroom accommodations, if needed.
- Model key skills.
- Break down tasks into concrete steps; provide a guiding template or a job card to outline the required steps.
- Teach compensatory skills for academic skill deficits.

Address Executive Function Deficits in Educational Plans: If the teenager has problems with executive function deficits that interfere with her ability to learn, educators should:

- **List specific deficits in the student's** IEP or Section 504 Plan as issues of concern (written expression, math computation, long-term project completion, homework completion, etc.).

- **Include accommodations in the plan.** Appropriate accommodations should be included in the IEP/504 Plan. See Summaries 46, 49, 51, and 52 for more on IEPs and 504 Plans.

SUMMARY 12 Impact of Executive Function Deficits on Academics and Behavior

Unfortunately, deficits in executive functions (EF) often are mistaken for laziness because it can seem as if the student has chosen not to get started on and complete her work. Students are often admonished to "try harder." In reality, these students may work very hard, but because of their attention and EF deficits, their productivity does not match their greater level of effort. Educating parents, teachers, and students about the components and impact of executive function on learning and behavior is critical.

"Students are often told they can do better in school if they try harder. And in fact, everyone does better when they try harder. However, students who try harder for long periods of time experience significant anxiety. At some point, students have to 'try normal'."

—*Real Life ADHD!* (video clip)
Ted Mandelkorn, M.D., Puget Sound Behavioral Health
(Dr. Mandelkorn is a physician who also has ADHD)

Researchers have not yet agreed on the exact elements of executive function, as research is still in the early stages. Two researchers who specialize in attention deficit disorders, however, have written helpful working definitions. The creators of the BRIEF (*Behavior Rating Inventory for Executive Function*) also provide useful guidance.

Dr. Russell Barkley describes "executive function" as it relates to students with ADD or ADHD this way: ***"actions we perform to ourselves and direct at ourselves so as to accomplish self-control, goal-directed behavior, and the maximization of future outcomes."*** Most of these actions are cognitive—in other words, "done in our heads," and thus not observable. Dr. Barkley has developed a rating scale to identify deficits in executive functions.

Dr. Tom Brown gives us a metaphor that compares executive function of the brain to the function of a conductor in an orchestra. The conductor organizes various instruments to begin playing alone or in combination, integrates the music by bringing in and fading certain actions, and controls the instruments' pace and level of intensity.

Components of Executive Function

Students with attention deficits may have difficulties with some, but not all of the characteristics of executive function listed in this section. (The first six of these components are adapted from the work of Drs. Barkley and Brown.)

1. **Working memory and recall** (actively processing information; holding facts in mind while manipulating the information to guide actions for performing another cognitive task; moment-to-moment processing of information in a timely manner, which is slower in many with inattentive form of ADHD; accessing facts; time awareness)

2. **Impulsivity** (inhibiting speech and actions; thinking before acting or speaking)

3. **Activation, arousal, and effort** (getting started, staying alert, paying attention, finishing work)

4. **Controlling emotions** (low frustration tolerance; emotional blow-ups; sensitivity to criticism)

5.**Internalizing language** (using "self-talk" to control one's behavior and direct future actions)

6. **Taking an issue apart, analyzing the pieces, reconstituting and organizing it into new ideas** (complex problem solving; writing an essay or report; completing a long-term project).

Dr. Gerard Gioia, Dr. Steven Guy, and their colleagues have identified a few additional EF components that are assessed in their test, the BRIEF.

1. **Shifting** (trouble with transitions and new situations; hyper-focusing [getting stuck] on disappointments, hurtful comments, or a specific topic; difficulty with problem-solving flexibly)

2. **Planning/organizing** (not turning in homework; getting overwhelmed by large, complex assignments; failing to bring needed school supplies; getting caught up in details and missing the big picture)

3. **Organizing materials** (losing homework, school money, lunchbox, clothes; disorganized backpack and locker)

4. **Monitoring** (making "careless errors"; not double checking completed work; unaware of impact of one's own behavior on others)

Executive Functions During the Teen Years

The demands for executive skills expand exponentially during the teenage years. Teens have more teachers and classes, are given more complex assignments, must be more organized and plan ahead, and are expected to work more independently. In some ways, teachers in elementary school *serve as* the child's executive function; younger students are told what, when, and how to do most everything. However, demands and expectations change radically in middle school because most teens (but not those with ADHD) are developmentally ready for the additional skill demands.

As explained earlier, two broad school-related areas are negatively affected by EF deficits:

1. **Academics** such as essay and report writing, algebra, memorization, reading comprehension, and long-term project completion, and

2. **Essential related skills** such as organization, getting started and finishing work, using self-talk to direct behavior, remembering tasks and due dates, time awareness and management, and planning ahead for the future.

Specific Challenges for each Executive Function Component
Poor Working Memory and Recall

As explained earlier, working memory is what allows us to hold bits of information briefly in mind while we are manipulating other key pieces of information. Practically speaking, if you want to buy two books at the store but aren't sure you have enough cash in your wallet, working memory is what enables you to remember the total price of the two books while you count your money to see if you have enough. At school, students with working memory and recall deficits struggle when writing essays, completing complex math problems (algebra), remembering what they read (comprehension), and memorizing isolated facts.

Students in general vary in their working memory capacity. However, children with ADD/ADHD have more limited working memory capacity than their peers, and this deficit often affects their academic performance and behavior at home and in the classroom. The development of their working memory is significantly delayed; according to one researcher, some teens have the working memory of a seven-year-old.

Researchers report that working memory is a strong predictor of academic success and higher achievement test scores, perhaps even more so than an IQ score. In fact, one magazine headline asked, "Is executive function the new IQ?" Strong working memory enables students to control their attention and is essential for successful reading comprehension, written expression, and completion of complex math. As a result of their weak working memory, students with attention deficits also have greater difficulty ignoring distracting information while completing school work.

1. Affects the ***here and now:***
   - limited working memory capacity; weak short-term memory
   - forgetfulness, can't keep several things in mind

   As a result, students have difficulty:
   - following directions
   - multitasking as required for more complex tasks: writing essays, math problem solving, reading comprehension
   - performing math computations or manipulating other information in their heads
   - processing large amounts of information; lengthy directions or complex, multistep tasks
   - remembering a "to do" list
   - remembering multiple requests; forget assignments, books, chores
   - with weak reading comprehension; need to reread pages, trouble remembering what is read

2. Affects the ***speed of processing incoming and outgoing information:***
   - slower processing speed for incoming and outgoing data
   - variable speeds in responding

   According to articles authored by Dr. Rosemary Tannock, research has shown that contrary to popular belief that children with ADHD are "driven by a motor," performances on both neuropsychological and real-world tasks indicate that children with ADHD are often slow at completing tasks, particularly when the task is cognitively demanding plus they tend to have highly variable speed of responding." Processing speed in children with the inattentive form of ADD is even slower and rates of response vary from day-to-day.

   As a result, students:
   - may not grasp all the instructions required for completion of work
   - may be slower at copying down information, completing assignments, and retrieving information
   - need more time to complete work and to process new information
   - need more time to formulate an answer in response to verbal or written questions
   - may need shortened assignments and/or extended time

3. Affects their sense of ***past events:***
   - difficulty recalling the past

   As a result, students:
   - don't study past actions
   - don't learn easily from past behavior
   - act without a sense of hindsight
   - repeat misbehavior

2

4. Affects their *sense of time:* students have difficulty:
   - holding events in mind (this skill is needed to develop a sense of time and awareness of the passage of time)
   - using their sense of time to prepare for upcoming events and the future
   - holding events in mind in the order they occurred (this ability is needed as a building block for a sense of time)

   As a result, students:
   - have difficulty judging the passage of time accurately
   - can't accurately estimate how much time it will take to finish a task (homework)
   - perceive time as passing slowly when tasks are rote, boring, or low interest
   - are impatient when asked to wait; time drags by
   - occasionally hyperfocus on high-interest tasks and lose all track of time
   - have a sense of time like younger children who do not have ADD or ADHD

5. Affects their sense of *self-awareness*
   - diminished sense of self-awareness (this awareness is needed to feel a sense of self-control)

   As a result, students don't:
   - examine their own behavior
   - easily change their own behavior
   - see how their behavior affects others
   - see another person's perspective

6. Affects their *sense of the future:*
   - limited foresight: students live in the present, focus on the here and now, rather than the future
   - less likely to talk about time or the future than their peers

   As a result, students have difficulty:
   - projecting lessons learned in the past forward into the future (foresight)
   - preparing for the future
   - being prepared for the future

Impulsivity and Difficulties in Inhibiting Behavior

1. Affects their *ability to inhibit their speech and behavior*
   - difficulty stopping and thinking before they act or speak
   - difficulty stopping their behavior, even when it isn't working, and changing to an effective behavior

   As a result, students:
   - blurt out remarks in class; butt into conversations
   - talk back to teachers before they think
   - have yelling matches or fights with other students
   - act impulsively and get into trouble, maybe even suspended
   - don't easily change or correct unproductive strategies

Activation, Arousal, and Effort

Students with ADD and ADHD have *difficulty getting started, staying alert, paying attention, and finishing work.*

1. Affects their *ability to start and complete a task*
   - appear unmotivated
   - have difficulty getting started
   - have difficulty maintaining their effort

   As a result, students:
   - procrastinate
   - don't follow through
   - fail to finish school work
   - may need a looming deadline or crisis that increases adrenalin and brain activity, thus enabling them to finally get started

2. Affects their *level of alertness and ability to pay attention*
   - difficulty becoming alert enough to pay attention
   - difficulty maintaining attention
   - serious sleep problems
   - low energy levels (in students with ADD)

   As a result, students:
   - are easily distracted
   - don't pay attention consistently
   - don't seem to have enough energy to get started or complete tasks (ADD)
   - are irritable, perhaps because of sleep deprivation
   - sleep in class

Controlling Their Emotions

1. Affects the *ability to control their emotions:* students have difficulty:
   - putting emotions on hold
   - separating emotions and actions (if a student is angry with a classmate, she may act without thinking of the consequences. For example, she may curse or hit another student even though she may be kicked off the basketball team that she dearly loves)
   - splitting facts from feelings (this skill is needed to be objective)

   As a result, students are:
   - more emotionally reactive
   - more sensitive to criticism
   - mainly concerned with their own feelings
   - more self-centered or immature
   - more selfish

2. Affects their *ability to direct behavior toward goals;* students have difficulty:
   - delaying gratification
   - regulating emotions to achieve goals
   - putting up with boring or tedious activities
   - focusing on future goals; immediate feelings (here and now) are most important
   - motivating themselves; rewards in school (grades) are too far in the future to be effective

As a result, students:
- want to quit if they become bored with homework, a job, or college
- don't stick with things; give up more easily than their peers
- must receive rewards immediately
- have difficulty generating their own intrinsic rewards (feeling good simply because the work is done)

Internalizing Language

1. ***Internalization of speech or self-talk is delayed;*** students have difficulty:
   - using language to control their own actions
   - directing their behavior with their own internal voice

   As a result, students have difficulty:
   - generating the thoughts necessary to guide their actions—for example, telling themselves to "get started on your homework"
   - managing their own behavior
   - reflecting on their thoughts and actions
   - thinking through their actions beforehand
   - using their past experiences
   - following rules

Taking an Issue Apart, Analyzing Pieces, Reconstituting, and Organizing into a New Entity

1. Affects their ability to do ***complex problem solving***

   As a result, students have difficulty:
   - analyzing and breaking down a problem
   - determining what caused a problem and developing a plan to correct it
   - knowing how and where to start to solve the problem; knowing what the finished product should look like

2. Affects their ***spoken and written communication***
   - weak verbal fluency, especially when responding to a question or giving a concise answer
   - difficulty communicating with others

   As a result, students have difficulty:
   - writing essays or reports and sequencing and organizing ideas
   - rapidly stringing words together
   - describing an issue in words
   - expressing themselves rapidly and effectively

Shifting

1. Affects their ability to ***shift from one issue or event to another***

   As a result, students:
   - have difficulty with transitions and new situations; difficulty shifting from one academic topic to another, from class to class, or from PE back to class
   - have difficulty with problem-solving flexibility
   - may hyperfocus on some activities (computers, video games)

- may act out when a substitute teacher is present or class schedules change
- perseverate; can't stop thinking about disappointments, hurtful comments, or a specific topic

Planning and Organizing; Organizing Materials

1. Affects their ability to **plan ahead, complete academic assignments, and organize themselves and their materials**

    As a result, students have difficulty:
    - planning ahead for the future (e.g., remembering to sign up for sports; fill out college applications and mail them in)
    - seeing the big picture (may get caught up in details)
    - writing essays (getting ideas down on paper and organizing them) and doing complex math
    - multi-tasking to organize and complete a task
    - planning and completing large, complex assignments
    - starting school assignments before the last minute
    - remembering to bring assignments and books home, or to bring homework back to school and turn it in
    - following through
    - bringing needed school supplies or getting permission slips signed
    - keeping up with possessions: they lose homework, school money, lunch box, clothes, equipment
    - organizing possessions; they have a disorganized, messy desk, backpack, and locker
    - cleaning up messes they make

Monitoring

1. Affects ability to *monitor self (academic work and behavior)*

    As a result, students:
    - Make "careless errors"
    - Produce sloppy school work
    - Don't double check completed work
    - Are unaware of the impact of their behavior on others
    - Talk too loudly or monopolize conversations

What You Can Do to Help

Strategies to address key executive skills are provided in several summaries in this book, as shown below:

1. **Working memory and recall: S 24, 33** (memory strategies; external prompts)

2. **Impulsivity: Section 5** (medication helps)

3. **Activation, arousal, and effort: S 37** (tips for "getting started)

4. **Controlling emotions: Section 5** (medication helps; academic success reduces likelihood of meltdowns)

5. **Internalizing language: Section 5** (medication helps; external prompts)

6. **Taking an issue apart, analyzing the pieces, reconstituting, and organizing it into new ideas: S 16-21, 38** (tips for writing essays and doing complex math; strategies for long-term projects)

7. **Shifting: S 60** (prompt before changes occur)

8. **Planning/organizing: S 32** (organizational tips)

9. **Organizing materials: S 18, 25, 27, 32, 39-40** (writing, long-term project, and organizational tips)

10. **Monitoring: S 67** (self-management tips)

Descriptions of each component of executive function deficits and its impact on learning and behavior from Drs. Barkley and Rosemary Tannock were invaluable in developing this section. Information from Steven Guy, Ph.D. and the BRIEF also was helpful in understanding the impact of deficits in shifting, monitoring, and planning and organizing.

Resources

Barkley, Russell. *ADHD and the Nature of Self-control*. New York: Guilford Press, 1997.

Barkley, Russell, Murphy, K. & Fischer, M. *ADHD in Adults: What the Science Says.* New York: Guilford Press, 2008.

Barkley, Russell. *Attention Deficit Hyperactivity Disorder.* 3rd ed. New York: Guilford Press, 2006.

Brown, Thomas E. *Attention Deficit Disorders and Comorbidities in Children, Adolescents, and Adults.* Washington, DC: American Psychiatric Press, 2000.

Dawson, Peg & Richard Guare. *Smart but Scattered*. New York: Guilford Press, 2008.

Gioia, Gerard, Peter K. Isquith, Steven C. Guy & Lauren Kenworthy, *BRIEF—Behavior Rating Inventory for Executive Function.* Lutz, FL: Psychological Assessment Resources (PAR).

Rethinking ADHD from a Cognitive Perspective. http://research.aboutkidshealth.ca/teachadhd

(Website sponsored by the Hospital for Sick Children, workplace of Dr. Rosemary Tannock and other leading researchers on ADD/ADHD).

SUMMARY 13 Learning Problems Commonly Associated with ADD and ADHD

Several learning problems are common among teenagers with ADD or ADHD. Some learning problems are the result of: 1) the actual symptoms of ADD or ADHD, and others occur because a student also has 2) deficits in executive functions, 3) a Specific Learning Disability (SLD), or 4) coexisting conditions such as depression or anxiety that are not being treated. Most studies of students with attention deficits have found that 25 to 50 percent have learning disabilities.

One study published in *ADHD Reports* found that up to 65 percent of students with ADHD had major problems with written expression. These problems, as well as practical implications for a student's school performance, are discussed below. However, keep in mind that each teenager with ADD or ADHD is *unique* and may have *some*, but not all of these learning difficulties.

Under the Individuals with Disabilities Education Act (IDEA), **students with attention deficits are clearly eligible for classroom accommodations** if their learning is adversely affected by their disorder. (See Summaries 43 & 44.) However, all too often behavior problems related to the ADD or ADHD become the primary focus of school interventions. Consequently, learning problems and related executive function deficits such as disorganization are often overlooked.

A study by Dr. Marc Atkins, professor, University of Illinois Chicago, clearly makes the point that academic issues should be addressed first when our students are struggling or misbehaving in the classroom. When Dr. Atkins implemented behavioral interventions for children with attention deficits in a classroom, their behavior did improve, but academics did not. Amazingly, when he next provided tutoring for similar students, not only did their academic performance improve, but their behavior improved also. **Many students with attention deficits are experiencing serious academic problems that may be at the root of much of their misbehavior!** Special efforts must be made to identify these academic problems and to provide appropriate accommodations in the classroom. Accommodations should be individualized and designed to address each student's specific learning problems.

Symptoms of ADD/ADHD That Interfere with Learning

Several characteristics that are a direct result of having an attention deficit cause serious learning problems. Most teens with ADD or ADHD have problems in these areas:

1. **Inattention/Poor Concentration**
    - Difficulty listening in class: may daydream, space out, and miss lecture content or homework assignments
    - Lack of attention to detail: makes "careless mistakes" in work; doesn't notice errors in grammar, punctuation, capitalization, spelling, or changes in signs (+,-, x) or exponents in math
    - Difficulty staying on task and finishing school work; distractible: moves from one uncompleted task to another; when distracted, has difficulty refocusing on work.
    - Lack of awareness of grades: may not know if passing or failing a class.

2. **Impulsivity**
    - Rushes through work: doesn't read directions; takes shortcuts in written work (such as doing math in his head); may not read the whole question before giving an answer; doesn't double check work (a greater problem among students with ADHD hyperactive/impulsive)

- Difficulty delaying gratification: gives up working for rewards occurring in too distant future (two weeks to six months or more). (Working for grades requires delaying gratification for six weeks or more.)

Executive Function Deficits That Have a Profound Effect on School Work

The majority of students with ADD/ADHD also have deficits in the key executive functions listed below. For more details, see Summary 12 and Section 3.

1. Poor organizational skills
2. Poor working memory
3. Difficulty activating and maintaining alertness
4. Reconstitution (taking issues apart, analyzing the pieces, and combining into a new whole)
5. Internalizing language
6. Controlling emotions
7. Shifting (from one issue or event to another)
8. Planning and organizing materials and assignments
9. Controlling emotions
10. Planning and organizing materials and assignments
11. Self-monitoring

Common Learning Problems Often Accompanying ADD and ADHD

Several learning problems, although not directly related to ADD or ADHD, often occur along with the disorder. If these problems are severe enough, the student will be diagnosed with a Specific Learning Disability (SLD). The ADD/SLD connection is discussed in more detail in Summary 50.

1. **Language Deficits:** Several language-processing problems are common among teenagers with ADD or ADHD. Deficits marked with an asterisk (*) are considered Specific Learning Disabilities.

   1.1. **Spoken Language* (Oral Expression)**
      - Talks a lot spontaneously (ADHD), if he can choose the topic.
      - Has difficulty responding to questions when he must think and give organized, concise answers; may talk less or give rambling answers.
      - Reluctant to speak in class (ADD) because of slow processing speed and difficulty organizing ideas; may even be willing to accept failing grade rather than speak in front of the class.

   1.2. **Written Language* (Verbal Expression; Input and Output)**
      - Slow reading and writing; takes longer to complete work, produces less written work.
      - Difficulty writing essays; difficulty organizing ideas and putting them in proper sequence.
      - Difficulty getting ideas out of head and on paper; written test answers, discussion questions, or essays may be brief.
      - Written expression is adversely affected by deficits in key executive skills: working memory and analysis, sequencing and synthesis.

1.3. Processing Speed: Low scores on the Processing Speed Index (PSI) of the Wechsler Intelligence Scale for Children (WISC-IV) or Wechsler Adult Intelligence Scale (WAIS-IV) may be indicative of problems with ***hand-eye coordination*** or ***slow processing speed.*** Several subtests are indicative of these problems: Coding and Symbol Search for both the WISC and WAIS, plus Cancellation for the WAIS. One way to rule out handwriting problems is to look at scores on the Symbol Search. Low scores on the Symbol Search alone may be indicative of problems with slow speed in processing of information since handwriting is not required on the subtest. These are the students who will need shorter assignments or extended time.

- Slow processing of information: reads, writes, and responds slowly; may take twice as long to do homework and class work and to complete tests; doesn't have time to double check answers;
- Recalls facts slowly;
- Can't quickly retrieve information stored in memory such as math facts, algebra formulas, foreign languages, history dates or facts, or grammar rules.

1.4. Math Computation*

- Difficulty automatizing basic math facts/slow math computation: cannot rapidly retrieve and use basic math facts such as multiplication tables, division, addition, or subtraction facts (Summaries 21-24).

1.5. Listening Comprehension

- Difficulty following directions: becomes confused with lengthy verbal directions, may not "hear" or pick out homework assignments from a teacher's lecture;
- Loses main point; difficulty identifying key points to write while taking notes.

1.6. Reading Comprehension*

- Can't remember what is read, then has to read it again; difficulty understanding and remembering what is read; difficulty with long reading passages.
- Makes errors when reading silently; may skip words, phrases, or lines; may lose place when reading.
- Difficulty identifying and remembering key facts from reading; linked to executive functioning deficits (holding key information in working memory).

2. Poor Memory: Students with ADD or ADHD may have difficulties with short-term, long-term, and/or working memory. Often these memory skills are interrelated. For example, if the student's working memory is limited, not as much information gets into storage or is retrieved from long-term memory.

2.1. Short-Term Memory Problems

- Difficulty remembering information in the here and now, for roughly 20 seconds: may not remember teacher requests, instructions, multi-step directions, or verbally presented math problems.

2.2. Working Memory Problems (an executive skill)

- Low scores on the Working Memory Index (WMI) of the Wechsler Intelligence Scale for Children (WISC-IV) or the Wechsler Adult Intelligence Scale (WAIS) are indicative of problems with ***working memory.***
- Difficulty holding information in mind while actively processing it; for example, may have difficulty holding a math problem in short-term memory while reaching into long-term memory to retrieve needed formulas and math facts to solve the problem.

- Difficulty retrieving information from long-term memory that is needed in working memory to solve a problem;
- May take longer on assignments and tests because of poor access to memory.

2.3. Long-Term Memory Problems

- Difficulty placing information into, and retrieving it from, long-term storage.
- Difficulty memorizing material such as multiplication tables, math facts, or formulas; spelling words; foreign languages; and/or history dates; lacks memorization strategies.
- Difficulty quickly retrieving information stored in long-term memory.
- May not recall information memorized the night before, such as math facts, spelling words, or history facts.
- May not do well on tests requiring recall of information from long-term memory, even though the student studies.
- Memory is consolidated during sleep; since 56 percent of our children have problems getting restful sleep, memorization and recall is often more difficult for them.

2.4. Forgetfulness Related to Short- and Long-Term Memory Problems

- May forget homework assignments.
- May forget to take books home.
- May forget to turn in completed assignments to the teacher.
- May forget special assignments or make-up work or tests.
- May forget to stay after school for teacher conferences or detention.

3. Poor Fine-Motor Coordination

- Handwriting is poor; sometimes, small and difficult to read.
- May write slowly; may avoid writing and homework because writing is difficult.
- May prefer to print rather than write cursive, even as an adult. Mel Levine, M.D., provides a good reason for their preferred printing: printing requires less memory than writing cursive. Produces less written work.
- May be artistic; motor coordination required for art may be quite good.

Difficulties in school may be caused by a combination of several learning problems. One student may not take good notes in class because he can't pay attention, can't pick out main points, and has poor fine-motor coordination. Another student may not do well on a test because he reads, thinks, and writes slowly, has difficulty organizing his thoughts, and has difficulty memorizing and quickly retrieving the information from memory.

Examples of how teachers and parents may use information about a student's specific learning problems and possible accommodations are provided in Summaries 48, 51, and 52.

Brain-Based Learning Strategies

In recent years, more and more teachers have been employing brain-based learning strategies in their classrooms. In other words, teachers are using information on the neuroscience of the brain and how the brain learns to guide their teaching strategies. The good news is that these brain-based teaching strategies are effective for all students, regardless of their learning challenges. Renate and Geoffrey Caine, founders of the Caine Learning Institute, suggest several principles to be considered by teachers. (I've added a simpler description of the Caines' principles in parentheses.)

- *The brain is a complex adaptive system.* (Brain neuroplasticity allows the growth of new brain cells.)

- *The brain is a social brain.* (It develops better when working in concert with other brains.)

- *The search for meaning is innate.* (Students do this automatically; meaning is more important than information alone.)

- *Emotions are critical to finding meaning in information.* (Positive emotions drive our attention and enhance learning and memory.)

- *Learning involves at least two ways of organizing memory—spatial and rote.* (Students learn best through their spatial memory.)

- *Learning is developmental.* (Younger children and students with delayed brain development, including students with ADD/ADHD, do not have the learning/ memory capacity of older students.)

- *Complex learning is enhanced by challenges and inhibited by threat.* (Students who fear failure or embarrassment can't learn easily.)

- *Every brain is uniquely organized.* (Information is stored in multiple areas of the brain and is retrieved through multiple memory and neural pathways.)

The Caines recommend three important interactive teaching strategies:

1. **Orchestrated immersion:** Create a learning environment that surrounds the student with interesting, related, hands-on activities.

2. **Relaxed alertness:** Eliminate fear while creating a challenging learning environment.

3. **Active processing:** Connect information to prior learning and allow the student to actively process the information.

Implementing Brain-based Learning Strategies in the Classroom

My sister, Dr. Billie Abney, a high school teacher, retired chiropractor, and an adult with ADHD, intuitively has created just such a brain-based learning environment for her students. For example, she brings pig parts to class for her anatomy students, who take turns inflating the pig lungs. One day the students took colored sidewalk chalk and textbook pictures of the heart, and went outside to draw and label parts of the heart on the parking lot in front of the school. She has also shown YouTube clips of teens having skateboarding accidents. After their initial emotional reactions, students name the bones that are broken and the muscles that are involved. For vocabulary reviews, her students form teams and text-message answers back and forth. Currently she is seeking donations of exercise cycles for her room, for those students who have trouble staying alert and may need a periodic brain boost. She has also been known to offer coffee to students who are not alert during her first period class.

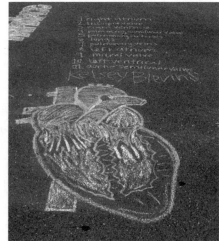

Maximizing Learning during Instructional Periods

Researchers tell us learning occurs best during shorter instructional periods. According to David Sousa, Ed.D., author of *How the Brain Learns*, an ideal lesson is divided into three sections.

1. Students best remember the information that comes first (***prime-time 1***),

2. They remember second best the information that comes last (***prime-time 2***).

3. Teens remember least the information that comes in the middle (***downtime).***

New information should be presented during "prime-time 1" and closure on the topic in "prime-time 2." During "downtime" (which allows the brain to process the new information), teachers may offer review activities such as a worksheet, games, or a lab activity to practice what they have learned.

Time Limits for Working Memory

Researchers such as Peter Russell have found that teens can engage their working memory intensively for only 10 to 20 minutes before brain fatigue sets in; preadolescents, only 5 to 10 minutes. However, because of their delayed brain development, teens with ADD/ADHD may have more limited working memory than the average teen.

For maximum learning, Dr. Sousa suggests packaging lessons into several 20- or 40-minute segments. For a 20-minute session, "prime-time 1" learning lasts roughly 10-15 minutes; "downtime," 2 minutes; and "prime-time 2," 3 minutes.

Amazing "Ah-Ha Moments"

In reading about brain-based learning, especially Sousa's *How the Brain Learns*, I've had some wonderful "ah-ha moments."

Regarding Movement:

■ ***Movement is critical.*** After twenty minutes of sitting, blood pools in our seat and feet. Within a minute of standing up and moving, 15 percent more blood and critical oxygen reach our brain. Linda Sorenson, a veteran teacher, encourages active "brain breaks" to reenergize the student, thus maximizing learning. (See Summary 16-A.) Exercise, fruit, and water have been shown to improve academic performance on tests.

■ ***Fidgeting and movement facilitate learning***. Mark Rapport, Ph.D., psychology professor at the University of Central Florida, found that students with attention deficits who were participating in routine class tasks were not especially active. However, when more complex tasks requiring working memory were introduced, activity levels increased significantly. He suggests that activity helped stimulate brain activity and blood flow, thus enhancing attention. Chewing gum has also been shown to improve attention for similar reasons.

Regarding Brain Fuel:

- *Glucose and oxygen are our brain's fuel.* The more challenging the task, the more fuel the brain requires. Water is essential since it helps move neuron signals through the brain and keeps the lungs moist so oxygen can get into the bloodstream more easily. So, utilize teaching strategies that increase the levels of glucose, oxygen, and water in the brain. Most students don't drink enough water each day.

- *Some snacks contain glucose (brain fuel).* Raisins are an excellent fruit source of glucose and can boost working memory, attention, and motor function.

Regarding Humor:

- *Laughter stimulates the frontal lobes of the brain.* Starting the class with a good joke or humorous tale creates laughter, which in turn increases the level of oxygen in the blood. Laughter also produces endorphins, which stimulate the brain's frontal lobes and give students a sense of well-being. Positive emotions enhance learning retention. Plus, when people laugh together, they bond and establish a community spirit.

Regarding Working Memory:

- *Working memory can stay activated for only 10-20 minutes for demanding tasks* (as explained in earlier paragraphs).

- *The capacity of working memory is limited to a few items.* On average, high schoolers can handle up to seven items. However, keep in mind the developmental brain delay in students with ADHD may limit the number of items they can address to five or fewer. According to David Sousa, teachers can't expect students to master in one lesson "the names and locations of the ten most important rivers in the world."

Regarding Retention:

- *Retention improves when information is connected to past experiences.* Researchers found that when new learning is easily understood (makes sense) and is connected to past experiences, activity in the brain increases and retention improves dramatically.

Regarding Emotion:

- *Emotion is the "on-off switch" to learning* according to Priscilla Vail, author of a book entitled *Emotion: The On/Off Switch for Learning*. Negative emotions such as anxiety, fear, sadness, or anger disrupt thinking, memory, and learning. Creating a positive classroom free of fear and anxiety is critical.

Regarding Exercise:

■ ***Exercise improves attention and working memory, plus facilitates growth of new brain cells.*** According to Dr. John Ratey, exercise has been shown to increase endorphins (makes you feel better), the neurotransmitters dopamine and serotonin (increases attention, working memory, and mood) and neurotrophin BDNF ("Miracle Gro" for brain cells).

Regarding Sleep:

■ ***Restful sleep is critical for remembering information.*** The process of absorbing new information into long-term memory occurs during deep sleep. Since over 50 percent of students with ADD/ADHD have sleep deficits, it's critical for teachers to encourage parents to seek treatment when needed.

Practical Implications

Several educational concepts may be used to implement good brain-based teaching principles:
■ mastery learning,
■ learning styles,
■ multiple intelligences,
■ cooperative learning,
■ practical simulations,
■ experiential learning,
■ problem-based learning, and
■ learning through movement.

Experiential learning, learning styles, and multiple intelligences are discussed in more detail in subsequent summaries.

SUMMARY 15 — Learning Styles

Most teachers today are well aware that students have different learning styles. Consequently, teachers know they can be more effective if they vary their teaching strategies. Although the issue of learning styles is a complex concept that obviously cannot be addressed in detail in this book, a brief overview may be helpful.

Although experts do not agree upon what constitutes intelligence, there is general agreement that different people learn certain types of information more easily than others. Students with ADD or ADHD are often visual learners and do not learn as easily in traditional lectures where they passively listen to teachers.

As discussed below, Howard Gardner and Robert Sternberg have come up with different ways to categorize the ways that students show their intelligence.

Howard Gardner's Theory of Multiple Intelligences

Although it would be impossible for teachers to read everything that educators and psychologists have written about learning styles, most teachers are familiar with Howard Gardner's eight different learning styles. Gardner believes that each of us is 100 percent smart, and that our total intelligence is made up of at least eight different types of "smartness." This is in contrast to traditional IQ tests, which primarily measure language and math intelligence.

Here is how Sandra Rief, author of several best-selling books on ADD or ADHD, summarizes Gardner's types of intelligence:

1. **Linguistic Learner**—*Word smart*: "learns best through oral and written language and by hearing, saying, and seeing words."

2. **Logical Mathematical Learner**—*Number smart*: "learns best by categorizing, making their own discoveries, classifying and working with abstract patterns and relationships."

3. **Visual-Spatial Learner**—*Art smart*: "learns best through visual presentations and by visualizing, using his mind's eye, and working with colors/pictures."

4. **Body-Kinesthetic Learner**—*Body smart*: "learns best through hands-on activities and by doing, touching, moving, and interacting with space."

5. **Musical Learner**—*Music smart:* "learns best through rhythm, music, and melody."

6. **Interpersonal Learner**—*People smart*: "learns best by sharing, relating, interacting, and cooperating with others."

7. **Intrapersonal Learner**—*Self smart*: "learns best by working alone, having self-paced instruction, and individualized projects."

8. **Naturalist Learner**—*Nature smart*. Gardner later added this eighth intelligence which refers to learning by being exposed to experiences in the natural world.

Although students with attention deficits are not all alike in their learning styles, many of them may learn **spatially** (by seeing) and **kinesthetically** (by doing). They seem to have greater difficulty with linguistic and logical mathematical learning.

Dean Robert Sternberg's Patterns of Intelligence

Dean Robert Sternberg, a professor at Tufts, categorizes learning skills differently than Gardner. He has identified three patterns of intelligence: analytical, creative, and practical.

1. Analytical intelligences enable students to analyze, critique, and evaluate information.

2. The creatively intelligent are skilled at discovering, inventing, and creating.

3. Practically intelligent students excel at applying, utilizing, and implementing.

Researchers have found that students learn best when they are taught in ways that best match their type of intelligence or achievement. Considering the differences in students with AADD/DHD, any single student may excel in any one of these intelligences. However, many students with attention deficits may be more likely to excel creatively or in areas involving practical intelligence.

Maximizing Student Learning

The National Training Laboratory (NTL) Institute has produced an informative diagram called the "Learning Pyramid." The NTL Pyramid (below) displays the best teaching strategies for maximum learning retention for up to twenty-four hours. According to the pyramid, lecture is the least effective teaching strategy.

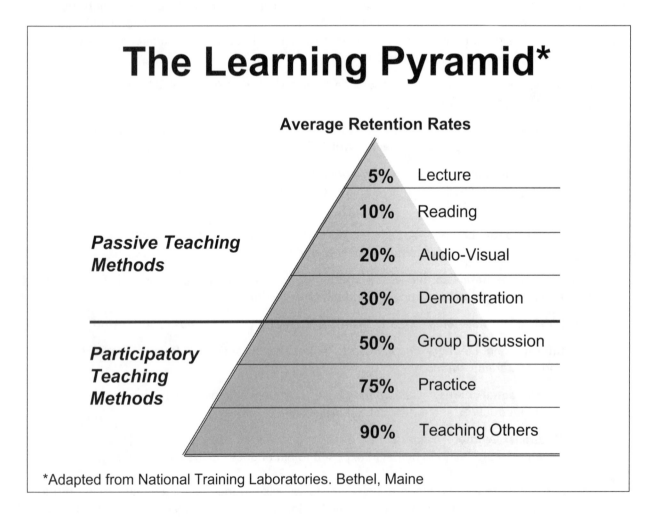

The Learning Pyramid*

Average Retention Rates

Passive Teaching Methods

5% Lecture

10% Reading

20% Audio-Visual

30% Demonstration

Participatory Teaching Methods

50% Group Discussion

75% Practice

90% Teaching Others

*Adapted from National Training Laboratories. Bethel, Maine

Auditory versus Visual Learners

Dr. Edna Copeland, author *of Attention, Please!* and one of the early pioneers in understanding the complexities of attention deficit disorders, reports that she has observed a shift in student learning styles from auditory to visual during the last thirty years or so. Judy Kranzler, a veteran reading specialist, estimates that ***65 percent of all students prefer and perform better with visual learning strategies!*** Furthermore, 30 percent do not learn well auditorily—that is, from just listening to the teacher. At least 50 percent of all students are frustrated with traditional left-brain, sequential type assignments.

In other words, school work that requires logical, linear sequencing and memorization of facts is difficult and our students prefer work that involves creative exploration. So, learning by listening to teachers lecture and by reading textbooks (*linguistic learning*) is often more challenging for students with attention deficits. Sometimes because these students learn differently from others, they may come to believe that they are not very smart.

Impact of Teacher Learning Style on Teaching

Since my own learning style is more *auditory, logical mathematical, linear, sequential, and convergent*, as a young teacher, I tended to teach that way. In other words, I gave lectures to my students and expected them to memorize the right answers. I wanted students to go step-by-step, in a logical order, and quickly narrow things down to one right answer. Since it comes naturally to teach using one's personal learning style, ***teachers should be aware of their personal style and make an effort to use a greater variety of teaching strategies***.

Students with attention deficits may have a more innovative, intuitive, and divergent learning style. So, being creative and finding their own way of solving a problem may be more appealing to them. Although these students must learn to produce school work that is logical, linear, and sequential, it is often very difficult for them. Consequently, ***students with ADD or ADHD often need more hands-on activities that incorporate visual cues*** to master challenging academics such as math or writing essays or book reports!

Numerous strategies that rely on visual cues and hands-on and interactive activities are included in Summaries 16A–16E. In addition, these learning and thinking differences, also referred to as ***left and right brain thinking***, are discussed in Summaries 35 and 36 with regard to their impact on time management.

Resources

Caine, Renate and Geoffrey Caine. *Making Connections: Teaching and the Human Brain.* 3rd ed. Palo Alto, CA: Dale Seymour Publications, 1994.

Copeland, Edna. "We Have Treated the ADD: Now We Shall Begin." ADDA National Conference workshop. Atlanta, GA, May 2000.

Gardner, Howard. *Multiple Intelligences: New Horizons in Theory and Practice.* New York, NY: Basic Books, 2006.

"Hyperactivity Enables Children with ADHD to Stay Alert: Teachers Urged Not to Severely Limit That Activity." *ScienceDaily,* March 11, 2009.

Ratey, John. *Spark: The Revolutionary New Science of Exercise and the Brain.* London: Little, Brown and Company, 2008.

Rief, Sandra. *How to Reach and Teach Children with ADD/ADHD,* 2nd ed. San Francisco, CA: Jossey Bass, 2005. (Additional helpful information is available at www.sandrarief.com).

Sousa, David. *How The Brain Learns.* 3rd ed. Thousand Oaks, CA: Corwin Press, 2006.

Ⓢᵁᴹᴹᴬᴿʸ 16 General Teaching Tips

Teaching today is such a demanding job, especially when individualized instruction is required to meet each student's needs. It's incredibly difficult for a teacher to single-handedly tailor his or her teaching to meet everyone's needs. So, tapping other resources is critical. Remember that **you don't have to be the only teacher** in your class! Seek assistance from students, computer technology, classroom aides, or parents.

If you've done everything you can and the student with ADD or ADHD continues to struggle, ask for help. Talk with veteran teachers or the guidance counselor to come up with some new ideas. Revisions to IDEA, the federal education law, require that when a child is struggling in class, teachers must implement interventions, known as Response to Intervention (RTI), to ameliorate problem areas…even if students aren't eligible for special education.

In addition, most states have established teams of educators who meet to brainstorm ideas to help students struggling with more severe problems. In Georgia, they are called "Student Support Teams" but these groups may go by different names in different states. Typically, a team of educators is available to help any student who is struggling academically, whether or not she needs special education services. However, if problems are serious, this team may refer the student to the IEP team for an evaluation for special education services.

The IEP Team, comprised of a group of teachers and administrators, meets to discuss the strengths and needs of students receiving special education and to develop educational plans for them. For more information, see Summary 55.

Summary of Strategies

A summary of teaching strategies that I have culled from local colleagues, nationally recognized educators, and my own experiences as a teacher and school psychologist is provided below. These tips may be helpful in teaching all students, not just those with attention deficits.

Although it goes without saying, these strategies will *not* work with *all* students with ADD or ADHD. Choose strategies from this section that you think are most likely to work with a specific student and that fit comfortably with your teaching philosophy. Revise the plan or try a different strategy until you find the ones that work best for each student.

If you want to know if an accommodation is working, look at a few key barometers:

1. Is the student completing more school work?
2. Are grades improving?
3. Does the student seem less tense and happier? Does she, in fact, seem to enjoy class?
4. Don't overlook the value of asking the real experts—the teenagers themselves—whether it's working.

Some General Advice

1. **A positive student-teacher relationship is essential.** Dr. Robert Marzano reports a *31 percent reduction in discipline problems* in classrooms where a strong positive relationship exists.

2. **Simple interventions are usually best!** Don't give more accommodations than are necessary to help the student become successful academically.

3. **Seek student input and approval.** As accommodations are developed for individual students, remember to involve them in making decisions. Student buy-in is a critical part of this process. You may develop the most extraordinary plan, but if the student is too embarrassed or overwhelmed to use it, the plan won't work. So, give the student some choices. For example, you might say something like this:

   "Students with ADD often have difficulty with math. I think there are a few things we could do to help you in class. Here are two or three choices.... Would you like to try one of these options?" If you want to be more direct: *"Which one would you like to try?"* If you feel strongly that one particular accommodation would be helpful, then say just that: *"Many students with ADD find it helpful to . . . do every third problem. Why don't you try that?"*

4. **Remember the most common problem areas.** Although each student's problem areas will vary, often the greatest challenges occur in written expression, complex, multi-step math, memorization, spelling, punctuation, or foreign languages.

5. **Consider learning retention when selecting teaching strategies.** Review The National Training Laboratories "Learning Pyramid" (Summary 15) for information regarding learning retention rates after 24 hours and effectiveness of teaching strategies.

6. **Use teaching strategies that actively engage students in learning.** Dr. Martha Denckla, noted neuroscientist, offers this metaphor to describe the primary attentional deficits these students face in a classroom: Students with ADHD use an overactive "radar beam" that sweeps over the surroundings. These students are weak in "spotlighting" and processing information that requires narrow, linear, steady, sequential, or intensive thinking ...*unless* the topic is intrinsically interesting or rewarding. In other words, students address class work in a superficial manner.

7. **Use new brain research to guide teaching strategies.** As we learn more about how the brain learns best, the importance of *movement and brain rest times* cannot be emphasized too much. Research by Eric Jensen, David Sousa, and others has demonstrated that the brain's ability to retain newly learned information, and subsequently transfer that information into long-term memory, is enhanced when teaching is carried out in episodes of 10 to 20 minutes (even in adults!). Between episodes, teachers should lead students in paradoxically named "downtime" activities consisting of anything from quiet reflection and paired discussions to jumping jacks and classroom exercises. The important thing is that the learner's brain be given a chance to "reset" and reenergize to get ready for more learning.

   The Importance of Fidgeting: Dr. Mark D. Rapport's research indicates that children with ADHD need to move more to maintain the required level of alertness while performing tasks that challenge their working memory. In other words, fidgeting can be beneficial for students with ADHD. Rapport suggests that "When they are doing homework, let them fidget, stand up or chew gum. Unless their behavior is destructive, severely limiting their activity could be counterproductive." In short, it's important to remember that the hands-on and experiential strategies that are successful in elementary school are also effective in the middle and high school setting. The new research on brain-based learning is telling us that teachers should return to the basic time-tested strategies discussed in Summaries 16A–E.

8. **Assignment of teachers is critical.** Teenagers with attention deficits tend to do well in classes where the teacher likes them and may fail the same subject with a teacher who doesn't like them. Students *and* teachers do better when students are matched with teachers who:

   ■ create a safe, positive learning environment,
   ■ use a variety of learning strategies,

- have a hands-on, active classroom learning environment,
- can channel their students' energy and cope with their learning challenges, and
- enjoy working with them.

The strategies mentioned below are explained in greater detail in Summaries 16-A through 16-E (on classroom accommodations) and Summaries 57-61 (on general classroom management and behavioral strategies).

Use these strategies:	to make these needed changes in class
Modify Teaching *Methods* (16-A)	to match the teaching style to students' learning strengths.
Modify *Resources* for students (16-A)	to give more individualized help.
Modify *Assignments* (16-B)	to match student skill level & to reduce written work.
Modify *Testing and Grading* (16-C)	to give adequate time to complete work & tests.
Modify *Level of Supervision* (16-D)	to increase student monitoring with help from others.
Use *Technology* (16-E)	to maximize learning and to take advantage of the student's strengths.
Modify *Classroom Management Strategies* (58)	to provide needed structure and prevent behavior problems.
Modify *Classroom Set-up* (58)	to provide the best seating assignment.
Modify *Class Schedule* (58)	to ensure that medication "peak work" time occurs during difficult classes.
Monitor *Medication Effectiveness* (52-57)	To ensure that medication is providing maximum academic benefit.

Resources for Section 2

Crutsinger, Carla. *Thinking Smarter: Skills for Academic* Success. Carrollton, TX: Brainworks, 1992. (This book offers strategies and reproducible worksheets for teaching memory techniques, time management, note taking, test taking, and homework skills.)

Denckla, Martha B. "The Syndrome Called ADHD and the Symptom 'Attention Deficit' Overlap Only Partially." Presented at the 26th annual Learning and the Brain Conference. Washington, DC, 2010.

Dendy, Chris A. Zeigler, Ellison, Anne Teeter, and Helbing, Joan. *CHADD Educator's Manual on ADHD.* Landover, MD, 2006. (CHADD gave free copies of this manual to every public school in the country.)

Dendy, Chris. *Teenagers with ADD and ADHD.* 2nd ed. Bethesda, MD: Woodbine House, 2006.

Deshler, Don and Schumaker, Jean. *Teaching Adolescents with Disabilities: Accessing the General Education Curriculum.* Thousand Oaks, CA: Corwin Press, 2005.

Desler, Don et al. *SIMS: The Strategic Instruction Model.* Lawrence, KS: University of Kansas Center for Research on Learning. (An intensive teacher-training curriculum; see www.ku-crl.org for information.)

Dornbush, Marilyn and Pruitt, Sheryl. *Tigers Two.* Atlanta, GA: Parkaire Associates, 2008.

Ellis, Ed. *Using Graphic Organizers to Make Sense of the Curriculum.* Tusculoosa, AL: MasterMinds, 1998. (mastrmnds@aol.com).

Graphic organizers available free from www.freeology.com.

Greene, Jane Fell. *Language! The Comprehensive Literacy Curriculum—Grades 3-12.* Longmont, CO: Sopris West, 2005. (Dr. Greene originally developed the program for incarcerated middle and high school age youths. The students gained three years in reading in only twenty-two weeks.)

Jensen, Eric. *Teaching with the Brain in Mind.* 2nd ed. Alexandria, VA: Association for Supervision & Curriculum Development, 2005.

Jones, Clare. *Attention Deficit Disorders: Strategies for School-Age Children.* San Antonio, TX: Communication Skills Builders, 1994.

Jones, Clare. "Strategies for School Success: Middle School through High School." CHADD National Conference workshop. New York, NY, 1998.

Kohn, Alfie. *The Homework Myth: Why Our Kids Get Too Much of a Bad Thing.* Cambridge, MA: Da Capo Press, 2006.

The Learning Pyramid. Arlington, VA: National Training Laboratories. (800-777-5227).

Levine, Mel. *Educational Care, 2nd ed.* Cambridge, MA: Educators Publishing Service, 2000.

Marzano, R.J. *What Works in Schools: Translating Research into Action.* Alexandria, VA: Association for Supervision and Curriculum, 2003.

Mastropieri, Margo and Scruggs, Thomas. *The Inclusive Classroom: Strategies for Effective Instruction.* 4th ed. Upper Saddle River, NJ: Prentice Hall, 2009.

Promethean Boards & ActivSlates, interactive white boards (classroom and individual) that enhance teacher effectiveness. Manufactured by Promethean, www.prometheanworld.com

Rapport, Mark D. "Hyperactivity Enables Children with ADHD to Stay Alert: Teachers Urged Not to Severely Limit That Activity." *ScienceDaily, March* 2009.

Rief, Sandra. *How to Reach and Teach Children wih ADD/ADHD,* 2nd ed. San Francisco: Jossey-Bass, 2005. (Although this book is for elementary-age children, many of the suggestions may be modified for middle and high school students. Rief has developed numerous materials, including videotapes, that educators will find helpful. See www.sandrarief.com.)

Rief, Sandra and Heimburge, Julie. *How to Reach and Teach All Students in the Inclusive Classroom,* 2nd ed. San Francisco: Jossey-Bass, 2006.

Schnoes, Connie, Reid, Robert, Wagner, Mary & Marder, Camille. "ADHD among Students Receiving Special Education Services: A National Survey." Farmington Hills, MI: Exceptional Children, Council for Exceptional Children, June 2, 2006.

Smart Boards and Slates, interactive white boards (classroom and individual) that enhance teacher effectiveness. Manufactured by Smart Technologies, www.smartboards.com.

Sousa, David. *How the Brain Learns.* 3rd ed. Thousand Oaks, CA: Corwin Press, 2005.

Welch, Ann. "Increasing Academic Engagement of Students with ADHD." *ADHD Reports,* June 1999, Vol. 7, No.3.

Judy Wood Publishing Company, 12411 Southbridge Dr., Midlothian VA 23113. (Visit Dr. Wood's website for several helpful teaching tips: www.judywood.com.)

Zentall, Sydney. "Theory- and Evidence-based Strategies for Children with Attentional Problems." *Psychology in the Schools*, 2005, Vol. 42, No. 8.

Modify Teaching Methods and Resources to Enhance Attention and Learning

1. **Provide More Visual Cues and Reminders:** Since students with ADD or ADHD frequently have multiple learning problems, they may benefit from teaching styles that use a multisensory approach. In other words, they remember more if they *hear* the teacher say something while *seeing* her demonstrate the skill. Later they may see pictures of the skill or words in their minds. Obviously, students are more likely to remember material that is related to their personal experience.

    1.1. **Model skills for students.** Since students with attention deficits are often visual learners, modeling by the teacher can be extremely effective. Overhead projectors and interactive boards such as Smart Boards or Promethean Boards are especially helpful for this purpose. In addition, teachers can face the class when they write on the overhead or interactive board rather than having their backs to students. One teacher writes in different colors to denote important information to remember.

        1.1.1. In Language Arts class, teach students *how to write an essay* by actually writing one in class. See Summaries 17-20.

    1.2. **Post Key Points on Board.** Leave *key points* being taught on the overhead or on the board for the whole class. For example, leave rules for grammar or conjugation of foreign language verbs. Preferably leave information in the same location on the board so students know where to look for it. Number steps rather than use letters of the alphabet.

    1.3. **Post New Concepts around the Room.** Place *key concepts/phrases* from the lecture around the room and point to them when discussed. Ron Walker, an educational consultant in Georgia, developed this creative strategy, known as *visual posting*. The teacher writes key words on strips of bright poster board and places them around the room in easy sight—for example, on the wall, board, or filing cabinet. The strips may also be placed in areas where students tend to focus when they tune out, such as near the window. Then as the teacher lectures, he points to each key fact as he discusses it.

        1.3.1. **Pretest before instruction.** The students are tested on key information before the lesson is presented. The teacher states in advance what the key facts are that she wants students to learn.

        1.3.2. **Quiz briefly after the lecture.** After the lecture is completed, the teacher does a brief oral quiz. "Who sailed across the ocean and discovered America?" Point to the correct strip on the wall and the whole class repeats the answer.

        1.3.3. **Give brief review; test with strips in place.** The students are given the test with all the information still on the wall in plain sight.

        1.3.4. **Give the final test.** Take all the material down from the walls and give the final test on the material. Students can see the information in their minds and will look at the wall where the answer was posted

        1.3.5. **Post important information near the pencil sharpener.** The teacher may post spelling words or a reminder for a test near the pencil sharpener, the classroom door, or other areas where students may stand for a short period of time.

    1.4. **Use color to highlight important facts.** If a student continually makes the same spelling or grammar error, highlight the corrected word or letters within the word that she usually misses. Dr. Sydney Zentall found that color helps students remember things better. Red (or hot pink) may be the most memorable of colors.

1.5. Give guided lecture notes daily to all students (also known as guided practice). Give students copies of the teacher's daily lecture notes in outline form with key points marked. Use skeletal outlines that allow space between sentences for the student to write notes. Guided practice is extremely valuable because it provides detailed or outlined structured guidance to help students complete assignments. This guidance provides compensation for their impaired memory.

1.6. Show sample finished projects. Researchers report that the quality of long-term projects improves greatly when students are shown completed sample projects. Indicate the grade earned for each one; in other words this is what you have to do to earn an A, B, C, or D.

1.7. Make a wallet-size laminated copy of key facts for reference (basic math facts, formulas, verb conjugation for Spanish). Allow the student to keep a copy of the card for use in class.

1.8. Use Desktop Helpers. Desktop Helpers (3 x 12) provide a handy reference to aid memory deficits and are available on a variety of topics (common math facts, fractions, punctuation rules, state capitals). "Helpers" can be inserted in clear sleeves that adhere to the desktop. They are available from the "Really Good Stuff" company at www.reallygoodstuff.com.

1.9. Use informative posters in the classroom. Posters may provide visual reminders of important historical events, grammar rules, or math concepts. "Wild and wacky" illustrations will help students commit these facts to memory more easily. Students may be able to picture the poster in their minds during the test. An example of a memorable poster that helps in teaching multiplication tables is available in Summary 22. See Summary 24 for memory tips.

1.10. Use graphic organizers. Numerous books of graphic organizers are commercially available at school supply stores. Graphic organizers are often helpful because they: 1) make abstract concepts concrete, 2) help students visually organize material, and 3) assist with memory recall. These preprinted reproducible blank forms provide great visual cues for these students, increasing the likelihood of their remembering the information. A few examples of graphic organizers are listed at the end of this section under Resources, plus two blank organizers (Appendices A2 and A3) are provided for writing essays. One form includes drawings that help a student visually organize her thoughts and the other provides an outline for writing the essay. For example:

- The student practices *sequencing skills* for describing a novel or historical event by filling words or pictures in sections of movie film frames or railroad tracks;
- She develops essay ideas by brainstorming and *writing the ideas in clusters*. This process is sometimes referred to as "mind mapping" or "webbing";
- She may use *guides for comparison* or persuasive writing;
- She uses a *summary organizer* to prepare to write a book summary.
- She learns to make choices by *listing pros and cons* on a form and deciding which option is best;
- She identifies *the five Ws of report or essay writing* on the drawings ("who" is written on a face, "when" on a clock, and "where" on a state outline.)
- She can use a *double Venn diagram* (two overlapping circles) to show how two issues are alike and how they are different.

- She uses a *content organizer* to learn terms and definitions in a new chapter. Terms and definitions are listed in columns and the student is asked to match them.
- She uses a *content diagram* to place key information in columns such as type of rock, how formed, and examples of each.
- She classifies and describes triangles by angles and sides.

Dr. Ed Ellis, professor of Special Education at the University of Alabama, has done extensive work in the development of graphic organizers. Teachers may find his books, *Using Graphic Organizers to Make Sense of the Curriculum* and *Strategic Graphic Organizer Instruction,* especially helpful. (More information on these and other teaching strategies is available at mastrmnds@aol.com.)

1.11. Review for exams in class. Review materials in class that will be on tests.

1.11.1. Give review summaries for exams. Outline a summary of material being reviewed. Write each fact on an overhead projector or interactive board. By writing the outline in class, teachers slow the pace of their lecture, which makes it easier for students to keep up with taking notes.

1.11.2. Identify key points as such. State the obvious: "This is a key point. Mark it. This will be on the test."

1.11.3. Teach review skills. Show students how to review material—for example, look for **bold** or *italicized* print, capitalized headings for each section, captions under pictures, and summaries at the end of the chapter.

1.11.4. Record reviews for MP3s or iPods. Dr. Billie Abney, a high school anatomy teacher who also happens to be my sister, records her test reviews so that students can listen to them on their iPods or MP3 players. She ends the review with an (awful) joke and then gives students extra credit on the test if they have listened to the test review and know the joke.

1.12. Use visual cues to enhance attention.

1.12.1. Place a mirror in front of students. According to Dr. Sydney Zentall, when distractible students work while sitting in front of a mirror, they are more likely to stay on-task.

1.12.2. Post a reminder target in the student's line of sight. The target or picture serves as a private visual cue for the student to refocus her attention on her class work.

1.13. Schedule virtual field trips. Virtual field trips offer interesting learning experiences. Information regarding virtual field trips is available at several websites. "The Slave Trade" is available from history.org/trips. Utah Education Network (www.uen.org) has student interactives for all ages: examples for grades 7-12 include: "Make a Mad Neuron," "Blood Typing," "Operation: Heart Transplant." The Center for Interactive Learning and Collaboration offers trips to zoos, museums, libraries, and theaters: www.cilc.org. The virtual trips typically cost less than $200.

2. **Give additional individualized help:** If you are too busy, ask others to help. You can make your teaching even more effective by seeking other "teachers" to help you.

2.1. Use "paired learning." Provide class time for students to pair off, solve a problem, and discuss (teach each other) the new concepts in an assignment. Each student creates a sample problem, works it, swaps the unsolved problem with their partner, compares answers, and then discusses any differences. This method of instruction is also referred to as class-wide peer tutoring. See discussion in Summary 21 as it relates to math and peer tutors.

2.2. Use peer tutors. Ask the student with ADD or ADHD to tutor a younger student or a classmate who is learning similar concepts. Tutors usually learn more than the person receiving the tutoring does. According to the learning pyramid, students who teach others remember 90 percent of what they learn.

2.3. Use classroom aides. Classroom aides may help give the student more individualized attention when working on academics or monitoring homework assignments and completion. Typically, this accommodation is available only to students who qualify for special education under federal law. Inclusion of a classroom aide must be written into the student's individualized educational program (IEP) or Section 504 Plan.

3. **Increase active class participation of all students:**

   3.1. Use group response. Some teachers increase student participation by asking a question, then having *all the students* respond with a card, hand signal system, or an answer written on a dry erase board. The teacher calls on a student to give the correct answer. The teacher also may use choral response, asking everyone to repeat the correct answer.

   This teaching strategy has significant advantages over the traditional system of having one student at a time answer a question or come to the board and work a problem. For example, more students are involved, plus it gives the teacher a sense of which students don't understand the material. Additionally, use of dry erase boards involves frequent movement: writing down an answer by every student, movement to hold up the board and show teacher the answer; and then movement again to erase and write the next answer. These strategies may work better for students with an attention deficit since there are fewer opportunities to daydream or space-out.

   High tech options such as Interactive boards (Smart or Promethean) and individual slates (Smart Slates and AtivSlates) are also available and will be discussed in Summary 16-E. However some schools may find them cost prohibitive.

   3.1.1. Hand signals may include:
   - thumbs up, if the answer to the question is yes, thumbs down (no), or palm out flat (uncertain or don't know).

   3.1.2. Response cards may include:
   - three colored cards: red (no), green (yes), and yellow (don't know).
   - *Yes* and *no* cards with the same answer printed on both sides of the card so the student can see which word she is holding up and not get confused about her answer.
   - Other cards may include the words: *True/false, noun/verb, or add/ subtract.*

   3.1.3. Card fans may be made by fastening cards together with a ring or fastener. Categories may be listed on the card and the students hold up the correct card in response to the teacher's question. For example, list categories such as *parts of speech (noun, verb, adjective); states of matter (solid, liquid or gas), or A/B/C/D for multiple choice questions.*

   3.1.4. Dry erase boards are better when specific, brief answers can be given to questions. My colleague Joan Helbing shared this tip: teachers can make cheap substitute "dry erase" boards by laminating light colored construction paper for student to write upon. These thin "boards" require little storage space.

3.1.5. Use choral response. Students answer questions in unison. See Summary 24 on memory.

3.2. Provide active, hands-on learning experiences.

3.2.1. Develop a play to act out major historical events or the storyline of a book.

3.2.2. Make a pop-up book. Create a book with pictures and drawings that explain a story or event. Directions for making a pop-up book are provided in Summary 25.

3.2.3. Use videotape. Allow the student to videotape herself giving a book report or research on a specific event or topic.

3.2.4. Use physical movement. Try the teaching strategy referred to as *total physical response (TPR)*. As the term implies, the student is physically involved in the learning. For example, students might arm wrestle to demonstrate the importance of creating equally powerful protagonists and antagonists.

3.3. Give "brain breaks." Linda Sorensen, a master teacher and trainer from Bountiful, Utah, encourages teachers to give students brain breaks—physical activities that reenergize the brain. Tell the students why you are asking them to participate in these activities—"school work is demanding; you **need to reenergize your** brain." Here are several of Sorenson's strategies:

- Take turns clapping a rhythm for others to mimic.
- Toss Koosh balls.
- Dance or jump up and down to some music.
- Do chair pushups or stand up and stretch.
- Give a visual break by asking students to look out the window and count to five.

4. **Encourage students to schedule hands-on active classes:** Some classes, such as home economics, physical education, computer classes, and agriculture education, typically involve active hands-on learning activities. Through conversations with Sara Clark, a veteran teacher, horticulturist, and licensed landscaper, I have developed a deep respect for agriculture education programs. These programs provide wonderful opportunities for developing leadership skills, character, and increasing personal competence and confidence. Students have the opportunity to participate in local, state, and national competitions in numerous areas including public speaking, plant identification, and livestock judging.

   Students Teaching Each Other. One of Ms. Clark's favorite teaching strategies is to have her students teach each other. According to the Learning Pyramid in Summary 15, that is the most effective strategy for ensuring retention of information. She provides students a very structured learning experience that involves summarizing, organizing, and public speaking in front of the class. Students are given a choice of speaking aids: a poster or a PowerPoint presentation. Students who are fearful of public speaking may do their presentation to her in private. An example of the required structure for presenting information on insects is shown on the next page.

5. **Allow students to use manipulatives to increase alertness and attention:** Manipulatives and seemingly purposeless fidgeting or doodling may actually help students learn, according to Dr. Sydney Zentall, a leading educational researcher on attention deficits and coauthor of *Seven Steps to Homework Success.* Dr. Mark Rapport also reports that this **physical activity seems to help the student maintain a higher level of mental alertness** so that she can listen to the teacher or work on an assignment. Otherwise the student's attention and alertness may begin to fade.

   One school psychologist explained that when students with attention deficits were being tested, they seemed to concentrate better if they were allowed to handle a Koosh Ball while they were

Sample Content of Powerpoint Presentation on Insects	
Slide 1	Genus (use correct scientific notations) Species (use correct scientific notations) Common name Your name
Slide 2	Type of metamorphosis (complete or incomplete) Overall picture of insect
Slide 3	Egg picture of insect
Slide 4	Larva or nymph picture of insect
Slide 5	Pupa or nymph picture of insect
Slide 6	Adult picture of insect
Slide 7	Type of mouthpart Close-up picture of type of mouthpart
Slide 8	Beneficial or Harmful Picture of benefit or damage
Slide 9	List of three plants damaged and picture of each plant OR List of three insects that are controlled and picture of each insect
Slide 10	Picture of insect

thinking. One parent reported that when her son studies for a test, he holds and rubs a strand of worry beads. Pipe cleaners, "Wikki Stix," Tangle toys, or paper clips are other good manipulatives for students to use.

6. **Teach students to create "foldables."** Foldables enhance the learning process by providing a three-dimensional graphic organizer. Students are more likely to remember foldables because they involve a hands-on activity that also incorporates a strong visual component. Students are given careful directions and shown how to fold the paper for each assignment. Foldable styles include: matchbook, layered books, accordion books, tri-folds, shutters, envelopes, and door folds. After folding, students write key facts on each surface of the foldable. Three of my colleagues recommend foldables as a very effective teaching strategy: Linda Smith and Linda Sorenson from Utah and Selena Conley from Georgia. For clever examples of foldables, including specific suggestions for a variety of subjects, visit these websites:

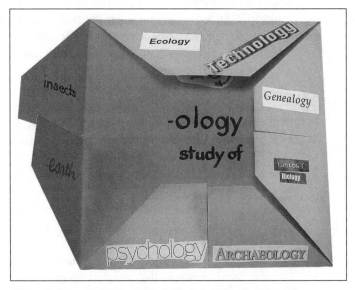

(This activity was taken from Dinah Zike's Foldables®, Notebook Foldables®, and VKVs® for Spelling and Vocabulary 4th -12th (2009) and used with permission. See more of her ideas at www.dinah.com. Foldable® is a registered trademark of McGraw-Hill School Solutions Group. Visual Kinesthetic Vocabulary® and VKV® are registered trademarks of Dinah-Might Adventures, LP.)

- www.dinah.com
- www.fultonschools.org/k12/math/documents/foldablesbook.pdf
- www.cataba.k12.nc.us
- www.registereastconn.org/sblceastconn/nutmeglesson12008.htm
- www.foldables.wikispaces.com

7. Use supplies that are helpful to students:

7.1. Use mechanical pencils. Many students with an attention deficit like to write with mechanical pencils. Some students even have included use of these pencils in their IEP as an accommodation. Although the reasons for this preference aren't totally clear, the students believe it helps them with their handwriting difficulties. Perhaps the pencils provide better writing control, greater accuracy in writing, tactile sensitivity, and novelty.

Pentel has a "Quicker Clicker" that is popular. Students like the textured grip plus the location of the fingertip "clicker." The student can extend the lead without having to mash a button on the top. Number 9 lead is preferable since it is the strongest.

7.2. Use a textured pencil grip. Some students like to put textured grips on their regular number two pencils to improve their writing grip.

7.3. Use a clipboard. Some students find they can work more efficiently if they put their paper on a clipboard. This seems to give them more working desk space and keeps their paper from sliding away.

8. Teach learning strategies for specific academic skills: Students with ADD or ADHD may lack basic academic skills such as reading, comprehension, and written expression. Teachers may have to backtrack and teach basic skills such as the learning strategies taught at the University of Kansas that are discussed below.

8.1. Provide teacher training. With special education students increasingly being included in regular classes, demands on teachers' skills have increased significantly. Teachers may need specialized training for teaching students with learning problems. Examples of training curricula include:

- *The Strategic Instruction Model* for teaching learning strategies. The University of Kansas Center for Research on Learning is one of the national leaders in studying learning issues. They have developed an intensive teacher training curriculum known as *SIMS, the Strategic Instruction Model.* This curriculum breaks down skills such as sentence and paragraph writing and shows teachers how to teach these skills more effectively. Training sessions are scheduled at several sites around the country. The 26 learning strategies included in their curriculum include a paraphrasing strategy, four strategies to help with memory, test taking strategies, cooperative thinking strategies, self-advocacy, and basic math strategies. Additional information is available from www.ku-crl.org. Local school systems and education agencies also sponsor numerous training opportunities that may be helpful.
- *Language!, 4th ed.* for teaching reading and comprehension. Dr. Jane Fell Greene developed *Language!*, a special program to help improve the reading skills of students who were significantly below grade level. Dr. Greene created this program for incarcerated middle and high school age students. The students who participated in the program gained three years in reading in twenty-two weeks. This could be a great resource for middle

and high students who are having trouble reading and comprehending material. (Program available from Sopris West at www.sopriswest.com.)

- *CHADD Teacher to Teacher (T2T),* a training program. From 2007 to 2010, a group of CHADD volunteers has worked on developing in-service training modules on ADD/ADHD for teachers. I, along with Anne Teeter Ellison, Ed.D., professor emeritus at University of Wisconsin and Joan Helbing, M.S., ADHD consultant/diagnostician, have been fine-tuning this two-day program. It is offered two or three times a year including at the annual CHADD conference each October/November. Online classes are also being planned for the future (www.chadd.org; 800-233-4050).

SUMMARY 16-B Modify Assignments

If a student consistently fails to complete homework, teachers should assess whether the assignment is too long or too difficult—since these two issues are the primary reasons for failure to complete school work. Another critical factor is slow processing speed, which results in these students taking up to twice as long as their peers to complete homework. Shortening assignments and designing assignments that are skill-level appropriate are both essential. Additionally, adding novelty to the assignment can increase the likelihood that students will complete work. For example, try awarding homework passes, giving choices on assignments, and adding an element of gaming.

1. **Reduce written work:** As discussed in Summary 12, many students with ADD or ADHD may have difficulties with verbal expression, complex multi-step math, slow processing speed, fine motor coordination, or other problems that make written work more challenging. As a result, these teenagers often take much longer to complete class- and homework. This may explain why students with attention deficits so studiously avoid homework. It takes a lot more effort for them to complete written work than their peers. This is not to suggest that teachers should never give written class- and homework to students. Rather, the length of assignments should be modified so that these students are not spending significantly more time than their peers on the same assignments.

   To help determine "How much homework is too much?" see Summary 26. Typically, **teachers can reduce the amount of written work pretty easily without compromising the amount of academic material mastered.**

   Since completing written work—especially homework—is often the biggest academic challenge that these teenagers face, reducing written work is very important. Suggestions for the best ways to reduce written work are given below.

   1.1. Reduce the amount of homework. Estimate how long homework should take, and then ask the student to report how long it actually takes her to complete homework. If it is taking too much time, reduce the amount of homework. For example, a National NEA/PTA policy suggests that a sixth grade student should spend up to a total of about one hour each evening on all homework (10 minutes per grade; Summary 27).

     1.1.1. Assign fewer problems or questions. Where feasible, assign fewer problems, sentences, or questions, if that still covers the necessary skills and mastery of major concepts. For some students with ADD or ADHD, math homework may be the biggest problem and should be reduced. For example, the student may be asked to complete every second or third problem.

     1.1.2. Write the correct answers only. Have the student write only the correct answers, rather than the whole sentence or question. The goal is to see whether the student knows the answer to the question, not to see if she can copy the question.

     1.1.3. Fill in the blanks. Allow students to photocopy math problems or scan in science or history questions from the book and fill in the blanks instead of writing the whole problem or sentences.

     1.1.4. Allow students to dictate schoolwork. Sometimes the student may dictate a report to a parent or friend (scribe) who types up the information. Researchers have found that the quality and length of reports and essays were better when students with learning problems dictated their work.

1.1.5. Substitute creative activities for written assignments. Develop an **Assignment Menu** that offers students the choice of creative, active assignments as a substitute for written assignments. For example, one Language Arts teacher allowed her students to give book reports accompanied by a videotape of two or three favorite scenes from a book, a cake as described in a book, and an oil painting of a famous poet. Other examples include writing a play, building a model, writing about imaginary travels, and contacting a space center and getting their reaction to the topic.

1.2. Teach tips to improve note taking.

1.2.1. Teach shorthand. For common words, help the student create her own shorthand to speed up taking notes. Don't use this strategy if this becomes too complicated, distracting, or difficult. One unexpected benefit of the current texting craze is that using shorthand notations may be second nature to today's students.

Examples: wrds tht R commly u'd 2 cre8 y'r own short/hd.

T = the	sp = spelling
rd = read	hw = homework
wr = write	w/i = within
w/o = without	< = less than
> = more than	$ = money
? = question	bks = books
– = negative or subtract	+ = plus or positive
# = number	EZ = easy
mtg = meeting	cap = capital
wr/u = write up	p. = page
wrk = work	ex = example
B4 = before	wkly = weekly
@ = at	impt = important
& = and	asign = assignment
% = percent	y = why
c = with	gov = government
whn = when	

1.2.2. Take notes in two columns. Show the student how to take notes in two columns, one for the main idea and the second column for more details about the main idea. The student may fold her notebook paper in half lengthwise or simply draw a vertical line to divide the paper in half.

1.2.3. Identify key points. Tell the student, "This is important, write it down."

1.3. Reduce notetaking. Students with ADD or ADHD can have trouble focusing on what is being said in class because of their limited working memory capacity and difficulties in identifying key points to record. Try these strategies to enable them to listen better:

1.3.1. Identify a notetaker for the whole class. Ask another student who is good in the subject to take notes and star the important issues of the lesson. The designated student takes notes, makes ten copies, and places them in a box in the room available to any student in need.

1.3.2. Jointly identify a notetaker. Sometimes a student with an attention deficit does better with a personal notetaker. Try to involve her in the selection process. Perhaps give a choice of two or three students. Sometimes, the notetaker and student don't even know each other since the notetaker may be in another class. The notetaker in one class takes notes and leaves them in a designated spot for pickup later. The big question is, "Will the student with ADD or ADHD remember to pick it up?" If she consistently forgets, develop a way to help her remember.

1.3.3. Use NCR (carbonless) notebook paper, or even carbon paper, to make notetaking easier. For example, duplicate checks are made from this special paper. You simply tear off the bottom copy of notes and give it to the student. Unfortunately, the paper is not always easy to find in stores. Try asking the director of special education where to get the paper. Hayden-McNeil is one publisher of carbonless notebooks. Distributors can be located via an Internet search.

1.3.4. Provide guided lecture notes. The need for notetaking is reduced when a student has guided lecture notes to follow, as described in Summary 16-A.

1.4. Shorten keyboarding assignments. Although working on a computer can be a lifesaving skill for students with attention deficits, initially their keyboarding skills are often terrible. Their combined learning problems related to memorization, slow retrieval, slow processing, and fine motor skills are horrendous obstacles to mastering keyboarding skills. Teachers may consider using the *Type to Learn* program discussed in Summary 16-E, which uses memory tricks to help students learn. Some teachers are reluctant to reduce keyboarding assignments but it is a *critical accommodation* for most of these students!

1.5. Accept unfinished class work, sometimes. Occasionally, if the student seems to understand the concepts or is in crisis, accept unfinished class work without piling it on in addition to homework assignments. These students may reach a point where the amount of overdue school work is overwhelming. They may give up because they feel they can never catch up.

1.6. Don't assign sentences to be written as punishment. Years ago, it was common to have a student write a "hundred sentences" for punishment for failing to pay attention in class, running in the hall, not turning in homework, or chewing gum. Obviously, this old-fashioned punishment does not help these students pay attention or complete homework.

2. **Break assignments and long-term projects into segments:** When assignments or projects seem long or complicated, students with attention deficit disorders may feel overwhelmed and struggle to get started. Breaking the task into segments can be extremely helpful, thus releasing the logjam. In addition, long-term projects often cause problems because students forget them, lack the organizational skills and awareness of time to plan ahead, or fail to budget enough time to complete the project. See Summaries 33-36.

Russell Barkley explains that any assignment involving a significant time lag between the assignment and due date creates a disability for students with ADD/ADHD. Their impaired sense of time and delayed "self-talk" skills make completion of these tasks incredibly difficult. Notification of parents of any long-term projects should be part of all educational plans (IEPs or 504 Plans).

> **2.1. Read to the clip.** For reading assignments, the late Dr. Clare Jones suggested dividing the material into three or four manageable sections and marking the sections with colorful paper clips. The student tells herself to "read to the clip." Now she can "see" how close she is to being finished.
>
> **2.2. Divide assignments into sections.** Divide math or other homework into manageable sections. The student may take a break when she finishes a section. Worksheets may actually be cut or folded in half so the student can "see" how much she has left to complete.
>
> **2.3. Assign separate due dates** for different parts of a long-term project.
>
> **2.4. Grade each section of the project independently.**

3. **Give students some choices with regard to assignments:** Students who are allowed to select from several homework options produce more work and are more compliant. Students can be given choices related to the manner in which they present a project: a written report, a video, or a diorama. One teacher set up a *100 point list of spelling options,* as shown in Summary 25. Students select from ten or so hands-on options each with different point values; ultimately the student must earn 100 points during the week.

> **3.1. Tic Tac Toe Assignments.** Teachers list nine assignment choices, one within each block of the Tic Tac Toe grid. Students are instructed to select choices either three across, three down, or three diagonally

4. **Award homework passes:** Give a **homework pass** to reward good work, effort, or a positive attitude. "This student is awarded a homework pass for any daily homework assignment other than studying for a test." Students may save the coupon and use it one day to skip a homework assignment. Discuss the possibility of saving it for a day when they have forgotten or lost an assignment.

5. **Give a job or cue card for difficult tasks:** One reason students with attention deficits often procrastinate is that they feel overwhelmed by large, multi-step projects. They lack the skills necessary to break the assignment down into the required action steps. Consequently, they need more supervision and must be taught this skill. Sometimes they truly don't know what to do or where to begin. Providing a job card with a brief outline of the steps necessary to complete the project can help. Working on these skills provides the opportunity to teach or *shape* the new skill. (For a discussion of shaping behavior, see Summary 66.) For example, the teacher may initially:
   - Discuss the steps required to complete the assignment with the whole class.
   - Then write the steps on the board.
   - Ask the class to copy the steps down on paper.
   - If the student seems to have trouble getting started on the assignment, discuss the steps required and help her write them down on the job card.

6. **Seek quality, not quantity:** Ann Welch, a veteran special education teacher, says, "Fewer high quality responses are preferable to more poor quality responses." She explains that when teachers give assignments, they are often looking for three things: 1) speed, 2) completeness (number of problems done), and 3) accuracy. For example, a teachers may want students to finish 30 problems (number), before the end of class or by tomorrow (speed), and have the right answers (accuracy). Since some students with attention deficits work very slowly, typically they will complete fewer problems. Unfortunately, grading criteria "that focus only on speed or completeness, encourage many students to do poor quality work." Welch suggests that modified assignments of reasonable length and difficulty are more likely to produce quality work. For example: "Write three complete, interesting sentences with no more than two spelling or punctuation errors."

SUMMARY 16-C Modify Testing and Grading

Let's assume that the primary goal of testing is to measure what a student knows, *not* how well the student takes a particular type of test. Since students with ADD or ADHD have learning problems that make some types of tests much more difficult for them, it makes sense to modify the style of testing. Test modifications have been a lifesaver for many students with attention deficits. In fact, many students with attention deficits say that receiving extended time on tests, long-term projects, and homework has been their most helpful classroom accommodation.

Giving **extended test time** is a great idea, but it may be difficult to provide easily in middle and high school:

- Finding uncommitted class time to finish the test is difficult. Students may change classes every hour. Or, under the block scheduling system, they may be expected to finish the test the first forty-five minutes and then start a new lecture the second half of the period. If students continue working on the test, they will miss their next class or lecture material from the second half of the block class. They will also have difficulty concentrating on the test if the rest of the class is listening to a lecture.

- Maintaining the integrity of the test, also known as preventing cheating, is a primary concern in giving extended time on tests. Teachers and administrators are concerned that if test times are broken up, some students might look up correct answers before they return to finish the test. Most teachers prefer that students finish the test the same day they start work on it.

Test integrity is very difficult to maintain even under normal circumstances. For example, if a teacher has four sections of the same class and gives the same test to each, students in earlier classes can share test information with students in later classes.

However, most students with ADD or ADHD are hoping simply to pass the test, not make an A. These students often don't remember or plan ahead to get answers or ask friends for help. I don't think it ever occurred to my son to ask other students or look up answers to the remainder of the test questions. Of course, if a student with an attention deficit were in the running for class valedictorian, maintaining test integrity would take on more urgency.

1. **Give extended test time while preserving test integrity:**

   1.1. **Find alternatives times for test completion.**

      1.1.1. **Include a special education supervision period or study hall in the student's schedule.** This period may be used for several purposes such as finishing tests, doing make-up work, receiving assistance, or collecting the right books and homework assignments to take home.

      1.1.2. **Give the test before or after school or during a portion of lunch.** The student could stay after school or come early in the morning to start the test or complete any unfinished questions. Or the test could be tied into a lunch period. Perhaps, the student may bring lunch from home or another student may bring her something from the lunchroom. For students with sleep disturbances, tests before school may not be a good choice.

      1.1.3. **Complete the test during the second half of a block scheduled class.** Some students can learn the new information that is missed with notes from a notetaker.

1.1.4. Allow a tutor to monitor test completion. Some students with attention deficits receive tutoring after school as required in the IEP/504 Plan or because the parents have paid for private tutoring. If there is a comfortable working relationship between the school and tutor, the tutor could monitor all or a portion of the test.

2. **Select a good test location:** Students need a quiet place away from traffic or others talking. In block classes, students with ADD or ADHD may be too distracted to continue working on the test in the same classroom while the teacher gives instruction for the remainder of class.

   2.1. Send the student to the library or guidance office to finish the test, especially during the last half of a two-hour block class.

   2.2. Select a test location without distractions even if a student doesn't need extended time.

3. **Implement honor system testing:** Depending on the student, this may or may not be a good choice. Because of their impulsivity, students with attention deficits are more likely to speak before they think. So if another student either asks them or tells them about the test, the student may talk before she remembers that she has signed an honor code pledge. Don't institute a system that you know won't work because it just sets the student up for failure. Discuss the difficulty of this system with the student and ask her if she thinks she can do it. If so, ask her to sign an honor system form indicating that she has not given or received information from other students about this test.

4. **Modify the format of the exam to test for a student's true knowledge:** Even when these students know the material, they may not do well on tests because of slow processing speed and information retrieval, weak verbal expression skills, and limited working memory capacity. Some methods of testing are more difficult for all students, not just those with attention deficits. For example, tests requiring cold recall of information rather than recognition are usually more difficult. Typically, students with ADD or ADHD do better with a test format that provides word cues to jog their memory.

   4.1. Use multiple choice or true-false questions. Since slow processing speed and slow information retrieval may be a problem, consider giving multiple choice tests or true-false questions. This may not work for younger students who are too impulsive and mark their answers without reading all the options.

   4.2. Use "word banks." Consider using word banks that include a list of words from which to choose the correct answer or two columns that require matching answers. Since these students often have trouble quickly retrieving stored information, word banks can be a better way to accurately measure their knowledge. The words provide a visual prompt for the student so that she does not have to rely on her deficient retrieval skills. Advise students beforehand if an uneven number of words and matching phrases are given.

   4.3. Allow the student to carry a small laminated card. This is another way to make accommodations for the student's memory problems. The card may contain secondary facts such as formulas, acronyms, rules for verb conjugation in foreign languages, or grammar rules to help trigger memory of key information during tests.

   4.4. Avoid lengthy essay exams, especially if the student has deficits in verbal expression. The student may know the material but be unable to express her thoughts in a clear, organized manner.

      4.4.1. Give a word bank for essay exams. Supply the student with a word bank of key issues that must be discussed on the essay.

2

4.5. Shorten the test. Develop a shortened version of the test for students with special needs. One drawback is that with fewer questions, each one missed counts off more points, which may increase the likelihood of failure.

4.6. Consider oral exams. A few students have such severe written expression problems they can't pass written tests. Typically, these students do better on oral exams. Sometimes the teacher reads the questions and the student responds orally. Or another student may read the questions to the teenager, who then dictates her answers into a tape recorder or to a scribe. Occasionally, teachers may give an oral test to a student who obviously knows the material but has failed a written test.

4.7 Consider giving open book tests.

5. **Use an online quiz generator with immediate feedback:** Class Marker is an inexpensive online service for generating tests ($25 annual fee; students have free unlimited access). After the student completes the test, answers are provided immediately so the student can see where she made mistakes. Giving immediate feedback is an excellent strategy. Visit www.classmarker.com for more information.

6. **Adjust grading techniques:** Try adjusting grading techniques so that they don't punish a student's learning deficits, an "off day," or lapse in memory:

   6.1. Drop the student's lowest daily or test grade.

   6.2. Don't count off for spelling on written assignments, unless spelling is the subject being tested. Allow the use of a spell checker if spelling is an important part of the assignment. At a minimum, allow the student to earn full credit by correcting misspelled words. Or ask the student to record the correct spelling of the word five times into a tape recorder.

   6.3. Allow the student to earn extra credit, especially in classes she is in danger of failing. If possible, identify creative projects related to the subject that may be completed for extra credit. (Unfortunately, some school systems don't allow teachers to give extra credit under any circumstance.)
   - Videotape an interview of a war veteran for a history class.
   - Audio- or videotape an interview with someone who speaks Spanish for a foreign language class.
   - Create a scrapbook on a related topic.
   - Cut articles or pictures from newspapers or magazines on issues related to class.
   - Or the student may earn extra credit by correcting errors on tests or completing additional work or projects.

   6.4. Award bonuses to students for good work. In their book, *Teach and Reach Students with ADD*, Dr. Nancy Eisenberg and Pam Esser, Executive Director of ADDA-SR, give samples of blank forms roughly 4" x 6" for teachers to award *bonus points or a homework pass*.
   - Give coupons for **bonus points** to be added to a grade. For example, if a student turns in her book report on time, three bonus points may be added to her final grade. Five bonus points may be awarded for 1) correcting spelling and grammar errors on an essay or 2) writing in the correct answers to missed questions or problems on a test.

   6.5. Grade completed material. Base the grade only upon the amount of work the student turns in or allow extended time to complete the test.

7. **Teach test-taking skills:** Frequently, our children do not intuitively use effective test-taking strategies. Dr. Don Deshler and his colleagues found that test scores increased by as much as 10 points when test-taking skills were taught. Specific strategies are provided in Summary 16-C.

8. **Institute a "failure is not an option" policy:** Missouri school principals Tim Crutchley and Kristen Pelster turned their failing school around by establishing a "failure is not an option" policy. Student cannot receive a zero for missing work. They must make up missing homework during lunch hour. The principals also go to truant students' homes and bring them to school. The principals partnered with Marvin Berkowitz and the Leadership Academy of Character Education to develop their own character education program that provided the underpinning of this school's success. Basically, the school's culture was changed significantly for the better; teachers who did not genuinely care about helping children succeed in school were encouraged to leave.

    Personally, I think we send the wrong message to students when we give them zeros: don't do your homework now, and you'll never have to do it. The Missouri message is better: if you don't do your homework now, you'll just have to do it during lunch.

9. **Allow the student to make up work:** Weak organizational skills and an impaired sense of time often interfere with prompt completion of school work, unless accommodations are put in place. So, allow these students to make up work but develop a plan to correct the problem. Since completing work on time is such a major problem, expect occasional backsliding and failure of the plan. **Nothing works all the time with these students!** Make adjustments and try again.

10. **Choose the right accommodations for special testing situations:** Several special testing situations can pose significant challenges for students with either ADD or ADHD, including:
    1. the mandatory state tests that measure the student's academic achievement,
    2. benchmark tests to determine whether a student passes to the next grade,
    3. competency exams for high school graduation, and
    4. college entrance tests such as the ACT or SAT.

    Some schools assume that students with attention deficit disorders cannot have accommodations for these special tests. However, **federal law mandates that students with ADD or ADHD whose learning is adversely affected are eligible for accommodations.**

Examples of Accommodations Used During Achievement or Graduation Tests

Most states have compiled a list of accommodations for statewide achievement tests that are available to eligible students. The examples below are taken from the lists of Arizona and Georgia. Each state may have different requirements, so check with your state department of education for a copy of their guidelines.

Extended time	Reread directions
Administer test in shorter sessions, perhaps over several days	Simplify language in the directions
Allow frequent breaks	Highlight verbs in the directions
Mark answers in the test booklet	Provide a calculator
Increase size of answer bubbles	Provide a word processor
Change the time of day for giving the test	Provide a dictionary or spell checker
Test in small groups in a separate location	

Typically, to be eligible for accommodations on these special tests, students must currently be receiving those accommodations as part of an IEP or Section 504 Plan. (See Summaries 49-50.) There must be a notation in the IEP (or 504 Plan) indicating which accommodations and/or modifications are required for testing situations. Eligibility for extended time for these students may be determined by test scores or classroom performance indicating related problems such as slow information processing speed.

Information on accommodations available for the SAT is available from the Educational Testing Service (866 630-9305.; www.ets.org); on accommodations for the ACT, from ACT, Inc. (319-337-1270; www.act.org). SAT and ACT are discussed in much greater detail in *Teenagers with ADD & ADHD,* 2nd edition.

SUMMARY 16-D Modify Supervision and Structure

Teenagers with attention deficit disorders are less mature and will require more supervision and structured guidance than their peers. Experts explain that the ADD/ADHD brain matures at a rate that is three years behind those without the disorder. This means that a fourteen-year-old student with an attention deficit may have the organizational skills and planning abilities of a ten- or eleven-year-old. In addition, the working memory skills of many of these teens are comparable to those of a seven-year-old. Young people with an attention deficit *will* act more responsibly in the future, but at a later age than their peers. In the meantime, students with attention deficits need more supervision and structure and need their work to be monitored more closely.

For teachers, it is a good idea to recruit others to help with routine monitoring. It doesn't matter who provides the supervision (a student or teacher's aide) as long as the job is done.

Strategies to provide increased structure are provided throughout this section and in Section 6. Ensuring that teacher instructions and expectations are clear is critical. For example, show students completed sample projects or create rubrics or academic contracts that clearly spell out requirements for earning a good grade.

1. **Ask other students to help with monitoring:**

    1.1. Designate "row captains." Select captains in each row to assist you by checking that work is complete and homework assignments are written down, and by collecting homework.

    1.2. Pair off all students. Students can check each other's work to see that it is completed and assignments are written down. Devote the last 3 to 5 minutes of class to this task.

    1.3. Monitor the assignment book. Give paired students five minutes at the end of class and ask them to initial that assignments are written down.

    1.4. Recruit a friend or other student to be a "coach." Typically, this close level of monitoring is necessary only when the student is in danger of failing a class. One "coach" may be selected for all classes or a coach may be assigned in those classes where the student is struggling. The coach checks to see that assignments are written down or reminds the student to turn in homework. The coach may even meet her after school to review which books and assignments should be taken home. Sometimes, girlfriends or boyfriends help with this task. For some students, being monitored this closely can be embarrassing. So, if the student is passing, a "coach" could be offered as one option that might result in more success at school. See Summary 71 on coaching.

    1.5 Hire a coach. Parents might pay a senior to meet their freshman daughter at her locker at the end of the school day. This coach could double check to see that all assignments and books are taken home.

2. **Ask parents to monitor:** Since these students are developmentally four to six years behind their peers, don't hesitate to give parents permission to be more involved in monitoring schoolwork. Parents of students with attention deficits must be involved longer and to a greater degree in moni-

toring school work than either the teacher or they want to be! In essence, most parents who are still involved in their middle or high school student's schoolwork are providing "developmentally appropriate supervision." Please don't make them feel guilty for doing this.

Remember, too, that a fair number of parents of these students may also have an attention deficit and have their own difficulties with memory and organization. So, if parents forget to check that assignments are completed, you might tactfully ask them to develop a reminder system or ask whether someone else (non-ADD/ADHD) parent or sibling (non-ADD/ADHD) is available to help with monitoring. Obviously, teachers would not talk about the parent's attention deficit unless the parent brings the issue up first. However, some parents are fully aware of their own personal challenges and are very open to discussing them.

> **2.1. Advise parents when monitoring may be necessary.** Let them know if a particular assignment requires greater organizational skills and if they may need to provide more guidance than usual to the student.
>
> **2.2. Involve parents as partners in completion of homework.** Assignment books and weekly reports are excellent tools for ensuring homework completion. See Summary 28 for suggestions for helping parents coach students through homework.
>
> **2.3. When the student is in danger of failing, communicate with parents** by phone, e-mail, or telephone answering machine.
>
> **2.4. Ask parents to check assignments.** When a student with an attention deficit is struggling academically, take time to talk with parents about assignments. Explain that they should ask to see and sign the student's assignment book each night. They can also help make certain it is returned to school each day. The parent's role also may be spelled out in the IEP or Section 504 Plan.

3. Involve other adults in monitoring:

> **3.1. Ask a classroom aide to monitor** class work, homework, or assignments, as described in 1.3 in this summary. When the classroom aide is provided as part of special education services, the aide may provide support to several students, not just the one with ADD or ADHD. This avoids embarrassing the student by singling her out as being different.
>
> **3.2. Ask a special education teacher to monitor.** Some students meet with a special education teacher near the end of the day and review which assignments and books must be taken home.
>
> **3.3. Ask a case manager to monitor.** A few schools have additional staff designated as "case managers" to monitor the progress of students who are at risk of failure.

4. Decide how you, the teacher, can help with monitoring:

> **4.1. Use an assignment book that the student takes home each day.** Assignment books have become one of the primary ways teachers monitor school work and communicate with parents. To use these books effectively, students with ADD or ADHD will require more supervision. They often have trouble using assignment books due to their memory deficits. For example, they have to remember to write down assignments, get their book signed by six teachers, take it home, get it signed, and return it to school.

4.2. Check the book daily. Teachers may check the assignment book themselves to ensure that assignments are written down and then initial it. When the book is sent home, parents review, initial, and return the book to school. It is critically important to make a plan to ensure that the assignment book is successfully carried between home and school. If the plan doesn't work, modify it. Avoid punishing the student for forgetting the book.

4.3. Develop a plan to make the assignment book process work. See Summary 30 for ideas to help the student remember her assignment book. For example, a *row captain* may remind the student to write down assignments, her best friend may remind her to take it home, or she may set her wrist alarm or cell phone alarm (if allowed in school) to remind her to take it home. If the student goes home without her book, her parents should take her or send her back to school to get it. Avoid punishing the student for this forgetful ADD/ADHD behavior. Punishment teaches the student what *not* to do. It doesn't help her learn what she *should* do. Teach the student to compensate for her challenging ADD/ADHD behaviors.

4.4. Use a weekly report. Weekly reports may be sent home to let parents know how the student has been doing on assignments and tests. Teachers may write a note listing any uncompleted assignments, plus grades for the week. Reports are very helpful for getting students back on track academically if they are not doing their school work. When the student brings her grades up, she is rewarded by no longer having to do weekly reports. Remembering to get any papers signed is very difficult for these students, so limit the number of subjects monitored and try to keep document signing to a minimum. For tips on effective use of weekly reports, see Summary 39 and 40.

SUMMARY 16-E Use Regular and Assistive Technology

Computers, word processors, and other electronic devices can sometimes be the answer to the problems with memory, organization, or handwriting that students with ADD or ADHD face at school. The decision as to which technology to use, however, must be made with some caution. Sometimes technology may complicate an issue rather than simplify it. For example, it may take a student longer to accomplish a task with technology than without, or she may become so involved in playing with a gadget that she may not use it for its intended purpose. It is best to try a specific technology and see if it is really practical and helpful before committing to use it.

1. **Encourage use of a computer or word processor:** Working on a computer solves several problems for students with attention deficits. They are not slowed down by their problems with handwriting. They can get their ideas down on paper more quickly before they lose them from their working memory. Plus, their grades may actually improve since teachers who cannot read their messy handwriting can easily read typed work. Because students with ADD or ADHD are often forgetful and lose assignments, having a backup copy of work done on a computer is a major advantage for them. Allow students to use computers for as much of their work as possible.

   1.1. **Teach keyboarding skills.** Many students with attention deficits have a terrible time learning keyboarding skills because of their deficits in working memory and visual memory, and their slow access to stored information in long-term memory. Their keyboarding skills are usually extremely slow and they have difficulty completing assignments in regular keyboarding classes. Many instructional programs are rather traditional and rely on rote memorization, which is difficult for students with ADD or ADHD. Obviously, *classroom assignments in keyboarding must be shortened.* Students may do better with keyboarding software, if carefully chosen as discussed in 1.3. Once these students master keyboarding, they will do extremely well working on the computer.

   1.2. **Consider a netbook or AlphaSmart.** In recent years, smaller, lighter weight, less sophisticated, and inexpensive computers known as netbooks have been produced. Prices range from $250 to $500. A typical netbook has a screen that is roughly 10 by 7 inches and weighs about a pound with a memory size of 1 GB and 160 GB capacity. This is a great alternative to the more expensive full-size computers.

   AlphaSmart is a simple, portable, affordable computer companion that allows students to type, edit, and electronically store written work. However, the small display area of up to six lines is a major drawback. A student may write a report or essay, compose e-mail messages, or take notes and then transfer them to any computer for formatting or directly to a printer. Some school systems are using the NEO 2 AlphaSmart in conjunction with their regular computers. More information is available at www.alphasmart.com. AlphaSmart features include:
   - a full-size keyboard,
   - a two- to six-line display with adjustable size fonts,
   - memory storage areas for daily schedule, assignments, or questions,
   - battery power (runs on 3 AA batteries for up to 700 hours),
   - additional software; e.g., Text2Speech and Accelerated Reader,
   - a relatively low price (roughly $200).

Assignments completed on netbooks or AlphaSmart are easy to read, so take less time to grade. Teachers can send vocabulary lists, questions, or assignments electronically to the student's computer. At this cost, if the machine is lost, as can happen with the student who has ADD or ADHD, it's not as bad as losing a $1,000 laptop computer. Check out netbooks and the AlphaSmart and see if either is practical for everyday use at school.

1.3. Find effective computer software programs. Find computer programs that will assist the student with difficult subjects. Ask the school media specialist for suggestions or call the school district office and talk with the person in charge of assistive technology. Some parents can afford to buy computer programs for use at home. Below are some software packages recommended by several educators as well as reviewers in a CHADD newsletter:

- **Keyboarding software**: One keyboarding program, **Type to Learn 4** by Sunburst Communications, incorporates memory tricks to help students ages 8 to 14 memorize the keyboard. Twenty-two lessons are provided (www.sunburst.com). It is available for approximately $100, or sometimes less on sale.

- **Concept mapping software: Inspiration Software** (http://www.inspiration.com; 800-877-4292) is a type of concept mapping software. The software allows you to manipulate information to organize it in various written and graphic formats. For example, students can develop ideas for papers using a web organizer and then convert them automatically to an outline prior to writing. Teachers can also create blank webs for students to use. Both downloaded and package versions are available from $70-$100.

- **Academic subject software**: Teens with ADD or ADHD often find computer games highly motivating and can sustain their attention longer than when listening to lectures. Software programs are constantly changing and being updated. Check current reviews to determine best software buys. Examples of software programs that may be useful include:

  - **Writer's Helper**—which prompts a student through the writing process by asking a series of questions or presenting reminders. Several functions such as brainstorming, freewriting, categorizing, and structured questions are included. Teachers may also lock in test questions and then have the student type in the answers between the questions.
  - **SkillsBank 4** (InstallShield Corporation, Inc.) and **CornerStone 2** (Houghton, Mifflin, Harcourt)—two self-paced, comprehensive programs that address reading, math, vocabulary, and language. Students can work at their own skill level.
  - **Math Companion 3**—which allows teachers to create worksheets, posters, games, and game cards to help students learn math concepts such as fractions, percents, and geometry. Single copies are available for roughly $50; 10 copies for $200.00.
  - **NovaNET** (Pearson)— a comprehensive, online software program covering multiple academic courses for students in grades 6 to 12 that may help reduce drop-out rates. Students who are struggling can recover graduation credits so that they can graduate on time. One parent wrote that this school-wide software allowed her daughter to finally pass algebra after two other attempts; she was able to work at her own pace. This program qualifies under Titles I, V, and IDEA funding and is now being used in 2,000 schools.

- **Webpage Development software: Microsoft Front Page** is a user-friendly software program for creating a webpage. You can view the page as you have written it, as it looks in code and a browser. To really do a web page right, a student should also know HTML code. Occasionally, web-authoring software will have an error that can only be corrected by using HTML code. **First Page 2000** was designed by Evrsoft to help people learn to use HTML very easily. Best of all, it is free.

- **Desktop Publishing software: Microsoft Publisher, Adobe, and Corel** are all good desktop publishing software programs that are available at local book, computer, or office supply stores.

- **Software for earning make-up credits:** Teachers participating in the Kenosha (WI) Schools model ADD Program use self-paced instructional software from the Plato Company for students who want to earn make-up credits toward graduation. **Plato** offers a wide range of courses including algebra, science, chemistry, social studies, and a writing series. Although the program is expensive, probably close to $2,000, the long-range benefits far outweigh the initial cost. (**NovaNET,** above, is a similar school-wide program that has shown positive results in over 2,000 schools.)

  Since most students who use the program have already failed the course once, they already have mastered some of the knowledge taught in the class. Plato courses allow the student to quickly review a chapter and then take a test to indicate mastery. Typically, the student may move fairly rapidly until she reaches the chapters where she does not know the material. Once the student reaches this point, then she will have to read all the material, answer questions, or work all the problems before she is ready to take the next test. For students who are poor readers, Plato also has an audio component. More information is available at www.plato.com.

- **Other technology:** More sophisticated technology is available and may be helpful for students with more severe learning problems. For example, a speech synthesizer can read what a student has written aloud so that she can listen for errors or ways to strengthen the essay.

1.4. Use computer spell check. Allow students with serious spelling deficits to use spell check when writing an essay or taking an essay test at school. Obviously, most students will use spell check at home, if they have computers.

2. **Use an interactive Board:** Interactive Boards from Smart (www.smarttech.com) and Promethean (www.prometheanworld.com) offer high tech teaching strategies that are visual and generate high interest among students. They will be impressed with the ability to drag pictures or words that appear on the screen from one place to another. However, discounted educational prices for Smart Boards of $2,000 (Promethean $1,400) may be too pricey for many schools.

   Use Individual Slates. Smart Slates and ActivSlates are also available now for individual students. As students write on the Slate, their words or numbers appear on the screen. Obviously their novelty is a big plus for students with ADD/ADHD. However both interactive tools still limit activities to just one student at a time. Smart Slates are priced at roughly $400 each; ActivSlates, $80 apiece (in quantities of 25 or 32).

3. **Use an iPod Touch—an amazing resource:** Not only are students are enthralled with them, iPods are a great teaching tool, offering a wide variety of academically related activities including applications (apps). Here are a few examples:

- Access to research on academic topics via WiFi
- A microphone and voice recorder
- Several helpful tools such as a dictionary and maps
- Teachers can record spelling lists or create flashcards for use on the iPod
- Teachers also can create podcasts on specific subjects including materials for a test review
- Access to iTunes, including apps and movies
- Subject-specific games are available through these apps; some free, some costing a nominal amount.
- Educational movies like *School House Rock* also are available. Episodes such as "Conjunction Junction" and "Verb: That's What's Happening" are available for purchase at 99 cents each.
- Parents and teachers can browse the iTunes store to identify other appropriate resources.

4. **Use noise reduction headphones**: Headphones may be worn during class or homework sessions to reduce noise distractions. For example, JVC NC100 received good reviews at www.goodcans.com/HeadphoneReviews/noisereductionreview.htm. Some students also use white noise from their iPod to block distractions.

5. **Use a cell phone for texting academics**: Dr. Billie Abney, an innovative high school anatomy teacher who also has ADHD, has her students text-message to review their anatomy vocabulary. Teams are established and score is kept. The teacher asks a review question and one team texts their answers to a different team. A member of the receiving team then reports the answer to the teacher who records team scores on the board.

6. **Use YouTube or TeacherTube clips for teaching purposes**: Clips from either of these two sites can be used to pique the interest of students. No matter what subject you teach, chances are, someone has uploaded a video to YouTube (www.youtube.com) or TeacherTube (www.teachertube.com) that may be helpful in getting the information across to your students visually.

7. **Use a tape recorder**: Tape recorders offer a low-tech way to reduce the amount of written work for students with ADD or ADHD.

   7.1. Assign reports on the tape recorder. For subjects such as Language Arts, History, or Government, a student with ADD or ADHD could sometimes dictate a brief report, summary of a newspaper article, or interview with a war veteran on the tape recorder and give the teacher the tape as a substitute for a written report. Or the student may dictate the information to a scribe (another student or a parent), who writes the information down.

   7.2. Allow students with attention deficits to tape class lectures instead of taking notes. This is helpful for some students, but for other students, it is a waste of time because they will not listen to the same material a second time.

   7.3. Consider buying an inexpensive handheld memo or tape recorder. The student could dictate homework assignments to a small tape recorder rather than writing them down. Such recorders are usually available at K-Mart, WalMart, or Radio Shack.

8. **Use a video camera**: As another alternative to written reports, students with ADD or ADHD can videotape themselves or others. Making a video may help them remember more about the subject than they would from writing a traditional report, and allowing them to use their creative instincts may enrich the learning experience.

9. **Use Books on Tape:** These audiotapes provide an alternative resource for students who are slow readers or have reading comprehension problems. The multisensory approach enables the student to see the book while at the same time hearing it. Fiction, nonfiction, and textbooks on audiotape, plus the equipment on which to play it, are available in each community. Check with your local school or regional library, or contact either of these two organizations:

> National Library Service for the Blind and Physically Handicapped (NLS)
> Library of Congress
> Washington, DC 20542
> Phone: 202-707-5100
> E-mail: nls@loc.gov
> www.loc.gov/nls
>
> Recording for the Blind and Dyslexic (RFB&D)
> 20 Roszel Road
> Princeton, NJ 08540
> Phone: (800) 221-4792
> www.rfbd.org

10. **Get a copy of the textbook on CD/DVD:** Complete textbooks are available on CD/DVDs. The student may get a disk from the school or may purchase one from the book publisher. In addition, some classic novels, whose copyrights have expired, can be downloaded free to your computer.

   In the future students will likely be able to use a *Kindle or other e-book reader*. However, the device still has some drawbacks for practical classroom use. In a university study, students found that underlining and taking notes on the Kindle was very difficult. Students also had trouble finding specific information within the book text. For now, Kindles also don't have a reader function so blind students would not be able to use them. The manufacturer, Amazon, is working to address accessibility issues.

11. **Allow use of a calculator for class work and homework:** Some students may *never* master multiplication tables. In the real world, most adults use a calculator for doing everyday math calculations. Even the SAT now allows use of a calculator during testing. See Summaries 21-22 for more information on math accommodations.

12. **Use electronic tools to help students with reminders and organization:**

   12.1. Consider using electronic organizers such as a Sharp Wizard or Palm Pilot. These may be helpful for some students, but the Palm Pilot may actually be too sophisticated and a distraction for some students with ADD or ADHD. They may be tempted to play chess or send e-mail messages rather than just write down homework assignments. Wizard is priced at roughly $20 and Palm Pilot as high at $170-$200.

   12.2. Try prompting devices. Several tools are available to remind students with attention deficits of things they need to do:
   - *WatchMinder2™*: This wrist alarm may be programmed as a reminder to take medication, stay after school, or go by the locker and pick up books. (www.watchminder.com)
   - *Electronic reminder applications (apps).* Several electronic tools have apps that will provide reminders of things to do. For example iPhone has three free helpful apps, EverNote, ReQall, and Easy Task that allow you to text notes to yourself, record voice reminders, and use a reminder service and memory aid. Applications that provide reminders are also available for use on computers. Most computers already have calendars that can be programmed to ring an alarm reminder of key events.

12.3. Use ADHD-friendly clocks.
- *TimeTimer:* This product makes the passage of time visible, plus has an optional audible signal. Clocks (three different sizes), a wristwatch, and a software program show movement of time with an exposed red area that decreases in size as time passes. Available for $30-$40 from www.timetimer.com.

12.4. **Check out "Smartpens."**
- The "Livescribe Pulse" and "Echo" digital pens write on special paper, record lectures with sound, and will transfer notes to your computer as a digital copy (www.livescribe.com). This could be a great help for students who have trouble taking notes accurately and quickly. Although currently the pens cost between $175 and $200, the price should drop over time. The special paper is available online or at Best Buy, Target, and Staples.

Resources

- **The DO-IT (Disabilities, Opportunities, Internetworking, and Technology) website** at www.washington.edu/doit/ offers helpful information for students and teachers. The information was developed to promote computer and networking technologies for teens and young adults with disabilities who are in need of academic assistance, independent work skills, and career guidance. Numerous brief videos and publications are available on assistive technology and computers.

- **Georgia Tools for Life Program** (www.gatfl.org) offers several publications regarding specific assistive technology (AT) tools. Includes numerous resources such as software for writing or math difficulties, plus a list of Internet resources. Georgia has regional AT centers where you can actually try out specific AT tools. Check in your home state to see if similar resources are available.

Common Problems with Written Expression

SUMMARY 17

Teenagers with ADD or ADHD may have very creative ideas for writing essays, but often have great difficulty getting their ideas down on paper. In fact, in a study published in *ADHD Reports*, 65 percent of students with ADD or ADHD were found to have problems with written expression, making it the most common learning problem they experienced (see Summary 13). This is not surprising, considering that written expression involves many complex executive skills requiring organizing, analyzing, synthesizing, sequencing, and remembering—skills that are often challenging for students with attention deficit disorders. The suggestions in this summary and the next one on writing an essay may help address these problems.

Five Common Writing Problems

Dr. Mel Levine, the author of numerous books on teaching students with learning problems, has identified five common problems that interfere with written expression for many middle and high school students:

1. **Organizational Problems**—Often students don't have a good organizational plan for where and how to begin writing or what the next step should be. Sequencing of key information is also difficult. Students must think about what they are writing, figure out what comes next, and organize the essay or report.

2. **Poor Retrieval Memory or "Exceeded Memory Capacity"**– Students, especially those with attention deficits, often lack sufficient memory capacity to write well. Students must access their long-term memory for correct spelling and to find rules of grammar, punctuation, and capitalization. At the same time, students have to use their working memory to remember what they are writing about and decide which thought they want to express next. Simply holding that thought or a chunk of information in working memory long enough to write it down is often difficult.

3. **Graphomotor Dysfunction**—For students with fine motor problems, writing may be very slow and laborious. Some students with ADD or ADHD, even as adults, prefer printing instead of cursive writing for good reasons. According to Mel Levine, M.D., cursive writing requires more memory than printing does. Plus our students often have fine motor coordination problems.

4. **Unsophisticated Ideation**—*Ideation,* or generation of thoughts, includes selection of a topic, analysis of the topic, development of related ideas for the topic, elaboration on the ideas, and incorporation of information learned previously.

5. **Written Language Problems**—Students who have weak language production, or difficulty putting thoughts into words, may write very simple essays using brief sentences. Problems in the first four areas listed may contribute to written language problems.

Resources

Levine, Mel. *Educational Care.* 2nd ed. Cambridge, MA: Educators Publishing Service, 2000.

Mayes, Susan D. & Susan Calhoun. "Prevalence and Degree of Attention and Learning Problems in ADHD and LD." *ADHD Reports*, April 2000, Vol.8, No. 2.

Improving Written Expression

1. Create a safe writing environment: Most students with ADD or ADHD are extremely anxious about writing assignments. This is such a difficult task for them, they avoid writing as much as possible. When they do finally write something, the words may not flow easily and they dread criticism from the teacher. Teachers and parents will find helpful information at www.grammar.ccc.commnet.edu/grammar. The graphic organizers for adverbs and adjectives included below are reprinted with permission from this site. Strategies for building skills and reducing anxiety include:

1.1 Work on fluency first. Claudia Jordan, a veteran high school Language Arts teacher, recommends building student confidence by establishing writing fluency first. She does not grade early writing. Instead she gives students credit for giving their best effort.

- **Sentences first.** Start with two- to three-sentence assignments. Jordan starts out by asking students to write two to three sentences every day about an interesting paragraph or short story she reads them or a picture or cartoon shown on an overhead. *Masterpiece Sentences,* a part of the *Language!* program developed by Dr. Jane Fell Greene, offers another way to give students guided practice writing creative sentences. See the discussion in Summary 16-A and the resources listed in Summary 16 for more information.

- **Paragraphs next.** Marcy Winograd, an experienced middle school Language Arts teacher, says, "Students need lots of practice with this type of writing [paragraphs] before putting pen to paper on a five paragraph essay." Winograd asks students to write daily paragraphs "in the air." She writes a topic sentence on the overhead—for example, "Students should wear uniforms at school." She then throws a beach ball to select a student to write a sentence. Students who voluntarily catch the ball must use a transition word before giving a supporting statement. (Transition words are written on posters on the wall: For example; In addition; First; Second; Third; Finally; Consequently.) Each student's statement is written on the posters or the overhead. For the conclusion, she may ask, "What difference will it make if students wear uniforms? What is the bottom line?" Again, students respond with sentences beginning with transition words such as "then" or "as a result": "Consequently, students who wear uniforms to school will learn more."

- **Allow dictation to a "scribe" if needed.** Initially students may benefit from dictating their writing to a scribe, who may be another student or parent.

- **Lengthen assignments.** Increase the length of writing assignments gradually. Next, students may begin writing at least one brief paragraph four or five days a week.

- **Finally, polish.** After writing fluency is achieved, Dr. Greene suggests enriching writing by "painting" nouns and verbs with additional adjectives and adverbs. The Royal Order of Adjectives graphic organizer from the *Capital Community College's Guide to Grammar and Writing* (Hartford, CT) should help students select adjectives and put them in the proper sequence in a series. (See example on the next page.) Finally, polish grammar, spelling, and punctuation.

THE ROYAL ORDER OF ADJECTIVES									
Determiner	Observation	Physical Description				Origin	Material	Qualifier	Noun
		Size	Shape	Age	Color				
a	beautiful			old		Italian		touring	car
an	expensive			antique			silver		mirror
four	gorgeous		long-stemmed		red		silk		roses
her			short		black				hair
our		big		old		English			sheepdog
those			square				wooden	hat	boxes
that	dilapidated	little						hunting	cabin
several		enormous		young		American		basketball	players
some	delicious					Thai			food

Royal Order of Adjectives, reprinted with permission from Capital Community College's Guide to Grammar and Writing, by Charles Darling (http://grammar.ccc.commnet.edu/grammar). Royal Order of Adverbs also available on this site.

1.2. Encourage journal writing. Set aside time in class and ask students to write two sentences about what they are feeling or thinking at that exact moment. Since the work may be personal, teachers may tell the students they will not read any journal unless a student asks them to do so. Don't grade the content but simply give credit when the student shows you a completed paragraph.

- Read from inspirational books. One teacher reads from the "Chicken Soup" books each Friday and gives her students ten minutes to free write in their journal.
- Show pictures or cartoons on the overhead to trigger ideas. For example, you might show a picture of a smiling person, then briefly discuss examples of happy times given by students and ask them to write their memories of a happy time.

1.3. Be sensitive and caring about students' writing anxieties. Many students with ADD or ADHD feel inadequate because of problems expressing themselves in writing and poor handwriting. Do not embarrass students about their messy written work or put it on display without their permission. If the student has written a good essay, the teacher may read it in class. However, if the student is embarrassed about her writing or is a poor reader, don't ask her to read it in class.

2. **Model skills for students:** Show, don't just tell, students how to do specific types of writing assignments. Claudia Jordan **writes with her students.** She actually writes essays or poetry in class and walks students through the process step by step while using an overhead projector. Students contribute to her essay by brainstorming and giving suggestions for topics to address, identifying four or five paragraph topics, developing supportive sentences for each topic, and writing an opening and closing paragraph. After the teacher models these steps in class, the students complete the same steps for their own personal essays. This process is completed over a period of weeks.

3. **Teach concepts:** Teach concepts related to sequencing: first-second-then-next-finally, before-after, yesterday-today-tomorrow, past-present-future.

4. **Modify assignments:** See Summary 16-B for more details on modifying assignments.

   4.1. Give extended time. Allow more time for written assignments and essay questions on tests.

   4.2. Reduce written work. Shorten reports or assignments. Expect that answers to essay questions will be brief; comprised of only a few short sentences.

   4.3. Bypass writing. For students who are overwhelmed by the writing process, periodically substitute other types of assignments such as a recorded or oral report, a project instead of a written report, or multiple-choice or true-false tests.

   4.4. Allow students to print their work. Do not require cursive writing if students are more comfortable and write more rapidly with printing.

   4.5. Allow students to write in pencil. Some students are more comfortable writing with a pencil because of frequent errors and erasures.

   4.6. Give cooperative writing projects.
   - Group projects: Allow a group of students to write a report cooperatively. Students may be assigned different roles: researcher, brainstormer, proofreader, and illustrator.
   - Joint projects: Sometimes students may alternate working on the computer as they jointly compose an essay. This process encourages scaffolding or building upon the other student's work and improving the final product. Researchers have found that the quality of student writing improves as one student learns from another.
   - Telecommunication network collaboration: A few schools have tried teleconferencing with local and distant school systems as they share writing products.

   4.7. Select topics related to personal growth. Coyle Bryan teaches an applied communication class to high school seniors in Whitfield County, Georgia. The content is related to real-world work experience, as well as personal growth. Students talk and then write about important topics such as self-esteem, values, self-awareness of personality characteristics, recognizing these traits in others, and getting along with peers and coworkers.

5. **Modify testing and grading:** See Summary 16-C for more details.

   5.1. Don't grade early work. Do not grade the content but simply give the student credit (e.g., 25 points) for completing the assignment. Too much criticism early on is terribly discouraging and may result in the student giving up.

   5.2. Prioritize key elements of the assignment. Next, focus on the content, but don't count off for spelling or grammar errors the first time around. Mark errors and have students revise and make corrections. Or consider giving the student a word bank with the correct spelling of key words to be incorporated into the essay.

   5.3. Grade only one aspect of the essay. For example, sometimes Coyle Bryan grades the students only on their use of verbs, nouns, spelling, or capitalization. She tells the students in advance so they will know which element to review most carefully.

   5.4. Assign each essay two grades and average. If grammar, spelling, and punctuation are being graded, give the student two grades, one for creative content and one for grammar, spelling, and punctuation. Then average the two grades. The late Clare Jones, Ph.D., author of *Attention Deficit Disorder: Strategies* *for School-Age Children*, suggested including this as an accommodation in the student's IEP or Section 504 Plan.

5.5. Give tests that measure recognition rather than recall.

- Provide word banks on tests. Give the student a list of words from which to choose the correct answer.
- Give prompts for essay tests by providing a bank of words that should be included in the paper.
- Provide "starter sentences" to help students organize their thoughts. For example, "Both the North and South are to 'blame' for the start of the Civil War. In the years preceding the war, both sides took actions that angered the other side. For example, the North...."

6. **Use Technology:** For more information on electronic resources, refer to Summary 16-E.

6.1. Allow use of a computer. Students with ADD or ADHD should be encouraged to use computers for written work as early as possible. Keyboarding is often extremely difficult (see Summary 16-B for software for teaching this critical skill).

6.2. Use a spell and grammar check. Allow students with ADD or ADHD to use spell check as part of a computer program or use a handheld spell check. Handheld Franklin Spellers are available for less than $20. Computer spell check is also helpful.

6.3. Make students and parents aware of helpful websites:

- www.ldonline.com—This informative site includes articles and books about teaching writing, suggested software for math and writing instruction, articles about software such as Inspiration, and suggestions for helping with organizational skills.
- www.sdcoe.k12.ca.us—This website, developed by the San Diego County Office of Education, includes graphic organizers for journaling, literature, and rubrics that may be duplicated. Click on Learning Resources and Educational Technology, and then view Score Language Arts.
- www.grammar.ccc.commnet.edu — "A Guide to Grammar and Writing" is available on this site. Adverb and adjective graphic organizers also are available here.
- www.essaywritinghelp.com—This helpful website offers tips on writing several different types of essays: persuasive, compare and contrast, and narrative. The site is a great resource for parents who are trying to help their child with essay writing.

7. **Share at-home tips with parents:**

7.1. Help your child write the essay. If your child has hit a "brick wall" with essay writing, help her write the essay—and don't feel guilty about it. Visit some of the suggested websites for tips. If needed, let her dictate to you while you type what she says. If she gets stuck, suggest a sentence and then let her rewrite it in her own words. As you do this with her, you are also teaching her. If she is starting at "ground zero" (can't even get started), by working it with her you may move her to a level three on a ten-point scale. When you work on the next essay with her, maybe you'll move her to eight. If she's struggling this much, extra help is clearly needed.

7.2. Visit www.essaywritinghelp.com. Print out their action steps and use it as an informal outline for writing the essay, leaving several spaces between steps. Handwrite ideas and facts for each step; then begin writing the first draft of the essay.

SUMMARY 19

Writing an Essay

Most teachers divide essay-writing assignments into stages such as brainstorming, outlining, first draft, revisions, second draft, revisions, and final version. Students with ADD or ADHD may need to have these stages broken down into even smaller parts or be guided through them step by step if they are going to succeed in writing an essay.

1. **"Think it"/Brainstorm:** Brainstorming for ideas to include in the essay is often the most difficult step for students with ADD or ADHD. Sometimes students almost panic because they have such difficulty quickly retrieving ideas or information from their brain. It's as though their brain is frozen or stuck. Teachers can help them break ideas loose and get started in several ways.

   1.1. **Provide guidance on topic selection.** Students with attention deficits often have a terrible time narrowing down and selecting a writing topic. Limit the number of topics from which they may select to two or three. Since it is easier to write about what the student knows, tell him to select the topic he feels strongest about or knows the most about. Or if he can't select one right away, ask him to eliminate one idea.
      - Topic ideas may include: something you believed was true; the most beautiful place you've ever been; an enemy who isn't a person; foods you love; something that got you in trouble; secrets you had; a time you were scared or sick; things you did with a brother or sister; or a favorite book, TV show, or movie. Then, to stimulate thinking, briefly talk through one idea with the students.

   1.2. **Break the idea logjam.** Encourage students to write down their ideas in whatever form they occur—for example, global ideas, phrases, or specific details. Don't do anything to stop or slow the flow of the student's ideas.

   1.3. **Use Post-It notes.** Encourage the student to freely throw out ideas and then write them on Post-It notes. Write down all ideas. Don't make judgments of what is good or bad or what to keep or eliminate.

   1.4. **Provide prompts to stimulate thinking.**
      - Give visual prompts. Show students pictures, cartoons, newspaper headlines.
      - Have a class discussion or read them a short story. Help students bring a picture to mind of their topics.
      - Use manipulatives. One teacher gave each student a pipe cleaner or clay and told them to form it into something that was of interest to them or that stood as a symbol for themselves and then write about the topic.
      - Act out plays. Read and act out a classic play such as *Romeo and Juliet*. Later have the students write an essay on a related topic.

   1.5. **Answer key questions.** Have students answer who, what, when, where, and why regarding their topic.

   1.6. **Reinforce with physical activity.** Teacher Marcy Winograd uses a physical activity to reinforce the elements of a conclusion:
      - "Touch back"—she has the students bring their pinky to their thumb to illustrate touching back on the thesis of the essay.

- "Go to the heart"—students touch their hearts to show that you have to explain the bottom line—what difference the thesis makes—otherwise, who cares?
- "Look to the future"—hand on forehead, looking outward.
- "End strong"—flex the biceps to emphasize the need to express a strong opinion.

Students usually think these activities are fun and are learning at the same time. Asking students to write a "How to do something" narrative also helps them become physically involved in writing. For example, explain step by step how to change the oil in your car.

1.7. Use graphic organizers. Several graphic organizers are available to help students brainstorm by using *clusters, webs, or mind maps* to develop and expand upon ideas. Summary 16-A lists resources that contain graphic organizers.

- Draw your own graphic organizer. (See Appendix A2.) Have the student draw a circle in the center of the page, draw six lines radiating out from the center, add small circles, and draw additional lines away from the small circles.
- Use the student's hand as a graphic organizer. At Paul Revere Middle school in Los Angeles, students
  - ➤ trace their hand,
  - ➤ label the thumb with the thesis statement,
  - ➤ label the index finger with the topic sentence of the first supporting paragraph,
  - ➤ label the middle finger with the topic sentence for the second supporting paragraph,
  - ➤ label the ring finger with the topic sentence of the third supporting paragraph, and
  - ➤ label the pinky with the conclusion.

2. **"Write it":**

   2.1. **Begin organizing thoughts.**
   - **Regroup Post-It notes.** If students recorded ideas on Post-It notes as described in 1.3, move Post-It notes into clusters. Perhaps group by who, what, when, and where or other logical categories (such as by pros and cons about the issue).
   - **Cut and paste.** Type ideas into a computer and print them out. Either physically cut up the words on paper or cut and paste on the computer to move ideas around, group them together, and begin thinking of a logical writing sequence.
   - **Dictate ideas to a "scribe" or parent.**

   2.2. **Provide writing prompts.**
   - **Use an Essay Organizer.** Refer to information on the graphic organizer as the student begins writing (Appendix A2). Usually the information listed under "who, what, when, and where" sections is included in the first paragraph of the essay. Information under "why and how" is expanded to provide the body paragraphs of the essay. The small circles by each of these six sections may be numbered to indicate the order in which they are included in the essay.
   - **Develop guided writing tips.** When students are just beginning and believe that they cannot write a good essay, guided writing tips will help them succeed and gain confidence. Here is an example from one class:
     - ➤ Picture in your mind a pleasant place from your childhood, a special time when you felt really happy. Try to see it in your mind's eye. Where

are you? Draw a picture of the place where you are. Who is there? What time of year and time of day is it?

- ➤ Ask questions regarding the five senses to help enrich the essay.
    - ⟩ *Sight*. What do you see? Picture yourself as a little kid. Who else is there? Describe yourself and them. What are you wearing?
    - ⟩ *Smell*. What do you smell? (food, granddad's aftershave) *Taste*. What do you taste? (cake, salty tears)
    - ⟩ *Hearing*. What do you hear? What does it sound like? (AC, fan, buzz of talking)
    - ⟩ *Touch*. What does it feel like? (scratchy, smooth, cold, soft)
- ➤ After the student has written this material, ask him to go back and add two adjectives to each sentence.

2.3. Share tips with parents. Since parents are often involved in helping students write essays and reports for numerous subjects, teachers may want to share with them the information in Appendix B1 on writing a three-part essay.

3. **"Fix it":**

3.1. Allow students to use computer editing and proofreading functions to polish their first draft.

3.2. Use peer review. Ask students to swap papers with each other. Each student tells: 1) one thing the writer did well, and 2) one thing the writer could improve. The students may go through two or three rounds of peer review. Students are much more likely to remember writing tips that they learn by "teaching" or sharing corrections with another student.

3.3. Provide teacher review. While students are doing peer review, the teacher can begin reading each student's paper and asking questions. Sometimes the teacher may say, "Read this to me. Does it sound right to you?"

3.4. Provide editing practice. Give students material that someone else has written or that the teacher has created for practice editing and have them make needed changes and corrections.

3.5. Do not correct all errors. Don't correct all the errors in a student's early writings. Correct major errors such as sentence fragments or run-on sentences. Otherwise, he may be too discouraged to even attempt to write anything.

4. **Evaluate and polish it:** Many teachers develop rubrics or checklists of questions a student may ask himself after he has written an essay. For example, here are some questions to answer yes or no about the essay.
    - ▪ I begin with a topic or thesis sentence.
    - ▪ I provide details to support the topic sentence.
    - ▪ All my sentences have a subject and a verb, begin with a capital letter, and end with a punctuation mark.

Winograd asks her students these questions when they write a mystery story:
- ▪ Did your mystery have a beginning, middle, and end?
- ▪ Did it include a crime, clues, suspects, and alibis?
- ▪ Did it include some element of conflict?
- ▪ Was your detective character believable?
- ▪ Did you create a detailed setting that intrigued the reader?
- ▪ Did you create a climax where all the action came to a head?

5. **"Share it":**

    5.1. Have students hand in final papers.

    5.2. Ask students to read their essays in class. Or the student may ask the teacher or another student to read it.

    5.3. Publish it in a school or class newspaper or magazine. In Georgia, *Foxfire* is an excellent, well-known publication of student writings. Graduating students from Winograd's classes have work published in their very own *Story Walk*, a literary arts magazine. You could also find a good desktop publishing program (Summary 16-E) and publish student writings. Researchers have found that the quality of written work improves when writing is published.

    5.4. Display student papers on the class or school bulletin board or teacher website. Sometimes private businesses display student art; why not display student writing in private businesses or the school administrative offices? Or their work could also be displayed on the school or teacher's webpage.

Other Written Assignments

1. **Book Reports:** Some Language Arts teachers are shying away from traditional written book reports. Written reports do not provide assurance the book has actually been read since reports are easily available from the Internet and other students. Instead, students may be asked to do a project and then give an oral report on the book. There are also a variety of other options that may work better for students with ADD or ADHD than the written book report.

   1.1. Use "Books on Tape." If a student has problems with reading, allow her to listen to books on audiotape. See Summary 16-E for details on Books on Tape.

   1.2. Assign book projects. For example, one student baked a cake like Mrs. Haversham's from *Great Expectations*. Fake spider webs and roaches were added to make it look fifty years old. Another student did an oil painting of Emily Dickinson and told about her life.

   1.3. Give verbal book reports. Students are asked to report on their book, show their project, and then answer questions from the class. Students are not asked to stand up to speak unless they wish to do so.

   1.4. Read classic books in class. The teacher may read two chapters to the class and then ask students to read one chapter at home on their own.

   1.5. Assign creative alternatives to nonfiction book reports. Sometimes students have to do book reports for other classes such as social studies, history, or government. Make these books memorable by assigning creative projects. Susie Smith, a language arts teacher at Lullwater School in Decatur, Georgia, has her students make pop-up books to accompany their oral book reports. (See Summary 25.) A secondary benefit for students with attention deficits is that these projects frequently call for little or no writing. For example:
      - videotape interviews of war veterans,
      - draw a poster of how a bill becomes a law,
      - design a movie poster to sell the book,
      - do videos of key scenes in the book,
      - create a three-dimensional sculpture depicting at least three of the major characters.

   1.6. Use a graphic organizer. Allow students to fill in the blanks in a "who, what, when, where, why, and how" graphic organizer.

2. **Creative Writing:**

   2.1 Provide prompts for creative writing assignments. Teacher Marcy Winograd explains that she gives her students prompts to help them write more interesting creative stories. For example, when writing to create suspense, she "slows down the moment" by asking students to *go slow and raise doubt.*
   "She thought she heard someone in the house."
      - Describe the sound.
      - What is she thinking?
      - What does she smell? Connect the smell to a memory.
      - Bring the feeling back to the present.

"It reminded him of the time he got lost in the woods and was dying for a drink of water. Now his throat felt parched, too. He was so scared he couldn't swallow."

➤ Have the character notice something visually different about the scene.

➤ What is she thinking now?

➤ Have her do something; keep moving closer until she makes a discovery.

3. **Poetry:** With poetry, students are learning to use imagery and paint pictures with words.

3.1. Act out narrative poems. Marcy Winograd assigns students roles in *Casey at the Bat* or *Paul Revere's Ride* and has them dress for their parts. The students act out the poems as a class. They have a batter, people on bases, a pitcher, and fans in the audience. People in the stands may yell at the umpire.

3.2. Provide prompts for inspiration. For example, give students a theme for their poetry. Winograd taught a "Fruit Poetry Lesson." She brought a bowl of fruit including mangos, apples, strawberries, limes, and others. She picked a fruit and then talked about what it was like on the outside and on the inside. Then the class as a group wrote a poem about fruit. Students looked for outside/inside parallels between fruit and key events in their lives such as a girlfriend who makes them happy or their parents' divorce. Here is a "Strawberry Poem" the class wrote as a group:

> *On the outside*
> *The strawberry is rough*
> *Like the hands of the farmworker who toils*
> *Back bent in the fields*
> *On the inside*
> *The strawberry is a ruby*
> *A heart*
> *A tunnel to a new beginning*
> *Taste the Strawberry*
> *And savor the sweetness of summer.*

3.3. Use the five senses to help enrich the description, as explained earlier about writing an essay.

3.4. Provide written prompts. Winograd gives her students a graphic organizer to write either a poem or essay on "Where you're from." Each student is given a map of a town, complete with roads and descriptive words to help her write a poem on the topic, "I'm from...." In addition to "you" in the center of the map, other words on the map include town and street names, parent's work, relatives near you, central events, smells, tastes, religious experience, hiding place, what grew in your yard, and a wild card (any topic of the student's choice).

3.5. Write poetry that is imitative of famous poems. For example, read "The Raven" in class and have students write a poem with the same rhythm or rhyme scheme or with a repeated line such as "Quoth the raven, nevermore."

3.6. Publish student poetry. Winograd has helped her students get their poetry published in *Story Walk,* a literary magazine. Kevin Cooper, a student with ADHD, wrote this lovely poem in class. He takes his medication just before her class begins.

First Interest ...
By Kevin Cooper

When I started I only knew one thing
About the amber-brown violin.
I was the greatest, the best violinist in the world.
My dad tells me to practice
Everybody knows
That the best violinist needs no practice.
My posture was like celery
That had been left out for three months;
Limp, slouching, bad, and worse;
My hand was flat as if it had been steam rolled
And my bow hand clutched my bow
Like a crab clutches a stick.
How was I to know good posture from bad
And I was the best in the world.

After that year I took private lessons
The bird-like screech of before
Was now a cricket's chirp.
My posture slowly improved.
Old celery was replaced with new.
Flat sharps and sharp flats went away
I saw and heard those who were far ahead of me
As if I were racing the fastest men in the world.
The one thing I wonder is
If I have improved since I began
How is it that then I was the best
And now I am not.

4. **Reports or long-term projects:** Long-term projects with delayed due dates present major challenges to students with ADD/ADHD. Semester projects and reports are discussed in two sections: 1) Summaries 37-38 provide tips for completing a long-term project and 2) Summaries 34-36 suggest organizational and time management strategies for long-term projects.

Common Math Difficulties

Basic math skills such as numbers, addition, subtraction, simple multiplication, simple division, simple weights and measures, money counting, and telling time are often weaker in students with ADD or ADHD than in their peers. (The basic symbols and processes of arithmetic are known as numeracy skills.) These difficulties with math have been confirmed by research; math achievement scores for students with ADHD were 10 percent lower than for non-ADHD students in a control group.

Computation

Poor math performance, especially weak math computation, is one of the most challenging problems facing students with ADD or ADHD. Even those students who don't qualify as having a learning disability can still have terrible problems with math. Typically, most students with attention deficits don't *automatize* basic math facts. In other words, they are unable to quickly retrieve addition, subtraction, multiplication, and division facts. Unfortunately, this gaping hole in their "math foundation" interferes with their ability to complete math problems quickly. In spite of this serious deficit, however, these students may learn complex math concepts as easily as other students.

It is critical for teachers to allow the students to move on to more advanced math concepts and give them accommodations to compensate for their deficits in basic math skills!

Common sense tells us that time spent struggling to retrieve multiplication facts is wasteful and could be more wisely spent mastering advanced math concepts. This makes it vital to provide appropriate classroom accommodations, such as use of a calculator or a chart of math facts, or shortened assignments. These accommodations enable students to focus on mastering concepts rather than having to agonize over their faulty rote memorization skills or slow processing speed. Although students may use calculators for figuring basic math facts, it is critical that they also know how it is done—for example "how to" multiply fractions. Periodic review of these basic procedures may be necessary as students move through more advanced math topics.

Complex Multistep Math

Algebra is often extremely challenging for students with ADD or ADHD. Algebra presents a major shift from concrete arithmetic to more abstract advanced math concepts. Because of their delayed brain maturity, the demands for working memory capacity, manipulation of abstract concepts, and rapid use of memorized math facts may be overwhelming for our children. These students may also fail to use more sophisticated strategies during problem solving. Word problems can be especially problematic since they have difficulty ignoring irrelevant information in the problems. Furthermore, students must have strong linguistic skills to properly interpret a word problem and then set up and solve the problem correctly. Helpful strategies include job cards, mnemonics, paired learning, guided practice, and frequent monitoring of progress. These strategies are explained in Summaries 25, 22, and 16-A.

One of the most effective ways to help them master algebra is to use hands-on concrete activities to teach these abstract concepts. See www.msalgebra.com. Once concepts are mastered, the hands-on strategies are no longer needed. Self-paced math curricula are also helpful. See Summaries 22-23 for additional strategies.

Factors Contributing to Difficulties in Math

1. Deficits in working memory (difficulty holding information in mind while performing math functions);
2. Slow processing speed and difficulty retrieving information from long-term memory (slow retrieval of stored math information);
3. Weak linguistic skills (difficulty in solving word problems);
4. Weak visual perceptual skills (difficulty judging placement on paper, aligning columns, carrying numbers from one column to the next);
5. Poor fine motor skills (poor handwriting).

According to *Rethinking ADHD in the Classroom* (published online at http://research.aboutkidshealth.ca/teachadhd), researchers identified these additional math weaknesses:

- procedural errors (for example, subtracting a larger number from smaller number, failing to carry a number);
- tendency to rely on finger counting rather than direct retrieval of facts;
- more overt (out-loud) self-talk to guide actions (rather than using inner speech);
- difficulty ignoring irrelevant information in word problems;
- difficulty solving math problems with multiple procedures or steps.

Without extensive testing, one of the easiest ways to spot a student's math deficits is to look for lower than average scores on standardized tests such as the IOWA, especially the Math Computation section, or the Arithmetic subtest of the WISC-IV or WAIS-IV. Actually, these deficits can be identified as early as kindergarten. Children who have difficulty with letter knowledge and counting have been shown to have lower scores on working memory/executive function tests. Early screening for deficits in executive functions, working memory, or processing speed is very important.

How These Factors Affect School Performance

1. Some students with ADD or ADHD work math problems more slowly than their peers and may not finish assignments or tests during the time allotted in class.
2. They may take twice as long as other students to finish homework. See Summaries 27-29 for suggestions to help with homework.
3. Since students cannot quickly retrieve basic addition, subtraction, multiplication, or division facts, they take more time to complete more complex math problems.
4. Organizational and sequencing skills are often deficient, making multistep math problems extremely difficult.
5. They may learn multiplication tables one night and seem to forget them by the next evening. Even intellectually gifted students with ADD or ADHD may never master their multiplication tables.
6. Students may attempt to "do the work in their heads" and write down the answer only. However, when they do work in their heads, they may skip steps and make "careless" errors.
7. They may write their numbers very small, too close together, and all on one line rather than spacing the problem properly so that it is more easily read and errors more easily detected.
8. Forgetting to write down homework assignments and to take assignments and the appropriate books home are also major challenges.

With all these challenges to overcome, doing math homework may be overwhelming. Students may avoid homework by telling parents they don't have any or that they completed it at school. Accommodations including calculators and shorter assignments are beneficial to many of these students.

General Tips for Mastering Math

Students must learn many complex math concepts, especially in algebra, geometry, and advanced math courses. Obviously, this summary cannot provide tips for every single math concept to be taught. Instead, it offers tips that can be generalized for teaching other math concepts. Teachers will find it helpful to use this summary in conjunction with Summaries 21 and 23 as well as Summaries 16-A to 16-E on providing accommodations.

Words of Wisdom from Math Teachers

Several middle, high school, and college math teachers, a few of whom have children with ADD or ADHD, contributed excellent ideas for this summary. Their suggestions for accommodating math deficits are below:

1. **Modify assignments:**

    1.1. **Modify/shorten homework assignments.** Assign every second, third, or fourth math problem that still covers the necessary skills and mastery of major math concepts.

    1.2. **Reduce writing.** Photocopy pages for students so they do not have to rewrite the math problems. Enlarging the original copy may give the student more room to show her work and write answers.

    1.3. **Reduce notetaking.** Jointly identify a note-taker. Ask another student who is good in math to take notes and underline the important issues of the lesson. NCR (carbonless) paper makes notetaking easier. See the suggestions for notetaking in Summary 16-B.

2. **Modify teaching methods:**

    2.1. **List steps for completion of math problems on the board.** As examples are written on the board, especially multistep math problems, Denise Vogelesang, chairman of a high school special education department, suggests listing the steps taken for solving the problem on the board. She always puts the problem in the same spot on the board and leaves it there throughout class. Number (don't use letters) the steps in the order they are to be completed.

    2.2. **Keep a sample math problem on the board.** Keep a step-by-step model of the problem on the board for the student to refer to while the concept is being taught.
        * If students have working memory problems and can't hold the problem in mind as they look back and forth from the board, ask them to copy the problem on a colored card and put it by their paper as they work. If they are unable to remember to do this, ask another student to write the problem down and give them a copy.

    2.3. **Provide visual cues for common math facts.** Desktop Helpers (3x12) provide a handy reference to aid memory deficits and are available on a variety of topics (math facts, fractions, punctuation rules) from the Really Good Stuff company (www.reallygoodstuff.com).

2.4. Use a "paired-learning" teaching strategy. Paired learning, also known as *class-wide peer tutoring,* is a very effective interactive learning strategy. After the teacher demonstrates a problem, students are paired off and each student within the pairs makes up her own problem, solves it, and writes the answer down. Next the student gives her partner the blank problem to work and they compare answers to the problem. If their answers are not the same, the students discuss their differences and make corrections.

Dr. Ed Thomas, a veteran math educator and president/senior math consultant for Dimension 2000, recommends this strategy for teaching middle, high school, and college math classes. This technique was extremely effective with my college-age son who had always struggled and barely passed his math classes. He earned his first ever "A" in a math course with a 100 average in Dr. Thomas's Calculus course.

2.5. Pair with another student. If unable to use a full blown paired-learning teaching strategy with the whole class, jointly identify a nearby student who: 1) is willing and capable of answering questions the student may ask, and 2) can double check to see if homework assignments are written down.

2.6. Use an overhead or interactive board. Write sample problems on an overhead projector or interactive board. Since the teacher is facing the class, students can hear and see the work, plus the teacher can see them. Mary Kay Wells, chairman of a high school math department, uses different color markers for each new step of a problem and for different lines on a graph. Plus, with an Interactive Slate, students can write on the board too. See Summary 16-E for more details.

2.7. Use group response. As suggested in Summary 16-A, increase student involvement in class by using a group response. All students are asked to work a math problem, then write their answers on dry erase boards and hold them up for the teacher to see. A teacher can quickly see which students don't understand the material.

2.8. Give review summaries for exams. Review summaries are very helpful for students with attention deficits. Summaries are even more critical for parents who may help their teenager study for the test.

2.9. Use concrete strategies to teach abstract concepts. Dr. Brad Witzel's math program, *Multisensory Algebra,* discussed in Summary 23, uses concrete strategies to teach new abstract math concept. When students achieve mastery, they transition to representational learning. Finally, they complete algebra problems, just like other students do.

2.10. Use self-paced algebra software. *NOVAnet* software has enabled students who have failed traditional classes to successfully pass algebra. (See Summary 23.)

2.11. Use foldables as a review strategy. Foldables are discussed in detail in 16-A.

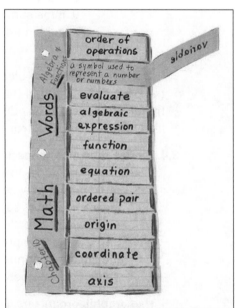

This activity was taken from Dinah Zike's Foldables®, Notebook Foldables®, and VKVs® for Spelling and Vocabulary 4th -12th (2009) and used with permission. See more of her ideas at www.dinah.com.

2.12. Minimize copying problems from the board. Provide sample problems in written handouts.

2.13. Link math problems to real world situations.

2.14. Identify key words and concepts in word problems. See Summary 23.

3. **Modify Teaching Resources.** Use more visual cues and allow students to use prompts to compensate for their memory and retrieval deficits. See Summary 16-A for more details.

   3.1. Allow use of a calculator for class- and homework. However, students may become "calculator dependent." They punch the numbers in the calculator to multiply fractions but may not remember how to do the basic problem. Students must understand these basic math skills for use in higher math courses such as Algebra I, II, and Trigonometry. So, periodic review of how to perform basic math skills may be necessary.

   3.2. Laminate a copy of important math facts. Shrink multiplication tables to a size that will fit in a student's wallet and allow her to use it when a calculator is not permitted or is unavailable. Also allow the student to keep a small card with formulas or acronyms. These cards will help trigger her memory of important math facts.
   - Or print divisibility rules on a small wallet-size card and laminate. Understanding divisibility is important because it helps the student reduce fractions or factor problems more quickly. A student who understands divisibility rules won't have to do long division on a problem to find the factors.

     Divisibility Rules: *You'll know if a number is divisible by*
       2 if the number is even (ends in 0, 2, 4, 6, or 8);
       3 if the sum of the digits is divisible by 3;
       4 if the number in the last two digits is divisible by 4;
       5 if the number ends in 0 or 5;
       6 if the number meets the rules for 2 & 3 above;
       8 if the number in the last three digits is divisible by 8 (less often used);
       9 if the sum of the digits is divisible by 9;
      10 if the number ends in 0

   3.3. Use graph paper for place value instruction. Graph paper helps separate the places and decimal (ones, tens, hundreds, thousands; one-tenth, one-hundredth, one-thousandth). This keeps columns straight, reducing the likelihood of making errors.

   3.4. Model appropriate spacing of math problems.
   - Use graph paper to demonstrate proper spacing of a problem. Show the student how to write a few math problems correctly. Place numbers in separate squares so that they are not too close together and the numbers are aligned correctly.
   - Turn notebook paper 90 degrees to help students organize math problems and line up their numbers. When the paper is turned sideways, the student writes numbers between the vertical lines.

   3.5. Use graphic organizers. Development of graphic organizers for math is more difficult but nonetheless extremely valuable. Foldables are also useful as a graphic organizer. An example of a graphic organizer that helps with classification of triangles by angles and sides is shown in Summary 23.

3.6. Use informative posters in the classroom. Posters provide visual reminders of important mathematical facts or concepts. The more interesting and novel the illustrations are, the more likely the student will remember them. For example, the information contained in Summary 23 on multiplying and dividing numbers with decimals could be drawn up as a poster.

3.7. Use color to highlight key facts. *Before* beginning work on math problems, ask students to highlight key "math operations" or issues. For example, students with ADD or ADHD often don't notice when the sign changes from + to –. Highlight each time the sign changes. In geometry, highlight the words perimeter, area, or volume and the name of the shape you're working with (triangle, square, trapezoid). Use different colored highlighters to help differentiate what is being emphasized.

If your school won't allow students to mark in their books, have the student highlight worksheets or scanned or photocopied pages from the textbook. Students may also purchase erasable highlighters.

3.8. Provide an extra textbook at home. Having a math book at home is often helpful for a couple of reasons: 1) Students with ADD or ADHD are so forgetful and disorganized they often forget their books. 2) Since math is one of their most challenging subjects, forgetting a book and not doing homework may make the difference between passing and failing the class.

4. **Modify testing and grading:** More detailed suggestions are provided in Summary 16-C.

    4.1. Give extended time on tests.

    4.2. Use "word banks" for tests. Provide the student with a list of the formulas required for the math test. The student must understand the information to know which formula to use in each problem. Also allow the student to use these word banks, perhaps on laminated cards, as she works on class- and homework.

    4.3. Allow use of a laminated card with key math facts, as described in 3.2 above.

    4.4. Adjust grading techniques by allowing the student to drop her lowest grade, earn extra credit, or do make-up work. Some teachers prefer not to make adjustments to grades after the fact, but have found other ways to adjust grading. For example, one teacher only gives four tests in a grading period. She doesn't drop the lowest grade but allows students to replace it with the final exam score, if they earn at least a C on the final exam. For example, if a student made test grades of 51, 71, 77, and 75, plus 72 on her final exam, she could substitute the 72 for the failing grade of 51.

5. **Modify the level of supervision:** As explained in Summary 16-D, these students will need more supervision than their peers. Utilization of weekly reports in challenging classes is often beneficial. See Summary 39 on weekly reports.

6. **Modify class schedules:** A more detailed discussion is given in Summary 62 on Classroom Management.

    6.1. Schedule math class during peak medication times. Work with school officials to schedule challenging classes like algebra during morning hours. See Summaries 56-60 for information on peak medication effectiveness.

    6.2. Reschedule with math teachers with whom the student has been successful. Suggest that parents talk with or write the administration—for example, the assistant principal for curriculum—requesting the same teacher and explaining why it is so important. Hopefully the school will honor this type of request.

SUMMARY 23 Challenging Middle and High School Math Skills

Teachers and parents alike have identified the following math skills as being especially challenging for middle and high school students with ADD or ADHD.

Multiplication Tables

By the middle school years, if students are still struggling with multiplication tables, allow them to use calculators or other aids. If remedial instruction is continuing, several additional resources are identified in the Resources section at the end of this summary.

- **Use assistive technology.** Allow students to use a **calculator** or **laminated chart** of these tables during class and for homework.

- **Provide visual cues.** Use resources that provide more visual cues, such as *Times Tables the Fun Way!* by Judy Liautaud and Dave Rodriguez (see illustration at right). Included in the *Times Tables the Fun Way!* kits are multiplication books, cards, workbooks, and posters that utilize mnemonic tips. Their latest product, *Times Alive* (CD-Rom software), provides a colorful, animated version of key multiplication facts. Available from City Creek (800-585-6059; www.citycreek.com).

- **Use songs or chants.** *Multiplication Rap* offers math facts set to rap music. Available from Remedia Publications (800-826-4740; www.rempub.com).

- **Teach multiplication short cuts.** For problems remembering the nines multiplication tables, try this finger counting technique. Hold your hands out in front of you and spread your fingers. For 9 x 7, count from left to right until you reach the seventh finger. Hold that finger down and then count the remaining fingers on either side to obtain the answer. There are six fingers to the left and three fingers to the right. The correct answer is 63.

Remember: When it's 4 x 4, the fours become a 4 by 4 (4 x 4) and you have to be 16 to drive it.

From Times Tables the Fun Way!

9 x 7 = 63

- **Give simple, easily understood rules when possible.** For example:

    If multiplying by 10, add one zero. (10 x 5 = 50)

    If multiplying by 100, add two zeros. (100 x 5 = 500)

    If multiplying by 1000, add three zeros. (1000 x 5 = 5000)

Long Division

- **Develop mnemonics** to help students remember math concepts or facts. Here's an example of an acronym to help students remember the steps of long division. (Teachers or students are encouraged to make up their own mnemonics.)

Dumb **M**onkeys **S**ell **B**ananas

Divide	[39 by 22]
Multiply	[1 times 22]
Subtract	[39-22=17]
Bring down	[6]

[repeat the process with 176]

```
          1 8
  2 2 | 3 9 6
      2 2
      1 7 6
      1 7 6
            0
```

Fractions and Decimals

- *Use* **concrete visual examples.** Susan Jessup, a middle school math teacher, uses money when she begins teaching students how to change fractions to decimals and then percentages. Many students find it easier to learn abstract concepts when using a concrete example with which they are already familiar.

    ½ of one dollar = $.50 = 50%

    ¼ of one dollar = $.25 = 25%

    ¾ of one dollar = $.75 = 75%

    ¹⁄₁₀ of one dollar = $.10 = 10%

Multiplying and Dividing Numbers with Decimals

- **Give a mnemonic.** Jessup gives students these rules of thumb for multiplying and dividing numbers with decimals.

```
      .25
  x   .33
      75
      75
    .0825
```

When *multiplying* numbers with decimals the new number is always smaller and the decimal moves to the left.

$$\begin{array}{r} 1.2 \\ .25\overline{\smash{)}.300} \\ \underline{25} \\ 50 \\ \underline{50} \\ 0 \end{array}$$

When **dividing** numbers with decimals the new number is always larger and the decimal moves to the right.

■ **Draw a poster of this information and post it in the room.**

Algebra: A Challenging Abstract Subject
Explaining Algebraic Equations

It can help to explain to students that an equation is like a balance scale. If you subtract the same number from each side, the equation stays balanced. So, "To solve the problem, whatever you do to one side of an equation, you need to do to the other side (add, subtract, multiply, divide)."

$$\begin{array}{rcl} 27 + x & = & 93 \\ -27 & & -27 \\ \hline 0 + x & = & 66 \end{array}$$

Multisensory Algebra

Most schools use prescribed curriculums and curricular materials in class. After class or at home, though, teachers can recommend that parents/students try some of these supplemental methods to help with understanding algebra. Sometimes students with ADHD/ADD benefit from working with manipulatives because they are more likely to understand and remember information when they use concrete, hands-on learning strategies.

Several resources are listed below. However, one of my favorites that has proven successful is by Dr. Brad Witzel, a math professor at Winthrop University. Dr. Witzel has created a wonderful hands-on program that features use of concrete teaching strategies for an often difficult abstract subject. This program was created to help all students but especially those who had previously struggled with or failed algebra. The program uses manipulatives (tongue depressors or craft sticks and cups) and representational pictures (slashes and circles to represent depressors/craft sticks and cups) to represent number units and math functions. Dr. Witzel suggests *"using concrete learning when knowledge is new or difficult."* Then *"use representational learning when students show accuracy without hesitation with concrete manipulations."* In other words, as students gain confidence with this concrete system, they can use slashes and circles to represent the sticks and cups. More detailed information is available at www.msalgebra.com.

Additional Multisensory Resources for Algebra

■ Algeblocks—www.etacuisenaire.com/algeblocks/algeblocks.jsp

■ Algebra Tiles—www.learningresources.com

■ Hands-on Equations—www.borenson.com

■ *PreAlgebra Blastoff* by Josh Rappaport—www.singingturtle.com

NOVAnet

NOVAnet is a relatively expensive school-wide software program that allows students to work at their own pace and even make up graduation credits. One parent told me that her daughter with ADHD passed algebra thanks to the program after two previous unsuccessful tries. Visit www.novanet.com for more information. An individual student's family would not be able to purchase it, so if your school doesn't use it, you may be better off trying one of the multisensory programs listed in the box.

Linear Equations

Linear functions are described by both a formula and a line drawing on a graph. Typically, students have problems in two special cases—1) when the line has no slope (a vertical line), and 2) when the line has a 0 slope (horizontal line).

■ **Ask the student to try using a mnemonic to remember their differences.** Liteena, a high school senior, was struggling with linear equations and made up this acronym that her teacher now uses for other students:

Slope of a Horizontal Line: **HOY— H**orizontal, **0** slope, **Y**=?

> *Example:* A **H**orizontal line has a slope of **0** and is represented by an equation, **Y** = a constant. (For example, y = 5.)
>
> (If you know HOY, then it is easier to remember that a vertical line has no slope and is represented by an equation x = a constant)

Problem-Solving (Word Problems)

Problem solving typically involves completing word problems. Many students with ADD or ADHD have difficulty setting up the equation correctly for these problems.

■ **Make the process more concrete and visual.** Jessup asks her student to **label** parts of the problem to make it easier to solve. Circles and X's are drawn on the key words in the math problem.

> **1. CIRCLE** needed facts in the problem.
>
>> *Example:* Mr. Fuller paid his son Brian $10 each time he mowed the lawn. If Brian mowed the lawn 12 times, how much did he earn?
>
> **2. MARK OUT** any unnecessary facts.
>
>> *Example:* Ten members of a drama club each bought a $4.75 ticket to see a play on Tuesday night. The play ran for 3 nights. How much did it cost for the group to see the play?
>
> **3. UNDERLINE** the strategy word or phrase.
>
>> *Example:* Mary spent $9.95 on a tape and $12.95 on a CD. <u>How much</u> did she spend?
>
> **4. FOR A 2-STEP PROBLEM,** place 1 LINE under the first step and 2 LINES under the second step.
>
>> *Example:* Stacy has 1 yard of ribbon. She needs <u>5/6</u> of a foot, <u>1 1/3</u> feet, and <u>3/4</u> of a foot. Does she <u>have enough</u> of the ribbon?

■ **Give students a list of strategy or action words** and the appropriate math procedures they translate into. Sometimes the terms in word problems such as "combined," "what amount," or "how much less" can confuse students so they are unsure which math procedure to use. This list should help students avoid confusion when these terms are found in word problems. Obviously, the student must understand the problem to be able to find the answer and to interpret it. Teachers may want to reduce or expand the list based upon the grade level being taught.

Addition	Subtraction	Multiplication	Division
how many?	the difference	product	quotient
altogether	how much less?	times	how many groups?
total*	how many more?	times as much	divided into
sum	more than	multiple of	divided by
combined	less than	twice	one-half of
in all*	subtracted from	(a number) times	one-third of
perimeter	less	multiplied by	one-fourth of
total cost*	increase	times as much	what part?
surface area*	decrease	times as many	make equal parts
	fewer	area	factor
	minus	volume	per unit
	how much change	surface area*	unit cost
	have enough?	squared	
		total*	
		in all*	
		total cost*	

These words may mean to either add or multiply, so read problems carefully.

■ **Use association** with something familiar in setting up the problem. Try using a student's name in sample word problems. Or use metaphors, analogies, or examples from the student's daily life. For example, if there are eight slices of pizza and your brother eats three of them, how much is left? Express in a fraction (5/8), percent (62.5%), or decimal (.625).

Using Math Ratios in Problem Solving

Math ratios are used to set up a proportion in a math equation. A ratio compares two numbers and can be shown as a "fraction" (3/4), "colon" (3:4) and "to" (3 to 4).

■ Use a **mnemonic**. When setting up an equation using a math proportion or ratio as a fraction, this mnemonic may be helpful:

When there are two numbers in a problem before a comma (,) or period (.), set up the ratio between the first two numbers.
Then the second two numbers must be set up in the same order—in other words, comparing apples to apples and money to money.

If 10 apples cost $2.50, how much will 20 apples cost?

$$\frac{\#\ apples}{cost} = \frac{\#\ apples}{X} \qquad\qquad \frac{10}{2.50} = \frac{20}{X}$$

$$10X = 50.00$$

$$X = 5$$

The cost of 20 apples is $5.00

Classifying Shapes

- **Create a Mind Map** (graphic organizer) to classify geometric shapes. To help students understand and remember the difference between shapes, teachers may classify them in more than one way. As shown here, triangles may be classified by naming angles and by describing their sides.

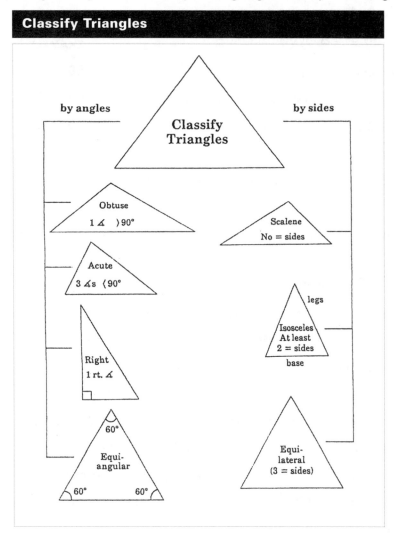

- **Use color and visual cues** to teach students to distinguish between similar and congruent figures. Cut out shapes from color-coordinated construction paper (or transparent colored sheets for use on an overhead) to illustrate various shapes and concepts.

Similar figures have the same shapes but one may be larger or smaller.

Congruent figures are exactly alike and will match identically if laid on top of each other.

- 2 congruent squares
- 2 similar triangles
- 2 similar rectangles

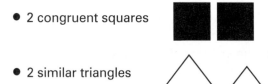

The Order of Operations

Math teachers Denise Vogelesang and Mary Kay Wells both use **mnemonics** (acronyms) frequently. When addition, subtraction, multiplication, or division may be mixed into a problem, they suggest using this acrostic to help students remember the order to follow in solving the problem. PEMDAS is one of the most frequently used mnemonics in math.

<u>P</u>lease <u>e</u>xcuse <u>m</u>y <u>d</u>ear <u>A</u>unt <u>S</u>ally (**PEMDAS**):

EXAMPLE

<u>P</u>arenthesis: Do the operations in parenthesis first. $50 \div (3-8)^2 \cdot 4 + 3$

<u>E</u>xponents: Do numbers with exponents next. $50 \div (-5)^2 \cdot 4 + 3$

<u>M</u>ultiply or <u>D</u>ivide: Do whichever comes first, left to right $50 \div 25 \quad \cdot 4 + 3$

$$2 \quad \cdot 4 + 3$$

<u>A</u>dd or <u>S</u>ubtract: Do whichever comes first, left to right $8 \quad + 3$

$$11$$

(Many math problems involve only MDAS, My Dear Aunt Sally, and do not include exponents or parentheses.)

Multiplying Binomials

Another commonly used mnemonic—**FOIL**—can help students remember how to multiply binominals.

EXAMPLE: $(X + 2)(3X - 5) = ?$

Perform multiplication of terms in the following order:

<u>**FOIL**</u>

<u>F</u>irst $\quad x \cdot (3X) = 3X^2$ (Multiply the first terms in each set of parentheses.)

<u>O</u>utside $\quad x \cdot (-5) = -5X$ (Multiply outside terms.)

<u>I</u>nside $\quad 2 \cdot (3X) = 6X$ (Multiply inside terms.)

<u>L</u>ast $\quad 2 \cdot (-5) = -10$ (Multiply the last terms.)

$$3X^2 - 5X + 6X - 10$$

$$3X^2 + X - 10 \quad \text{Combine like terms.}$$

Properties of Whole Numbers

There are five common properties of whole numbers, but typically two of them are especially confusing for students. The challenge here is to differentiate between Commutative and Associative property: CO and AP.

■ Use a **mnemonic.**

COmmutative Property: <u>**CO**</u> allows a <u>C</u>hange in <u>O</u>rder of numbers.
It applies:

- to addition and multiplication $\quad 5 + 7 = 7 + 5;$
- even though the order changes $\quad a + b = b + a;$

- the sum or product is still the same   **3 x 7 = 7 x 3**

Associative **P**roperty of Addition: **AP A**rranges **P**arenthesis:

- even though the parentheses move   **(12 + 8) + 5 = 12 + (8 + 5)**
- (the grouping of numbers   **(3x + 2) + 2x = 3x + (2 + 2x)**
  changes) the sum is still the same

Resources

Liautaud, Judy, Dave Rodriguez & Val Bagley. *Times Tables the Fun Way!* 3rd ed. Minneapolis, MN: City Creek Press, 1999. A picture method of learning multiplication tables. Audio and CD versions are also available. (800-585-6059; www.citycreek.com)

NOVA Net. An online math software program sometimes used to help students who have been unsuccessful in traditional algebra classes. Courses are offered in several additional topics. (www.novanet.com)

Really Good Stuff. This company's catalog contains many of the teaching tools mentioned in this section. These items have been created by former teachers who have firsthand teaching experience. (448 Pepper St., Monroe, CT 06468. 800-366-1920. www.reallygoodstuff.com)

Remedia Publications. This company, founded by special education teachers, specializes in educational materials for students who have trouble learning in traditional ways. Request a publications catalog. (15887 N. 76th St., Suite 120, Scotsdale, AZ 85260. 800-826-4740. www.rempub.com)

Thomas, Ed. *Styles and Strategies for Teaching Middle Grades Mathematics*. Woodbridge, NJ: Thoughtful Education Press, 1999.

Thomas, Ed. *Dr. Thomas' P3CR Paired Learner Math Activities for General Math, Pre-Algebra, Algebra, and Geometry.* Woodbridge, NJ: Dimension 2000, 1999.

Witzel, Brad. *The Multisensory Algebra Guide*. Fort Hill, SC: The Effective Teacher, 2007. Multisensory Algebra was designed to help students grasp difficult math concepts associated with abstract thinking. This algebra model helps students through the proven *concrete-to-representational-to-abstract* sequence of instruction, helping students understand how to solve for variables. (www.msalgebra.com)

Math Games

Some middle and high school teachers occasionally allow their students to play math games, especially on the day before a holiday or as part of review for a test. Games that actively involve all students at once are preferable. Dry erase boards for each student are helpful learning tools. Teams might also work math problems together and then text answers by cell phone to each other, provided your school allows cell phone use during school hours. Students with ADD or ADHD especially enjoy math games because they are fun and involve activity and novelty. To find additional games that may appeal to your students, check the local library for books on math games.

Math Competition

Susan Jessup, a middle school math teacher, organizes math competitions to motivate her students to review for tests. She selects the game problems from a math review sheet that was assigned for homework the night before. Students may even use their homework paper to copy the problem onto the board. The first student to finish the problem with the right answer is awarded a point. Up to four students can work simultaneously at the board, which actively involves more students than many other math games.

Teams, Games, and Tournaments

Dr. Ed Thomas uses math games as a form of cooperative learning. In his book *Styles and Strategies for Middle Grades Mathematics*, Dr. Thomas describes a game in which he privately ranks his students by grade average or performance levels and spreads them across four home teams. Team members practice and review key concepts before the game. Members of each team may then rank order their team members based upon their skill level. Four competitive tables are set up in the room. The number one ranked members of each team go to table number one for their game. Number two players go to table number two and so on. There are cards with questions on each table. One student draws an index card containing a math problem from the center of the table. After she gives her answer to the problem, the next student may challenge her answer. The student who has the correct answer gets to keep the card. At the end of the competition, the top four winners at each table are declared. Points are awarded and then added together for their home team members.

Math Baseball or Kickball

In math baseball or kickball, the class is divided into teams. The first student from each team comes to the board, is given a problem, and works out the answer. If she works the problem correctly, she advances to first base (a designated desk or other landmark in the classroom). Each time a student gets a problem correct, players move forward to the next base. Students keep walking around the bases until they score or their team gets three outs. Dr. Thomas makes the game more interesting by creating questions of varying difficulty that may earn a single, double, triple, or home run.

The Multiplication Facts WAR game

Dr. Thomas describes a game to help with reviewing multiplication facts. A deck of cards is shuffled and divided evenly between two players. On command, each player turns a card up. The first player to multiply the two numbers shown and say the correct answer wins the cards. (Face cards are worth ten and Aces are worth one.) One team member tells players when to start and another may act as the calculator judge.

The game may be modified to review other math facts such as squares and integers, positive and negative numbers. In *Integer War*, black cards are negative and red cards are positive numbers. Each of the two players turns up a card. The student who has the highest positive number wins the cards. Math war games are also available commercially for addition, subtraction, multiplication, and division facts.

Math Bingo

Students are given bingo cards with numbers written on them. Math problems are read aloud, students solve the problem, and look for the answer on their card. The math problems can be tailored to the unit the class is studying, or be used to review basic concepts. In his book, Dr. Thomas explains how teachers may make their own cards and gives samples of Bingo questions.

ZOOM Multiplication Card Game

This math card game provides fun practice for students who are weak in basic math skills. Players add cards and wild cards can send their scores zooming forward, backward, or nowhere at all. The game reinforces multiplication and other basic skills. It is available from several websites including www.amazon.com.

Who Wants to Be a Millionaire?

This math game, which uses a format similar to the popular television program *Who Wants To Be a Millionaire?*, would likely pique the interest of many students, with and without ADD or ADHD. Divide the class into two teams. Let each student on a team take turns answering one question posed by the teacher. The teacher gives the students four answers to choose from. As questions become increasingly difficult, students have the opportunity to stop, giving up their turn, and keep the points they have won for their team. To add challenge, students may risk losing the points they have won if they continue on to harder questions and give an incorrect answer. A total of three "lifelines" are allowed for the whole team and may include: 1) polling teammates for the correct answer, 2) eliminating two wrong answers from the list of four possible answers, and 3) asking another student for help with one question.

Math Snowball Fights

Susan Putman, a middle school math teacher, uses one math game her students love. Students make up three math problems, solve them, copy each blank problem onto a separate piece of paper, and write their names on their papers. They then wad up each paper separately. For two to three minutes, the students throw the wads of paper at each other. Then they stop and each collect three wads of paper with math problems on them and solve them. Next they compare answers with the person who made up the problem and correct any errors.

Settling Down after the Game

Any time students are active, getting them to settle down afterwards can present a problem. So, explicitly teach the students what they should do as they stop playing the game. Explain the rules for the math game, then how to change from being active to sitting down. For example:

> *"When it's time to stop, I'll say, 'The snowball fight is over. Get your three problems and sit down at your desk.'"*

> *"I'll count to five. If anyone is still standing when I say 6, then we won't be able to play the Math game tomorrow."*

Strategies for Improving Memory and Reading Comprehension

On the surface, memorizing information and remembering what you have read seem like simple tasks. Consequently, they are often taken for granted. However, these complex skills are a major challenge for many students with ADD or ADHD. (See Summaries 12 and 13.) The major problems that contribute to these skill deficits appear to be difficulties with:

1. limited working memory capacity,
2. getting information into long-term memory (to remember facts any longer than twenty seconds, information must be transferred from short-term into long-term memory),
3. quickly retrieving information when needed.

Practically speaking, students with attention deficits often have difficulty remembering information such as assignments, chores, multiplication tables, spelling and vocabulary words, foreign languages, and material they have read. They may learn multiplication tables or vocabulary words one night, only to forget them by the next day. Or read a whole page, only to look up and say, "I don't remember a single thing I read." Rote memorization of isolated facts, dates, numbers, or "boring" information is especially difficult. Because students with ADD/ADHD lack strategies for memorization, they seem to superficially glide over math facts.

Tips on Reading Comprehension

Let's start with a few tips for improving reading comprehension. It will be important to teach students strategies for reading and remembering. Since these students have limited memory capacity, they must learn to use external prompts such as sticky notes or a highlighter to assist with their retention of important information.

1. Review paragraph structure, reminding students that the main idea is usually included in the first sentence.
2. Break down the reading into segments that are not overwhelming (for example, use the "read to the clip" strategy described in Summary 16-B).
3. Write a key fact on a sticky note for each paragraph and put it in the margins.
4. Several general reading strategies such as SQ3R and SSR are discussed in Summary 69. Since SSR is simpler, students with ADD or ADHD may be more receptive to using this method. Of course these skim, read, review strategies including review of pictures, drawing, chapter heading, and sidebars.
5. Teach vocabulary before reading the required material.
6. Consider taking two column notes, as described in Summary 16-B.
7. Take time to discuss the material in pairs after reading is complete. To help students read with clear purpose, teachers may give specific questions for them to answer regarding their reading assignment.
8. Students may also read each question in the chapter and then go back and search for each answer as described in Summary 69.
9. Creating a "foldable" or "pop-up" book about the reading material will help the student use memory strategies that provide more hands-on involvement, elaboration of information, and discussion. See Summary 16-A for "foldables" and the discussion on "pop-up" books in this summary.

Strategies for Addressing Deficits in Memorization Skills

Memorization strategies such as those discussed in this summary must be specifically taught. Further complicating memorization tasks, over half of students with ADHD have problems getting restful sleep, and memory is consolidated during sleep. If a student's sleep problems are significant, encourage parents to talk with their child's doctor.

Actually, it may be wise to ***minimize requirements for memorization*** as much as possible. Ask yourself: "Is it critical to this student's life to stress her limited skills to memorize this material?" If the answer is no, allow the student to refer to basic facts on a small card. Another strategy for saving limited memory capacity for the critical elements of a task is to ***provide accommodations*** such as graphic organizers or job cards that provide supplemental information that is essential for completing the job. When memorization is necessary, consider the following strategies:

1. **Use mnemonics:** Mnemonics are devices or techniques consciously used as aids in remembering. They are among the most effective memory tools for all students, not just those with ADD or ADHD. Students may use mnemonics created by others, or make up ones that are more meaningful to them—and therefore easier to remember.

    1.1. Make an acronym. Use the first letters of the information to make a word. One of the best known acronyms is **HOMES,** an acronym for the Great Lakes: **H**uron, **O**ntario, **M**ichigan, **E**rie, and **S**uperior.

    1.2. Make an acrostic. Use the first letters of key words to make a new word or sentence. For example, the metric measurements in order: **K**ing **H**enry **D**ied **M**onday **D**rinking **C**hocolate **M**ilk; (kilo, hecto, deka, meter, deci, centi, milli. Margo A. Mastropieri, a George Mason University professor and coauthor of *The Inclusive Classroom: Strategies for Effective Instruction,* is known for her research on effective memory strategies. Here is an example adapted from Dr. Mastropieri's suggested use of two strategies, "mnemonics & key word" for remembering the World War II Axis powers.

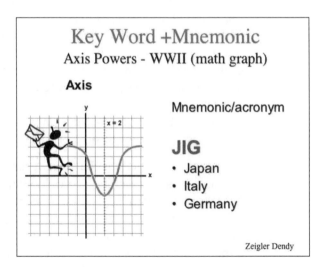

    1.3. Categorize and chunk. Divide information into smaller categories. If twenty vocabulary or spelling words are given, group them by three or four common categories: 1) people, places, events; 2) verbs, nouns, adjectives; 3) words related to science or history; or 4) words starting with the same letters. Then study them.

    1.4. Chant, or use rhymes or choral response. Use rhyme or a beat to help remember information. Younger middle school students may find "math rap tapes" or "Times Tables the Fun Way" helpful. See Summary 23 for math resources.

2. **Use concept imagery.** Help students create a mental picture or draw a picture of the object to be remembered. Exaggerating features or adding absurdities will make it easier to remember. For example, the late Dr. Claire Jones, a learning disabilities and ADD consultant, suggested picturing a bay with pigs each wearing a T-shirt with 1961 on it to remember details about the Bay of Pigs. My embellishment would be to picture these pigs in a boat and the names, Kennedy, Castro, etc. written

on the shirts. For political science, draw a picture of how a bill becomes law: the idea (a light bulb), first draft (a curtain blowing in a drafty window), and the introduction of the bill ("Hi, Bill"). Ideally, when students hear the keyword on the test, the mental picture pops into their heads to help them remember the correct answer.

2.1. Try visual posting. As suggested in Summary 16-A, write key information on colorful poster board or put pictures on the wall in the classroom. As you talk, point to the material to be learned. Later, ask questions on this material, point to the correct card, and have students answer in unison. Students are much more likely to remember information presented in this manner.

2.2. Use mental visualization. In another example, Dr. Jones asked three students independently what they saw in the word "opulent." Then they were asked to make a mental picture of what they saw in order to remember the meaning of opulent. Responses included: "if wealthy, *lent* money," "buy *opals*," "buy *OP*"— Ocean Pacific clothes). The key was allowing the student to pick the association that was meaningful to her, rather than make up one for her.

2.3. Create a "pop-up" book. Susie Smith, a middle school teacher at Lullwater School (Decatur, GA), teaches her students to make pop-up books. Students create four or five scenes that capture the essence of the novel they are reading and put them in a "pop-up" book. They make the book by folding construction paper in half to make pages 4 x 5½", cutting the fold in two or three places (1" wide x 1" deep), and folding the cut strip outward so that it stands up when the book is opened to a 45 degree angle. Then pictures are glued on the standup parts. Book elements might include the book cover, picture of author, key characters, and a key scene in the story.

3. **Use color cues:** Dr. Sydney Zentall, special education professor at Purdue University, has found that using color helps students with ADD or ADHD remember information.

3.1. Use color to highlight the correct response. For example, if the student transposes letters within a word, highlight the letters where the error occurs but not the whole word. Highlight the correct response, not the error. For example, if a student consistently spells "girl" as "gril," then highlight the "ir" in "girl." Dr. Zentall suggests a possible rank order for use of colors for highlighting. Red is a memorable choice since researchers indicate that it is the color most quickly recognized by recovering stroke victims, then green, blue, and yellow.

3.2. Use color to highlight key facts or unique aspects of spelling or vocabulary words. Highlight who, what, when, where, or why in an essay or the three sets of double letters in Mississippi.

3.3. Color code materials. Students may use color-coded items to denote each subject. For example, for math, use red book covers and assignment folder, or circle or write assignments in red ink.

3.4. Color code test review information. Teachers may divide study material for tests and print it on different color paper: key facts on a blue sheet; important names on yellow; themes/issues on pink. Or, in Language Arts or foreign language class, put nouns on blue cards, verbs on pink, adjectives on yellow.

4. **Use contextual cues:** Students are more likely to recall vocabulary words and facts that are used in a sentence, especially if the example is funny or unusual. Here are a few examples: "This honey is too *viscous*," she said in a syrupy voice. OR: The *supercilious* cheerleader looked super silly with

her nose in the air. OR: The long-distance runners raced along the line of *longitude* from the North Pole to the South Pole.

5. **Try the Loci Method:** Using this method, you label familiar local settings as a frame of reference for learning. You use visual cues to help make the topic three-dimensional and bring it to life. For example, when teaching about World War II, arrange large hand-drawn maps of the key countries involved around the room to portray their relationships to each other. Put the map of the U.S. on the file cabinet at the front left side of the classroom, England on the left side of the board, France and Germany on the right, and Africa hanging off the front of the teacher's desk. Have students cut out pictures of people, label them to represent the key leaders, and place them in their countries. Cut out pictures of buildings and label them to represent key cities in each country. In another lesson, start with clean maps and add major battles. As Germany advances, use clear red plastic wrap to cover the countries that fell under its control.

6. **Rehearse information (the right way):** Frequently, when new vocabulary words are introduced, students are asked to "rehearse," or write each of them five or more times. This strategy is not especially effective with students with ADD or ADHD. Adding a verbal element to the rehearsal makes it more helpful. Ask students to say the word aloud, repeat it to themselves, record it on a tape recorder using unusual speech (vary timing or pitch), and then listen to it for review.

7. **Use a multisensory approach:** As Summary 15 on Learning Styles discusses, students with ADD/ADHD often benefit from a multisensory approach to learning. They may learn better by watching *and* listening, for instance.

   7.1. Use popular DVDs. Allow students to watch videos of classic novels or war portrayals at home or school.

   7.2. Use "Books on Tape." Books on audiotape can be helpful for students who have trouble concentrating and remembering the content of material they read. This multisensory approach involves both auditory and visual cues. See Summary 16-E.

8. **Provide study guides and review sheets.** Several strategies are helpful here:

   8.1. Give the student a study guide with key points identified.

   8.2. Teach students to use foldables as a method of review as explained in Summary 16-A.

   8.3. Allow students to use a "cheat sheet." Students may write all the key information needed for a test on a Post-it note. Selena Conley, veteran special education teacher, uses this strategy in a very structured way. Students spend a period in small groups reviewing key concepts to be addressed on a test and then identifying the things they don't know. For example, a teen might list specific formulas on his cheat sheet, especially the ones he fears he may forget. Some students write a lot of information on their sheet in really small letters and then bring a magnifying glass so they can see everything. This strategy teaches the student to study and identify deficits in select skills, plus increases the likelihood that he will learn the desired information.

9. **Externalize prompts.** Since students with attention deficits have limited working memory capacity, give concrete guidance for completion of their assignments.

   9.1 Use a job card. Make a list of steps required for completing the task and give it to the student.

10. **Remember the keys to learning for students with ADD or ADHD:** Two educators I admire, Dr. Sydney Zentall and the late Dr. Claire Jones, have identified what they feel are the key elements for improving memory. As I mentioned earlier, Dr. Zentall emphasizes the **use of color**. Dr. Jones stressed:

- **the use of association** to help link isolated information to things we already know. Allowing the student to identify his own "personal association" for information is also critical.
- **the use of exaggeration,** since it is easier to remember the "wild and wacky" than the "same and similar."

Remember, too, that information that is presented with both *auditory and visual cues* is usually easier to remember.

11. **Provide compensatory tools.** For students who can't remember math facts, draw up a multiplication grid and tape it on the desk or allow the student to use a calculator. Or provide a word bank for a student who has difficulty memorizing French or Spanish vocabulary words.

A Summary of Tips for Mastering Spelling and Vocabulary Words

100 Point Spelling Contract

Jonathan Jones, a former learning disabilities teacher and CEO of the SOAR Camping Program, shared this 100 Point Spelling Contract, which his son's teacher used very effectively. Each child selects several activities totaling 100 points as a way of mastering the spelling words. Parents sign a note indicating that the work was completed.

- 20—Write words on flashcards.
- 20—Write words 5 times.
- 20—Type words 5 times.
- 40—Use words in a sentence.
- 20—Write words in ABC order.
- 40—Write antonyms for words.
- 40—Write definitions for words.
- 20—Illustrate words.
- 20—Air write words.
- 20—Build words with letter tiles (Scrabble).

Developmental Spelling

Dr. J. Richard Gentry, a former Western Carolina University professor who is an expert on spelling and reading, has developed a program known as Developmental Spelling. Dr. Gentry has an online test that can be used to identify the student's developmental stage of spelling mastery. Based upon this information, the teacher can prepare a specific spelling list for the student to master. See Resources, below.

Additional Strategies

Linda Blondi, a New Jersey teacher, and Dr. Kathleen Duryea, a physician in Alabama, shared these strategies:

- Paint spelling words on a shower glass door using watercolors.
- "Rainbow" words with different colored pens by tracing over them.
- Draw a tree and put the new words on leaves.
- Write words creatively in different fonts—block, 3-D, etc.

- "Backwriting": write words in lotion on someone's back. Parents can initial that the task is completed.
- Write words using a variety of things: nuts, raisins, M&Ms, Scrabble letters. The student can eat the food afterward.
- Use each word in written questions regarding a specific topic: cartoon, superhero.
- Include each word in a list of rules for dogs or astronauts.
- Write about one of your proudest moments.
- Describe an imaginary underwater creature.

Resources

Barnwell, William & Robert Dees. *The Resourceful Writer: A Basic Writing Course* . Florence, KY: Cengage Learning, 1998.

Gentry, J. Richard. "Monster Test: You Can Analyze Developmental Spelling." www.gse.uci.edu/docs/DEVELOPMENTAL_SPELLING.pdf.

Rzadiewicz, Carol. "How to Improve Reading Comprehension." www.suite101.com.

SECTION 3

The Impact of ADD or ADHD and Executive Function Deficits on Essential Related Academic Skills:

Getting Started, Finishing, Organizing, Completing Homework and Long-term Projects, Processing Information, Managing Time, and Planning Ahead

As explained in Section Two, the impact of executive function deficits can be divided into two general categories: 1) specific *academic challenges* such as writing essays, memorizing information, completing complex math, and 2) *essential related skills* such as organization of self, possessions, and projects; starting and finishing work; remembering tasks and due dates; timely completion of homework and long-term projects; processing information in an efficient and timely manner; having good time awareness and management skills; using self-talk to direct behavior; and planning ahead for projects and longer-term for the future.

Difficulties with essential related skills may be mistaken for laziness. Since academic deficits such as a writing disability are easily recognizable, teachers are more willing to provide necessary accommodations. However, educators may be reluctant to provide supports for executive skill deficits such as disorganization and failure to submit completed homework in a timely manner. Unfortunately, when a student fails to perform these tasks, it can look like he made a simple choice to be lazy and not complete the work. In fact, a neurological deficit makes these tasks extremely difficult for students with ADHD. Consequently, parents and teachers must always keep in mind that, first and foremost, this is a neurological problem, not laziness.

A Metaphor for Executive Function

Dr. Russell Barkley, one of the leading international researchers on attention deficit disorder, uses this metaphor to describe how attention and executive function deficits profoundly affect a student's life:

When a student has an attention deficit disorder, it's as if he is walking down the railroad tracks (of life) with an opaque curtain hanging in front of him that obscures his view of the track ahead (the future). His view is limited to the nails or smashed pennies on the tracks right in front of him (the here and now). He does not look ahead to see or plan for the future. Further down the tracks, he cannot see the upcoming railroad crossing (the due date for the Chemistry semester project) nor the train coming from the other direction (major crisis).

Strategies for Teachers and Parents

Teachers and parents also must take into consideration the three-year brain delay in children with ADHD. These students will need more support and supervision than their peers. As Dr. Barkley explains, teachers and parents help the student by *bringing the future into the here and now*. In other words, teachers and parents must:

1. **Give external prompts.** Provide *auditory or visual cues* to remind the student of key events and due dates that lie ahead,
2. **Intervene at the point of performance.** To ensure that students take home the right books, remind them right when they go to their locker to get the proper books and assignments to take home.
3. **Increase support and supervision.** Provide increased support and supervision commensurate with the student's delayed development of key executive skills.
4. **Teach skills or compensatory strategies such as organizational skills, time management, and scheduling time backward to meet due dates.**
5. **Provide accommodations to address deficits in essential related academic skills.**
6. **Consider finding an "organizational or academic coach,"** or providing a study/ organizational skills class.
7. **Work with the family and doctor to ensure medications are effective.**
8. **Address executive function deficits in educational plans.** If the teenager has problems with executive function deficits that interfere with his ability to learn:
   - **List specific deficits** in the IEP or Section 504 Plan as issues of concern (difficulty getting started, disorganization, etc.).
   - **Include appropriate accommodations in the IEP or 504 Plan.** See Summaries 46, 48, 49, and 51 for more on IEPs and 504 Plans.

Summaries 51 and 52 offer guidance regarding specific intervention strategies to address common academic and behavioral challenges.

Problematic Behaviors Linked to Executive Skill Deficits: Tips for Eliminating School Failure

Educators I have worked with have identified several factors as primary reasons for school failure among students with ADD or ADHD. Most all these difficulties are linked to deficits in the executive skills identified in the introduction to Section 2. Two of these major challenges, disorganization and an impaired sense of time, are not included here but are discussed in more detail in Summaries 30 and 32. Seven additional challenges are displayed in the chart below. References to other related summaries are noted by (S-#).

Problems	General Intervention Strategies
1. Not completing and turning in homework/getting zeros	Increase level of supervision and provide accommodations for EF deficits (S 16-D).
(Not writing down assignments, disorganization, forgetfulness)	1.1. Have the student write down assignments in an agenda or *assignment notebook.* 1.2. Designate "row captains" to double check that assignments are written down and then submitted. 1.3. Have a classmate double check assignments. 1.4. Allow the student to ask a classmate to write down assignments for her. 1.5. Teacher double checks assignment and initials it. 1.6. Give assignments earlier in class rather than during the rush at end of class. 1.7. Suggest that students write the assignment on their hand or arm in a pinch.
(Forgets assignments)	1.1. Provide a variety of ways for student to get assignments. 1.2. Post homework assignments on the school or teacher web page. 1.3. Provide a couple of classmates' phone numbers so the student can phone them at home for the assignment. 1.4. Email, text, or fax a copy of assignments to parents, perhaps daily or weekly. 1.5. Ask a student or teacher's aide to write down assignments to send home. 1.6. Give assignments and test dates in writing (every week or month). 1.7. Record homework assignments on a classroom answering machine or teacher voice mail. 1.8. Have a "homework hotline," a school operated phone line that students can call to get homework assignments. 1.9. Post homework assignments on an outside window so students can return to check it after school hours. 1.10. Tell parents the homework pattern, e.g., Algebra: homework four nights weekly; test every two weeks or at the end of a chapter.

(Forgets books)	1.1. Allow students to keep an extra book (or set) at home. 1.2. Suggest that the student contact a classmate to borrow a book after school hours. 1.3. Place a Post-it note reminder inside the locker. 1.4. Schedule a reminder alarm on the student's cell phone.
(Forgets to turn in assignments)	1.1. Enlist other students' help. 1.2. Ask "row captains" to check that assignments are written down and to collect homework. 1.3. Pair all students. Ask them to spend the last five minutes checking to see that assignments are written down and homework turned in. 1.4. Be flexible: allow work to be turned in late. 1.4.1 Develop a plan to turn work in on time. 1.5. Use a weekly report to reinforce completion of work. See Summary 39 on weekly reports.
(Medication wears off doing homework time)	1.1. Talk with doctor about adding a short-acting medication for the homework hours. 1.2. Start homework during the time when medication is still effective.
(Too much homework)	1.1. Determine whether too much homework is being assigned (S-27). If appropriate, reduce the amount of homework
2. Difficulty getting started and finishing work *(difficulty initiating work on routine or "boring" tasks, inattention, organizing materials and a study plan)*	2.1. Give verbal or auditory external prompts. 2.2. Set a timer to ring indicating that it is time to start work. 2.3. The teacher may tap the student's desk as a reminder to continue working. 2.4. Have the student write his name on the completed paper to receive extra credit for submitting it on time. (S-65) 2.5. A teacher or other student can review the instructions for the assignment and answer questions. 2.6. Break the assignment into segments and complete them one at a time; then take a short break. 2.7. Draw a mind map or brainstorm the assignment's content. 2.8. Use a graphic organizer. 2.9. At home, student can call a classmate for clarification of assignments.
3. Failing tests *(Due to lack of study and test taking skills, poor working memory and lack of effective memory strategies)*	Modify testing or grading (S 16-C). Teach test-taking strategies (S 69) .

(Does not do homework or study)	3.1. Ensure homework completion, using strategies listed above.
	
	3.2. Provide a study review sheet of key facts.
	
	3.3. Modify testing format (S 16-C).
	    ➤ Use word banks.
	    ➤ Avoid essay exams.
	
	3.4. Allow the student to earn extra credit.

(Does not have time to finish tests)	3.1. Give extended time on tests. 3.2. Give tests in an area without distractions or interruptions.
4. Forgetting key assignments, tests, and long-term projects *(forgetfulness, immature self-talk skills to remind oneself to begin working, and lack of awareness of the passage of time)*	4.1. The teacher or row captain reminds the student of due dates. 4.2. Send a notice home to parents regarding special projects or tests. 4.3. Break projects into three or four segments. ➤ Grade each segment separately (S 16-B). 4.4. Teach time management (S 34-37). ➤ Complete a weekly/monthly schedule. ➤ Divide task into required steps. ➤ Schedule each step. ➤ Work backward to complete the timeline.
5. Not taking notes/Difficulty copying from the board *(limited working memory capacity, difficulty identifying key facts within a lecture and paraphrasing that information, lack of note taking skills)*	5.1. Teach the student to take notes (S 16-B). 5.2. Teach students to make up their own shorthand. 5.3. Designate a notetaker for the whole class. 5.4. Make photocopies of a student's notes and leave them in a designated spot for any student who needs them. 5.5. Have the notetaker use Carbonless Copy Paper (CCP) and tear off the bottom copy to give to the student with ADD or ADHD. 5.6. Give guided lecture notes. 5.7. Outline the key points, leaving spaces for students to write additional notes. 5.8. Allow the student to tape record the class lecture. (This strategy may be ineffective for students who are unwilling to listen to the same material twice.) 5.9. Minimize copying from the board. When copying is necessary, allow the student to copy from the book or a handout.
6. Difficulties making the transition from elementary to middle to high school *(difficulty adjusting to changes in routine, shifting and starting a new activity; increased demands for immature executive skills at the secondary level)*	6.1. Encourage parents to notify a new school about ADD or ADHD. Notify in April-June, or check with the guidance counselor at the new school to find out when student schedules are developed. Provide input on the Fall schedule (S 60). 6.2. Develop an IEP for special education students before they transition to the next school. 6.3. Schedule a student support team meeting (SST).* 6.4. Assign an upper class mentor to help with the transition. 6.5. Give parents an update on grades after 2-3 weeks in the new school.
7. Undiagnosed coexisting conditions including learning disabilities and executive function (EF) deficits.	7.1. Use strategies to address difficulties with executive functions, both academics and essential related skills (S 2 & 3). 7.2. Ensure that coexisting conditions are diagnosed and treated (S 1, S 72, and Chapter 7 in my book *Teenagers with ADD & ADHD,* 2nd ed.).

Many states have developed teams of educators that meet to discuss ways of helping students who are struggling. These teams may have different names such as student support team (SST) or child study team (CST). Team members may include veteran teachers and ideally also a guidance counselor, school psychologist, or social worker.

An SST is not the same thing as an IEP team. IEP teams are mandated by federal law to screen students for special education eligibility. The SST team is available to help any student, whether or not she is eligible for special education services.

SUMMARY 27

What Is "Good Homework" for Students with ADD or ADHD?

Teenagers with ADD or ADHD are notorious for getting lots of "zeros" because they don't always complete and turn in their homework. In addition, their school performance is often erratic: one day they do well and the next day they do poorly. For example, my son once scored 87 on a final exam but failed a class because he didn't complete all his homework and a make-up test. The seemingly simple task of completing and handing in assignments often erupts into a major battle between teenagers and their parents and teachers.

This challenging scenario illustrates the profound impact of deficits in key executive skills on school performance. When students can't complete the "simple tasks" of getting started and finishing work, it's easy to understand why parents and teachers get frustrated. To the uninformed, these skill deficits appear to be a reflection of the student's lack of motivation and laziness.

Since homework, by definition, is done at home, *a partnership between teachers, parents, and the teen is critical* to ensure that students with attention deficits successfully complete their work. So, suggestions are given on two levels: 1) for teachers (this summary), and 2) for parents (the next summary). Consider developing your own homework tips for parents (or using Summary 29) and sending a copy home.

Best Practice for Homework

The popularity of homework fluctuates over time; sometimes it is in favor and at other times, news headlines question whether our children are being given too much of it. The U.S. Department of Education provides some guidance about homework in their publication, *Homework Tips for Parents* (available free from www.ed.gov).

Let's talk briefly about what we know is *best practice for giving homework.* First, the DOE homework document cites the National PTA and National Education Association (NEA) general guidance for time spent on homework. They suggest that roughly ten minutes per grade be spent on homework each night through about the sixth grade. So, a sixth grader could spend a total of from 30 minutes to an hour (60 minutes) on his homework for all his subjects. If this formula is applied to a ninth grader, the student would spent up to an hour and a half (90 minutes) on homework.

Drs. Sydney Zentall and Sam Goldstein, in *Seven Steps to Homework Success*, suggest a general homework time range for middle school of one to two hours and for high school, up to two and a half hours. Remember, researchers advise that homework doesn't have to be lengthy to be effective! *Newsweek* gave an example of a seventh grader who was given 15 minutes of math homework every school night through eleventh grade who wound up one full grade ahead in achievement.

How Much Homework Is Too Much?

When homework is a problem, two key issues must be considered:

1. How do teachers, especially in middle and high school, know how much homework students are getting from other teachers?
2. How much longer does the student take to complete the work than the teacher expects it to take?

A conference can be scheduled to answer the first question. As for the second question, Zentall and Goldstein have a suggestion that may be helpful. If there are problems with homework completion:

1. The teacher writes on the student's paper how long she thinks homework should take.
2. Parents and the teenager write on the homework paper how long it actually takes to complete and then return it to school.

Zentall and Goldstein point out that many teachers underestimate how long students with learning problems actually take to complete homework! When assigning homework, also keep in mind the general homework guidelines given by the NEA and PTA.

Selena Latham Conley, a veteran special education teacher in Georgia, suggests allowing students to *"time out"* of an assignment. For example, set a timer for a limited time frame, say thirty minutes to an hour; when time has elapsed, the student stops working and submits the partially completed homework.

Negative Consequences of Too Much Homework

National researchers have found that there is a tipping point where too much homework can have negative consequences by turning students off to school and a love of learning.

School is an especially stressful environment for students with ADD or ADHD, according to Dr. Robert Reid, special education professor, University of Nebraska. A vicious cycle may develop if the student returns to school upset because he did not complete his homework, fails to complete class work, and is assigned even more homework. During this cycle, the student's behavior usually deteriorates rapidly. "Therefore homework should be kept to the absolute minimum and the teacher should not assign uncompleted class work as homework," recommends Dr. Reid. Although Dr. Reid's advice is directed at students in special education, it is also good advice for students with ADD or ADHD who are in regular education classes.

When students struggle with an overwhelming amount of homework, grades aren't the only thing to suffer. Fighting between parents and their children over homework completion may seriously damage the crucial parent-teen relationship. When parents press too hard, teenagers may withdraw, avoid interactions with them, and become defiant. In addition, too much homework keeps students from sports and community or religious activities that build self-esteem and teach important values. According to a Columbia University education professor, **when homework turns kids off to school, it becomes a part of the problem rather than the solution.**

What Is Homework in Middle and High School Typically Like?

Dr. Zentall and Dr. Goldstein found in their research that, typically, most teachers assign two types of homework:

1. questions or problems from textbooks, and
2. worksheets.

Students say these types of assignments are often boring. Boredom may lead to:

1. decreased attention to assignments,
2. reduced student motivation,
3. completion of less school work (half of all students don't finish these assignments),
4. reduced accuracy on completed work (only 40 percent of students complete work with 80-100 percent accuracy),
5. negative evaluation of school by students,
6. disinterest in school, which may result in a student dropping out of school.

What Is Good Homework for Students with ADD or ADHD Like?

Good homework can help reduce boredom. It should:

1. Promote a love of learning.
2. Be meaningful and not too hard, long, or repetitive.
3. Be brief: completed in a reasonable time.
4. Review material taught in class, not introduce new material.
5. Be critical for the next day's work.
6. Be broken into smaller chunks (20-30 minutes at a time).
7. Develop understanding through experience and discovery.
8. Provide a novel or creative learning experience. For example, have the student interview a relative about his or her experiences in the military rather than write a boring essay on the war.
9. Help students in application of knowledge, in discovery thinking, and transfer of learning to new settings.
10. Use a variety of ways to demonstrate competency, rather than just writing. For example, the student could:
    - Dictate the learned information on audiotape.
    - Dictate the information to a scribe (another student or adult), who types the information for him.
    - Produce a videotape of the information to be learned—for example, his interpretation of the way a bill becomes law.
11. Give students some choices, such as a choice of two or three topics for writing an essay or report. When students are given limited choices, they:
    - complete more assignments,
    - are more compliant,
    - are less aggressive.
12. Give math and reading homework on alternate days.
13. Allow students with learning problems to begin assignments in class to see whether they understand the material.
14. Consider giving each student five to ten "Homework Passes" that may be substituted for any zeros received for homework. This allows the student to skip or submit partial homework for full credit.

It is important for teachers to keep these tips in mind when they assign homework! Remember, homework doesn't have to be extremely long to help students learn the information.

Barriers to Homework Completion

According to Dr. Reid, the two most common reasons students fail to complete school and homework are that: 1) assignments are too long; or 2) assignments are too difficult. Other common barriers for students getting full credit for doing homework are listed below. Summaries that discuss each issue are noted as follows (S-#):

1. Forgetting books and assignments (S 25 & 32),
2. Failing to complete assignments (S 25 & 32),
3. Failing to turn in completed assignments (S 25 & 32),
4. Avoiding homework assignments because they are too long or difficult and thus overwhelming (S 26),

5. Attempting homework when medication has completely worn off; the student can't easily pay attention and has difficulty getting started and completing work (S 26, 54-59),

6. Parents don't know how to monitor homework and provide guidance to the student (S 26-28, 67).

Families may need help correcting each of these problems. Sharing copies of the summaries noted in parentheses will be helpful for parents who want to be involved.

Teacher Homework Tips for Parents

Parents often want to help their child succeed in completing and promptly submitting homework, but don't always know how. Teachers should consider sending home some homework guidelines for parents such as those in Summary 29. Teachers are encouraged to adapt this list for the student's age and the parent's ability to assist with providing homework support. Many potential problem areas that prevent homework completion are addressed: remembering assignments, setting up the homework session, supervision during homework session, improving attention during homework, returning homework to school and to the teacher, after the homework session, teaching organizational skills, and maintaining teacher communication.

Closing Thoughts on Homework

Teachers and parents must work to ensure that homework is a helpful learning experience. If a student continues to struggle with completing homework, teachers should determine how long homework is taking. Although giving extended time on assignments is helpful, that accommodation alone is often not enough. Ultimately, if assignments are taking students with ADD or ADHD longer to complete than their classmates, the *amount of homework must be reduced!*

Resources

The Brown Center on Education Policy, *Brown Center Report on American Education: Do Students Have Too Much Homework?* Washington, DC: The Brookings Institution, 2003.

Dendy, Chris A. Zeigler. Teenagers with ADD & ADHD: A Guide for Parents and Professionals. 2nd ed. Bethesda, MD: Woodbine House, 2006.

Helbing, Joan. "Handling the Homework Hurdle." *Focus on ADD,* the Wisconsin Consortium Newsletter, February 1998.

NEA Reviews of the Research on Best Practices in Education. NEA & PTA Policy Paper on homework. Available from www.nea.org.

Reid, Robert. "Attention Deficit Hyperactivity Disorder: Effective Methods for the Classroom." *Focus on Exceptional Children*, Dec. 1999, Vol. 32, No. 4.

U.S. Department of Education. *Homework Tips for Parents*. Washington, DC: DOE, 2006. (Search for Homework Tips for Parents at www.ed.gov.)

Zentall, Sydney & Sam Goldstein. *Seven Steps to Homework Success*. Plantation, FL: Specialty Press, 1998.

Helping Parents Cope with Homework

Parents often complain that the greatest challenge in parenting a teenager with ADD or ADHD is getting him or her to complete homework! Parents are often frustrated by their teen's failure to do homework independently and sometimes also feel guilty for having to be so involved. Nightly emotional blow-ups may be common, leaving many parents and teenagers feeling angry and overwhelmed. The teacher is often the key to helping families solve the homework problem. Typically, part of the teacher's job is to help parents learn how to provide the right level of support for their teenager. Remember, however, that these teenagers are developmentally behind their peers and therefore need more supervision and support than their peers. Finding the proper "developmentally appropriate level of supervision" is very difficult for both parents and teachers.

Appropriate Parental Involvement

The level of parental involvement in homework supervision will vary for each student depending on the severity of ADD or ADHD symptoms, presence of learning problems, and level of maturity. Because of the teen's learning problems and 30 percent developmental delay, parents are involved far longer and to a greater degree in monitoring school work than they would like to be! It is critical for teachers to convey the message that it is okay for parents to guide and monitor their teenager's schoolwork. Teachers must keep in mind that these parents are simply providing *developmentally appropriate supervision*.

A strong bond between parents and the teenager is critical for coping successfully. One way to help solidify this bond is to treat the teenager as a respected partner in the problem-solving process. Remember, attention deficit disorder is not a picnic for teenagers. They did not ask to be born with this challenging biochemical condition. If supervision becomes too intense and begins to damage the parent-teen relationship, parents may have to back off and develop a new monitoring plan. Ultimately, parents will be able to reduce their level of supervision over time, but some degree of supervision may be needed into college and young adulthood.

Suggestions for Teachers to Share with Parents

If a student is not completing homework, many parents are stymied and don't know what to do to help their child succeed. I have developed a handout (Summary 29) for teachers to share with these parents. Feel free to adapt this handout to meet the needs of a student and the capabilities of the parent. Here are a few other tips:

1. **Parents should consider talking with their doctor about giving a short-acting medication later in the afternoon to assist with homework hours.** Granted, teachers can't tell parents to consider medication, but you can give them a copy of this summary. Parents may use a trial and error approach to determine how late the student can take medication without it interfering with her sleep.

2. **Ask the teen to complete the homework survey** in Appendix A6: "What Helps Me Study Best at Home?"

3. **Take a break on days when no homework is assigned.** Some parents require their child to study at home even when no homework has been assigned. Personally, I fail to see any value in this practice. This time could be spent more productively

with the parents and teen participating in a fun event together. These joint activities can achieve the more important goals of deepening family relationships and building the teenager's self-esteem so as to withstand future academic challenges that may lie ahead.

See Summary 39 on *Weekly Reports* and Summary 66 on *"Shaping" Behavior* for more suggestions on homework. Additional suggestions for dealing with homework issues are discussed in detail in Chapter 12 of *Teenagers with ADD & ADHD, 2nd ed.*

Helping Families Avoid Bloody Homework Battles

We all know that students with ADD or ADHD are more likely to have **emotional blow-ups** than their peers. Obviously, tense homework sessions are high-risk times for these flare-ups. It is important to remember that these students are attempting homework under less than optimal conditions.

■ The effects of medication have usually worn off completely by evening.

■ Attention, executive function, and learning problems, plus lack of medication in the evening, all interfere with the teenager's ability to complete homework successfully.

■ Furthermore, the student is probably tired and may have trouble getting started and paying attention long enough to complete the assignment.

Teachers may want to give parents some or all of the following suggestions to help them lessen homework conflicts:

1. If tempers flare, **take a brief break** to allow things to cool down. Both parents and the student may need a brief break from homework and from arguing with each other.

2. If the teenager blows up, **stay calm and lower your voice.** A loud emotional response from parents tends to escalate the problem, generating an even louder emotional response from the teen.

3. If homework becomes a constant battlefield, parents, teachers, and the teenager should **develop a joint plan to resolve the problems.** (See "Changes to Consider," below.)

Teachers should ask parents to advise them if problems continue. If parents report that terrible nightly battles are still raging, encourage them to back off some, change strategies, or ask someone else to monitor homework (the other parent, an older sibling, an upperclassman, or adult tutor). Changes should be made if screaming battles are the rule, if the teen gets so upset she frequently cries, or if she has to stay up too late to complete work.

Changes to Consider

Teachers who know a family is struggling with homework battles may want to advise parents that these options are available to them:

1. One of the first changes to consider is **reducing the amount of homework** (S 27). If the total time spent on all homework is more than one to two hours, reducing the amount of work assigned may be necessary, depending on the student's grade level. Ask parents to time how long each subject takes to complete. Identify which subject is taking an inordinate amount of time and reduce the length of the assignments.

2. During emotional crises, it may also be necessary to let the teenager go to bed, ***request a time extension, and complete the assigned work at a later time*** when both the teen and parents are less frazzled.

3. Or parents can be empowered to ***determine when "enough" homework has been completed:***

Ivan Vance, a special educator/parent of a teenager with an attention deficit, included this accommodation in his child's IEP: "The parents will determine when 'enough' homework has been completed at night." Parents are in the best position to judge the emotional climate at home and know whether or not the student is capable of finishing the assignment. The parent's signature on homework returned to school should be sufficient justification for not penalizing the student with a failing grade.

The teacher must decide on a case-by-case basis whether or not to accept the work completed "as is" or to ask for some additional work. However, if make-up work is simply piled on a lengthy assignment for the next night, the student may well become depressed and overwhelmed. In my experience, the majority of parents and students will not abuse use of this accommodation. Obviously, if the accommodation does not work, and the student is not learning the basic material, the educational plan must be revised.

SUMMARY 29 — Homework Tips for Parents

By Chris Dendy, with input from Joan Helbing, M.S.

Dear Parents:

If your child often forgets homework assignments, has trouble getting started on the work, forgets to turn in completed work, and is disorganized, he or she will need more support to ensure work completion; in other words, "developmentally age appropriate supervision." Remember, the brains of students with ADD or ADHD mature more slowly than their classmates' brains. For example, a 12-year-old may be more like an 8-year-old (a 30% delay) when it comes to basic homework skills such as getting started and finishing, being organized, prioritizing tasks, and managing time. Here are some helpful hints you can use at home.

Remembering Homework Assignments

Forgetfulness is characteristic of ADHD.

Help your child develop a unique system for remembering homework assignments that works for him or her. Students with ADHD benefit from **visual or auditory reminders "at the point of performance."** In other words, they need to "see or hear" the reminder, near the end of the day when they make the decision of what books to bring home. Helpful strategies include:

1. Use an assignment book, a note card kept in a pocket, a Zire or Palm Pilot, or folded incomplete work that is put in a book to take home.
2. Ask a friend or behavioral aide to meet the student at his or her locker as a reminder.
3. Tape a homework reminder checklist on the inside of the locker door.
4. Get your child a watch with a reminder system or suggest he set a vibrating alarm on his cell phone as a reminder.
5. Check the school website for assignments.
6. Get a phone number for a classmate to confirm assignments.
7. Get the teacher's email address, if she is willing to share it.
8. Ask teachers about assignment routines: e.g., algebra homework four nights a week.
9. Get an extra textbook for home—especially if your child is in danger of failing a class, often forgets his book, or is eligible for an IEP or 504 educational plan.

Setting Up the Homework Session

Involve your child in decisions.

1. Jointly set a starting time: give two choices, for example 7:00 or 7:15.
2. Make a list of assignments to be done and estimate time required for each.
3. Jointly select a reminder procedure: kitchen timer or an alarm on a cell phone.
4. Monitor closely if your teenager is in danger of failing. Consider having him do school work at the kitchen table. While you're cleaning up the kitchen, you can gently nudge him back on task when his attention wanders. Or take the laundry to his room and fold it while he works. But if the teen is adamantly opposed, don't insist that he work in the kitchen. This is not one of the major issues worth fighting over.

5. Jointly select a good working location—clear the desktop.
6. Encourage use of a computer for work completion. Having a back-up copy is helpful if the original is never submitted.
7. Work away from "screens"—especially TV and other electronic gadgets.
8. Occasionally allow your child to invite a friend over to do homework together, especially if the other student is a good role model.
9. Keep needed school supplies like paper and pencils nearby.
10. For "unexpected" long-term projects that are due the next day, keep extra poster board, markers, and report covers on hand.

During the Homework Session

Executive function deficits may cause difficulties: 1) getting started and maintaining attention, 2) with slower processing (slower reading and writing—homework takes longer), 3) finishing work.

1. If necessary, sit with your child until he or she gets started. Then check back periodically to make certain he is still working.
2. Limit homework sessions to 10-30 minutes at a time, then give your child a break to reenergize his brain (age appropriate).
3. For children who seem overwhelmed and can't get started, fold the worksheet in half or have them complete 10 of the 30 problems. They can bring you their work when they finish the ten problems.
4. Take short physical breaks (activity improves attention by increasing blood flow to the brain).
5. During the break, drink some water (to help the lungs send more oxygen to the brain) and eat a snack (raisins provide fuel for the brain).
6. Monitor how long it takes your child to complete homework assignments for each class. If your child is spending significantly longer than 80 minutes for completion of all assignments (for middle schoolers) or 120 minutes total on homework (for high schoolers), notify the teacher. Your child may need shortened assignments.

Supervision of Homework Sessions

Delayed maturity means more supervision is required.

1. Parents should decide who is better suited to work with the child. Being patient and positive is important.
2. If one parent also has ADHD and has trouble being organized or patient, the other parent should probably take on this role.
3. Consider hiring a tutor or asking an older student in the neighborhood to help.
4. Review completed work for accuracy and completion. Have your child correct any errors. Some students with ADD or ADHD will be able to double check their work; most won't.
5. Praise your teen's effort and willingness to tackle this challenging task.
6. Allow your teenager to take brief breaks at 20- to 30-minute intervals: snack, stretch, walk, or listen to music. Or allow him to take breaks after completion of work by subject or segments thereof (15 of 30 math problems).
7. Reward your child when he is completing homework regularly, by allowing him to study where he chooses, without close supervision, or without requiring a weekly report.

Improving Attention During Homework

1. Most ADHD medication wears off by late in the afternoon.
2. If your child is struggling to pay attention during homework time, talk with your doctor.
3. Some physicians prescribe small doses of medication in the late afternoon to last until homework is completed.

After the Homework Session

If your child is forgetful or a slow processor, consider requesting accommodations in the IEP or Section 504 Plan to allow shortened assignments and/or late submission of work.

1. Keep copies of all completed homework assignments, including written and computer work.
2. Don't throw assignments away for the school year until you've confirmed with the teacher that all assignments have been submitted. These old assignments and tests may be useful for studying for final exams or completing projects.

Returning Homework to School

Help your child learn to use visual or auditory reminders to assist him in remembering to bring his homework with him.

1. Put finished work in a specific place, perhaps in a colored folder.
2. After homework is finished, put everything back in the folder or backpack.
3. Put the backpack near the door that exits to the car or bus (a visual cue).

Teaching Organizational and Memory Skills

Disorganization and weak memorization skills are characteristic of ADHD.

1. Once a week go through the notebook and backpack with your child and help him or her organize papers.
2. Pull out and keep completed assignments in a folder.
3. Look for notes from the teacher or assignments that are incomplete.
4. Ask the teacher for a list of strategies to help with memorization. See Summary 31.

Maintaining Communication with the Teacher

1. Maintain regular communication with the teacher if your child is struggling.
2. Please notify the teacher if the work takes longer than ___ minutes. If it takes your child significantly longer than 10 minutes per grade level to complete all his homework for the day, discuss this with the teacher who assigns the most homework. You may need to request an IEP or 504 Plan meeting if many teachers are involved. (See Summary 27.)
3. If your child is not completing assignments, ask the teacher to call or email an update on any overdue assignments at the end of the week. (If grades are reported online, be sure to select the option to receive an email alert whenever grade reports are updated.)
4. If your child is in danger of failing, ask for a weekly or daily report. Closer to the end of the grading period, check with the teacher and ask if any assignments are missing. Submit missing work.

SUMMARY 30 Disorganization

Most teenagers with ADD or ADHD appear to be extremely disorganized! Any teacher or parent who has worked with these students can tell you that losing books, homework, written assignments, reports, backpacks, jackets, gym clothes, shoes, band instruments, jewelry, tools, or keys is often a daily occurrence. Messy desks, backpacks, school lockers, and rooms are also common. Problems with disorganization are often compounded by poor memory. This makes it difficult to identify which skill deficit is causing a problem. Most likely, many of the difficulties these students face at school result from a combination of several problems.

On the surface, disorganization may look like simple laziness. In reality, however, it is a much more complicated issue. Problems with organization spill over into academics, where students with attention deficits may have difficulty with:

- having basic school supplies for class participation,
- bringing homework to class and remembering to turn it in,
- knowing how and where to get started on long-term school projects,
- remembering the sequencing procedure for solving complex math problems,
- remembering what they have read and synthesizing a summary,
- organizing a plan of action to complete a project,
- organizing information into a logical, flowing written essay or report.

The last two issues relating to organization of projects and assignments are addressed in Summaries 18 and 19.

Maintenance time is required. To help these students learn organizational skills, "maintenance time" must be set aside both at school and home to master key skills. For example, a teacher, aide, or classmate may meet the student near the end of the school day to review assignments and books needed for homework. This is an example of important behavioral strategies—"intervening at the point of performance" and giving visual cues.

Teach organizational strategies for home. As explained in Summary 2, there are differences in the "reward" center of the ADHD brain that impair the ability to sustain interest in boring tasks, including organizing a backpack, locker, or room. At home, parents should therefore help their teen set up an organized homework system (See Summaries 27-28.) Establish a routine of always putting completed homework in a backpack or notebook. Kathleen Nadeau, Ph.D., author of numerous ADHD books, and Judith Kolberg, a professional organizer, refer to this area as a "launching pad." Consider designating a basket near the exit door to the car or bus as the "launching pad." See Table below for additional strategies.

Make sure papers get from home to school and back. Erin Scussel, a reading teacher at Sonoraville (GA) High School, has found an innovative way to manage this challenging task. She staples a name label to a plastic shopping bag and has the student put in all her papers that need to go home. She always gets her papers back within two or three days.

Keep all old papers until grades are submitted. Encourage parents to periodically go through their teenager's notebook with her to sort, file, and identify papers that should have been turned in at school. Don't ever throw away any completed papers until the semester is over and grades have been posted. These papers may be helpful when studying for tests or working on projects. Often parents may find assignments that were never submitted that resulted in a zero being recorded. Parents should check with the teacher for any missing assignments before the end of the semester.

Keep school supplies on hand. Parents are also encouraged to keep critical school supplies on hand for last minute completion of assignments. Selena Conley, a special education teacher, advises students to keep a "School Supply Tackle Box" that contains a stapler, paper clips, scissors, a hole punch, high-lighter, tape, glue stick, and pencils. In addition, keep some sheets of poster board, markers, and report covers. At the beginning of school, Conley explains the importance of being organized and how having a Tackle Box at home can be of help to them. Then after about three weeks, she allows the students to vote and select a good citizen to be given the Box as a prize.

Notify parents of organizational issues at the first PTA. A discussion with the parents at the first PTA "open house" should alert them to potential problem areas such as a required long-term project. Addressing this issue in the IEP/504 Plan is also important.

Establish new habits. Helping students to establish routines at both home and school to address organizational challenges is critical. When new habits are taught, practice them for 30 days so they become automatic. Put reminder cues everywhere and make them visual. You can put a sticky note on a student's desk; at home, a "launching pad" basket near the door works well. Reward the student when she is successful; praise or physical rewards are often effective.

If any of the behaviors in the table below occur on a regular basis and interfere with the student's ability to learn, they should be:

1. **described in Section 1, "present performance," of the IEP/Section 504 Plan,** and
2. **included in the IEP/504 Plan** to teach the student a) the needed skill or b) methods for compensating for the problem (Summaries 44 and 46)

Strategies to Combat Disorganization

Problem	My Favorite Strategies
1. Loses school supplies. *(comes to class without pencils, books, papers, or folders)*	1.1. Keep extra pencils, paper, and books in the classroom. Ask parents to donate supplies. 1.2 Suggest that parents keep extra school supplies on hand at home.
2. Loses gym uniform, sports equipment, or musical instruments.	2.1. Put the student's name on all school supplies, band uniform, instruments, or other items. 2.2. Put belongings in the gym or band room first thing in the morning. 2.3. Reduce the number of times the student must transport uniforms or instruments back and forth to school.
3. Loses class work and homework.	3.1. Put all school work in one colorful pocket folder; place work to be completed on the left side and finished work on the right side.
4.1 Does not turn in homework to teacher; forgets to turn in homework. **Leaves schoolwork at home.** *(Does not **hear** the request to turn in homework before leaving class; homework may be completed but at home, in the locker, backpack, book, or car.)*	4.1. Establish routine that homework is always turned in to the teacher's same "red" box or folder at the end of class. 4.2. Ask "row captains" to collect homework or to check to see that homework is turned in at the end of class. 4.3. Establish routine at home; put finished schoolwork away immediately; place in backpack and set the backpack on the "launching pad," a basket near the door to the car/bus. 4.4. Place papers in a shopping bag that has the student's name stapled on it. Have the student take papers home and return them in the same bag.

5. Loses or forgets, but never makes it home with homework assignments or the right books.	5.1. Establish an *"organizational homeroom"*; the student returns at the end of each day; teacher or an aide reviews assignments, needed books, due dates, and projected timelines.
	5.2. Use an *"organizational coach"* (classmate, teacher, or parent) to help with organization and memory.
	5.3. Use an assignment notebook.
	5.4. Ask "row captains" to remind the student.
	5.5. Post all assignments on teacher or school website. Consider listing materials needed to do a task.
	5.6. Have student call a classmate for assignments. (Get phone numbers for a couple of other students.)
	5.7. E-mail, text, or fax assignments home.
	5.8. Record assignments on cell phone, PDA, or computer.
	5.9. See Summary 26 for more detailed suggestions for remembering assignments.
	5.10. Goldberg suggests using three clear pocket folders. "Homework to do," Homework done," "Notices."
6. Has a messy notebook, backpack, desk, or locker.	6.1. Use an organizational notebook that contains a sealed plastic pouch for pencils or calculators; a colorful folder (with pockets for uncompleted class work and finished homework).
	6.2. Arrange the locker for maximum organization: ➤ top shelf/put the books for morning classes; ➤ middle shelf/books for afternoon classes; ➤ after each class, put books on the bottom shelf; ➤ at the end of day put the books back in order. ➤ if only one shelf is available, put a divider, small box, or stand-up magazine holder in the bottom to create a third compartment. ➤ have the student create her own unique system of organization for the locker.
	6.3. Have someone meet the student after school to practice this routine until she does it automatically.
	6.4. Ask parents to regularly schedule time to clean out backpacks, desks, or lockers. Notebook should be cleaned out every few weeks. Save all completed work until after the end of the grading period just in case the student forgot to turn it in to the teacher.
7. Has great difficulty keeping an organized log of daily assignments, grades, test scores, and table of contents written in sequential order. *(Some classes require this to practice organizational skills; however, it requires specific instruction, support, daily monitoring, or an accommodation for students with attention deficits.)*	7.1. Teach and monitor this skill until mastery is reached.
	7.2. If this task is mandatory, provide daily assistance from another student or an "organizational coach." Generally speaking, if teachers can't provide the necessary instruction and support, avoid requiring this level of detail from students with ADD or ADHD.
	7.3. Do not deduct points from a student's grade for failure to keep these records. Grade the student on the subject (English), rather than organization.

8. Does not know grades and whether passing or failing. *(Some students will be able to keep up with grades and others will not.)*	8.1. If the student wants to and is capable of keeping up with his grades, staple a sheet in the front of the student planner; the teacher or another student checks to see that grades for homework and tests for each class are written on that sheet. 8.2. The teacher or aide may e-mail her grades for the week to the family. 8.3. If school uses Internet-based grade reporting system such as Edline, encourage the student and/or parents to view and print out her grades.
9. Has difficulty writing an essay or report.	9.1. Summaries 17-19 contain suggested strategies for improving written expression and essay writing.
10. Has difficulty organizing and completing long-term projects.	10.1. Summaries 38-40 provide guidance for completion of long-term projects.
11. Poor time management and organizational skills; has difficulty developing a plan of action and following through.	11.1. Getting organized and developing a plan of action are discussed in Summaries 32, and 38-40.

Resources

Dendy, Chris A. Zeigler. *Teenagers with ADD and ADHD*, 2nd ed. Woodbine House: Bethesda, MD, 2006.

Goldberg, Donna. "School Organization Tips for Students with ADHD or Learning Disabilities." *ADDitude* magazine (www.additudemag.com), 2004.

Kolberg, Judith & Kathleen Nadeau. *ADD-Friendly Ways to Organize Your Life*. New York: Brunner-Routledge, 2002.

Lehmkuhl, Dorothy & Dolores Cotter Lamping. *Organizing for the Creative Person*. New York: Crown Publishing, 1993.

3

Section 3 | The Impact of ADD or ADHD and Executive Function Deficits on Essential Related Academic Skills

SUMMARY 31 Impaired Working Memory and Forgetfulness

Forgetfulness is one of the primary characteristics of teenagers with attention deficits! Forgetfulness is one of those ADD/ADHD behaviors that may look like laziness or a bad attitude but in reality is a classic characteristic of the disability. Punishment for forgetfulness is inappropriate; instead, teach compensatory skills for coping with the challenge.

In reality, remembering is a more complex task than we often realize. A student must:
- pay attention,
- select key information,
- store information,
- find information,
- quickly retrieve it, and then
- act upon the information.

Many students with ADD/ADHD have difficulties with two types of memory: 1) working memory, and 2) long-term memory.

Working Memory

Difficulty with working memory is perceived by some experts as the core deficit that teens with ADD/ADHD experience in executive functions. As you recall, working memory is what enables us to hold information in mind while manipulating it, then sequence and organize it and subsequently take action (writing a paper, solving a problem). Working memory is critical for key academic tasks: writing essays, solving complex math, remembering what is read, completing long-term projects, and problem solving. (See Summaries 25 and 31.) Unfortunately, one study reported that the average teen with ADHD has a working memory comparable to that of a seven-year-old. This deficit presents significant challenges in the classroom.

Teachers should also be aware that **working memory fluctuates daily in kids with ADHD.** According to Dr. Julie Schweitzer, a professor of psychiatry at UC Davis, children with ADHD are unable to consistently respond during working memory tasks. So, just because your student is able to remember and process information one day does not mean he can perform these same skills the next day.

Long-term Memory

Additionally, **getting information into long-term memory is especially difficult** for students with ADD/ADHD. Two factors interfere with this task: lack of strategies for memorization and sleep deprivation. Over half of all students with ADHD have serious sleep problems. More importantly, researchers report that memory is consolidated during sleep. So students who don't get restful sleep will have more difficulty memorizing information.

Even when information is stored properly, students with attention deficits still have trouble quickly accessing information when they need it. Typically, they know they have a terrible memory. As a result, they are often chronically anxious that they are going to forget something important! Over time, they may learn to hide their anxiety by acting as though they really don't care.

Punishment will not grow more white matter or improve attention. Instead, teach compensatory skills for coping with the challenge. A two-pronged approach may help:

1. Teach students the **memory strategies** discussed in Summary 25.
2. Simultaneously, teach students **how to compensate** for their memory problems.

In this summary, the discussion will focus primarily on teaching them to *compensate* for their forgetfulness.

Since memory deficits are often a lifelong problem, ask another student to be a backup memory or "coach" who reminds the student of important tasks. Remember to give the student with an attention deficit some control in choosing who will provide the reminder and how and when assistance is provided. Obviously, the student doesn't want to be embarrassed or made to feel stupid for having a poor memory.

It can also help to allow the student to fidget, stand up, or chew gum while he is trying to use his working memory. Dr. Mark Rapport, a psychology professor at UCF, found that students were more active during activities that required working memory. They were less active during more routine academic activities. In other words, they're using movement to help keep themselves alert. According to Rapport, "They have a hard time sitting still unless they're in a highly stimulating environment where they don't need to use much working memory." If any of the behaviors in the following table occur on a regular basis and interfere with the student's ability to learn, they should be

1. **described in Section 1, "present performance," of the IEP/Section 504 Plan,** and
2. **included in the IEP/504 Plan** to teach the student: a) the needed skill or b) methods for compensating for the problem (Summaries 46, 48, and 51).

Strategies to Combat Impaired Working Memory and Forgetfulness	
Problem	**My Favorite Strategies**
1. Forgets to write down home-work assignments. *(also may not **hear** the assignment; may be too rushed at the end of period; puts books away early to sprint to the next class or visit with friends at the locker)*	1.1. Ask another student or "row captain" to double check to see that assignments are written down for the student with an attention deficit or the whole class. 1.2. Use an assignment notebook/student planner. 1.3. Allow student to create his own reminder system; a 4x6 card pre-printed with a class list may suffice; assignments are written; card placed in pocket. 1.4. Allow students to dictate assignments into a voice reminder recorder (under $20). 1.5. Record assignments in cell phone or computer. 1.6. Schedule adequate time for students to write down assignments and put papers and folders away (perhaps earlier in the period when students aren't rushed). 1.7. E-mail, text, or fax assignments home. 1.8. See Summaries 16-D and 25.
2. Forgets to bring home the correct assignments and books.	2.1. Put a checklist on the door of his locker (check algebra homework, get books). 2.2. Write a reminder note in the palm of the hand. 2.3. If assignment is forgotten, the student may check "Homework Hotlines," school websites, teacher voice mail, or teacher assignment board for homework.

3

	2.4. Give students a class syllabus with general timelines for assignments & tests; especially for classes at high risk for failure. 2.5. Staple the teacher's weekly lesson plan in the student's planner. 2.6. Ask someone to be an "organizational coach" and meet with the student after school to ensure that homework assignments and appropriate books make it home. 2.7. The Really Good Stuff company has stylish "reminder loop" bracelets (like hospital ID bracelets but in leopard or zebra skin designs) on which students may write items to remember or things to do (www.reallygoodstuff.com). 2.8. Get classmates' phone numbers. 2.9. Keep an extra book at home, or set if needed. 2.10. See Summaries 25 & 31 for more detailed suggestions.
3. Forgets to return things to school, especially if they must be signed: ➤ Homework, reports, papers ➤ Tests ➤ Weekly reports ➤ Assignments initialed in a student planner ➤ Money for school photos ➤ Sign-up for sports or field trips	3.1. Notify parents that papers will be sent home regularly, if this is true. 3.2. Establish a routine, e.g., papers or weekly reports are sent home on Fridays. 3.3. Suggest that parents ask the student to place the completed paper in the same folder or book each day; place in book bag and set on the "launching pad" near the door. 3.4. Reduce the number of papers sent home to be signed. 3.5. E-mail reminder home.
4. Forgets to stay after school for a teacher conference or detention. *(Medication has often worn off, so memory is even less efficient.)*	4.1. Ask a friend to remind him. 4.2. Put a Post-It note on a notebook for the last class or in his locker. 4.3. Set a wrist-alarm (WatchMinder™) with a message reminder. (It vibrates and gives a message, S 16-E.) 4.4. Friends/parent can send a text message reminder. 4.5. Wear a "reminder loop" bracelet containing written reminder. See 2.7. above. 4.6. Identify the problem (antecedent behavior) resulting in detentions (tardy to school caused by sleep disturbances); implement a behavior intervention plan to correct the problem; refer to doctor.
5. Forgets to put his name on his paper.	5.1. Tape a 3x5 cue card on his desk that states what to do: "1) "Write name on paper. 2) "Turn in homework." 5.2. Give the student a name stamp or stick-on name labels. 5.3. Give him pre-stamped or pre-labeled papers. 5.4. Ask another student to remind him to write his name. 5.5. Don't take off points for failing to put a name on the paper. Help the student master the skill. 5.6. Row captains check for names on papers.
6. Forgets to bring pencils, papers, books to class.	6.1. Keep an extra supply of pencils and paper for forgetful students. Parents may volunteer to pay for this or buy these supplies for their teen to keep at school. 6.2. Ask a classmate to remind the student to return the pencil.

	6.3. Keep one or two extra loaner textbooks in the classroom.
	6.4. Remind student to write down in the assignment book any extra or unusual materials that are needed for class the next day.
7. Forgets to complete long-term projects. *(These projects depend upon skills that are deficient in these students; thus must be addressed as a disability for some.)*	7.1. Break projects into segments, each with a separate due date. (See Summaries 35-37.) 7.2. Send a reminder to parents of projects and due dates. 7.3. Include in IEP/504 Plan need for notification of parents. 7.4. See Summaries 36-38 for more detailed suggestions regarding completion of long-term projects.
8. Forgets how to complete in-class assignments or steps in solving problems.	8.1. Reduce demands on working memory by providing written instructions. 8.2. Simplify multi-step directions; use task checklists

Impaired *Sense of Time/Impatience*

Many teens with ADD or ADHD ***don't accurately judge the passage of time.*** One student lamented, "I have no sense of time." Researchers report that when asked to indicate the end of a ten-second time interval, students with ADHD are unsuccessful, but those who don't have ADHD come very close to accurately measuring the interval. What's more, students with attention deficits have great difficulty estimating how much time a task will take. So, they may feel overwhelmed by a homework assignment because they have no sense of how long it will take to complete nor how and where to begin work. In addition, time seems to creep, especially if they have to do "boring," repetitious work or wait for someone. These students are often described as "living in the here and now."

Their impaired sense of time contributes to several problems:
- tardiness,
- avoidance of homework assignments since they "will take forever,"
- late completion of class assignments,
- inability to accurately estimate time requirements for tasks,
- not allowing enough time to complete work,
- not planning ahead for homework completion or major class projects,
- delayed start on major projects.

A Lifelong Challenge Requiring Supports and Accommodations

The impaired sense of time is another lifelong problem that shows only limited improvement, even with medication. Helping the student learn to compensate or providing accommodations is essential. These students also will need closer monitoring and provision of external reminders. An accurate sense of time is an executive function that is essential for succeeding in school or planning ahead for the future.

Dr. Russell Barkley believes that teachers and parents need to help bring the future into the moment to help teenagers cope successfully with their attention deficit. For example, adults must use strategies to assist students in remembering homework assignments or planning ahead and completing applications for college or vocational schools. In other words, teachers and parents may have to provide more guidance and support for a longer period than usual. **Provision of auditory or visual external cues is essential!**

Continually punishing ADD/ADHD behaviors by sending students to detention or penalizing grades is not especially effective in changing their behavior. In fact, punishment may create even more anxiety and even poorer school work. When their forgetfulness and disorganization are combined with their impaired sense of time, these students often find themselves rushed and overwhelmed as they confront major long-term projects that are due "tomorrow."

If a student is often late to class, don't automatically assume that her tardiness is intentional. Instead, talk with her and try to determine why she was late. Review her routine between each class and develop a plan to adjust her trips to the locker so she isn't late. If she can't find the right books, help her organize her locker (Summary 30).

The Time Timer© makes times concrete and visual (www.timetimer.com).

If any of the behaviors in the following table occur on a regular basis and interfere with the student's ability to learn, they should be

1. **described in Section 1, "present performance," of the IEP/Section 504 Plan,** and
2. **included in the IEP/504 Plan** to teach the student: a) the needed skill, or b) methods for compensating for the problem. (Summaries 46, 48, and 51 .)

The following strategies may be helpful:

Impaired Sense of Time	
Problem	**My Favorite Strategies**
1. Tardiness: late to class *(a few of our students are dis- oriented spatially and become easily lost, especially early in the school year when transitioning to a new school)*	1.1. Review routes taken between each class and change routes that contribute to tardiness. 1.2. Ask a student "shadow" to walk with her as a reminder to keep moving. 1.3. Advise student not to go by the locker between each class, but to take 2-3 books at a time from the locker. 1.4. Advise student to pick up books when there is more time, such as before school or during lunch. 1.5. Keep a couple of extra textbooks in the classroom. When the student must borrow a book, ask someone to remind her to leave it in the room. 1.6. Let the student leave a couple of minutes early for her next class. 1.7. Help the student find books more quickly by organizing her locker more efficiently. (See Summary 30, suggestion 6.2) 1.8. Ask the student to set a wristwatch alarm with a five-minute reminder that school is starting (WatchMinder™ S16-E). 1.9. Consider assigning the student two lockers: one to hold books for morning classes and one for afternoon classes.

2. Late to school *(often related to a sleep distur- bance, lack of awareness of the passage of time, and problems getting organized to leave home on time)*	2.1. Use auditory or visual time prompts as reminders for leaving home.
	    2.1.1.*Tel-Time©* talking timer announces the passage of time in de- creasing time intervals.
	    2.1.2. *Time Timer©* makes time concrete and visual by showing the remaining time in red. As time passes, the red shrinks. Available in different sizes plus a watch and computer software program.
	
	 2.2. If parents ask for help, suggest they involve the student and pick one of these options:
	    2.2.1. Have the student get up earlier, if necessary.
	    2.2.2. Doctors may prescribe a faster, short-acting medication like regular Ritalin for mornings. Parents wake the child a half hour early; give medication, allowing the child to return to sleep; 30 minutes later a more alert, organized child wakes up and dresses more easily.
	    2.2.3. Set her own alarm clock to wake up. Connect a timer to the radio, TV, and lights. Novel alarm clocks like "Clocky" roll off the table and hide.
	    2.2.4. Tape a wake-up message from her or a friend.
	    2.2.5. Ask a friend or girlfriend to call.
	    2.2.6. Advise of the passage of time. "You need to leave for school in 30 (10) minutes (now)."
	    2.2.7. Lay clothes out and put books together in one place the night before.

	2.2.8. Schedule school departure time backward from school start time. Estimate time required for driving/walking, parking, locker visit, visits with friends, and getting to class. Students with ADHD underestimate time requirements. 2.2.9. Ask the family to consider an evaluation for a sleep disturbance, which is common in attention deficit (56%). 2.2.10. Medication may help. See discussion of sleep problems in *Teenagers with ADD and ADHD* (Dendy, 2006).
3. Late turning in homework & projects	3.1. Establish a homework collection routine: Ask an aide, "row captain," or an "organizational coach" to remind the student of assignments or to turn in completed work. 3.2. Allow flexibility in turning in late assignments while working to develop a plan to correct the problem. 3.3. Create and keep calendars of assignments and due dates. 3.4. Post a large calendar in a central place that is visible to all. 3.5. Keep a calendar on the computer also. 3.6. See more detailed suggestions regarding homework in Summary 27.
4. Does not plan ahead for long-term projects	4.1. See the discussion on long-term projects in Summaries 36-38. 4.2. Teach the time management skills discussed in Summaries 34-35.
5. Impatient; hates waiting	5.1. Give students desk signs, "Need help." Students set up sign on desk and continue working. 5.2. Color-coded "I need help" flip charts are available from Really Good Stuff company. Red signifies "I need help now—can't continue working" and yellow indicates "I need help but can wait." 5.3. Give the student something to do while she is waiting for the teacher to help her or answer her question. "Go on to the next problem while I finish this." 5.4. Allow students to help each other. 5.5. Reduce waiting time.

6. Impaired time awareness	6.1. Make time concrete and visual.
	
	6.1.1. Place a clock in sight in the room. Consider *Time Timer©*, a clock that visually shows the passage of time.
	    6.1.2. At home, set an alarm or use a timer to announce a homework "break time."
	
	6.2. Practice time awareness and time estimation. This strategy may not be effective long-term, but may at least increases student's awareness of her time challenges. (Don't spend a lot of time on practice.)
	    6.2.1. Notify of the passage of time. "It has been twenty minutes since you started. You have ten minutes to go before break."
	    6.2.2. Ask the student to estimate how long the homework assignment will take to complete. Write her answer down. Compare it to actual time spent. This practice may help students realize that tasks don't take as long as they think they will.

7. Difficulty sitting still	7.1. Reduce sitting time; use active teaching strategies.
	7.2. Assign errands that require movement; notes to office, sharpening pencils, returning or collecting homework.
	7.3. Give fidget toys; a tangle toy, rubber pencil grip, Silly Putty, "Koosh Ball"; or attach a small piece of Velcro under the desk—the student can scratch it or attach and remove a small piece of Velcro from it.
	7.4. Consider allowing chewing gum.
	7.5. Assign the student two seats; side-by-side or at a table near the back of the room.
	7.6. Provide a stand-up desk; some have a swinging foot rest.
	7.7. Allow student to use an exercise bike in the rear of the room.
	7.8. Place student desk at end of row; allow her to stand or kneel in desk.
	7.9. For younger students, use tape on the floor to mark an area immediately around the desk in which they can move freely.
	7.10. Give the student an air-filled rubber disk to sit on that allows wiggling ("sit fit" cushion). Although often used with younger children, teachers report that even middle school students like to sit on these cushions.

The ADD/ADHD Window on Time

Dr. Russell Barkley explains that **acquiring a sense of time is a developmental skill that is significantly delayed in students with attention deficit disorder.** Even for the average person without ADD or ADHD, a mature sense of time is not completely developed until the *early thirties,* when the prefrontal cortex reaches full maturity. He describes this maturational process as a **"window on time"** that opens more slowly for students with attention deficits. The chart below explains how time should develop for the average student who does *not* have ADD or ADHD.

When students are in preschool, their window on time is closed and everything is "now." As they reach the teenage years, the typical high school student can plan ahead up to two days. However, the student with an attention deficit is more likely to have a window on time that is closer to 12 hours. Without any prompts, his semester chemistry project doesn't enter his narrow window of time until the night before it is due (roughly 12 hours). So, teachers and parents often hear a familiar refrain, "I forgot my project is due tomorrow."

The Window on Time for People Who Don't Have ADHD:

- **Preschool:** the window on time awareness is closed for all children; they are time unaware

- **3–6 years old:** aware of time for only a few minutes

- **7–8 years old:** aware of time for up to 12 hours

- **Teenagers:** aware up to 2 days ahead (ADHD only aware up to 12 hours ahead)

- **Adults:** 8–12 weeks and more

The ADHD Window on Time:

- An "invisible disability"
- Has no "sense of time"
- Does not get ready on time
- Does not anticipate coming events
- Does not plan for the future
- Does not estimate time correctly
- Crises may be frequent due to failure to manage time well!

NAGGING WILL NOT CHANGE THIS BEHAVIOR! An event must enter the student's "window on time" before he will take action!!

As Barkley points out, ***"Time is the enemy of everyone with ADHD."*** He offers the acronym ERO to help explain why these students can successfully complete assignments in class and submit them, but are often "disabled" when asked to complete long-term projects.

E—event: a request to write a paper

R—response: the student writes the paper

O—outcome: the paper is submitted.

If there is no time lag between the "Event and "Outcome," the student can successfully complete the assignment. For instance, our students find it easier to complete an assignment that is given to complete in class and then turn in at the end of the period. However, if a time lag is present—for example, the project is due in one month—the student will have great difficulty completing the assignment. According to Barkley, *the time delay creates a disability because of the student's impaired sense of time.*

The Need for Extended Time

Because of multiple deficits in executive skills—delayed development of time awareness, slow processing speed, difficulty initiating and finishing projects—students with ADD or ADHD often need extended time on assignments and projects. Here is a first-person account documenting the need for more time. Lynne Rucinski, director of special education at Knoxville Catholic High School, shared this timeline for a high school senior we'll call "Christina":

A day in the life of a high school student with ADHD:

10:45	Christina comes to the office; she can't remember why. My assistant reminds her she needs to take a calculus test.
10:50	Christina remembers she needs a calculator.
10:55	She realizes her calculator needs batteries.
10:58	My assistant finds a spare calculator for her to use.
11:00	Christina realizes she needs a pencil.
11:10	She realizes she needs her notes.
11:20	She finds her notes; starts the test.
11:25	The bell rings—she finished three out of fourteen problems.

Time Management and ADD/ADHD (A Brief Discussion of the Issues)

Traditional time management strategies à la Stephen Covey typically rely on a four-step process:
- planning,
- prioritizing,
- scheduling, and
- following a plan.

Using this strategy is essential for success in school. Unfortunately, without some modifications, this system doesn't work very well for students who have an attention deficit. This should come as no surprise, since we know these students are forgetful, disorganized, and often have trouble planning ahead and judging the passage of time. Even adults with attention deficits still have problems with time management; so don't expect miracles from teenagers. According to Dr. Joan Teach, an educational consultant and expert on educating students with ADD and ADHD, the best strategy is to *"expose students to a variety of organizational and time management strategies and hope that something sticks."* In other words, they will ideally adapt the strategies that you teach to their own unique organizational style.

Why Is Time Management a Challenge?
Left Brain vs. Right Brain Thinking

Traditional time management systems are often designed by people who are: *left brain dominant, logical, convergent, linear, and sequential thinkers.* Unfortunately, many people with attention deficits may be described as the exact opposite: *right brain dominant, divergent, innovative, and intuitive thinkers.* This style of thinking is not just limited to people with attention deficits. One time management consultant explains that nearly half the population is right brain dominant. Actually, most people use both sides of their brains, but typically one side is dominant.

Traditional time management is usually introduced to enhance productivity and efficiency in contrast to the right-brain organizing style that is creative, spontaneous, and flexible. Right brain organizing styles are not bad, just different! Although this style of organizing may not be a major problem in adulthood, it causes significant problems while a teenager is still in school. Let's look at a few of the differences between left-brain and right-brain approaches to time management.

Time Management Strategies	Left-Brain Thinkers	Right-Brain Thinkers
1. Plan	1. Asks, "What *should* be done?"; develops a manageable list.	1. Asks, "What *could* be done?"; brainstorming occurs; "to do" list expands greatly and becomes unmanageable.
2. Prioritize	2. Lists items in order of priority: important, next in importance; 1, 2, 3 or A, B, C.	2. Everything is important or it wouldn't be on the list; can't narrow list down and pick just one; priorities change quickly.
3. Schedule	3. Writes dates and times on a calendar.	3. Can't decide which calendar to buy; must research all options; writes notes and misplaces them; forgets to write on calendar; then loses the calendar.
4. Follow plan	4. Follow-through is fun and satisfactory; completion is a reward in itself.	4. Once steps 1-3 are completed, the student becomes bored and weary; craves fresh ideas and new challenges. Joy and rewards come from producing new ideas and finding new challenges, not follow-up.

Visual vs. Abstract Organization

Students who have difficulty with traditional organizational strategies may in fact be **visual processors.** They remember and locate things visually, not abstractly. In other words, these students find their algebra homework by seeing a picture in their mind of where they left it, rather than remembering the name of a specific folder or location in a drawer.

Perhaps the key to good organization for students with attention deficits is to help them **maximize their skills as visual organizers** rather than try to convert them to an abstract system that may never work for them. For example, organize school materials on open shelves that are labeled. Post a large month-at-a-glance calendar on the wall and write scheduled events and due dates on it.

Interestingly, I have found that within their apparent disorganization, they often have their own unique organizational system. Amazingly, they often do find things within the "chaos." So, if a student's system works, don't make any changes. One time management consultant offers an easy test of whether or not a system is effective: "If you can find most things in three minutes or less, your system is working. Don't change it." If a student's system *doesn't* work, see the next summary for suggestions on teaching time management.

Resources

Covey, Stephen R. *Seven Habits of Highly Effective People*. New York: Simon and Schuster, 1990.

McGee-Cooper, Anne, with Duane Trammell. *Time Management for Unmanageable People.* New York: Bantam Books, 1994.

Teaching Time Management

Frequently students with attention deficits must be taught skills most of us do quite naturally. Since organizational and time management skills are often major deficits, an IEP/504 goal should be written to help improve these skills. Even if a teacher has time to teach the skills, parents should also be given a copy of Summaries 33-36. To help parents teach and reinforce use of these skills at home, perhaps the guidance counselor or special education teacher could provide a training session on time management for parents of all students who have special needs. Obviously, having similar time management systems in place at school and home is helpful.

The four traditional steps in time management are listed below, along with suggestions for helping students with attention deficits improve these skills. Some of these suggestions may sound great, but in reality, the student may be unable or unwilling to do them. For example, it's a great idea to do homework while waiting for a ride or for basketball practice to start. In reality, I don't know too many students with ADD or ADHD who will actually do that. However, it is still worth the effort to teach students these skills. Even if they aren't developmentally ready now, they may be able to use these strategies in later life. Don't get discouraged and give up, but rather try a different strategy.

I. Plan

1. **Develop a "to do" list (master list):** An **organizational coach**—usually parents, a good friend, or a girlfriend—may help the student develop a list of things he has to do each day. For example, turn in picture money, sign up for the basketball team, audition for the school play, check a book out of the library for next week's report, or do chores.

2. **Keep a calendar:** List all assignments, projects, and due dates on a central month-at-a glance calendar that is visible to all.

3. **Keep a student planner or assignment notebook:** To help students be better organized, many PTA groups buy school-mandated student planners. If the school does not have a standard planner for everyone, suggest that parents help the student find a planner he likes. Then show him how to use it. Someone at school or the parents should spend time with the student each day checking or writing in the planner until it becomes part of his routine.

    Allow the student to develop his own unique system for keeping up with assignments—as long as it works. One student writes down assignments, folds the paper in half, and places it in his textbook. Another student has his classes listed on a preprinted 4x6 index card he created. He carries the card in his jeans pocket every day and writes his assignments down during each class.

    Help the student decide exactly what kinds of things to write down—for example, assignments, sports practice, a teacher conference, and tests. Consider color-coding or using stars or something to make test dates stand out.

    If the student continues to forget to write down assignments, see Summary 25 for suggestions to ensure that assignments make it home.

4. **Review the list each day:** Ask parents to review the "to do list" the night before, then remind the student about urgent things as he leaves the next morning. Handing him a written reminder, such as a Post-It note for his notebook, backpack, locker, or car, or asking him to set his wrist alarm may be helpful.

II. Prioritize

1. **Practice setting priorities:** Teachers and parents must guide students in setting priorities. Many students with attention deficits have trouble ranking things to do in priority order. They often get sidetracked and spend too much time considering all the options for ranking items. The options below may help streamline this process.

   1.1. Divide items into two groups. Have the student write items on Post-It notes or cards, move the important ones to the top of the table, and others to the bottom. In this system, items are considered either: *1) important (do it now)* or *2) unimportant (do it any time)*. Students may need a third stack for undetermined or semi-important items. Those items may be pushed to the side, out of the way.

   1.2. Pick the top three items. Ask the student to look over the cards at the top of the table and select the three most important topics. If he can pick the top three items, proceed to scheduling tasks. However, if he has problems, a parent or teacher should select cards for three of the most important tasks. Ask the student to eliminate one or two of the cards. If he can't make a quick decision, briefly discuss why the top three are the most important.

   1.3. Or divide the list into four groups. Time management à la Stephen Covey and other time management trainers typically involves dividing a "to do list" into the four groups shown below. But one of the major problems here is the age-old conflict between parents and teens regarding what is important! A teen's definition of important and urgent most likely will not be the same as an adult's. Teens' priorities tend to become crises, deadlines, and fun activities. Planning ahead to avoid a crisis is often not particularly important to some teens. More importantly, most students with attention deficits are not developmentally ready for this level of organizational planning. For example, below is how one teenager with ADHD ranked a number of events on a "to do" list.

I. Urgent & Important	II. Important But Not Urgent
➤ forgot money for school field trip; must go to teacher's house tonight and turn it in ➤ practice clarinet for marching band tryouts tomorrow ➤ spend time with girlfriend ➤ read a car magazine or comic book	➤ read a book/begin work on the book report ➤ do homework for tomorrow ➤ visit library, get material for semester project due in 2 weeks ➤ develop a web page for Mom ➤ watch a good movie on TV ➤ set up a tent in the woods near home ➤ play Nintendo
III. Urgent But Not Important	IV. Not Important or Urgent
➤ start reading book for book report due tomorrow ➤ install a friend's stereo in the car today ➤ answer phone calls during dinner or homework	➤ develop a weekly schedule ➤ spend time with family ➤ copy homework over ➤ correct errors on an essay for extra credit ➤ clean room ➤ mow yard

Ideally, students should spend most of their time on "Urgent and Important" or "Important But Not Urgent" items, planning to avoid crises. But in reality, even adults with attention deficits put things off until they become "Urgent and Important" and spend far too much time on items in Group I, as well as fun things that seem "Urgent But Not Important." In other words, time management for teens with attention deficits is incredibly difficult! To successfully manage their time, teens must tailor-make a system that is interesting and meaningful to them.

1.4. Put Post-It notes on a calendar. Place small Post-It notes in priority order on a large, easily visible wall calendar. Simply move Post-It notes from one square to another as priorities change or throw them away when they're finished. The student could use different colored notes: hot pink to denote an urgent deadline; sports events on yellow.

1.5. Put items on a stand-up clipboard. Post-It notes may also be placed in priority order on a clear acrylic clipboard or a frame that will stand up. This way you don't have the dreaded task of recopying "to do lists." Simply move Post-It notes from one column to another as priorities change or throw them away when they're finished. Columns on the clipboard might be selected to help the student arrange notes by priority or by activity: "Today, Soon, Do Anytime" vs. "Family, School, Sports, or Religious Activities." As noted in 1.4, he could color code notes. If the student needs a copy at school, place the Post-It notes on a piece of paper and photocopy it. Or simply place the plastic stand face down on a copy machine to make a copy.

1.6. Put reminders of priority tasks in a cell phone or on a computer calendar. The tips given in 1.4 and 1.5 can be applied to monitoring tasks on a computer calendar, a PDA, or cell phone.

III. Schedule

1. **Transfer the "To Do List" onto a daily planner, small calendar, or the large family calendar.**

2. **Teach the student to allow enough time for activities.** Major activities to be scheduled may include school work, extracurricular activities, chores, community or religious events, and activities with friends. Students need to learn to allow adequate time to complete chores or special projects for school before they go out with friends. **Schedule backwards.** Show the student that if he has a ball game at 7:00, then he should schedule time to work on homework at 3:00 or 4:00. The steps necessary to complete a long-term project must be scheduled well in advance of the final due date. Time also must be allowed for cleaning up, dressing, and traveling to an event. Tips for scheduling backward are available in the sample schedule in Summary 38 and the blank form in Appendix A8.

3. **Practice time estimation.** If the student has an impaired sense of time, practice may or may not help. At Brainworks, an educational consulting program specializing in ADD and ADHD in Carrollton, TX, Carla Crutsinger recommends having students practice time estimation for tasks. Ask the student to write his estimate down. Then record how long it actually took to complete the job. If nothing else, the student may learn that he consistently tends to over- or underestimate the time required for certain jobs.

4. **Try a Palm Pilot or cheaper PDA.** Some older teenagers may benefit from using a handheld computerized planner, such as a Palm Pilot ($100), Palm Zire ($60+), or perhaps a less sophisticated, cheaper version such as a Sharp Wizard ($15—$100). Students with attention deficits love gadgets and might actually enjoy keeping a computerized schedule of homework and appointments. However, the downside is that forgetful teens also may lose it. Plus, the Pilot has e-mail capacity and so many options and games that it may be too much of a distraction in class. See Summary 16-E for other electronic devices.

5. **Look ahead in the planner or calendar.** Remind the student to check the upcoming week in his weekly planner or calendar on a regular basis. One parent explains that the next week does not exist in her

daughter's mind until she turns the page. So the student does not know that something is due on Monday until she turns the page in her planner late Sunday night or on Monday morning. Consider writing tasks on the larger family calendar so you have a month-at-a-glance.

6. **Block time for homework.** Suggest to the teen and parents that they establish an evening routine by blocking off time four nights a week for homework. For example, the student will choose the time to start homework, perhaps after dinner at around 7:00 each evening, lasting approximately until 8:00 or 9:00. No other commitments are made for that time unless the student has no homework or does it earlier so that he can attend a school or religious event. Or the student may do half the homework before the event and half afterward. Obviously, if the student has no homework, there is no need for him to sit down and study something simply to be studying.

7. **Use a weekly or monthly schedule for long-term projects.** When planning for a long-term project, have the student use a planner/calendar with the hours and days marked. The calendar makes an abstract concept (time) concrete because the student can see the hours and days. See Summaries 36-38 for more information. Blank forms are available in Appendices A5 and A6.

8. **Put a master calendar in the teen's room and perhaps at school.** Suggest that the student hang a large monthly calendar in his room that includes all events (school, family, religious, sports), as well as long-term projects. Chances are that the student will need prompting from teachers and/or parents to start early enough to finish long-term projects. Parents will also need to work with the student to keep the calendar up-to-date and review it on a regular basis.

   Teachers may want to post a large monthly calendar on the classroom wall and refer to it regularly. This may help make time more concrete and make students more aware of due dates.

9. **Make the planner or calendar interesting.** Consider adding an element of color and design to the planner/calendar. Use colored pens to write down assignments for different classes. Use colored dots, such as red for due dates. If the student seems to enjoy it, use colorful stickers when an assignment is finished. Of course, these teens will need ongoing help to make this system work. Help them monitor time and develop a fairly simple system. Teachers/parents may need to nudge them along because they could spend hours picking calendars, colors, stickers, or a system.

10. **Use procrastination wisely.** Sometimes procrastination, otherwise called *idea incubation*, really can make a contribution to a project. Allowing some time to think about a project or sleep on it may give the brain time to subconsciously come up with solutions or creative ideas.

11. **Allow some things to die a natural death.** Parents or teachers may need to explain that everything on a "to do list" does not have to be finished. If the project is a low priority, the student should not feel guilty. Sometimes the best thing is to let a task die, especially if it keeps ending up on the bottom of the priority list.

IV. Follow the Plan

1. **Keep the "to do" list in sight. Think visual!** Students may find it helpful to have the "to do" list stand above everything on the desk. Write the to do's on Post-It notes and put them on the clear acrylic standup frame/clipboard. Or for variety, write them on 3x5 cards and put them on a corkboard. Use push pins so you can move them around when needed.

2. **Use a cell phone, Palm Pilot, or a WatchMinder™.** These computerized gadgets have the capacity to provide a prompt (beep) or written reminder to start projects. See Summary 16-E.

3. **"Jump start" reluctant students.** Sometimes when a student is having trouble getting started, he may get stuck and then cover up his frustration with defiance. Getting started on tasks is an executive skill that is extremely difficult for students with ADHD and often remains a lifelong problem. The

student may be willing to work but need prompting to get started, or he may feel totally overwhelmed and have no clue where to start. Teachers and parents can help jump-start the student a number of ways. Help him understand that this challenge is related to his ADHD: "Alex, most students with ADHD have trouble getting started. Let's find some strategies to help you start on your work." See Summaries 38 and 65.

4. **Skip missing information.** Not surprisingly, these students often look for excuses to stop doing their homework. So, if needed information is missing, have the student work around it, leaving a blank that can be filled in later that night or the next day.

5. **Teach "quick and dirty" shortcuts.** Some students with attention deficits have a **compulsive need to do things perfectly,** so the work takes forever to complete. Perfection-seeking behavior combined with executive function deficits may mean that an essay takes three hours to draft rather than the expected hour. So the student looks at the assignment, knows it will take three hours, and groans a silent "Oh, no!" Sometimes he may avoid the assignment completely.

    Teach students how to use "quick and dirty" shortcuts or adaptations. For example, a crisis arises when the student suddenly remembers at 9:30 p.m. that an essay is due tomorrow. The student may dictate ideas to a parent, who types the first draft. Then the student can cut and paste the paragraphs, either on the computer or the paper itself, and arrange the paragraphs in order. See Summaries 19 and 20 on written expression for other ways to help a student get ideas down on paper.

6. **Discuss the concept that there is never enough time to do everything.** Help students understand that there is never enough time to complete every task to perfection. Help them learn to distinguish between projects that require their "best work" and those they can complete by doing them well enough to "get by." The example in the preceding section is one of those occasions when the student cannot expect to achieve perfection and must accept lower standards. Even though the work may not earn an A, a grade of C or D is better than an F for not turning in anything.

7. **Work during peak energy times.** Recommend scheduling homework during times when the student's energy is more likely to be at a peak. Each day there are times when our brains seem to think more clearly and working is easier. In addition, medication affects the times of peak attention for students with ADD/ADHD. Parents may talk with their doctor about prescribing a dose of short-acting medication such as Focalin to help the teen focus during the homework hours. Otherwise, students are attempting homework without medication coverage and thus are unable to pay attention. (See Summary 58 to determine peak times.)

8. **If a task is boring, add something to spice things up.** Play music or TV (no story plot) at low volume. When reading, break assignments into segments marked by colored paper clips. When the student "reads to the clip," he can take a break or have free reading.

9. **Avoid interruptions.** Once the student begins homework, hold any telephone calls until break time or homework is completed. Parents may have to take his cell phone away so he is not constantly texting. Many teens are in the habit of keeping their cell phones on vibrate in their pockets and texting constantly throughout the day.

10. **Schedule a "joy or brain break."** At home, suggest that the student renew energy and at the same time reward completion of work by taking a short walk, exercising, calling a friend, drinking a glass of water, eating a snack, or playing video games for a brief period. Some students may actually do better with breaks at the end of an assignment rather than the middle. Figure out what works best for each teen.

Putting Time Management to Work: Long-term Project Completion

Failing to complete a major long-term project is one of the primary reasons students with ADD/ADHD may fail a class. Not surprisingly, **deficits in executive skills are a major factor interfering with completion of these projects!** In fact, Russell Barkley explains that the time delay associated with long-term projects creates a disability for our students. The typical student with an attention deficit immediately feels overwhelmed when she is assigned a large project. She has no idea how to break this huge project down into smaller segments or where to begin working on it. Since the due date is usually a few weeks away, she often procrastinates or forgets the project until the night before it is due.

Projects requiring more than a couple of days to complete are often complex and present major challenges for students with ADHD. Skill requirements include getting organized, knowing exactly what the project requirements are, figuring out where to begin, analyzing, synthesizing, organizing, and then doing the required work, and last but not least, getting started. Often, once the student starts working, she really doesn't mind the work.

Suggested Organizational Strategies

Teachers will find that specific steps for helping students use organizational and time management strategies will vary depending on the student's skill level. The first time a student has a fairly complicated semester project, the teacher will probably walk the student through the project, step-by-step. Using an overhead, the teacher may show the student how to do a sample project. Here are a few suggested strategies:

Notification, Reminders, and Monitoring

1. **Notify parents.** Send a notice home to parents regarding due dates for special projects or tests.
2. **Include in IEP/504.** Include an accommodation requiring notification of the parent in the IEP/504 Plan if this is a major challenge for the student.
3. **Remind student.** Periodic reminders from the teacher or row captain will be helpful to these students.
4. **Monitor work.** Monitor progress with emails to parents if the student falls behind.

Project Management

5. **Break-up project.** Break projects into three or four segments with separate due dates.
6. **Give several grades.** Grade each segment of the project separately. (S 16-B)

Provide Support and Guidance

7. **Give a job card.** Provide a 3x5 index card that outlines specific steps required to complete a job.
8. **Use a graphic organizer.** Provide a graphic organizer for the project (Summary 37) and teach the student how to use it.
9. **Show finished projects.** Provide completed model projects or reports (reports that earned As, Bs, Cs, and a failing grade; students make better grades when this guidance is provided).
10. **Use a grading rubric.** Give a grading rubric, so that students know what they have to do to earn a certain grade.

Teach Skills

11. Teach time management. (S 35-38)
- Complete a weekly/monthly schedule.
- Divide task into required steps.
- Schedule each step.
- Teach the student to schedule time backward.

Tips for "Jump Starting" Students

Parents and teachers are often surprised to learn that activation of the brain—getting started on school work—is a critical executive skill. For people who *don't* have ADHD, getting started seems like such a simple task. However, brain chemicals must work properly for a student to use self-talk to guide her behavior and actually start work on homework or projects. Unfortunately, failure to get started looks like laziness or a matter of choosing not to do the work. Dr. Steven Guy, coauthor of the *BRIEF* test of executive function, believes that a major reason for difficulties getting started is that the child with ADHD cannot "see" a clear path to a solution or a good plan for tackling the problem. Consequently, she may try briefly to start but quickly become frustrated and give up.

Teachers may try some of the suggestions below at school and suggest others to parents to try at home.

1. **Read directions aloud.** Review the instructions with the student.
2. **Call a classmate.** At home, she could call a friend for clarification.
3. **Divide the work.** Help the student break the assignment into manageable segments.
4. **Begin working.** Sometimes if the student will simply begin working, the assignment becomes clearer.
5. **Brainstorm on paper.** Draw a mind map or brainstorm using similar graphic organizers to get creative ideas flowing. See Summary 16-A for a discussion of graphic organizers plus names of websites that offer examples.
6. **"Get physical."** Sometimes if a student starts with physical activities, it may increase her alertness enough so that she can start mental activities such as reading. Dr. Sydney Zentall tells us that *physical activity often primes mental activity.*" The student could:
   - walk around, reading aloud from a book, until she can settle down and read while sitting in a chair.
   - Fiddle with Wikki Stix or pipe cleaners, or a squeeze or Koosh ball while studying.
   - Walk on a treadmill while reading; put the book on the stand attached to the treadmill; but be careful, this is not for the uncoordinated.
7. **Make a game of it.** Have the student play a game with herself: "I'll just read for 15 minutes and then I'll stop whenever I want to." Once students get started, they usually continue.
8. **Read during TV commercials.** Suggest the student watch a TV program and read material during the *muted* commercials (for short reading assignments). This may be too difficult for many students.
9. **Give her some company.** Sit with the teen and help her talk through what needs to be done. Parents may sit with her and fold laundry, knit, or read while she is working. Offer encouragement and support.
10. **Take a "brain break."** Linda Sorenson, a Utah master teacher, explains that the brain needs breaks to reenergize itself in order to work at peak efficiency. Suggest the student consider a "brain break" after 30 minutes or so—shoot a few baskets, get a snack, drink some water, take a short walk, ride her skateboard or bike, or listen to music.

The tools in this summary will give teachers and parents ideas of how to help the student break down and organize her project. An example of a semester project for Jerry, a high school junior, is described here. The forms contained in the next two summaries will help the teenager and parents organize their thoughts and develop a plan for timely completion of a project. Although blank forms are available in Appendices A5 and A6, teachers and parents should feel free to create their own forms to help organize this process. The software "Inspiration" may also help students organize their materials for projects or essays.

A Sample Project

Let's put organizational skills and time management tips to work on Jerry's semester project.

Jerry has been given a major project in history. He was overwhelmed by the three-page single-spaced project narrative provided by the teacher. Each student must develop a portfolio of his best work on Operation Desert Storm (Persian Gulf War I). From a list of twenty-two activities related to the war, the student must complete six mandatory and four optional activities. This student will need assistance to identify the suggested activities and then narrow down his selection to ten.

The Organizational Plan

An organizational plan using the time management strategies discussed in Summary 35 includes these four steps:

1. plan,
2. prioritize,
3. schedule,
4. follow the plan.

A teacher, or perhaps a coach, will need to go through all these steps with the student to *shape behavior,* or, in other words, to teach him or her how to complete a major project. With enough supervised practice, students with ADD/ADHD will eventually learn to do a major project on their own.

1. Plan:

- **Complete a graphic organizer.** Don, Jerry's father, used this amusing example to help his son understand how to tackle a big project. *"How do you eat an elephant? One bite at a time."* He then helped Jerry complete a graphic organizer to visually present all the project requirements. He knew that giving a student with ADD/ADHD a graphic organizer may help him "eat the project one bite at a time"—in other words, break the project into manageable sections.

  Teachers may help students complete the graphic organizer in Summary 37 to visually present all the project requirements on one page. First, write all the important information regarding the assignment on this page so the student can tell at a glance what the requirements are. Later, check off each task as it is done. A blank form is available in Appendix A5.

- **Post a class calendar for the project.** Joan Helbing, an ADD Consultant and diagnostician in Wisconsin, recommends posting a monthly calendar (as shown on the next page) for the whole class. Note major dates and information and remind students as those dates draw near. This concrete, visual reminder is more likely to help them "see" and remember the due dates.

Mon	Tues	Wed	Thurs	Fri
1	2	3 Project assigned	4	5 Turn in topic choice
8	9	10 Turn in list of 4 sources	11	12
15	16 Turn in note cards (or outline)	17	18	19 Rough draft due
22	23 Charts & graphs due	24	25 Final copy check	26 Project due

- **Display a completed project.** Teachers have found that the quality of student projects improves when completed projects are displayed for them to review. Students are able to visualize what the final project should look like and create their project accordingly.

2. Prioritize:

- **Decide which of the ten steps should be done first.** First, review the requirements and decide if any of them require special time considerations. For example, allow adequate time in case a book must be requested from another library or the book has been checked out by someone else. Or, for instance, does the family need to schedule a visit to a relative's house for an interview about the war?

- **Then rank order the steps.** List the steps in the order in which they should be done. However, after the first two or three steps, the order may not be important.

3. Schedule:

- **Schedule activities on a weekly calendar** as shown in Summary 38. Once the material is written out on the graphic organizer and the student knows all her assignments, she can begin scheduling each step by writing it on her calendar. As explained in Summary 35 schedule each step backward from the due date. A blank form is available in Appendix A7.

4. Follow the plan:

- **Help the student get started and monitor regularly.** First the student will collect all the information needed for one or several segments of the project. Jerry completed all his research during several visits to the library, photocopied important material, and was then ready to start writing the report.

  As explained above, sometimes parents have to "jump-start" students to get them working on the project. More than likely they'll need prompting to simply select a topic to start researching or writing on first. The teacher or parent may also need to limit choices to help the student make decisions more quickly. If the student is struggling, the parent may arbitrarily narrow the choices to two and say, "Would you rather do 1 or 2?"

- **Set up folders or binders for collected material.** Help the student organize a storage system, using either folders or binders with separators. Put all the various pieces of the project into these folders—for example, label a folder for the cover, the table of contents, the written content, photocopies of reading materials, pictures/ graphs/charts, bibliography, and resources.

- **Set up a "wiki" for shared information.** Students who are working on a group project can establish a wiki account online at one of several sites, including www.wikispaces.com. The wiki allows sharing and editing of information on the site. This process allows the group to share information even when they are not together. YouTube offers short videos that explain how wiki works.

- **Keep an up-to-date list of references.** Nothing is more frustrating than finishing up the report late the night before it is due and discovering to your chagrin that you don't have the author's full name, the publisher's name, publication date, and city in which a reference book was published. Photocopy the front and back of the title page of each book consulted. Most of the needed information is typically found on those two pages. As a backup, you can also search Amazon.com or Barnesandnoble.com for information on the year of publication and the publisher.

- **Set up pocket folders.** Any work that is done at school should be collected in one folder for each student.

Advice for Coaches

Anyone who is helping coach a student through a major project may appreciate this humorous advice from Penny, Jerry's mother.

"My son is totally overwhelmed by most projects. He doesn't know where to begin." Somewhat tongue in cheek, she explains the best strategy: "Lie! Don't ever tell your teenager everything at once. Even though he has the papers, he doesn't understand what it all means. Keep things simple. Break the project into sections and start working on them. Feed the material to him one "bite" or section at a time.

"You can't write on the schedule to do two of ten sections of the project each visit to the library. You have to be flexible. Because it all depends on how he feels or the mood he's in or whether or not his medicine has worn off. Today he may do work on four of them, but on the next visit to the library, he may just barely be able to finish one."

SUMMARY
37   Project Graphic Organizer

Name: _____Jerry_____   Class/Teacher: ___Jenkins_____

Project Title or Focus: __Operation Desert Storm__   Due Date: May 14
                         (Persian Gulf War 1)

I. <u>Plan</u>: What do you have to do? What are all the project requirements?

Check box when complete.

① ___Saddam Hussein___ □☑ __Map Work__ ②

15 facts   Pictures   timeline/main events   write a map key   color it   label it

Profile:
③ Gen. Norman Schwarzkopf ☑□ Patriot missiles & scuds ④

25 facts   Pictures   1 picture each   10 facts each

⑤ Liberation of Kuwait □□ Interview Gulf War Veteran ⑥

create newspaper front page   write articles, briefs; get pics   name & date paper   picture   write 5-8 facts (age, where sent, memories)   schedule visit

Project Graphic Organizer

Projects may be complex and involve multiple steps. Sometimes in the rush of completing the project some key information may be overlooked. Record all requirements on this page so that no steps will be forgotten. Good luck!

I. Plan: What are all the project requirements? What do I need?

- Complete the Project Graphic Organizer on the other side.

Check resources needed:

- **X** library visit
- ____ books
- ____ magazine articles
- **X** Internet
- **X** interviews
- _____
- _____

Check products needed:

- **X** written report   ____ build a model
- **X** report cover   **X** maps
- ____ poster   *create newspaper*
- **X** pictures   _____
- **X** bibliography   _____
- **X** timelines with dates
- _____

II. Prioritize: Do I need to set priorities? **X** yes   _____ no

- Which one do I need to do first? *#5 & 6*
- Which one is most complicated and will take the most time? *#5 -- newspaper*
- Do I need to allow time to order a book from the library or schedule a visit for an interview? *yes--schedule to visit veteran*
- Number the remaining parts of the project on the organizer in the order you will do them. *do 5 & 6 first; no special order after that*

III. Schedule: How long will the project take? *2 weeks* (estimate)

- Put steps on the Weekly Project Calendar in Appendix A7.

IV. Do it: Complete all the steps on the Weekly Project Calendar.

- Check each step off in color marker on the Project Graphic Organizer when it is completed.

Weekly Project Planner

Week 1

During the first week, the student completed all the research for this project, photocopied it, and put it in a folder.

Part of the work was completed at school during class and visits to the school library; the rest was done via the Internet at the local library and his computer at home.

Interviewing the veteran was completed while on spring break.

		Monday	Tuesday	Wednesday	Thursday	Friday	Saturday
	7:30						
	8:00						
	8:30						
	9:00						
	9:30						
	10:00						
	10:30						
	11:00						
	11:30						
	12:00						
	12:30						
	1:00	Research Liberation of Kuwait	Continue Research; Get pictures	Begin writing articles re: Kuwait Liberation	Write another article	Create newspaper front page	**Sunday**
	1:30	newspaper	newspaper	newspaper	newspaper	newspaper	
	2:00	group work	group work	group work	group work	group work	
	2:30						
	3:00						
	3:30						
	4:00						
	4:30						
	5:00						
	5:30						
	6:00						
	6:30						
	Evening	Interview veteran of Gulf war	Write up interview; include picture	Research & write up facts on Saddam Hussein	Research General Schwarzkopf; get pictures		write up info. on Schwarzkopf

3

Week 2

The student began working on the project one section at a time.

Activities were scheduled at regular intervals to provide ballpark guidance. Of course, flexible scheduling is required for these students. Some nights the student may do four activities and the next night, only one.

Teachers will check student progress at regular intervals, answer questions, problem-solve, plan, advise if on track, and give encouragement.

	Monday	**Tuesday**	**Wednesday**	**Thursday**	**Friday**	**Saturday**
7:30						
8:00						
8:30						
9:00						
9:30						
10:00						
10:30						
11:00						
11:30						
12:00						
12:30						
1:00	Map work; draw, label	Map work; write key	Patriot missiles & scuds research	Start putting report together	REPORT DUE	**Sunday**
1:30						
2:00						
2:30						
3:00						
3:30						
4:00						
4:30						
5:00						
5:30						
6:00						
6:30						
Evening	continue work on map	continue work on map	Write up research on missiles	Polish report		

SUMMARY 39 Using Weekly Reports to Ensure Completion of Schoolwork

Sometimes when students are not completing work consistently, parent-teacher conferences are scheduled. Typically, the purpose of the meeting is to identify problem areas and to develop an intervention plan. A first step is often to check whether the student is writing his homework down in his planner or assignment book each day. Next, teachers may try some of the strategies listed in Summaries 16-D and 25, such as asking row captains to check that assignments are written down or getting phone numbers for a classmate who usually knows the assignment. As the next step, teachers often begin sending home a weekly report to keep families posted on a student's progress.

A weekly report usually indicates whether class work and homework were completed and may give grades for school work or tests. These reports are often used for short periods to help students get back on track academically. Sometimes when students are struggling terribly, a "daily report" may be used. However, "weekly reports" work well for most teenagers.

Weekly Reports Are Challenging for These Students

Weekly reports are one of the most effective tools teachers can use, but asking teenagers with attention deficits to use them is often complicated. Because of their ADD or ADHD symptoms and learning problems, teenagers often forget to get reports signed or to take them home. In middle school, homeroom teachers may still give the student the form and remind him to get it signed by other teachers. By high school, however, the student must remember to pick up a blank form, take it to each class, and get it signed by the teacher. If forgetfulness is a problem, teachers may discuss the report with the student and then email it home to him and his parents or call and leave a message.

If asked the purpose of weekly reports, *students* would probably say they are for punishment. Since this process can be so aversive, look for a way to minimize its negative aspects. After all, ADD or ADHD is a serious disability for some students. The very skills (attention, memory, organization, and executive function) that are deficient in students with ADD or ADHD are often the underlying reasons that homework is incomplete and weekly reports are forgotten. So do not be surprised when these students have problems with weekly reports. Use weekly reports sparingly and in as few classes as possible. Expect to make adjustments to ensure that the weekly report works.

Purpose of Weekly Reports

Let's consider what most teachers and parents say is the purpose of these reports.

1. To **help students:**
   - complete their class work and homework,
   - learn the academic material, and
   - succeed in school,
   - rather than to simply punish them for failure to complete work!

2. To **help parents:**
   - stay informed of their teenager's progress so they may monitor homework when needed,
   - know when work is not done so they can ensure make-up work is completed.

Developing the Weekly Report

Weekly report forms should be simple and contain basic information. They should include:
1. **comments on the student's good work,** not just his failures;
2. **a statement of missing assignments** that must be done—for example, math, p. 89, 1-30, odd problems.

As a teacher, I preferred weekly reports that were "teacher friendly":
1. easy to read,
2. quick to complete,
3. required little writing,
4. used in as few classes as necessary.

A weekly report might look something like this one:

DAILY/WEEKLY REPORT

Name: _____ Date: _____

Class: _____

homework turned in this week ☐ Yes ☐ No

grades for the week: _____

Comments: _____
_____
_____

(Write something positive—for example, note improvement)

Unfinished assignments: _____
_____
_____

Teacher signature : (in ink) _____

Secrets for Making Weekly Reports Work

First and foremost, good communication between teachers and parents is essential. It is best if teachers and parents discuss how to implement the report, as well as rewards or consequences that might be used. Remember to keep the above goals in mind, involve the teenager in some decision-making, and don't let the weekly report simply become a form of punishment for the teen.

Rewards

Depending on the student, rewards may or may not be necessary. If a student is totally overwhelmed and depressed, a reward may give him the boost he needs to finish his work. Privileges and money are two of the most common rewards used. Parents may say, "If you get a good report this week, I'll pay for a movie and gas and let you drive my car." Eventually, when the student gets hooked on success and his grades improve, completion of homework without nagging from parents and teachers may be a reward in itself.

Negative Consequences

Restrictions and logical consequences are two of the most common strategies that parents use when homework is incomplete. However, be careful, because sometimes negative consequences can give the student the wrong unspoken message or can actually be a reward for the teen.

Typically, **harsh restrictions cause resentment and anger** between parents and teens and make the weekend miserable for the whole family. If students are placed on restrictions for a weekend or longer, they probably hear this unspoken message: "If you would just try harder, you could do your work. You're lazy. You don't care."

In contrast, **logical consequences give the correct unspoken message** and also meet our goals: "Do your class work/homework now or you'll still have to do it eventually, possibly Friday night or Saturday before you go out with friends." So, when the student comes home with the weekly report, parents may say, "When your homework is completed, you may go out." If the student finishes at 8:30 Friday night, then he may go to a movie.

If the student has a lot of homework, parents may divide it into reasonable segments: half due Friday and half Saturday. Thus, the student is rewarded for completing his school work, even though it is late, plus he learns the academic material. Parents create a win-win situation where both the parent and the teenager get something positive from this approach.

Logical consequences are not always easy to use effectively. See the discussion of this strategy in *Teenagers with ADD and ADHD, 2nd ed.*

A Word of Caution: Requiring completion of homework before the weekend may *not* be the best strategy if the amount of unfinished work is overwhelming. In this situation, go back to the drawing board and revise the plan. Help the student get caught up with his work and then continue the plan. If a lot of homework must be "made-up," one way to help the student is to:

1. **Reduce the assignments to a manageable level** that will still teach the concepts the student may not have mastered.

2. Sometimes teachers may **forgive some assignments** when make-up work is too overwhelming, so the student can catch up with the rest of the class.

3. It may be necessary to **do daily monitoring of school work** for awhile.

The Wrong Sort of Rewards: For a student who hates doing homework, the "*best* reward" he can receive is for teachers to say, "You didn't do your work, so you get an F. We will not let you turn it in late." The unspoken message a depressed teenager hears is "If you don't do your math assignment today, you'll *never* have to do it."

The next step in "shaping" the student's behavior is to have him complete the school work when it is due. See Summary 64. (Homework and weekly reports are also discussed in more detail in Chapter 12 of *Teenagers with ADD & ADHD, 2nd ed.*)

SUMMARY 40 Ensuring Parents Receive the Weekly Report

Although weekly reports help adults monitor and ensure completion of school work, the secondary task, remembering to get the report signed and to bring it home, often becomes as great a challenge as homework completion. Remember, the report relies on a skill that is often deficient as a result of the student's ADD or ADHD. After all, forgetfulness and disorganization are major characteristics of this condition. So teachers have a choice. They can send a weekly report via email or the child can take it home. If teachers don't mind sending email, this is probably the best option for ensuring that the report makes it home. Consider giving the student a choice of the two options.

If parents and teachers are unreasonable, a student could complete all her school work, forget the report, and still be punished, even though her work was done. Teach the student to master this skill or compensate rather than just punish her for her disability! Or, as suggested below, find an innovative way to send the report home until she has mastered the most important skill, completion of school work! Some students with attention deficits can remember the report; others cannot and will need extra help.

If students are failing a class, master one step at a time!

FIRST,

Address completion of school work:

Get students hooked on academic success!

NEXT,

Work on the secondary skill:

Remembering the note.

If students cannot remember the note....

Find Alternate Ways to Send the Weekly Report Home

1. Teachers may e-mail or fax the report home or to the parent's office.

2. Another student, girlfriend, or boyfriend may remind the teenager to get the weekly report signed and returned home.

3. Have the student use a wrist alarm to help her remember to bring the note home. When the alarm rings, if the student has forgotten to get the note signed during each period, she can still get teacher signatures after school, providing she does not ride the school bus.

4. Ask each teacher to remember to give the student a signed note to take home.

5. The guidance counselor may send a note or e-mail around to teachers asking for the weekly report information.

6. Teachers may call home and leave a message on the answering machine.

7. Post assignments on a wiki. Parents and teachers can set up an account with a wiki on one of several websites. Teachers can post assignments on the site and then students and parents can access the information.

Coping with Executive Function Deficits

SUMMARY 41

Why Are Executive Skills So Important?

I hope that the preceding summaries in Sections 2 and 3 have clarified just how critical **organization, activation (getting started), working memory, use of self-talk to direct behavior, awareness of time and time management, controlling emotions, and reconstitution (analysis and synthesis)** are for making good grades in school.

One suggestion for addressing these challenges is to involve an "organizational coach," typically the parents or another student. Some schools have a teacher or aide who meets with the students at the end of the day to review assignments and books for the evening. One parent even went so far as to hire a senior to meet her freshman daughter after school to decide which books and assignments to take home. In other schools, the teachers or counselors may be too busy to spend class time teaching these skills. If so, then give appropriate summaries from this section to parents. It is critical that someone help teenagers with attention deficits master these basic skills. Tips for coaching are provided in Summary 71.

General Suggestions for Handling Executive Function Deficits

When students with attention deficits are struggling with any of these challenges, keep these four key pieces of advice in mind:

- *Keep it simple!*
  - *Keep it brief!*
    - *Keep it visual!*
      - *Keep it novel!*

Remember also to intervene at the "point of performance" and provide "external" visual and/or auditory prompts!

Provide Additional Guidance

As they learn to become more organized, students with ADD/ADHD need more hands-on guidance than their peers. Remember, adults will have to be involved in this teaching process longer for these students primarily because of their three-year delay in brain development and their 30 percent developmental delay in key executive skills. If parents are interested and want help, give them copies of selected summaries in Section 3.

Help Teens Understand and Cope with Executive Function Deficits

Review relevant summaries in this section with teens—for example, on organization, memory, time management, getting started. Ask them, "Does any of this sound like you? Which part?" Help them understand their own organizational system better and to choose ways to make it more effective.

Model Time Management and Organizational Strategies

A teacher, parent, or tutor may need to help the student develop an organizational system from the strategies listed in Summaries 32-39. Someone may have to show him how to write a "to do" list, pick priorities, make a schedule, schedule backward, and implement the plan. Remember, it is much harder for these students to get information into long-term memory, so they will need visual cues and tricks to help them remember these strategies. Frequent repetition will be required until the skill is mastered.

Limit Choices

Many students with attention deficits get bogged down if they have too many choices. For example, they may spend enormous amounts of time considering all their options for an essay topic. By the time they have selected a topic, they are mentally worn out and ready to move on to something else. Perhaps teachers and parents can help them find shortcuts around this time-consuming and exhausting process.

- Give only two choices of essay or report topics.
- Write topics on two or three 3x5 cards; tell the student to take one card away and then another. If he can't decide, have him flip a coin so he can save his precious time for writing the essay.
- If a teacher gives an open-ended choice ("write an essay on a topic of interest to you"), someone should help narrow the topics down to two choices.
- Even then, it may be necessary for teachers or parents to briefly discuss the topics, help the student make a decision, and, sometimes, arbitrarily select a topic.

Expect Students to Change Their Organizational Systems Periodically

These creative students become bored with sameness! So, most organizational systems lose their effectiveness after a while. Change is essential to hold their interest. Add something new and interesting to the system.

SECTION 4

Federal Laws Governing the Education of Students with ADD/ADHD

Three important federal laws impact the education of students with ADD or ADHD:

1. **IDEA (the Individuals with Disabilities Education Act)***: a federal **education** law guaranteeing a free appropriate public education to all students with disabilities in the United States. This law applies primarily to students served by public schools, ages birth through high school, and in some cases through age 21.

2. **Section 504 of the Rehabilitation Act of 1973**: A federal **civil rights** law prohibiting discrimination against people with disabilities in programs that receive *any* financial aid from the federal government, including schools, public and private, as well as colleges and technical schools.

3. **ADA (the Americans with Disabilities Act)**: a federal **civil rights** law, broader than 504, that prevents discrimination against people with disabilities in many settings, including public schools, private nonreligious schools, and the workplace. ADA supersedes other laws, including IDEA.

Initiate Early Intervention Services First: Researchers tell us that approximately 50 percent of students with ADD or ADHD qualify for services under IDEA and most qualify under Section 504. However, recent revisions to IDEA encourage earlier interventions in the classroom without requiring testing for special education eligibility or Section 504. Hopefully, services provided through Early Intervening Services (EIS) or Response to Intervention (RtI) will help many students succeed academically and prevent the need for special education referral.

---

* Recent revisions to IDEA (2004-2008) and ADA (2008) have had a major impact on students with ADD or ADHD. Revisions are noted in the appropriate Summary.

Evaluate Next: If these strategies are ineffective and students with ADD or ADHD continue struggling, then an evaluation for special education is required. Other Health Impairment (OHI) is the most commonly used eligibility category in IDEA for students with attention deficit disorders. Parents are sometimes told their child isn't eligible for special education if the student is evaluated for Learning Disabilities (SLD) only, and OHI is not considered. For those students who are ineligible for services either as OHI or SLD under IDEA, the school system must consider eligibility under Section 504.

Sometimes, if students need services that are more costly, the school may prefer to provide assistance under IDEA instead of Section 504. Under current funding guidelines, local school systems are reimbursed by the state for services provided under IDEA but *not* Section 504. Typically, qualifying for services under IDEA is more difficult than qualifying under Section 504.

Regardless of eligibility category, most students with attention deficits will spend the majority of their time in regular classrooms, rather than special education classes.

Complexities of Laws: Writing about these laws is very difficult because explanation of any law requires interpretation. If you ask two lawyers, you may get two different interpretations, just as you would if you asked a school official and a parent, or two different judges. In addition, the interpretations of the law may change overnight on the basis of a court ruling or policy memo. Furthermore, states may pass laws and regulations that provide more detail than the federal law does. For example, states may specify the number of days during which an evaluation and special education placement must occur, or add to the list of objects qualifying as weapons. So, please be aware that ***the information given in this section is stated in general terms and is not intended as legal advice. Please consult an attorney with any legal questions on this topic.***

Special Thanks: A simple thank you seems inadequate to express my appreciation to my friend and colleague Mary Durheim, an educational consultant, mediator, and expert on Section 504, who was so incredibly helpful in writing this chapter. Mary not only knows all the key legal issues related to ADHD but also where to find relevant statutory citations. Mary, a past president of CHADD, is also the co-creator of CHADD's model Parent-to-Parent (P2P) Training program.

Resources for Section Four

Helpful publications with a variety of viewpoints are available regarding IDEA and Section 504. With regard to any law, interpretation varies with the viewpoint of the person reading the law. Some of these resources speak from the perspective of the best interests of the parents, local schools, or state or federal education agency involved. However, in the end, the interpretation should be based upon the best interests of the student involved.

Helpful Websites

- CEC (www.cec.sped.org): A Primer on the IDEA 2004 Regulations. Council for Exceptional Children.
- GLRS (www.glrs.org): The Georgia Learning Resources System (GLRS) provides information regarding training, newsletters, books, and videos to help special education students.
- IDEA 2004 Summary (www.fape.org): IDEA Partnership (comprised of 55 member agencies funded by the U.S. Department of Education).
- IDEA Federal Statutes (www.idea.ed.gov): Public Law 108-446.
- NASDE (www.nasdse.org): The National Association of State Directors of Special Education has information on regulations and implementation of IDEA.

- National Center for Learning Disabilities (www.ncld.org): Useful resources include *NCLD: A Parent Guide to IDEA* and *NCLD: A Parent Guide to Response to Intervention.*
- NICHCY (www.nichcy.org): The National Information Center for Children and Youth with Disabilities offers excellent resources for educators, families, and other professionals. They have a wide variety of publications including fact sheets, bibliographies, issue papers, and information on IDEA that may be download from the Internet.
- PACER Center (www.pacer.org): The Parent Advocacy Coalition for Educational Rights (PACER) helps parents and families of children with disabilities. PACER provides many excellent, reader-friendly summaries on a range of topics, including their publication, *Honorable Intentions*.
- Reed Martin's Website (www.reedmartin.com): Reed Martin, an attorney who specializes in special education law, offers information on IDEA and Section 504.
- USDOE/OSEP (www.ed.gov/offices/OSERS): The Office of Special Education and Rehabilitative Service, U.S. Department of Education website offers more information about IDEA.
- Wrightslaw (www.wrightslaw.com): Several helpful summaries of key issues regarding IDEA 2004 are included on this website.

Books and Articles

Cohen, Mathew. "Response to Intervention Procedures for Children with ADH/HD and Learning Disabilities." Presented at the International CHADD conference. Anaheim, CA, 2008. (Cohen is a well-known attorney who is knowledgeable regarding ADHD and special education law.)

Dendy, Chris A. Zeigler. *Teenagers with ADD and ADHD (TWA): A Guide for Parents and Teachers.* 2nd ed. Bethesda, MD: Woodbine House, 2006. (Includes an in-depth discussion of IDEA, IEPS, and Section 504. Using the book in conjunction with this book will be very helpful to parents and teachers alike.)

Jordan, Dixie. *Honorable Intentions: A Guide to Educational Planning.* 2nd ed. Minneapolis, MN: Pacer Center, 2000.

Schnoes, Connie, Reid, Robert, Wagner, Mary, and Marder, Camille. "ADHD among Students Receiving Special Education Services: A National Survey." *Exceptional Children,* Summer, 2006.

"Section 504 Celebrates Its 25th Year: Top 15 Tips for Writing IEPS and Section 504 Plans." *Attention: The Magazine of Children and Adults with Attention-Deficit/Hyperactivity Disorder,* Winter 1999, Vol. 5, No. 3.

Volkow, N.D., Swanson, J.M., et al. "Evaluating Dopamine Reward Pathway in ADHD: Clinical Implications." *Journal of the American Medical Association,* Sept. 2009, Vol. 302, No. 10:1084-91.

Wright, Peter W. D. and Pamela Darr Wright. Wrightslaw: Special Education Law. 2nd ed. Hartfield, VA: Harbor House Law Press, 2007.

Regional Resources

Several states have ***regional education resource centers*** that can be helpful to parents and teachers. These centers operate independently of state and local school systems, are extremely knowledgeable about federal education laws, and focus on the best interests of the students. They have different names in each state. For example, in Georgia, the center is known as Georgia Learning Resources Services (GLRS), and in Texas, Education Service Centers (ESC). These centers often provide training for teachers and parents on special topics including ADD/ADHD.

Parent Training Information Centers (PTIC) are also available in each state. In Georgia, they are known as "Parents Educating Parents." If local officials do not know the phone number of your PTIC, contact your state department of education, special education division, or check on the website of the Technical Assistance Alliance for Parent Centers (www.taalliance.org).

Local Resources

Usually several individuals in each local school system are very knowledgeable regarding IDEA and Section 504 guidelines.

- Administrators and special education teachers at individual schools are knowledgeable regarding federal laws.
- Each school system has a ***Director of Special Education*** and a ***Section 504 Coordinator***. Teachers or parents may contact them if they have any questions about these federal laws or reasonable accommodations. Although IDEA doesn't apply in college, Section 504 does; so 504 coordinators are available.
- Related to "inclusion" of special education students in regular classes, ***special education teachers*** or ***consultants*** may be available to provide technical consultation regarding teaching strategies to regular classroom teachers.
- Some schools have an ***ADD/ADHD consultant*** who is also knowledgeable about IDEA and Section 504.
- Check also with ***local parent support groups*** such as CHADD, ADDA, or LDA. They often have very up-to-date information.

SUMMARY 42

17 Frequently Asked Questions about ADD, ADHD, and Education Law

These seventeen key questions provide a brief overview of the topics to be addressed in this chapter.

1. **Are ADD or ADHD Eligible Disabilities?** The answer is yes, in many situations. Federal policies state that students with "ADD or ADHD" should be evaluated and may be eligible for special education under either IDEA (Individuals with Disabilities Education Act) or Section 504 of the Rehabilitation Act. In 1991 the United States Offices of Special Education (OSEP), Office for Civil Rights (OCR), and Elementary and Secondary Education (ESE) issued a landmark joint memo clearly stating that many students with ADD or ADHD have significant learning problems and may be eligible for services. As is the case with other disabilities, ADD and ADHD exist on a continuum of severity from mild to severe. Consequently, students with more complex cases of ADHD and executive function deficits may need special education and accommodations.

   If the student's only qualifying disability is an attention deficit, she will be eligible for special education services under the category of "other health impairment" (OHI). However, most students with ADD or ADHD (67 percent) have co-occurring conditions, such as a learning disability or emotional disturbance, which are also qualifying disabilities under IDEA. In 2004, researchers reported that nearly two-thirds of children in classes for students with emotional problems also have ADHD. Since it is not unusual to find a student in a special education class who also has an undiagnosed attention deficit, it is important for multidisciplinary teams to also screen that population for ADHD-related problems. If a student appears to have more than one of the disabilities defined in IDEA, he or she should be evaluated in each of the disability categories, and the Individualized Education Program (IEP) should address the unique needs of the student related to each of the disabilities [34 C.F.R. §300.304(c)(4)(6)].

   Medical Diagnosis of ADHD: Not all states require a diagnosis by a medical doctor for eligibility under the OHI category. Regardless, a medical diagnosis of ADHD alone doesn't make a student eligible for services under either Section 504 or the IDEA. (Additional guidance is available with regard to 504 in the publication *Frequently Asked Questions about Section 504 and the Education of Children with Disabilities*—Question #24, March 2009—Office of Civil Rights, OCR.) A sample diagnostic report is provided in Summary 48. A more detailed report was written than usual because the school system, based upon their evaluation, originally indicated the student wasn't eligible for services.

2. **What Should I Do If a Student is Struggling and I Suspect ADD or ADHD?** Often, experienced teachers say that they "know" a student has an attention deficit, even though he or she has not been evaluated or labeled. In this situation, teachers may recommend that a child be screened, although they should never suggest a diagnosis of ADHD to parents. Teachers must walk the fine line between honoring their experience and avoiding premature conclusions and labels. Rather than ask, "Does this child have ADHD?" teachers may ask first, *"Is something interfering with this student's learning?"* If the answer is "yes," the next question should be, *"What should I do now?"*

   Teachers are encouraged by law to provide Early Intervening Services (EIS) and to implement a Response to Intervention (RtI) process when any student is struggling in class due to academic or behavioral challenges such as getting started and finishing work, remembering homework and long-term projects, and being organized. Read Summary 52 for more suggestions to incorporate accommodations and strategies into an effective RtI plan. Examples of steps to ensure teachers can take to ensure that students are successful at school are provided below. Additional information is available in the "Parent Brochure on RtI" on the National Center for Learning Disabilities website (www.NCLD.org).

3. **What "ADHD Behaviors" (in Addition to Inattention) Should be Addressed in an IEP or 504 Plan?** Several unique, yet less well-known, challenges face many students with attention deficits and should be addressed by the 504 Plan or IEP. Many of their "ADHD Behaviors" are linked to their three-year brain maturity delay and thirty percent delay in development of executive skills. See Summary 52 for more details.

- Deficits in working memory: memory skills that are essential for writing essays, doing complex math problem, and understanding what they read
- Difficulty getting started and finishing tasks
- An impaired sense of time: often late, don't manage time well
- Difficulty controlling emotions; more likely to speak impulsively or "blow up"
- Difficulty using "self-talk" to control behavior
- Difficulty analyzing, problem solving, synthesizing, and implementing a plan
- Slow reading and writing: produce less written work, read less material
- Disorganization: lose things; disorganized notebooks, backpacks, and lockers
- Forgetfulness
- Undiagnosed coexisting conditions like learning disabilities or depression that make it more difficult to learn (see Summary 78)

4. **What Is EIS?** Schools should develop early intervening services (EIS) for students who are not eligible for special education but are struggling and need academic or behavioral supports. Up to 15 percent of a district's federal special education budget may be spent on these services: evaluations, services, supports, scientifically based literacy instruction, and professional development.

5. **What Is RTI and Why Is It Important?** Response To Intervention (RtI) is a new term that was added to the 2004 revisions to IDEA. The National Association of State Directors of Special Education (NASDSE) define RtI as the practice of providing high-quality instruction and intervention matched to student need, monitoring progress frequently to make decisions about change in instruction and goals, and applying the child's response data to important educational decisions.

In a Wrightslaw article, Susan Bruce described it more simply: "the purpose of RtI is to catch struggling children early, provide appropriate instruction, and *prevent* the need to refer the child for special education." See Summary 44 for more details.

6. **What Are Positive Behavior Interventions and Supports?** The term positive behavior interventions and supports (PBIS) could almost be used interchangeably with Response to Intervention (RtI). Simply stated, PBIS refers to implementation of preventive strategies for helping students succeed in school even if they haven't been evaluated for special education eligibility. The services may be organized for an individual or schoolwide. A schoolwide system promotes a positive environment—for example, by focusing on teaching students specific actions such as showing respect, sharing, keeping your hands to yourself, or not bullying. Research results for the combined individual and schoolwide PBIS programs are impressive: reduced behavior problems, improved grades, reduced referrals for special education assessments.

The next section gives a better explanation of how PBIS works for an individual. Visit www.pbis.org for more detailed information on PBIS, Functional Behavior Assessments (FBA), and Behavior Intervention Plans (BIP). Additional information is available in Chapter 5.

7. **What Are Functional Behavior Assessments (FBA) and Behavior Intervention Plans (BIP)?** When students have shown a pattern of several disruptive incidents at school—especially if they place the student at-risk of a school suspension—a multidisciplinary team should meet to discuss strategies to prevent the problem behavior from recurring.

A good FBA will address several key issues: behavior, context, antecedent or "trigger" behavior, contributing factors, function of behavior, teacher response, student reaction, continuation of behavior, potential rewards, and previous effective interventions. This analysis of problem behaviors will help in the development of an effective behavioral intervention plan (BIP).

Here's an example: a student habitually failed to pay attention and complete his work in his 8 am language arts class. The teacher did a systematic assessment of the situation and discovered several things. There were three antecedents ("triggers" to the behavior): 1) the student took his ADHD medication as he rode to school in the car, and it wasn't effective until halfway through the class. 2) Based upon the ratings on the Dendy medication effectiveness rating scale for school (A9 and A10), it was highly likely that the medication dose was too low, since he was having problems paying attention in most of his classes. 3) The student was experiencing several deficits commonly associated with ADHD: limited working memory, difficult organizing, sequencing and paraphrasing written work, difficulty knowing where and how to begin on a lengthy project. Interventions suggested for challenges 1 and 2 were to take medication an hour earlier and show the doctor the medication rating scales to see if he would consider increasing medication. For challenge 3, the teacher provided graphic organizers to help with writing and practicing paraphrasing information and suggested some after school tutoring.

8. **Can Students with Attention Deficits Also Have Learning Disabilities?** Yes. Twenty-five to fifty percent of students with ADHD quality as having a specific learning disability under federal laws. Dr. Russell Barkley has reported significant learning disabilities in several areas: reading (8-39 percent), math (12-30 percent), and spelling (12-27 percent). In addition, two researchers, Dr. Susan Mayes and Susan Calhoun, found that 65 percent of these students had deficits in written expression. See Summary 50.

9. **What Can Be Done for Students Who Were Evaluated But Not Found Eligible for Services?** Sometimes school systems evaluate students for Specific Learning Disabilities only and mistakenly indicate that the student isn't eligible for special education services. If an evaluator states that a student is not eligible for services, the question must be asked, "What IDEA category was she evaluated under?" If the answer is SLD, then a request should be made to also assess under OHI. If OHI criteria are not met, then assessment under Section 504 is in order. Typically, testing for both SLD and OHI is most helpful. The evaluation can identify specific academic deficits.

10. **Does a Student Have to Be Failing Any Classes to Be Eligible for Services?** No. Federal law makes it clear that a student does *not* have to be failing to be eligible for services. According to the 2004 IDEA regulations [(300.101)(c)(1)] and an April 5, 1995 DOE policy statement (*Letter to Lillie*, 23 IDELR 714, OSEP):

> The evaluation should "consider information about outside or extra learning support provided to the child when determining whether a child who received satisfactory grades is nevertheless not achieving at age level. The child's current educational achievement may reflect the service augmentation not what the child's achievement would be without such help."

The 2004 regulations explain that students are eligible for a free appropriate public education, "even though the child has not failed or been retained in a course or grade, and is advancing from grade to grade."

In summary, a child may be making good grades primarily due to two reasons: 1) medication which the ADA refers to as a "mitigating measure" and 2) the academic scaffolding support provided by the parent. Both of these two reasons must be taken into consideration in determining eligibility. The question must be asked: "if you removed both of them would the student still be successful?" According to ADA, decisions of eligibility must be made "without regard to the ameliorative effects of mitigating measures, such as medication...." See Summary 49.

11. **What about Bright Children Who Are on Grade Level But Not Achieving Up to Their Ability?** These children may be eligible for service in certain situations. The 1995 OSEP memo also noted that:

> "...a student may be eligible for services 'if the team determines that the child does not achieve commensurate with his or her age and ability levels....'"

In this situation, specific interventions may be provided in their IEP or 504 Plan, however, these plans are not required to maximize a student's potential.

12. **Can Gifted Children with a High I.Q. Be Eligible for Services?** Sometimes; however, the determination is usually made on a case-by-case basis. Not all gifted children with ADHD will be eligible. The 1995 OSEP memo states that "there is no categorical exclusion for children with high IQs…therefore, if a student with a high I.Q. is not achieving at this expected performance standard," and also meets eligibility criteria, the student can be eligible for services. Researchers indicate that roughly one-sixth of gifted students have a disability. The student could have dual classification of Gifted-OHI or Gifted-LD. "Each child who is evaluated for a suspected learning disability must be measured against his own expected performance, and not against some arbitrary general standard." If gifted students are struggling academically yet are not considered for special education, parents should consider bringing this information to the teacher's attention. See Summary 10 for more general information.

13. **Should the beneficial effects of medication on academic performance be taken into consideration when determining eligibility for services under IDEA?** According to Federal law, ***absolutely yes!*** After all, if medication is working effectively, students will not exhibit as many symptoms of ADHD and will be more successful academically. According to Mary Durheim, the question the school should be asking is, "If the child is *not* taking her prescription medication on a daily basis, will there be a substantial limitation in her learning?" If the answer is yes, then the child is most likely eligible for services. Congress revised the Americans with Disabilities Act (ADA) in 2008 (S.3406) to say that schools must *not* consider the "ameliorative effects" of medication and present accommodations when determining eligibility. Durheim explains that ADA law trumps both IDEA and Section 504. Obviously, schools can't discriminate against people who have disabilities that interfere with their ability to learn. See Summary 49.

One parent who was also a doctor actually told school officials, "If you won't consider my child for special education, I'll be glad to take him off his medication for a month." That usually gets the school's attention. However, I'd advise against taking students off medicine, since the student may then have a serious blow-up or receive a school suspension.

If necessary, request a letter of support from the treating physician, who can point out that administering a test for ADHD to a child while she is on medication and then using that as the primary factor in determining eligibility is not a valid use of the test. A major drawback in these ADHD tests is that they don't identify deficits in executive functions, which may well be the primary reason for school failure. Consider requesting that a test to identify executive function deficits (such as the BRIEF) be conducted.

14. **What Should Be Done If a Student Has an IEP But Continues to Struggle?** Here's what advocate Dixie Jordan, PACER Center, has to say about students who have an IEP under IDEA, yet are failing in school:

> "We should never have a child with an IEP who is failing. That is a clear signal that something is terribly wrong with the IEP. Perhaps, expectations were too high, interventions were not intensive enough or the duration of the intervention was not long enough. School failure is a signal for scheduling an IEP meeting immediately and revising the goals or adding needed services."

Changes must be made to the IEP or 504 Plan so that the student is more likely to experience success in school! See Summary 44 for more details.

15. **Must Classroom Teachers Provide the Accommodations on a Student's IEP?** Yes. Teachers are obligated to comply with the IEPs developed by the local IEP team. In 1993, a West Virginia teacher refused to read tests orally to a student, as was required by the IEP. Even after urging by the principal and superintendent, the teacher refused to comply with the IEP. The student failed history and was barred from extracurricular activities. Subsequently, the parents sued and won a $15,000 judgment from the teacher alone. Because the school system, principal, and superintendent fully supported the provision of the accommodation, they did not have to pay any legal fines.

16. **If Students with ADHD Break School Rules, How Should They Be Disciplined?** A student with ADHD who breaks a major school rule can be disciplined like any other student, including being suspended from school for up to 10 days. After that time, the IEP team must hold a "manifestation determination hearing" to decide if the behavior was related to the disability or if it was the direct result of the school's failure to implement the IEP. See Summary 45 for additional information and suggestions.

17. **Why Is It Important to Establish Disability Eligibility No Later Than High School?**

Additional Support Needed for College: Some bright students with ADD or ADHD not previously evaluated under IDEA may just be getting by academically because they are on medication, their parents are providing intensive support, and their teachers are making teaching adjustments. If these supports are withdrawn when the student reaches college or technical school, she may flounder and fail. Consequently, establishing 504 or IDEA eligibility no later than the secondary school years is important for obtaining services later in college or vocational school environments. Postsecondary institutions will provide eligible students with reasonable accommodations similar to the ones they received in high school (but require documentation of the student's learning problems and the subsequent provision of specific accommodations that were provided previously in high school). Students must still meet the "essential elements"/basic requirements of the program, however. See *Teenagers with ADD & ADHD,* Chapter 15 for more information.

Accommodations on SAT/ACT: Since 1995, meeting eligibility criteria for accommodations on the SAT and ACT has become increasingly more difficult. Both SAT and ACT have endorsed a policy that was developed by a group known as the ADHD Consortium to determine eligibility criteria for accommodations on tests. According to this policy, having an IEP or Section 504 Plan is important, but in isolation is not sufficient documentation to receive testing accommodations. The new policy requires a lengthy comprehensive evaluation by a licensed professional that is not older than three years. A copy of the policy is posted on both the SAT and ACT websites.

Conclusion

Unaddressed academic and behavioral needs of students with attention deficits take a toll on their educational performance, as evidenced by higher dropout rates, lower graduation rates, lower grade averages, higher rates of suspensions and expulsions, and lower college attendance. Unfortunately, academic problems among these students also take a tremendous emotional toll on the whole family since the student is aware that she is smart enough to "do better" and yet is at a loss to explain why she can't do the work. The tragedy here is that most students with ADHD can be successful in school if the disorder is treated and effective intervention strategies are offered.

Resources

In addition to the federal laws, the following resources were helpful:

Durheim, Mary (educational consultant, Section 504 hearing officer, and mediator). Personal interviews, 2010.

Dendy, Chris A. Zeigler, Durheim, Mary, and Teeter, Anne. *CHADD Educator's Manual on ADHD.* Landover, MD: CHADD, 2006.

Office of Special Education and Rehabilitative Services. "Joint Policy Memorandum (ADD)." September 16, 1991. The full text of this landmark memo can be found online on many websites, including on the Wrightslaw site (www.wrightslaw.com/law/code_regs/OSEP_Memorandum_ADD_1991.html).

SUMMARY 43
Overview of IDEA: A Federal Education Law

The Individuals with Disabilities Education Act (IDEA), a federal education law, ***provides for a free appropriate public education to children with disabilities who have an educational need and meet eligibility criteria.*** Roughly 50 percent of students with attention deficit disorder may need services under IDEA, either in special classes or within a regular classroom setting. The remaining students who need help can be adequately served in their regular classroom with supports provided under Section 504. (See Summary 49.) Only a few students with attention deficits may *not* need or qualify for any extra classroom supports. Contrary to what the law requires, many students with ADHD are not being considered for, or are unfairly being denied, special education supports.

Definition of a Child with a Disability/Other Health Impairment (OHI)

Only children who have a disability are qualified for special education services under this federal education law. IDEA includes thirteen categories of disabilities under which children can qualify. If students with ADHD need services, IDEA makes it clear they should receive services under a category called ***Other Health Impairment*** (OHI). See Summary 47 for more detailed information about eligibility criteria.

The official definition of a "child with a disability" under the OHI category includes

- Attention Deficit Disorder (ADD), and
- Attention Deficit Hyperactivity Disorder (ADHD).

According to Federal regulations, **OHI** means:

"having limited strength, vitality or alertness, including a heightened alertness to environmental stimuli, that results in limited alertness with respect to the educational environment, that...

   a. is due to chronic or acute health problems such as asthma, attention deficit disorder, or attention deficit hyperactivity disorders, diabetes, epilepsy, a heart condition, hemophilia, lead poisoning, leukemia, nephritis, rheumatic fever, sickle cell anemia, and Tourette syndrome; and
   b. adversely affects a child's educational performance" [§300.8(c)(9)].

Key Provisions of IDEA

1. **A free appropriate public education (FAPE):** Schools must provide a free education for all students, even those with disabilities. Most school systems develop a range of services, including classroom accommodations, so that the student can be served in a local public school. Otherwise, if they can't serve the student, the school system may have to pay a larger public school system, a private school, or a residential school to provide an education. "Appropriate" means a program designed to provide some "educational benefit."

2. **An Individualized Education Program (IEP):** An IEP is a written plan jointly developed by teachers, parents, and the student that identifies strengths, challenges, goals, needed services, and expected benefits. Reasonable accommodations, supplemental aids, and services are provided based upon information from the evaluation. Amendments may be made to the IEP as needed without calling

an IEP meeting, if both parents and the school consent. If adequate progress is not being made on IEP goals, the IEP Team must review the IEP within 30 days. See Summaries 51 and 52.

3. **Parental involvement:** Parents are considered "equal participants" in making educational decisions as members of the IEP Team that determines eligibility and placement and develops the IEP.

4. **Right to remedy (due process):** If teachers and parents disagree about the evaluation, IEP, reasonable accommodations, or placement, then parents have the right to appeal decisions at an impartial hearing. Typically, a signature document is presented at the meeting. Sometimes signing the document means that parents agree with the IEP that is developed at the meeting, but sometimes it just means that they attended the meeting. If parents disagree with the findings and recommendation, they may choose to note this near their signature on the cover sheet.

5. **Education in the least restrictive environment (LRE):** The LRE is the educational setting that enables a student to have the most contact with typically developing peers and still meet his individual goals for learning. Schools must first provide services to the student in the regular classroom, with the help of reasonable accommodations, if necessary. For children with more serious challenges, supplementary aids and services such as a one-on-one behavioral aide or tutor may be provided as part of a Behavior Intervention Plan (Summaries 52 and 66). For some students, the LRE may be part-time or full-time placement in a special class, a separate school, a therapeutic day program, or other alternative.

6. **Nondiscriminatory evaluation:** Schools must do a comprehensive evaluation of academic, developmental, and functional behavior to determine whether a child qualifies for services. For ADD and ADHD, that may mean paying careful attention to test results in areas that are related to this condition, such as attention, working memory, cognitive processing, or organizational skills. (See Summary 6 for examples of diagnostic tests.)

7. **Positive Behavioral Supports: PBS means providing** positive behavioral intervention strategies for the student whose behavior impedes his learning or that of others. For example, when a student cannot focus on completing school work, it impedes his ability to learn and positive behavioral strategies (i.e., a Behavior Intervention Plan) should be implemented.

More on IEP Teams

All decisions regarding the student's educational placement, eligibility for classroom accommodations and/or modifications, or other supportive services must be made by the IEP team. IEP teams serve several major functions: 1) determining special education eligibility, 2) developing the IEP, 3) conducting Manifestation Determination Reviews, and 4) determining appropriate placement. In some states, one committee may serve all these functions. In other states, there may be two or three separate committees.

Each IEP team must include:

1. parents;
2. at least one special education teacher, if any time is or may be spent in special education;
3. at least one regular education teacher, if the student is or may be in regular classes or other activities;
4. at least one team member who is knowledgeable about the child and the disability;
5. a local school representative qualified to supervise special education who has the authority to allocate resources;
6. a person to interpret evaluation results, typically the school psychologist;
7. others at the parent's or school's discretion;
8. the student, once he reaches age 14 or 16, depending on the age that transition planning is initiated under state regulation. Ultimately, parents should encourage

their teen to attend the sessions, especially if the discussion will be a positive experience for him. Obviously, if the meeting may damage the student's self-esteem because negative comments may be made about him, it would not be in his best interests to attend. Instead, students may submit input in writing or through an earlier discussion with the parent or teacher. If parents/teachers have comments they don't want the teenager to hear, they should discuss them via email or phone *before* the meeting. When the student reaches the age of majority (18, in most states), he is the person who decides who can attend his IEP meetings. See Summary 69 for a discussion of self-advocacy.

Teacher attendance: Note that the 2004 revisions to IDEA state that teachers may be excused from the IEP meetings if the IEP issues to be discussed do not involve their curriculum area, but only with written parental permission. Teachers may be excused even if their curriculum issues are being discussed if they submit input in writing, and again with written permission from a parent.

Evaluation and Eligibility

- **Evaluation:** Suspicion that a disability exists triggers legal obligations requiring a formal evaluation. According to federal law, once parents sign a consent for an evaluation, the school system has 60 days to determine eligibility for special services. Reevaluation will be done every three years, unless the school and the parents agree that it is unnecessary.

- **Early Intervention Services:** Federal statutes encourage the provision of early intervention strategies prior to testing through two new services: *Early Intervening Services (EIS)* and *Response to Intervention (RtI)*.

- **Specific Learning Disability (SLD) eligibility:** The IDEA revisions of 2004 state that schools will "not be required to take into consideration whether a child has a severe discrepancy between achievement and intellectual ability" [Section 1414(b)].

- **Failing grades and IDEA eligibility:** Federal law makes it clear that a student does *not* have to be failing to be eligible for services. According to the 2004 IDEA regulations [(300.101)(c)(1)], a student is eligible for a free appropriate public education, "even though the child has not failed or been retained in a course or grade, and is advancing from grade to grade."

Academic, Student Assessment, and Testing Issues

In addition to the mandatory IEP requirements, the following issues must also be addressed:

- **Accommodations** (extended time, preferential seating) in the classroom or school day. Materials, instructional methods, testing methods, etc. may be adapted so that a student with disabilities can still receive the majority of instruction in a regular classroom. A list of *reasonable* classroom accommodations, such as tutors or one-on-one behavioral aides, is available in Summary 46.

- **Measurable annual goals,** complete with objective criteria showing how they will be assessed

- **Assistive technology** devices and services (such as a calculator, laptop computer, Alpha Smart, Phonic Ear, spell checker). See Summary 16-E for more details. Obviously, students must be taught to use these devices efficiently.

- **Supplementary aids and services** (notetaker, speech therapy, counseling, occupational therapy). See Summary 16-E.

- If English proficiency is limited, services to address the student's **language needs**

■ **Extent to which (the amount of time) the child is not in regular class and extracurricular activities**

■ If a student's disability prevents him from participating in **extracurricular events,** these barriers must be identified and appropriate accommodations provided. For example, teachers may need to repeat directions or double check to see that a student understands their instructions. To be eligible to participate, the student must meet the same grading criteria as other students—for example, maintain a C average. However, if the student qualifies under IDEA or Section 504, the student may receive accommodations in the classroom to help prevent future failure. In addition, students placed in classrooms outside of their neighborhood school may return to attend their home high school prom, participate in after school clubs, or go to their graduation ceremony.

■ **An extended school year (ESY),** if found necessary based upon the student's needs and his IEP. If needed services are currently not available, the school system will have to develop the services. See the discussion in Summary 51.

■ **Alternative testing** arrangements for state- or district-wide tests (modifications such as extended time, use of a calculator, testing in a room with no distractions. See below.)

■ **Progress reports and records,** including regular updates for parents (with reports on progress in the general curriculum given at least as often as for students in regular education) and parental access to all of the student's school records (not just "relevant" ones)

Disputes and Disciplinary Issues

■ **Mediation:** A dispute resolution proceeding conducted by an impartial third party must be offered if parents and school officials reach an impasse and cannot agree upon the student's evaluation, placement, or IEP.

■ **Disciplinary Action:** Disciplinary guidelines are detailed in Summary 45, including key revisions enacted in 2004.

■ **Change in placement:** IDEA 2004 gives school officials the authority on a "case by case" basis to consider unique circumstances when determining whether a student's placement should change because of rule violations. An IEP meeting must be called whenever the school considers any change in placement, including most suspensions of more than 10 school days (since a suspension or expulsion is considered a change in placement). The team must:
  ● review the behavior,
  ● determine if the behavior is related to the disability, and
  ● determine the punishment. In some school systems, punishment is predetermined for certain drug, alcohol, or physical violence offense. See Summaries 62-66 on behavioral strategies.

■ **Education at another school or tutoring in the home:** This must be provided if the student is suspended for more than 10 days or expelled (*if the misbehavior is related to the disability* and none of the offenses noted in the preceding paragraph have occurred).

■ **Limits on the length of suspensions:** Except for drug/alcohol or weapon offenses, or physical aggression, there are limits to how long a student may be suspended. See discussion in Summary 45.

Other Important IDEA Provisions

See Summary 44 for more details on some of these issues that were changed when IDEA was amended in 2004.

■ **Related Services:** Students may receive any "related services" recommended in the IEP—e.g., counseling groups, occupational therapy, instructions regarding study skills, organizational strategies, time management, problem solving, and/or anger management. (See Summaries 32-38 and 64-70 for tips on teaching these skills.)

■ **Supports for Regular Classroom Teachers:** Teachers must be provided the supports they need to implement the IEP. Teachers should be asked, "What do you need to make this IEP work?" For example, in some instances, the teacher may need a classroom or teacher's aide.

■ **Transfer Students:** Students with an IEP who transfer to another school system must receive comparable services at the new school until a new IEP is developed.

■ **Individualized Transition Plan (ITP):** By age 16, a detailed ITP must be developed and implemented to help students prepare for life after graduation (transition into a job, vocational training, or higher education). The 2004 revisions added the term "further education" and require "effective transition services to promote successful post-school employment and/or education." A student may receive these services at age 14 if the IEP team (or state law) deems it necessary. ITPs are discussed in more detail in Summary 53.

Impact of IDEA and Its Revisions on Students with ADD or ADHD

A summary of the impact of IDEA on students with ADD or ADHD is provided below. Obviously, this overview only touches on the highlights of the law and is not intended to serve as legal advice. The actual law itself is complex, totaling hundreds of pages in length. Of course, with a complicated law like IDEA, there will always be some exceptions to these general statements. A more careful review of the law and state regulations will be necessary if conflicts arise between the school and family.

Key IDEA Revisions Pursuant to 2004 Law

Major revisions to IDEA were enacted by Congress in 2004, and U.S. DOE regulations accompanying the law were released in 2006 and additional regulations in December 2008.

The IDEA revisions having a major impact on teachers and parents of these students include:

- **Early intervention:** Encourages early intervention strategies prior to testing through two services: *Early Intervening Services (EIS) and Response to Intervention (RtI)* (see below for an explanation);

- **Prompt evaluation:** Requires completion of an evaluation within a maximum of 60 days or less if mandated by the individual state after receipt of a signed parental consent;

- **IEP contents:** Mandates that IEPs must include statements regarding the student's present levels of academic achievement and developmental and functional performance (very important!). See Sections 2 & 3 for potential identification of areas to be addressed in the educational plan;

- **Goals:** Requires *measurable* annual goals, including academic and functional goals [Section 1414(d)(1)(A)]; goals cannot be broad, vague statements; eliminates short-term objectives for all students except those with the most significant disabilities;

- **Measuring IEP progress:** Requires IEPs to state how a student's progress will be measured; obviously, inclusion of short-term objectives would be a great way to accomplish this even though they are not mandated by law;

- **IEP Changes:** Allows changes to IEP without a meeting; IEP team members must be notified of changes;

- **IEP meeting attendance:** Allows IEP team members to be excused from meetings in certain situations;

- **Frequency of evaluations:** Allows the IEP team to ignore the requirement that reevaluations must be done every three years, if both parents and the team agree;

- **Services for transfer students:** Requires that students with an IEP who transfer to another school system must receive comparable services;

- **Transition services:** Requires the transition process (not just a plan) must begin at age 16;

- **Misbehavior linked to disability:** During "Manifestation Determination Reviews," shifts requirement to prove misbehavior is related to a student's disability from the school to parents;

■ **Placements in relation to disciplinary actions:** Eliminates the student's right to "stay put" in his current placement during disciplinary procedures;

■ **Removal of students from their regular placement:** Allows decisions to remove a student to be made on a case-by-case basis; this gives administrators more flexibility in determining disciplinary action;

■ **Length of suspensions:** Changes limits on removal of a student from class as a disciplinary action from 45 days to 45 *school* days;

■ **Requires written submission of due process complaint:** Parents must follow certain steps and submit a written report of the problem, including facts and contact information, and a proposed resolution to the local school system and state education office.

Highlights of IDEA—Part B

1. **Provision of Reasonable Classroom Accommodations:** Under IDEA, teachers must make a variety of changes in the classroom to help students with disabilities achieve some *"educational benefit."* For example, they might change the way the student is taught or tested, adjust class scheduling, or modify homework. A list of suggested accommodations is included in Summaries 16-A to 16-E, 46, and 51-52.

2. **Provision of Early Intervening Services (EIS):** Schools should develop early intervention services for students who are not eligible for special education but are struggling and need academic or behavioral supports. Up to 15 percent of the special education budget can be spent on these services: evaluations, services, supports, scientifically based literacy instruction, and professional development.

3. **Utilization of Response to Intervention (RtI):** Response to Intervention (RtI) is a new term that was added to the IDEA 2004 revisions. According to a Wrightslaw article written by Susan Bruce, "the purpose of RtI is to catch struggling children early, provide appropriate instruction, and prevent the need to refer the child for special education." According to Mary Durheim, an educational consultant, these early intervention strategies must be provided in addition to the core curriculum; they do not replace it.

Data must be collected to determine RtI eligibility. Durheim explains that before a student is considered for eligibility under RtI, the evaluation must look at two factors: 1) the effectiveness of the teacher, and 2) the response of other students to the curriculum. If the core curriculum has been shown to be effective for at least 75 to 80 percent of their same age, grade-level peers and the teacher's performance is judged to be effective, then the student will be fully assessed.

One commonly used model of RtI involves a three-tiered system:

■ Tier 1 includes provision of grade-level general education instruction with screening and identification of at-risk students;

■ Tier 2 requires more intensive supplemental instruction and intervention in a group of perhaps 3 to 5 students and progress monitoring conducted at least bi-weekly. For example, if a student had difficulties with written expression, specific instruction for improving writing skills could be taught in a small group of 3-5 students.

■ Tier 3 provides the most intensive supplemental instructions and interventions in a one-on-one setting. If a student's writing disability is so significant that he cannot benefit from small group instruction, then one-on-one instruction will be provided.

■ If the student still cannot perform up to grade-level after a month or so at Tier 3, an in-depth evaluation can be conducted to identify specific learning challenges and targeted intervention strategies. Although parents may request an evaluation any time through this process, the school system has the right to refuse to evaluate if the data clearly show that: 1) no interventions (RtI) have been tried first, or 2) the child doesn't have a disability.

Five key components of RtI include the following:

- **Scientifically research-based instruction:** All children should receive research-based instruction in the general education classroom.

- **School-wide screening:** Schools should screen all children early to determine if they are "at risk."

- **Continuous progress monitoring:** Schools should monitor the progress of all "at risk" children to determine if they are benefiting from instruction.

- **Fidelity:** Schools must use any program or curriculum correctly and as intended.

- **Procedural safeguards:** Schools must ensure parents are aware of their rights.

If well implemented, this strategy can be a huge help to struggling students with ADHD or ADD. Students may begin receiving help immediately, rather than waiting months for a formal evaluation.

If a student is still struggling, must she wait for an RtI plan to be implemented and fail before an evaluation can be done? The answer is no. OSEP addressed this issue in a February 12, 2011 policy memo that stated "it would be **inconsistent** with the evaluation provisions in the IDEA regulations for an LEA to. . . reject a referral and delay provision of an initial evaluation on the basis that a child has not participated in an RTI framework."

Academic Performance/Eligibility Criteria
1. Failing Grades and IDEA eligibility

Contrary to common belief, children with ADD/ADHD can be passing classes and still be eligible for services under IDEA. Occasionally teachers tell parents incorrectly that their child isn't eligible for special education services because the student is making passing grades. However, federal law makes it clear that a student does *not* have to be failing to be eligible for services. According to the 2004 IDEA regulations [(300.101)(c)(1)] and an April 5, 1995 DOE policy statement (*Letter to Lillie*, 23 IDELR 714, OSEP):

The evaluation should "consider information about outside or extra learning support provided to the child when determining whether a child who received satisfactory grades is nevertheless not achieving at age level. The child's current educational achievement may reflect the service augmentation not what the child's achievement would be without such help."

In other words, educators should take into consideration that students with attention deficits may be passing their classes primarily because of medication or the Herculean efforts of students, parents, or tutors. If these supports are withdrawn, the student's academic performance may decline significantly. Regardless of how bright a student is, if she is failing, extra supports will be needed.

The 2004 regulations explain that students are eligible for a free appropriate public education, "even though the child has not failed or been retained in a course or grade, and is advancing from grade to grade." Furthermore, according to *Wrightslaw,* "If the child is making progress on his IEP goals, but is receiving failing grades or is not making adequate progress in academic areas, this may be evidence that the child is not receiving a free appropriate public education." Provision of FAPE is mandated by law.

According to Dixie Jordan, PACER Center, the student's ability to meet "age/grade appropriate standards of personal independence and social responsibility" should also be taken into consideration during an evaluation. The importance of these skills is often overlooked. Unfortunately because of their significant developmental delay and executive function deficits, students with attention deficits often appear immature and unmotivated. In reality, they simply lack the necessary skills for independence.

2. Specific Learning Disability (SLD) eligibility

For a child to meet SLD eligibility in the past, she had to have a severe discrepancy between achievement and intellectual ability. However, thanks to changes in the IDEA revisions of 2004, schools now have the option of no longer requiring the severe discrepancy

[Section 1414(b)]. To determine eligibility now, the IEP team "may use a process that determines if the child responds to scientific research based interventions as part of the evaluation process."

The landmark 1991 OCR & DOE memorandum clarified that attention deficits may coexist with learning problems: "There is a growing awareness in the education community that attention deficit disorder (ADD) and attention deficit hyperactive disorder (ADHD) can result in significant learning problems for children with those conditions...."

Individualized Education Program (IEP)

The purpose of developing an IEP is to identify each student's strengths and needs, develop a plan to meet those needs, and then deliver needed services. It is important to remember that ***the student's needs, not the disability category, must drive the educational plan!*** So, if a student with ADD/ADHD needs specific services, such as tutoring in math, she may attend a class where she can receive that service, even if it is labeled the "SLD classroom" or "Varying Exceptionalities Resource classroom."

Mandated Components of the IEP

See Summary 51 for more details.

1. **Present level of academic achievement and related developmental needs,** including strengths, academic achievement and developmental and functional performance.

2. **Goals** for academic, developmental, and functional issues, including expected achievement; goals must be measurable.
    2.1.1. state how progress will be measured and when progress reports will be provided.

3. **Assessment;** justification for alternative assessments and evaluation tools selected.

4. **Research-based intervention:** IEP must include "a statement of the special education and related services and supplementary aids and services, *based on peer-reviewed research* to the extent practicable to be provided to the child" [Section 1414(d)(1)(A)(i)(IV)].

5. **Evaluation** procedures; completion of evaluation within 60 days from the time parents sign a consent form.

6. **Services** to be provided and time to be spent in regular education.

7. **Transition service** needs addressed by age 16 or earlier if needed or required by state law.

8. **Dates** of services.

Disciplinary Issues under IDEA

In general, the new IDEA revisions focus on helping students succeed by intervening early and using positive behavioral interventions to avoid as many behavior problems as possible. If students do have behavior problems, teachers must determine what may have triggered their failure or misbehavior (the antecedent behavior). Pursuant to Response to Intervention (RtI) guidelines, appropriate interventions must then be put in place to address behavioral and academic issues. Finally, if the student already has an IEP or 504 Plan, it must be reviewed and modified as needed.

1. **Consequences of Breaking Major School Rules.** A student with ADHD who breaks a major school rule can be disciplined like any other student, including being suspended from school for up to 10 days. After that time, the IEP team must hold a "manifestation determination hearing" to decide if the behavior was related to the disability or it was the direct result of the school's failure to implement the IEP. Alternative disciplinary procedures to existing school policies can be written into the IEP or 504 Plan.

   However, a child may be removed from his school and placed in an "Interim Alternative Educational Setting" for up to 45 school days for any of the following problems: drugs, weapon, inflicting serious bodily harm, or unique circumstances on a "case by case" basis. If a student does not have an IEP or Section 504 Plan, yet the school had reason to believe he had a disability because the parents had previously requested an evaluation or school personnel had expressed concerns, these same rules apply with certain exceptions (parents refused an evaluation or the evaluation showed no disability). However, accuracy of the evaluation could be an issue—frequently ADHD and executive function deficits are missed in school evaluations.

   When the characteristics of an attention deficit disorder (e.g., impulsivity or forgetfulness) are found to contribute to behavior problems, the school should conduct a Functional Behavior Assessment (FBA) plus develop a positive Behavior Intervention Plan (BIP) to address the behavior. The school should also reconsider any existing IEP or 504 Plans. The plan may have to be revised with more appropriate interventions or accommodations or teachers may need to be given instructions on how to implement the IEP correctly. Punishment alone is not sufficient and will not change behavior long-term. New skills must be taught. The teachers may also need training for coping with ADHD behaviors.

2. **A Behavior Intervention Plan (BIP).** When a student disrupts class, uses profanity with teachers, refuses to follow school rules, or misbehaves in other unacceptable ways, the school is required to focus on why the behavior occurred. After conducting a Functional Behavior Assessment (FBA), the school will typically develop a *Behavior Intervention Plan*. Implementing the strategies in the plan should prevent reoccurrence of these same problems. The school has a responsibility to develop a clear plan to teach the student positive behavioral skills to substitute for inappropriate behavior.

   Deficits in executive function may also be addressed in BI plans to help the student cope or compensate for attention deficits. The new law emphasizes using behavior plans *earlier* to prevent more serious problems. See Summary 68 for guidance on conducting an FBA and developing a Behavior Intervention Plan.

   - If a student's misbehavior cannot be handled by the classroom teacher, a *Functional Behavior Assessment* will be conducted and then a *Behavior Intervention Plan* developed as part of the IEP.
     - *Functional Behavior Assessment (FBA):* These assessments are intended to *identify the antecedent event* (the action that triggers misbehavior).

When a student is referred for an evaluation or staffing at an IEP meeting, the school psychologist or diagnostician will identify problem behaviors by talking with the student and teachers involved and ideally observing the student participating in a challenging academic situation. Based upon the assessment, the school may change antecedent behaviors or consequences of the student's misbehavior. See Summary 68 for more details.

- Next, a **Behavior Intervention Plan** is developed and implemented.
- If the present **Behavior Intervention Plan** isn't working, school personnel must revise and change it to address the behavior that resulted in the suspension.

■ A student who is **suspended for more than 10 days** in a school year and whose behavior is a manifestation of the disability must have a Functional Behavior Assessment and a Behavior Intervention Plan.

3. **Case-by-Case Determination of Removal.** The 2004 revisions to IDEA allow school personnel to consider any unique circumstances on a case-by-case basis when determining whether to suspend, expel, or place a student with disabilities in an Interim Alternative Education Setting (IAES). According to www.FAPE.org, this provision can be helpful for teachers or parents "to quote when they are having trouble proving that their child's behavior is a manifestation of the disability. It serves to remind the school personnel that common sense should prevail and all circumstances should be considered."

4. **Change of Placement.** Examples of changes of placement include school suspension beyond 10 days, expulsion, placement in an **Interim Alternative Educational Setting (IAES),** and high school graduation with the same diploma as any other student.

■ Only an IEP Team or occasionally a hearing officer may make a change in placement. Any time a change of placement occurs, an IEP Team meeting must be scheduled.

■ The school may remove a student to an *Interim Alternative Placement Setting (IAES)* immediately if drugs, weapons, or dangerous behavior are involved.
- However, if a school system wishes to quickly remove a student from his present placement because of alleged violent behavior, an **expedited due process hearing** must be held first and a hearing officer must determine if the violent behavior is dangerous. Typically, an immediate and substantial risk of injury or harm to self or others must be present before a student may be removed from his home school.
- If the school schedules an expedited due process hearing, the new IEP and recommended placement may take effect within 10 days unless the parents object.

5. **School Suspensions.** Most school suspensions beyond 10 days are considered a **change in placement,** so state and federal review policies must be followed. For disciplinary purposes, school systems may:

■ **suspend a student for up to 10 days** (for violations of school regulations), **without an IEP meeting**. Educational services are not required for the first 10 days of a suspension.
- If a suspension **exceeds 10 days during a school year,** the school must provide the educational services necessary for the student to appropriately progress in the general curriculum and advance toward achieving the goals in the IEP. The IEP Team will determine what services are needed.

■ **suspend a student for additional removals of up to ten days** as long as removals do not constitute a pattern
- If a student is repeatedly suspended for the same behaviors, an IEP meeting and a special review known as a **Manifest Determination Review** will be required before disciplinary action is taken.

- **remove** *the student to an Interim Alternative Education Setting for* up to 45 *school days,* for possession of drugs or weapons or for dangerous behavior, if students without disabilities are disciplined the same way for the same misbehavior.

6. **School Expulsions.** A school expulsion is different from a suspension. Typically, a student is suspended for less serious offenses for only two or three days, although it may be up to 45 school days. When a student is expelled, it is for more serious offenses and often involves a removal from the home school for perhaps a year or sometimes permanently. However, even when a special education student is expelled, the school system is still responsible for providing a free appropriate education.

   - When a student is expelled from school, it is considered a change of placement, so an IEP meeting and a Manifestation Determination Review must be held.

   - Some systems have alternative schools where these students are educated. For example, at a special program developed by the school system in Kenosha, Wisconsin, students receive a half-day of academic instruction. During the last half of the day, social services (child welfare, juvenile justice, and mental health staff) conduct groups to teach needed skills such as anger management, conflict resolution, and problem solving.

   - Smaller school systems may provide needed educational services through contracts with larger school districts.

7. **Interim Alternative Education Setting (IAES).** An IEP team or hearing officer now may place a student in an IAES (another school setting), but for no more than 45 *school* days, not calendar days. The following conditions must be met:

   - The student is allowed to participate in the general curriculum (continue the same subject content).

   - The student continues to receive special education services that enable him to meet the goals of his IEP.

   - School officials provide services designed to teach alternatives to problem behavior that led to placement in the IAES.

Timely notifications and reviews are required:

   - If a student is placed in an IAES, school officials must notify parents of that action no later than the day they make the decision.

   - As soon as possible, but within 10 days after the change of placement decision is made, the IEP team must determine if the behavior is a manifestation of the child's disability.

8. **"Stay Put" Requirement.** According to www.FAPE.org, the 2004 revisions to IDEA eliminated the right of a student with a disability to "stay put" in his current educational placement while the student or family appeals his alleged violations of the school code. This is in contrast to previous versions of IDEA that permitted the student to stay in his current placement pending an appeal. However, a student with an IEP plan cannot be removed from his current placement without a Manifestation Determination Review, below. Ultimately, when students are placed in any alternative setting, teachers and parents must remain vigilant to ensure that students receive FAPE services designed to meet goals that are outlined in the IEP/504 Plan.

9. **Manifestation Determination Review.** Before a student who is eligible for services under IDEA is suspended for more than 10 days, expelled, or placed in another setting, a Manifestation Determination Review must be conducted to determine whether the misbehavior is a manifestation of

the student's disability. According to a Wrightslaw publication, the IEP team must determine if the behavior "was caused by or had a direct and substantial relationship to the child's disability" or whether the behavior was the "direct result of the local education agency's failure to implement the IEP" [Section 1415(k)(1)(E)]. Current IDEA revisions shift the responsibility from the school system to parents to prove that the child's disability is linked to the behavior.

Because of these changes, teachers and parents must pay careful attention to the behavioral needs of the student that are written into the IEP or 504 Plan. Even if the child has not previously been subjected to disciplinary actions, parents must anticipate and identify potential problem areas in the "present level of academic achievement and *related* developmental needs" section or the IEP/504 Plan—e.g., impulsivity (actions and words), forgetfulness, lack of forethought (not thinking ahead of consequences), impaired sense of time, and oppositional behavior including talking back and fighting.

- If the parents and IEP team members can't agree that the conduct was caused by or had a direct and substantial relationship to the disability, parents should indicate their dissent. They may request mediation or a hearing.

- If the student's conduct was directly related to the district's failure to implement the IEP, then the district's failure must be considered when determining consequences for the student.

- If the behavior *is related* to the disability, the IEP Team must determine appropriate services and placement. In other words, special education students may be disciplined differently than the stated school discipline procedures. The school may impose a disciplinary action that is appropriate for the student's disability.

- If the misbehavior *is not related* to the student's disability, then the school may use the same discipline procedures it uses with all other students. However, the school must continue to educate the student.

Conducting a manifestation determination review a school must:
- consider the special education evaluation,
- observe the student,
- consider the IEP and the student's placement, and determine if the placement is appropriate.

In addition, the school must decide based upon documentation and teacher/school psychologist verbal reports:
- if the IEP and placement were implemented (i.e., if the behavior was the direct result of the school's failure to implement the IEP).
- if supplementary aids and services were provided,
- if behavioral intervention strategies were provided, The key issue here is whether the student has a neurological disorder such as ADD or ADHD that may interfere with his ability to control his impulsive behavior.

10. **Injury to Self or Others.** A due process hearing officer may also order placement in an IAES, even if the parents object, if the current placement is substantially likely to result in injury to the student or others. If the student has a previous history of causing harm to other students or himself, it will be provided to the hearing officer. Otherwise, it may be necessary for a professional with psychiatric training such as a medical doctor, nurse, or social worker to evaluate and report to the hearing officer.

11. **Definition of a Weapon.** IDEA defines a weapon as:

- "weapon, device, instrument, material, or substance, animate or inanimate, that is used for or is readily capable of, causing death or serious bodily injury,

- except..."a pocket knife of less than 2½ inches long."

12. **Students Not Yet Eligible for Services.** If a student has a disability that was never identified, and is facing major disciplinary action such as suspension or expulsion, he is eligible under the provisions of IDEA in certain circumstances:

   ■ If the school had knowledge that the child had a disability;

   ■ If the parents stated in writing that the child needed special education;

   ■ If the child's behavior or performance demonstrated the need for special education;

   ■ If the child's teacher expressed concern about the child's behavior or performance to other school personnel.

   The school must set aside disciplinary actions until an evaluation has been completed.

13. **Mediation or a Mandatory Resolution Session.** Before parents can participate in a due process hearing, they must first participate in mediation or a "resolution session." A meeting with the parents and key members of the IEP team will be held within 15 days of receipt of a "due process" complaint. Teachers may be asked to participate in this process, and, if so, may help by suggesting academic or behavioral interventions to address problem areas. The district has 30 days from when the complaint is filed to satisfactorily resolve the complaint with the parents; a due process hearing can occur after that. If parents seek legal advice, they will have to pay their own attorney's fees.

14. **Due Process Complaint Notice.** As explained earlier, if parents disagree with the school's disciplinary ruling, parents must file a complaint with their local school system and state. According to www.FAPE.org, a new provision provides that the school district shall file a response within 10 days unless the district within 15 days notifies the state hearing officer that it is challenging the sufficiency of the parent's due process complaint notice. In other words, the school disagrees with the parent's complaint and doesn't believe that they can work out a compromise with the parents. The State hearing officer has 5 more days to report his ruling.

15. **Avoid Due Process Hearings, If Possible.** Generally speaking, it is best for the school and parents alike to resolve their differences in mediation or resolution sessions. Due process hearings are lengthy and costly to all involved parties. According to www.wrightslaw.org, wounds created from the lengthy adversarial process never heal and the student may end up paying the ultimate price for this conflict. In addition, parents will have to pay legal costs if they lose their case.

4

SUMMARY 46

Reasonable Accommodations: 1991 U.S. DOE/OCR ADD/ADHD Policy Memo

Prior to 1991, federal IDEA guidelines regarding ADD/ADHD were nonexistent. As awareness grew about the impact of attention deficit disorders on school performance, the U.S. Department of Education and Office for Civil Rights jointly issued a key policy statement regarding the education of these students. The major elements of that policy memo were incorporated into the subsequent IDEA revisions. Policy memos are very important documents because they have the effect of law, and, as such, affect court decisions. A copy of this landmark policy is available at www.wrightslaw.com/info/add.index.htm under "Legal Resources."

This DOE/OCR memo contained specific suggestions regarding **reasonable accommodations** that teachers will find helpful. The memo, which applies to development of both IEPs and Section 504 Plans, basically states that if ADD or ADHD **"adversely affects a child's educational performance,"** then the student is entitled to extra supports and accommodations in the classroom. The accommodations provided in the column on the left are listed almost verbatim from the US DOE/OCR memo. The accommodations listed in the column on the right are suggestions from several veteran educators and from my own experience as a teacher and school psychologist. Frequently, experienced teachers have been providing accommodations such as these for many years. They automatically make adjustments for any students who are struggling, whether or not they are eligible for services under IDEA or Section 504. These accommodations are often listed in the student's IEP under educational services to be provided.

US DOE/OCR Memo (1991)

- structured learning environment
- repeat and simplify instructions
- provide visual aids
- use behavior management
- adjust class schedules
- modify test delivery
- use tape recorder
- computer-aided instruction
- audio-visual equipment
- modified textbooks or workbooks
- tailor homework assignments
- consultation
- reduce class size
- a notetaker
- one-on-one tutors
- special resources
- classroom aides
- modify nonacademic times (lunchroom, recess, PE)
- services coordinator or case manager to monitor student progress and ensure implementation of the IEP

Additional Suggestions

- give extended time on tests, homework, projects, if needed; teach skills, give supports for timely submission of work
- pair with student who checks that assignments are in writing
- appoint "row captains" who remind students to write assignments & take up work
- give guided lecture notes (S 16-A)
- use weekly progress reports
- break assignments into segments; grade sections separately
- use overhead projector or interactive whiteboard for teaching
- meet teacher at end of day; check homework & books
- model desired skill (teacher)
- send extra set of books home
- use of calculator
- reduce distractions (don't seat near door or pencil sharpener)
- give multiple choice tests
- give oral tests, if needed
- don't reduce grade for poor handwriting
- put month's assignments in writing
- use Books on Tape
- teach skills: organizational, time & anger management
- study skills class
- use multisensory approach
- seat positive role models nearby
- use flashcards
- use mnemonics
- give chapter outlines
- use two desks that the student moves between
- allow the student to stand if she chooses
- use color to note and avoid errors, e.g., highlight changes of math signs
- keep same teacher 2nd semester, if successful

SUMMARY 47 What Is Other Health Impairment (OHI)?

Before seeking an evaluation, a teacher who is concerned about the academic progress of a student with an attention deficit should seek advice from other school personnel. Veteran teachers may suggest interventions to eliminate the need for an evaluation. Fortunately, students no longer have to wait for a special education evaluation before receiving needed services, thanks to the 2004 IDEA revisions. For example, EIS (early intervening services) or RtI (response to intervention) are programs specifically developed to offer immediate services to struggling students. If these interventions do not help, teachers may then make a referral to the IEP eligibility team. The team will decide whether or not to ask a diagnostician or school psychologist to conduct an evaluation and determine the proper special education eligibility category.

Other Health Impairment (OHI) Definition

OHI means:

> "having limited strength, vitality or alertness, including a heightened alertness to environmental stimuli, that results in limited alertness with respect to the educational environment, that . . .

> is due to chronic or acute health problems such as asthma, attention deficit disorder, or attention deficit hyperactivity disorders, diabetes, epilepsy, a heart condition, hemophilia, lead poisoning, leukemia, nephritis, rheumatic fever, sickle cell anemia, Tourette syndrome; and adversely affects a child's educational performance" [§300.8(c)(9)].

Prior to 2004, many teachers thought students with attention deficits could qualify for special education services only under the categories of specific learning disability (SLD) or emotional/behavioral disorder (EBD). Some teachers hesitated to refer a student for special education evaluation if they were pretty certain the student didn't meet the stringent criteria for SLD or EBD.

When students with ADHD were referred for an evaluation, they were sometimes evaluated only for the presence of SLD or EBD. Many were then denied services under IDEA because "they did not have a significant discrepancy between the test scores for their intelligence (IQ) and academic achievement." Many school evaluators made this statement because they incorrectly believed that all students had to demonstrate a test score discrepancy for eligibility. However, the eligibility category of **Other Health Impairment** *has never required* a test discrepancy score. Regardless, the 2004 IDEA revisions now make it clear: no student, not even if seeking SLD eligibility, is evaluated *solely* on the basis of significant test score discrepancy!

Determining OHI Eligibility

Keep in mind that each state has its own specific requirements for OHI, which you may determine by asking a local special education teacher, the school psychologist, or the special education director for the school system.

OHI Guidelines

Although the information required by your state for the OHI label may not be precisely the same as in this example, most likely the same general types of information (academic and medical) may be needed. In Georgia, two key steps are necessary for determining OHI eligibility. They are: completion of

1. the school eligibility report, and
2. a diagnostic report from either the student's physician or a licensed psychologist.

School Eligibility Report: School personnel will gather relevant information and complete an eligibility report. Any required formal testing may be done by the school psychologist or an educational diagnostician, but the teacher may be asked:

1. to complete a behavior rating scale, and
2. to describe the student's academic performance and behavior with regard to alertness in class (paying attention, sleeping), class participation, independent work habits, getting started on and finishing tasks, completing homework, ability to complete tests within class timeframes, grades received in class to date, potential underachievement, relationship with peers, and compliance with rules. Related developmental needs should also be described, including strengths, academic achievement, and developmental and functional performance.

Remember, students with attention deficits can be passing classes and still be eligible for services under IDEA. Keep in mind that class failure is not the only determining factor for eligibility. Sometimes, students with ADD or ADHD may be passing their classes primarily because of the extraordinary efforts of parents and tutors. Clearly, however, failing a class is an obvious indicator that the "student's learning is adversely affected by his or her ADD/ADHD."

According to a policy memo from the Office of Special Education (OSEP) dated April 5, 1995, "the evaluation should consider information about outside or extra learning support provided to the child when determining whether a child who receives satisfactory grades is nevertheless not achieving at age-level. The child's current educational achievement may reflect the service augmentation, not what the child's achievement would be without such help." These policy statements have the same force as educational law.

Diagnostic Evaluation: A physician or licensed psychologist may complete a diagnostic report and include the information listed below. As part of this evaluation, a good social-medical history may be obtained. Sometimes, the doctor, psychologist, or school social worker may complete this type of interview. Whoever does the interview should look for coexisting conditions that may affect a student's school performance, including: anxiety, depression, executive function deficits, sleep disturbances, deficits in math computation, or problems with memorization. Examples of information that may be obtained in this interview are included below in parenthesis. A completed sample medical report is provided in Summary 48 and in Appendix 4, in my first book, *Teenagers with ADD and ADHD, 2nd ed.*

1. Diagnosis and medical history: *(ADD, ADHD, depression, anxiety, sleep disturbance)*
2. Current medication/side effects: *(Vyvance and Zoloft; even with medication, forgetfulness, disorganization, and an impaired sense of time may still be problematic)*
3. Conditions that may interfere with regular attendance or functioning in school; concerns identified by parents: *(difficulty paying attention, forgetfulness, disorganization; sleep disturbance, tardiness; academic problems, math computation deficits & slow processing speed; memory problems, difficulty getting started and finishing—common executive function deficits)*
4. Medical prognosis: *(excellent, if student continues to take medication and school provides needed supports, accommodations, and/or modifications)*
5. Recommendations and comments: *(schedule difficult classes earlier in the mornings, provide appropriate supports, classroom accommodations, and/or modifications)*
6. Signature: (doctor)

Next, the IEP team will review all relevant materials and make a decision regarding OHI eligibility.

General Observations

In the past, many teachers were unfamiliar with the term *Other Health Impairment (OHI)*, primarily because it was a seldom-used and relatively unknown special education category. However, **ADD and ADHD have been included in the list of eligible conditions under Other Health Impairment (OHI) since the 1997 IDEA revisions.**

Clearly, **the OHI category is a better diagnostic match for ADD and ADHD than SLD or EBD.** Most students with attention deficits never quite fit the criteria for a specific learning disability (SLD) or emotional and behavioral disorder (EBD). However, some schools have begun giving dual diagnoses—for example, when both ADHD and SLD are present.

Although up to 50 percent of students with ADD/ADHD have learning disabilities, they may not meet the strict eligibility criteria for a specific learning disability. See Summary 50. One major drawback to eligibility under SLD is that a student's academic performance may improve to the point the school declares him ineligible for SLD. Yet the organizational and memory challenges associated with executive function deficits remain.

Some students with attention deficits also qualify for the Gifted and Talented program. As explained in Summary 10, roughly one-sixth of students who are intellectually gifted have a learning challenge of some kind.

The remaining possibility is the EBD category. This category is not always appropriate either, since the behavior problems of students with attention deficits may not be as severe as those of their peers in the EBD class. Furthermore, the behavior problems of concern may be the direct result of the failure to address hidden academic and executive function challenges associated with ADD/ADHD. Not only is OHI a better diagnostic match, but parents and teenagers themselves may prefer OHI (or SLD) since these labels are often less stigmatizing than EBD.

Sample Diagnostic Report

The following report was developed for a student who was initially evaluated only under specific learning disabilities (SLD) and subsequently was declared ineligible for services under IDEA. The school failed to assess the child under the other health impairment (OHI) category or Section 504 eligibility criteria. The parents then asked that their son be evaluated for services under the OHI category. The report represents findings from a medical doctor and a school psychologist. If a psychologist or counselor does not work for the doctor or if the school seems unable to identify learning challenges, parents are encouraged to find someone locally to identify the student's academic and learning issues. This report also highlights issues that schools either fail to address as part of the evaluation or assess inappropriately. Since this particular student's school appeared to be unaware of some recent changes in the laws, the report cites specific statutes and is more detailed than may be necessary in most situations.

STUDENT DIAGNOSTIC REPORT
(medical and psychological)

Name: Hunter   **Age:** 13   **Date:** July 1, 2010

1. **Diagnosis and medical history:** Hunter is currently being treated for Attention Deficit Hyperactivity Disorder by Dr. Kathleen Smith. He was first diagnosed with ADHD combined type in 2007. His mother has discussed his academic struggles in conversations with both Dr. Smith and a private school psychologist throughout the school year.

2. **Current medication/list side effects:** Hunter is taking 40 mg. Vyvance once daily. If he forgets his medication, he may be inattentive, disorganized, and impulsive at school.

3. **Medical prognosis.** Good; if Hunter continues to take his medication and the school provides the additional supports and supervision that are needed. Medication helps with attention but never addresses all the related learning challenges associated with ADHD.

4. **Describe any condition that may interfere with regular attendance or functioning in school:** Based upon a review of the school evaluation that was completed in May, a consultation with the treating physician and with a former teacher and school psychologist, as well as a consultation from Hunter's mother, it is apparent that Hunter is experiencing several of the common challenges that students with ADHD often face at school. Hunter wants to do well in school but will need additional supports and supervision to achieve his potential.

   - **Deficits in executive function skills** resulting from the three-year brain delay associated with ADHD specifically affect organization of both materials and academic assignments, initiating and finishing work in a timely manner, and time management. These EF deficits have a profound impact on his academic struggles.

   - **Past School Performance:** At various time throughout the year, Hunter had 9-week grades in the 60s in two classes: English and Math. Hunter's grades vary from highs to lows. Fortunately, he finished the year with a passing grade in English; however, he barely passed Math with a D. Teachers reported that he had problems paying attention in class, getting started and completing assignments, and getting completed work into a notebook and properly organizing it in sequence. Teachers also reported that he seemed to daydream, didn't pay attention, and didn't always use his class time wisely. Of course, from outward appearances, he appeared not to be trying very hard, but in reality these are the manifestations of the symptoms of ADHD and executive function deficits.

■ **Specific learning challenges**: Hunter exhibits several learning deficits that have interfered with his ability to learn and be successful in school:

- *Difficulty getting started, organizing strategies to complete tasks, and then completing a task in a timely manner, especially in situations requiring the student to work independently.*
- *Difficulty organizing and completing class projects that take more than one or two days.*
- *Inattentive and forgetful;* may not pay attention, daydreams and drifts off task; forgets to turn in homework that is completed.
- *Slow cognitive processing* (reads and write slowly, slow calculation of basic math facts, which means the student will produce less written work and is more likely to have incomplete class and homework).
- *Poor memory and memorization skills* (difficulty remembering assignments and due dates, memorizing isolated facts such as multiplication tables, history or other math facts, and formulas.

Suggestions for addressing these challenges are provided in the final report section on recommendations.

■ **School evaluation**: Key issues identified in select sections of the school evaluation include the following:

- **Woodcock-Johnson III & State-Mandated Tests**: Hunter is learning despite his challenges paying attention, getting started and completing his work in a timely manner. His academic achievement scores are in the average range, with vocabulary scores above average.

- **ADDES-3**: The results of the ADDES are not relevant in this situation since Hunter's ADHD has already been diagnosed and he was on medication. If medication is working properly, as it obviously was, his behavior rating scores would be expected to be in a normal range. ADA laws provide guidance here:

    Revisions to the American's with Disabilities Act (ADA) effective January 1, 2009 addressed this issue. The ADA amendments are significant because they also apply to IDEA; otherwise the school would be guilty of discriminating against the student. The law states:

    "The determination of whether an impairment substantially limits a major life activity shall be made without regard to the ameliorative effects of mitigating measures such as—
    ➤ *Medication*, medical supplies
    ➤ Use of assistive technology
    ➤ Reasonable accommodations or auxiliary aids or services, or
    ➤ Learning behavioral or adaptive neurological modifications."

- **WISC-IV**: Perceptual reasoning was identified as one of Hunter's strengths. Differences between the highest and lowest scores on the WISC Indices totaled 27 points and that was greater than the 15-point standard deviation established by the test. This discrepancy is statistically significant and indicative of learning challenges in processing speed and working memory, both key executive skills. Practically speaking, slow processing speed results in the student producing less written work, assignments taking longer and not being completed within the allotted time. Working memory impacts the ability to hold information in mind and manipulate it to achieve an answer; working memory is a critical skill for writing essays and completing more complex multistep math problems. This may explain why English and Math are the two classes Hunter nearly failed.

- **Classroom observation:** The classroom observation was conducted during a high-interest math game. As expected, Hunter was on task during this time. Research has shown that students with ADHD can pay attention more easily when participating in active, high interest games. That's why active learning activities are helpful for these students. An observation during a more demanding classroom situation would have been more appropriate.

5. **Recommendations and Comments:** Based upon the data that we've collected, Hunter appears to be a child with a disability who has significant educational needs. His problems have continued from grade to grade. Each year his mother has to return to school, re-explain his learning challenges, talk with a new set of teachers, share information regarding ADHD, convince them of his educational need, and develop a new intervention plan.

Recommendations:

5.1. Assess Hunter for special education eligibility under the OHI category, and, if needed, Section 504 of the Civil Rights Law.

According to federal Education and Civil Rights laws:
- ➤ **OHI** "means having limited strength, vitality or alertness, including a heightened alertness to environmental stimuli, that results in limited alertness with respect to the educational environment, that . . .
  - ➢ is due to chronic or acute health problems such as asthma, **attention deficit disorder, or attention deficit hyperactivity disorders**, diabetes, epilepsy, a heart condition, hemophilia, lead poisoning, leukemia, nephritis, rheumatic fever, sickle cell anemia, and Tourette syndrome; and
  - ➢ adversely affects a child's educational performance" [§300.8(c)(9)].

Section 504 & ADA state:
"No otherwise qualified individual with a disability in the United States . . . shall, solely by reason of his or her disability, be excluded from participation in, be denied the benefits of, or be subjected to discrimination under any program or activity receiving Federal financial assistance...."
29 USC §794(a), 34 CFR §104.4(a)

Under the law, ***"qualified individuals with a disability"*** are those students who:
- ➤ *"have a physical or mental impairment which substantially limits one or more of such person's major life activities (Learning, reading, concentrating, thinking and communicating are specifically listed as examples of "major life activities."); or*
- ➤ *have a record of such an impairment; or*
- ➤ *be regarded as having such an impairment."*
34 CFR §104.3(j)(l)

5.2. Consider providing these accommodations to address his learning challenges:

- ➤ **Completion of class and homework;** provide more supervision and monitoring of class and homework, notify parent of incomplete work; as needed, send home weekly email notices; parent will ensure completion and return of work to school.

> ➤ **Inattention/difficulty starting and finishing:** additional prompts by the teacher or another student to help Hunter refocus; develop a private reminder—e.g., pull on ear, walk by and tap his desk.
> ➤ **Forgets assignments:** post homework assignments on a school website; identify a student in classroom Hunter can call as needed to determine assignments; leave an extra set of books at home.

➤ **Completion of long-term projects:** Hunter will need more prompts and supervision to finish any long-term project. The parent will be notified of any major project requiring ongoing work for more than two days; action steps for completion will be broken down into segments; progress will be monitored a couple of times during the project time frame; organizational strategies will be taught for these projects; a job card may be provided; teacher will show the parent how to break down the project into manageable segments.

➤ **Slow processing:** if needed, shorten some assignments, give extended time if needed.

SUMMARY 49

Federal Civil Rights Laws: Section 504 and ADA

Most teachers and parents are well acquainted with the major provisions of IDEA related to the education of students with disabilities. It is also important, however, to be acquainted with two federal civil rights acts—Section 504 of the Rehabilitation Act of 1973 and the Americans with Disabilities Act—because they extend different rights to students than IDEA does. In a nutshell, here is why it is important to understand the provisions of these two laws:

- **Section 504** protects the rights of *all* students with disabilities to a free and appropriate education, not just the rights of students who qualify under IDEA. In addition, whereas IDEA services terminate after high school graduation, provisions of 504 continue after students graduate from high school and attend technical school or college.

- **The Americans with Disabilities Act (ADA)** prohibits "public accommodations" (including most schools) from discriminating against individuals with disabilities, which again means that *all* students with disabilities are guaranteed equal access to programs and facilities at schools, and this equal access applies across the lifespan, not just until high school graduation.

(Both laws also prohibit discrimination in employment and other areas as well, but a discussion of the full extent of the laws is beyond the scope of this book.)

Basically, these two laws ***prohibit discrimination against people with disabilities*** by any agency that receives federal funding. This is very important for students with ADHD, since some students with this condition may not qualify for special education services under IDEA, yet still need accommodations to address their significant learning challenges.

Major Section 504 Provisions

Because Section 504 only applies to programs receiving federal funding, it generally covers students in public school, but not most private schools. Section 504 guidelines require the *provision of "appropriate educational services designed to meet the individual needs of such students to the same extent as the needs of student without disabilities are met."* The service array available pursuant to 504 includes, *"education in a regular classroom, education in a regular classroom with supplementary services, and/or special education and related services."* Section 504 guidelines are almost identical to IDEA, with a few exceptions:

- A Section 504 Plan is developed instead of an IEP.
- The Office of Civil Rights (OCR) clarified that a Section 504 reevaluation is similar to an IDEA re-evaluation.
  - Specifically, this applies to a change in placement for academic or disciplinary reasons. If the school wishes to suspend one of these students for more than 10 days, there must be a re-evaluation of the student's situation and services outlined in the 504 Plan.
  - Termination of services also requires a re-evaluation before the student can be dismissed from any program.
- When disagreements arise between the school and families, OCR may facilitate mediation through a procedure known as *"Early Complaint Resolution."*

There are also subtle differences in the level of services offered under IDEA vs. Section 504. Under Section 504, schools are only required to provide "commensurate opportunities" to students with disabilities when compared to their nondisabled peers. Under IDEA, schools must provide an education that provides some "educational benefit" to students with disabilities. Obviously, legal aspects of Section 504 are open to interpretation and vary widely, just as with IDEA. Generally, the intensity of services delivered under IDEA may be greater than under 504 to ensure that the student "benefits"—in other words, improves academically or behaviorally. However, most schools do their best to help all students regardless of IDEA or 504 eligibility.

Typically, the issue of educational benefit comes into play only if parents sue the school system because their child's academic achievement is below expected levels. For example, an eleventh-grade student with an above average IQ was provided half an hour of reading instruction weekly pursuant to his IEP but was still reading on a fourth-grade level. The school had met its obligations under Section 504 but *not* under IDEA. In 1993, the U.S. Supreme Court ruled in *South Carolina vs. Carter* that the student did not benefit from the educational program provided by the school and ordered that the parents be reimbursed for tuition in a private school. This type of ruling by the courts is the exception rather than the rule.

Steps for Obtaining Services Under Section 504

Before a student pursues eligibility for IDEA or Section 504, other interventions such as Response to Intervention must be implemented and proven unsuccessful. If a student fails to progress appropriately, he would most likely be referred for an evaluation under IDEA. If he was found ineligible under IDEA, he could then be evaluated under Section 504. Subsequently, the steps for obtaining services under Section 504 are similar to IDEA requirements. In general, a teacher would begin by talking with the person who chairs the Section 504 eligibility committee. (The school may have more than one committee that determines eligibility for services under IDEA and Section 504.)

Evaluation and Eligibility

Eligibility criteria for Section 504 are broader than IDEA, making it easier for children with neurobiological disorders like ADD/ADHD to receive services.

Both Section 504 & ADA state:
"No otherwise qualified individual with a disability in the United States . . . shall, solely by reason of his or her disability, be excluded from participation in, be denied the benefits of, or be subjected to discrimination under any program or activity receiving Federal financial assistance...."

29 USC §794(a), 34 CFR §104.4(a)

Under the law, a **"qualified individual with a disability"** is "a person who:
1. has a physical or mental impairment which substantially limits one or more of such person's major life activities [Learning, reading, concentrating, thinking and communicating are specifically listed as examples of "major life activities"]; or
2. has a record of such an impairment; or
3. is regarded as having such an impairment."

34 CFR §104.3(j)(I)
S.3406—4, E

So, the question that the school must answer is whether or not the student's ability to learn is impaired by his ADD or ADHD. To help teachers and parents understand this law, each local school system has developed a policy statement on Section 504 and has a designated Section 504 coordinator.

Although evaluation criteria vary from state to state, evaluations for 504 eligibility are usually not as formal as IDEA evaluations. ***Schools must consider a variety of sources;*** for example, a medical diagnosis, aptitude and achievement tests, teacher recommendations, physical condition, social and cultural background, and adaptive behavior. A medical diagnosis alone does not make a student eligible for services, but may be one of the many factors considered in the evaluation. In addition, an evaluation may involve a review of the cumulative folder, past grades, and classroom observation. Intelligence tests are not required and cannot be used as the only factor in determining eligibility for services. See Summary 48 for a discussion of what to look for when reviewing information.

When determining eligibility, *"mitigating measures"* such as medication, tutoring, or parental supervision that contribute to the child's current successes can't be considered. The question must be asked, "How would this child function without these supports?"

Development of a Section 504 Plan

Although there is no formal mandate for a written Section 504 Plan, most schools elect to develop one anyway. In addition, schools may keep minutes of the 504 meeting. Basically, a Section 504 Plan is like a stripped-down version of an IEP. Students with 504 Plans usually do not have as many needs as students with IEPs, so they may not receive as many accommodations. However, students served under Section 504 Plans have the right to access most of the same intervention strategies and classroom accommodations as students with IEPs. The information contained in Summaries 51-52 on developing an IEP will also help teachers develop a Section 504 Plan.

The Office for Civil Rights (OCR) provides limited guidance regarding the content of the 504 Plan. However, some local school systems have developed their own guidelines. Although a uniform format is not mandated, following the basic content of the IEP may be helpful. In particular, it is important to identify strengths, learning or behavior problems, and necessary classroom accommodations. Although transition plans are not addressed in Section 504, it would be in the student's best interest to provide some transition services. A member of the staffing team will be designated to write up the plan and distribute copies to each involved teacher, administrator, the parents, and the student's records.

Once a student has a 504 Plan, his disability must generally be taken into account in disciplinary actions by the school. Although not mandated under civil rights law, some current legal rulings have held that a Manifestation Determination Review must be held prior to any change of placement. See Summary 45 for an explanation of Manifestation Determination Reviews.

The Americans with Disabilities Act (ADA)

ADA often overlaps and complements Section 504. For example, Section 504 prohibits discrimination in federal grants and programs. However, ADA broadens the prohibition of discrimination from agencies receiving federal funding to *all* public entities, meaning facilities such as schools and universities that are open to the general public. (Generally speaking, it applies to all schools except those run by religious entities.) In addition, the ADA broadens anti-discrimination protection to before-school and after-school activities.

Although the definitions of an individual with a disability in ADA and Section 504 are identical, ADA is a statute that has broader application than Section 504. This means ADA and its regulations apply to Section 504.

In 2008, amendments were made to the ADA clarifying that eligibility must be made "based upon the child's disability as it presents itself without mitigating measures" (medications, hearing aids, accommodations, etc). In other words, if the child's academic success is the result of additional services that he received, he can't be declared ineligible for accommodations and other assistance at school. For example, students with ADD/ADHD may be succeeding academically because they are receiving medication, intensive tutoring, or supervision from parents who spend significant time keeping their child organized. Keep in mind that this applies for students being evaluated under IDEA also. The law states:

"(E)(i) The determination of whether an impairment substantially limits a major life activity shall be made ***without regard to the ameliorative effects of mitigating measures*** such as—

(I) ***medication,*** medical supplies, equipment, or appliances, low-vision devices (which do not include ordinary eyeglasses or contact lenses), prosthetics including limbs and devices, hearing aids and cochlear implants or other implantable hearing devices, mobility devices, or oxygen therapy equipment and supplies;

(II) use of assistive technology;

(III) reasonable accommodations or auxiliary aids or services; or

(IV) learned behavioral or adaptive neurological modifications."

S.3406—4, E

[bold print is the author's]

Also when the ADA was amended, Congress criticized some restrictive court rulings regarding the law and clarified that it was their intent to provide broad coverage under this act. Of primary importance, the ***definition of disability should be construed in favor of broad coverage of individuals to the maximum extent permitted by law.*** As a result of this statute change, many more children should receive services under Section 504. This is especially good news for students with attention deficits who may have been denied services under both Section 504 and IDEA.

Resources

Dendy, Chris A. Zeigler, Durheim, Mary, and Ellison, Anne Teeter. *CHADD Educator's Manual on ADHD*. Landover, MD: CHADD, 2006.

U.S. Department of Education. Articles on 504 include: "Frequently Asked Questions about Section 504 and the Education of Children with Disabilities" and "Free Appropriate Public Education for Students with Disabilities: Requirements under Section 504 of the Rehabilitation Act of 1973." www2.ed.gov.

Wright, Peter. Articles available on website include: "Civil Rights Law, Protection from Discrimination" and "Americans with Disabilities Act Amendments Act of 2008 (ADAAA)." www.wrightslaw.com.

The ADHD/SLD Connection: Specific Learning Disabilities (SLD)

SUMMARY 50

Specific Learning Disability (SLD) is an IDEA eligibility category that may apply to some students with ADD or ADHD. In the past, researchers have found that approximately *25 to 50 percent of students with attention deficits qualify for SLD in math, reading, or spelling*. In addition, research from Dr. Susan Mayes and Susan Calhoun has shown that nearly *65 percent of these students also have a learning disability in written expression.* This study of children who were referred to a child diagnostic center is one of the first clinical studies to evaluate the written expression skills of students with attention deficits. Of course, children who are referred to clinics for evaluation often have more serious learning problems, so the rate of problems found in this study is probably higher than a teacher would find in his or her own classroom.

The U.S. government first officially acknowledged the co-occurrence of ADHD and learning disabilities in the landmark 1991 Memorandum on ADD/ADHD that was jointly issued by the three premier agencies that control education for our children (see Summary 46). Specifically, education officials stated, "There is a growing awareness in the education community that ADD and ADHD can result in significant learning problems for children with those conditions."

A student may qualify for special education under the SLD category if she has significant learning problems in one or more of the seven areas listed below. These problems can't be otherwise explained by the presence of an intellectual disability, inadequate teaching, or speaking English as a second language.

- Oral Expression
- Listening Comprehension
- Written Expression
- Basic Reading Skills
- Reading Comprehension
- Mathematics Calculation
- Mathematical Reasoning

The ADHD/SLD Connection

Rates of learning disabilities found in children with ADHD:

- 8–39% in reading
- 12–30% in math
- 12–27% in spelling
- 65% in written expression (one study)

Determining SLD Eligibility

Sometimes scores on group achievement tests may be used for preliminary screening to determine whether further evaluation for SLD is needed. These tests include the IOWA Tests of Basic Skills (ITBS), as well as state achievement tests developed by many states.

Recent revisions to IDEA eligibility requirements for SLD reflect a significant improvement in identification of students with learning challenges. Prior to 2004, to qualify for SLD in many states, a student had to show a **severe discrepancy** between intellectual ability (IQ test scores) and academic achievement (reading and math grade level test scores from an achievement test). Key points from revisions to IDEA include:

1. Schools are not required to use the IQ-discrepancy model.
2. Schools must develop procedures to identify students with SLD that are based upon the child's response to scientific, research-based interventions.

Although severe discrepancies in test score are no longer mandated, a brief description of this model may be helpful.

1. a student receives a standardized achievement score on an individual achievement test such as the Woodcock-Johnson Psychoeducational Battery that is a significant number of points lower than
2. her cognitive ability score (IQ) on a test such as the Wechsler Intelligence Scale for Children (WISC-IV).

The point spread may need to be 20 points or higher, but varies from state to state.

Fortunately, states can no longer rely on the discrepancy formula as the sole determinant of eligibility for SLD. In addition, states now must consider not only academic achievement, but also functional and behavioral performance. Progressive states are relying less on point spreads and more on subtleties of the evaluation process. For example, the eligibility team may consider both **strengths and weaknesses** identified during the evaluation. Many states have broadened their definition of what constitutes a learning disability to include problems with processing information that is read, written, or spoken.

As discussed in Summary 44, IEP eligibility teams also consider information about the **student's classroom performance** in making their decisions. School psychologists may look at samples of written work, take current class performance into consideration, and compare the student's ability with her present achievement levels. Failure of classes is also taken into consideration. Students with passing grades may also be considered for eligibility, especially if the student is passing primarily due to the extraordinary efforts of parents and/or tutors

Gifted Students and SLD Eligibility. Unfortunately, in the past a student could have serious learning problems but not qualify for special education services. For example, a ninth-grade student with ADD/ADHD who had an IQ of 140 and achievement test scores for math and language skills on grade level probably would not have been eligible for special education under SLD even if she was failing five of six classes. Fortunately, today that is no longer true. The April 5, 1995 Office of Special Education (OSEP) Policy Memo also clarified this issue by stating that **students with high IQs may not be automatically excluded from the SLD disability category.** "Each child who is evaluated for a suspected learning disability must be measured against his own expected performance, and not against some arbitrary general standard."

Seeking Special Education Eligibility via ADHD vs. SLD: Generally speaking, it may be easier for students with ADHD and learning disabilities to receive special education eligibility under the Other Health Impairment category than the SLD category. Frequently students with ADHD do have significant learning challenges but they may not be severe enough to qualify for SLD eligibility. Furthermore, deficits in executive functions skills are more likely to be assessed in relation to ADHD but not SLD.

Resources

Barkley, Russell A. *Attention–Deficit Hyperactivity Disorder.* 2ⁿᵈ ed. New York: The Guilford Press, 1998.
Council for Exceptional Children. "A Primer on the IDEA 2004 Regulations." www.cec.sped.org.
Mayes, Susan Dickerson & Susan L. Calhoun. "Prevalence and Degree of Attention and Learning Problems in ADHD and LD," *ADHD Reports*, April 2000, Vol. 8, No. 2.
Wrightslaw. Helpful articles include: Is ADHD a Learning Disability? I've Been Told "No, It's Not" and "Response to Intervention (RTI): New Ways to Identify Specific Learning Disabilities." www.wrightslaw.com.

Writing an Individualized Education Program (IEP) for Students with ADD or ADHD

An IEP is a written plan that is mandated by federal education law (IDEA) for each eligible student with a disability. (See IEP discussion in Summary 43.) The IEP describes the special education and related services that each student needs.

To ensure that parents are actively involved in the development of the IEP, federal regulations state that the finalized IEP should *not* be written before the eligibility meeting. In other words, parents should not be given completed IEPs at the meeting and asked to sign them without ever having any meaningful input. This doesn't mean that there is no preparation for IEP meetings. Rather, most people, including parents, come to the IEP meeting ready to discuss several ideas. In fact, some teachers ask the parents' permission to develop a draft IEP in advance. However, they make it clear that it is only a draft and additions may be made easily.

Classroom teachers and parents play a key role in developing and implementing a successful IEP! Both of them have significant responsibility for:

1. identifying problem areas and strengths,
2. contributing suggestions for innovative interventions, and then
3. implementing the plan.

When developing an IEP, it is important to keep in mind that some of the student's behavior problems may actually be caused by unidentified learning disorders. So, addressing his academic problems is a critical step in the IEP process.

Typically, the school's role in implementing the IEP is the primary role that is written in the IEP. However, from a practical standpoint, the IEP reflects the teacher/parent partnership. So, I suggest spelling out in the IEP what teachers, parents, and the student will all do. The parent can be a more effective "equal participant" if actively involved in the IEP development and implementation.

Activities and responsibilities required by the IEP may be recorded in several different ways:

1. as a goal in the IEP,
2. as a program or service included in various sections, such as "special education program," "supplementary aides and services," "related services," or "assistive technology,"
3. checked off on a menu of services,
4. attached as a separate form such as an "Individualized Transition Plan,"
5. written in the minutes of the IEP meeting, or perhaps,
6. by verbal agreement, and not put in writing at all.

Mandatory Components of the IEP

IDEA requires that an IEP include these eight components:

1. **A statement of the child's present level of academic achievement and related developmental needs,** including strengths, academic achievement and developmental and functional performance. This section is very important; teachers and parents must identify strengths and needs, and especially executive function deficits in this section—such as difficulty getting started, disorganization,

difficulty completing long-term projects (impaired sense of time). Otherwise intervention strategies will not be targeted for these critical issues in the IEP unless they are first listed in this section as being problematic.)

2. **A statement of goals** for academic, developmental and functional issues including expected achievement; goals must be measurable.

    a. a statement of how progress will be measured and when progress reports will be provided (although objectives and benchmarks are no longer required except for those students who take alternative assessments). Progress toward goals must still be measured. (So parents may continue to request objectives; otherwise, it may be impossible to determine whether a student is making progress.)

3. **Assessment;** justification for alternative assessments and evaluation tools selected.

4. **Research-based intervention:** IEP must include "a statement of the special education and related services and supplementary aids and services, *based on peer-reviewed research* to the extent practicable to be provided to the child" [Section 1414(d)(1)(A)(i)(IV)].

5. **Evaluation procedures;** completion of evaluation within 60 days from the time parents sign a consent form.

6. **Services** to be provided and time to be spent in regular education,

7. **Transition service** needs. By age 16, goals for the transition after high school will be established and direct transition services will be provided. Services should focus on improving the academic and functional achievement of the child. For example, if the student plans to be a rock star, he should consider taking all the music courses that are offered. Services should include instruction, related services, community experiences, the development of employment objectives, and a vocational evaluation.

8. **Dates** of services; the projected dates for initiation of services and the anticipated duration.

What Should Be Done If a Student Has an IEP But Continues to Struggle?

Here's what Dixie Jordan, PACER Center, has to say about students who have an IEP under IDEA, yet are failing in school:

"We should never have a child with an IEP who is failing. That is a clear signal that something is terribly wrong with the IEP. Perhaps, expectations were too high, interventions were not intensive enough, or the duration of the intervention was not long enough. School failure is a signal for scheduling an IEP meeting immediately and revising the goals or adding needed services."

A 504 Plan or IEP may be ineffective for a variety of reasons; for example:

- All learning problems may not have been identified.
- Executive function deficits have not been addressed.
- Appropriate accommodations are not yet being provided.
- Effective accommodations are not being implemented consistently.
- Requirements of the IEP or 504 Plan are not being followed.

Regardless of the reasons for the ineffective IEP or 504 Plan, the bottom line is this—if the student has an educational plan and is still struggling or perhaps even failing, something is terribly wrong. ***Changes must be made to the IEP or 504 Plan so that the student is more likely to experience success in school!***

An IEP or 504 meeting may be requested at *any* time to revise the plan. A Functional Behavior Assessment (FBA) could be conducted to aid in development of a Behavior Intervention Plan (BIP) or Behavior Management Plan if the student also demonstrates behavior difficulties that interfere with his ability to learn.

Teacher Involvement in Developing an IEP

Usually, teachers are more heavily involved in developing certain sections of the IEP than others. Below are the areas where teachers are most likely to be asked to provide information or suggestions.

Identifying Problems and Strengths

Teachers should review the student's performance in their class and come to the meeting prepared to discuss his **academic and behavioral strengths and problems.** All too often, only behavior problems, such as emotional blow-ups, talking back and arguing, use of profanity, or other impulsive behaviors are addressed. Common academic problems and **executive function deficits** are frequently overlooked and should be considered. For example, problems with memorization, slow processing speed, written expression, complex multi-step math, disorganization, forgetfulness, or impaired sense of time are important to note.

When academic issues are dealt with effectively, behavior problems are often greatly reduced. For example, researchers tell us that when tutoring is provided for students with attention deficits, both academics and behavior improve. Conversely, when behavioral interventions alone are provided, academic performance may not improve.

Writing IEP Goals

Teachers should think ahead about the important issues to be addressed and come prepared to make suggestions for appropriate goals and intervention strategies. Although short-term objectives are no longer mandated for inclusion in IEPs, they remain the best indicator of whether or not goals are achieved. Even if objectives aren't written down, teachers must still use a similar mechanism to ensure that students achieve their IEP goals.

Objectives basically outline the action steps that must be taken to help the student achieve the IEP goal. With that idea in mind, several suggestions for goals and objectives are provided below as examples. Summaries in Section 2 (Academic Issues), Section 3 (Executive Function), and Section 6 (Classroom Management and Challenging Behaviors) should be especially helpful here.

Goals and objectives to address the important issues:

- **Goals:** Typically, goals are broader than objectives and cover a longer period of time such as a school year.
    1. *The student will improve written language skills so that he is on grade level by the end of the year.*
    2. *The student will maintain passing grades, C or higher.*
    3. *The student will improve memory skills by learning compensatory strategies.*
    4. *The student will explore career interests and become more aware of possible career opportunities.* (Example of a goal for an Individualized Transition Plan. See Summary 53 for more details on transition planning.)

- **Short-term Objectives:** Short-term objectives state what the student will learn and must be measurable. That is, the teacher must know when the student is successful. Objectives usually cover a shorter period of time, such as a grading period or quarter. Writing meaningful objectives is often very difficult. Here are several objectives to help the student complete homework, maintain passing grades, and improve memory or writing skills. A system for reminding the student to use the skills listed in these objectives will have to be built into the process. Progress will be assessed at the end of the grading period.

Objectives for meeting Goal 1: Improve written language skills

1. The student will improve written language skills from 6th grade level to an early 7th grade level (on grade level; based upon language arts teacher assessment compared with county writing standards; scores on the Woodcock Johnson Achievement Test);
2. The student will use pre-writing strategies to organize his thoughts using webs and outlines (skills in Section 2-4 taught and assessed by teacher);
3. The student will organize his writing into paragraphs with a topic sentence, supporting and concluding sentences;
4. The student will use editing strategies when completing weekly essays that are to be graded: spell check, grammar check, dictionary, and thesaurus.

Objectives for meeting Goal 2: Maintain passing grades

1. The student will know his homework assignments and take the right books home 80 percent of the time (improvement from 50 percent). A prompting system must be set up for the student, for example,
    1.1. the special education teacher sets up a system
    1.2. a teacher or behavioral aide meets with the student the last period of each day to check assignments and books needed
    1.3. a "row captain" will check that assignments are written down
    1.4. the student will dictate assignments into a small tape recorder
    1.5. teacher will post assignments on the school website
    1.6. the student will email or text assignments home
    1.7. the student sets a wrist or computer alarm as a reminder to get books from the locker
2. The student will improve homework completion and return from 50 percent to 80 percent of the time during this grading period.
    2.1. a reminder system will be established and monitored by the teacher
    2.2. a "row captain" will collect homework assignments
3. The teacher and parents will exchange emails to confirm that assignments are known and completed.
4. The student will complete assigned work in class and homework 80 percent of the time (improve from 50% completion rate; monitored by the teacher).

Objective for meeting Goal 3: Improve memory and compensatory skills

1. The student will use at least two memory strategies to compensate for memory deficits and to learn new information: mnemonics, visualization, sketching, chunking/associating, and application to familiar situations (skill taught to student and parents by special education teacher; skills jointly assessed by teacher and parent observations; discussed via phone conference).

Objectives for meeting Goal 4: Explore career interests and become aware of career opportunities

(During the semester, the student will participate in several activities that will be monitored by the special education teacher):

1. The student will complete a career interest inventory and meet with his parents and teacher to review the results.
2. The student will learn more about five career options of interest.
3. The student will learn about four job skills that are critical for maintaining employment.
4. The student will write a resume.
5. The student will participate in a job-shadowing program.

Sharing Responsibility for Achieving IEP Goals

An effective IEP outlines responsibilities of all parties involved in reaching an IEP goal, teachers, therapists, and parents included, not just the child. One common shortcoming of many IEPs is that responsibility for all corrective actions are placed on the child. That's like saying to a child who wears glasses, "You can read without your glasses if you'll just try harder." If they could do the skill, they would. Educators must keep in perspective that ADHD is a disability for some; that's why the child has an IEP.

Making Suggestions for Special Education and Related Services

Teachers may make suggestions about a student's ***special education program.*** For example, they might suggest:

- one hour of algebra in a self-contained special education resource room;
- one half-hour during the last period of the day for organizational assistance, instruction in study skills, and related services;
- remainder of time in regular education classrooms with classroom accommodations as needed.

Students are also entitled to any ***related services*** that are necessary for them to benefit from special education services. Related services may include:

- Education/counseling: Provide educational counseling on a range of topics:
  - the impact of ADD/ADHD on the student,
  - problem solving,
  - getting along with peers,
  - anger control,
  - time management,
  - study skills.
  - Train older students with ADD or ADHD to act as mentors or coaches for younger incoming students with the same condition. See Summaries 64-69 for tips on teaching these skills.
- Assistive technology—items that the school may have to purchase for one student; for example, the school may buy a relatively inexpensive laptop such as *AlphaSmart* that a student may type on but must later connect to a printer. The *Phonic Ear,* which amplifies the teacher's voice to help the student pay attention,

is another example of assistive technology. *Noise canceling headphones* may also help to reduce auditory distractions. Some electronic items such as a calculator or hand-held "spell checker" may be purchased by the family.

- health services (medication monitoring)
- speech therapy
- psychological services
- occupational therapy
- home-school liaison—a school social worker or special education teacher may be designated to act as a liaison to ensure that regular communication occurs between the school and home.
- parent training—for example, on ADD/ADHD or effective parenting and homework strategies.
- community resources—information for the family on available resources in the community, such as local ADD/ADHD groups (CHADD, ADDA-SR, Federation or Families for Children's Mental Health, National Mental Health Association, or Alliance for the Mentally III) or services from their local mental health center.

Teachers should also consider whether the student needs ***extended educational services*** for an extended school year (ESY). Sometimes when a student continues to do poorly in school, he can benefit from instruction beyond the traditional school day or year. The decision to provide an extended school year must be based upon the student's needs.

Although most students will not need ***year-round programming,*** a few may benefit from a summer program to keep them from falling behind academically. However, for some students, school is such a negative experience, they really need the three-month break.

Other types of extended educational services to consider include:

- instruction before or after school
- a tutor after school
- instruction on the weekend
- summer school classes
- a tutor during the summer
- a packet of materials sent home to the family during the summer with telephone monitoring from an educator.

Recommending Accommodations

Providing the right classroom accommodations is often the key to a student's success at school. There are therefore many suggestions on choosing and implementing accommodations throughout this book. Summary 46 contains a list of "reasonable" classroom accommodations and modifications. Summary 52 discusses specific learning problems and classroom accommodations for a student named Mark who has the inattentive form of ADD. Summaries 16 A-E and 17-25 also contain helpful suggestions regarding academic issues.

Many schools have a menu of accommodations/modifications for students. A sample menu from Walker County Schools in Georgia is contained in Appendix B3. One drawback to using menus, however, is that sometimes accommodations are limited to only those ideas on the list. Remember, these menus are only suggested lists and *any* needed accommodation may be added. In addition, the major reason for having all the summaries in this book is to give teachers, parents, and other educators a broad range of effective strategies to include in an IEP and use in the classroom!

Below are just a few examples of accommodations that may be appropriate for students with ADD/ADHD:

Accommodations for Related Academic Concerns:

- give untimed tests
- provide a notetaker
- give two sets of books
- give homework assignments in writing
- use a weekly report
- shorten tests
- shorten assignments
- provide supports for teacher to include weekly consultation between regular and special education teachers and consultation from the ADD consultant

Accommodations on Statewide Assessment Tests:

- give extended time
- allow use of a calculator
- repeat directions an unlimited number of times
- read parts of the test to the student in a small quiet group

Suggesting Intervention Strategies to Address Behavioral Issues

Most IEPs do not, but should, address behaviors related to *executive function deficits,* such as: disorganization, tardiness, forgetfulness, emotional blow-ups, impaired sense of time, sleep disturbances, talking back, and arguing. Examples of strategies that may be written in the IEP include:

- Help the student organize his locker, plan the best times to go by and pick up books, and review best routes from class to class to help avoid being late to class.
- Parents will be notified as soon as possible if the student is in danger of failing a class.
- In the event of a family or emotional crisis, parents will determine when enough homework has been completed.
- If the student suspects he is about to blow up, he has permission to go to the guidance office.
- Extra time, up to 5 days, will be given for completion of work. A plan will be developed to help the student turn in school work on time.
- If the student is continually late to school or class, consider these options:
  - Meet with parents to determine if a sleep disturbance exists; refer to a physician if needed.
  - Determine why the student is tardy to class and implement strategies to correct the behavior, e.g., a shadow walks with her to class, get books for a couple of classes instead of returning to the locker between classes, reward on-time behavior.
- See Summary 52 for a discussion of ten common ADD/ADHD related behaviors and suggested behavioral intervention strategies that may be incorporated into the IEP.

A *Behavior Intervention Plan* may be necessary if disruptive behaviors continue, especially if they result in suspension from school. See Summaries 63-66 for examples of common behaviors and intervention strategies, as well as more information on developing Behavior Intervention Plans. See also Summary 63 for information on identifying the antecedent behavior—the event that triggers the problem.

Implementing and Monitoring the IEP

Once the IEP is approved, teachers must implement academic or behavioral accommodations/modifications in the classroom as soon as possible. The IEP will note who is responsible for implementing the objectives in the IEP.

To **evaluate** whether or not the student is achieving his objectives, teachers must follow what the IEP says. The IEP states what measures or tests will be used and how often—for example: "daily work samples, weekly reports, teacher records, or grades."

Teachers are also involved in **monitoring and revising** the IEP and the student's progress on an ongoing basis. When the plan is not working effectively, teachers and parents must study and revise it. Parents or teachers may request a meeting at any time to revise the IEP.

IEP Attachments

IEP forms are often streamlined and do not tell the whole story with regard to the services the student will actually receive. Teachers and parents may attach a list of accommodations and/or modifications similar to those in Summaries 46 and 52 to provide more detail regarding specific accommodations the student will receive.

The information parents gather in preparing for the IEP meeting, such as a summary of their teenager's strengths, their concerns, and the student's needs, may also be attached to the IEP. A few schools may even ask parents to write a vision statement regarding their hopes and dreams for their teenager.

The Written vs. Unwritten IEP

IDEA mandates that IEPs must be recorded in writing. However, IEPs and Section 504 Plans are usually written fairly quickly and may not contain all the details regarding specific classroom accommodations that are actually provided to the student. In reality, an **informal plan** often exists in addition to the IEP. This informal plan is fluid, changing over time as teachers and parents try different strategies to help the student succeed.

As long as the student meets IEP goals and objectives, and parents and teachers are both happy, then it may not cause any problems if all the details are not recorded in the IEP. However, putting everything in writing is clearly the best policy. Just as "good fences make good neighbors," **putting IEP content in writing helps maintain the most positive relationship between teachers and parents.** This helps avoid misunderstandings and hurt, angry feelings later. So, if changes will be made over time, write that as an added step in the IEP: "In addition to the accommodations listed in the IEP, the teacher and parent will communicate with each other immediately if the student begins to struggle. Adjustments to the IEP may be made and accommodations may be added as needed in between IEP meetings."

The key to an effective IEP is to maintain regular communication between home and school! As long as parents and teachers are talking to each other, accommodations may be added or deleted as needed. Communication may be done by telephone, fax, or e-mail. Teachers might informally call or e-mail the parent as needed, brainstorm solutions, and then make needed accommodations in class.

SUMMARY 52 Accommodations and Strategies for Coping with ADD/ADHD Behaviors

As Section 3 discusses, several ADD/ADHD behaviors linked to deficits in executive function may cause major problems at school. These characteristics, often occurring in combination, have a profound impact on the student's school work and behavior. In addition, these characteristics often influence behavior in subtle ways that, on the surface, do not appear to be related to the student's condition. Frequently, these issues are not addressed in the IEP or Section 504 Plans. Ten specific challenges are described in more detail in the following section. See Section 3 for additional strategies.

Ten Challenging ADHD Behaviors

1. **Deficits in working memory:** Students have a limited capacity for holding information in mind, manipulating it, and then reorganizing it. This is a skill that is required for writing an essay, solving complex math problems (algebra), or comprehending what is read.

2. **Difficulty activating and maintaining effort:** These students often have difficulty getting started on tasks and persisting until the work is finished.

3. **An impaired sense of time:** Students don't accurately judge the passage of time. Consequently, they may be late and have difficulty estimating how long a task will take to complete. In addition, they have difficulty planning ahead and managing time and the work required for completing long-term projects.

4. **Poor regulation of emotions;** These students may be more emotionally reactive and have major problems with self-control, so are less likely to stop and think before they act or speak. Thus they may talk excessively, impulsively blurt out in class, talk back to teachers, or get into fights at school.

5. **Difficulty using "self-talk" to control behavior:** Self-talk refers to the internal messages that we use to direct our behavior; for example, "I need to get started on my homework now." "It's time to do my chores." Internalized speech is delayed, which means these students are less likely to use self-talk to direct their behavior for completion of future tasks or to control their own behavior. They may have trouble following rules, don't learn as easily from past mistakes, and may repeat misbehavior.

6. **Difficulty analyzing, reconstituting, and problem solving:** Students often have problems with complex problem solving required for critical tasks at school and in life. This deficit affects their verbal fluency and speed of verbal processing, as well as the ability to communicate clearly and concisely with others, complete complex math problems required in algebra, write essays, and sequence information and organize ideas. Students are often overwhelmed by complex tasks and don't know how or where to begin. They may also have great difficulty analyzing and subsequently changing inappropriate behavior.

7. **Slow processing speed and/or slow retrieval of information:** Another manifestation of executive function deficits is taking an abnormally long time to complete written work or to express thoughts verbally. Most often, students with ADD inattentive are more likely to have difficulty completing work as quickly as their peers and may avoid answering questions in class.

8. **Disorganization:** Many of these deficits contribute to a sense of chronic disorganization among students with attention deficits. Lockers are often a "black hole" where homework papers are lost forever. Homework may be completed but not turned in. These students need extensive supervision from parents or teachers to help them organize work materials and time. When disorganization is

debilitating and students are struggling in school, teachers must provide *developmentally appropriate supervision,* which means more supervision, more often, than for other students.

9. **Forgetfulness:** These students are extremely forgetful. Forgetfulness is not simply a matter of choice or laziness; it *is* one of the diagnostic criteria for attention deficits. Although they forget tasks they want to avoid, they also forget enjoyable events and activities in which they *want* to participate. Homework assignments are often forgotten or postponed, resulting in failure to submit homework in a timely manner. Students may forget to stay after school for detention or to take home books needed for homework. Simply put, don't punish students for characteristics of their disorder; provide needed supervision or accommodations.

10. **Undiagnosed Coexisting Conditions:** Teachers should be watchful for coexisting conditions such as learning disabilities, depression, anxiety, or bipolar disorder. Sleep disturbances are present in over half of these children, resulting in extreme difficulty falling asleep, waking up, and getting restful sleep. As a result, students may be late to school or appear tired and sleep in class. If other conditions are suspected, discuss the issue with your multidisciplinary team. You may decide to encourage parents to talk with their doctor.

If these behaviors result in academic failure or disciplinary action being taken against a student, then each ***challenging issue should be identified in the IEP or Behavior Intervention Plan (BIP).*** Specific objectives should also be included in the IEP or BIP to teach the necessary coping skills. Then teachers can work with the student to learn the skills, provide supportive intervention strategies, or make accommodations to reduce the frequency of these problems. Remember, discipline should be *instructive,* not just punitive!

Several common ADD/ADHD-related behaviors and intervention strategies are discussed below. Since each student with this condition exhibits different problem behaviors at school, each IEP will be different and may not necessarily address all the issues raised in this summary. Statements in *italics* are examples of accommodations or intervention strategies that may help the student cope with or compensate for the ADD/ADHD behaviors. These strategies may be formally listed as part of the IEP, checked off on a menu of services, or simply discussed and written in the minutes.

Strategies for Addressing ADD/ADHD Behaviors
Organizational and Memory Problems

Below are suggestions for addressing organizational and memory problems. For more detail about these problems, see Summaries 25, 30, and 31.

1. **Forgetting Homework Assignments and Not Turning in Work:** Frequently, disorganization and forgetfulness are lifelong problems for people with attention deficits. Students often don't know their homework or forget to turn in completed assignments. In addition, long-term projects may be completely forgotten or remembered the night before they are due. When students with ADD or ADHD get behind, they sometimes feel so overwhelmed they need help getting back on track. A Behavioral Intervention Plan should be developed to help the student correct or compensate for her organizational deficits and forgetfulness.

If the objectives for the IEP are for the student to: 1) know daily assignments and 2) turn in homework, intervention strategies such as the following may be needed. Obviously some students will not need all these accommodations to be successful.

- *Row captains will pick up homework from all students and check to see that assignments are written down.*
- *An organizational coach (teacher or another student) will meet the student at the end of the day to check that assignments are written down and proper books taken home.*

- *Extra time (up to 5 days) will be given for completion of work.*
- *The student may keep an extra book at home, especially for difficult subjects.*
- *Parents will be notified in advance about long-term assignments and their due dates.*
- *Reduce homework if appropriate.* (See discussion in next paragraph, plus S-24.)

2. **Not Completing Homework/Getting Zeros:** Several factors may contribute to the student getting zeros for not turning in homework: disorganization, forgetfulness, slow processing speed, lack of medication, or emotionality. Most of these issues are addressed in the previous paragraph and Summaries 25-26. However, one issue most teachers and parents don't fully consider is whether too much homework is being assigned. According to Drs. Sydney Zentall and Sam Goldstein, **teachers often underestimate the amount of time it will take students with special needs to complete homework.** (See Summary 27.) When homework takes more than a couple of hours to complete, the amount of homework must be reduced. To help a student consistently complete homework, several strategies from Summaries 27-29 may be used:

    - *Identify learning problems and make adjustments in the classroom.* (See Summaries 13 and 17-A.)
    - *Determine whether homework is taking too long. If necessary, reduce assignments accordingly.* (Generally, the total time spent on homework in all subjects should be no more than 1 ½ hours for a ninth grader and no more than 2 hours or so for a senior. See Summary 27.)
    - *In periods of high stress, parents will determine how much homework should be done, even though it may be less than the teacher originally assigned. Parents will sign and return the homework paper indicating that it is completed.* (See Summaries 27-29.)

3. **Failing a Class:** When academic and executive function deficits are not addressed, the student may be in danger of failing a class. It is important for the teacher to work with the teenager and her family to prevent school failure. As explained in Summary 1, these students don't learn as easily from punishment and reward as other students. So, when a student with an attention deficit is failing, she is more likely to feel overwhelmed and give up. Obviously, the most important thing to do is provide accommodations that will prevent class failure. The suggestions above will help. Including this statement in the minutes of the IEP meeting may also be helpful:

    - *Parents will be notified in a timely manner if the student is failing so that steps may be taken to get her back on track academically.*

Impulsive Behaviors

4. **Using Bad Language or Talking Back:** It is not unusual for students with attention deficits to speak or act impulsively, especially when their medication has worn off. Often they regret the action but cannot take it back. Sometimes students talk back to a teacher or use bad language. Of course, these are not acceptable behaviors, nor is ADD or ADHD an excuse for misbehaving. But it may be helpful if teachers can determine whether characteristics of ADD/ADHD are contributing to the misbehavior. For example, talking back may occur when medication has worn off. Typically, teachers can handle these misbehaviors without imposing severe consequences.

    - *Ignore minor muttering, especially if the student is actually following teacher instructions.*
    - *If bad language is used in front of a teacher, depending on the severity, loudness, and to whom the profanity is directed, the teacher has several options. See Summary 65 for suggestions.*
    - *Determine whether the blow-up occurred during a time when medication has worn off. If so, parents may ask their doctor for help in adjusting the medication.*

- *Make certain that learning problems have been identified and the student is receiving appropriate accommodations in the classroom.*
- *If the problem continues, refer the student to the vice principal in charge of discipline, who will determine appropriate discipline.*
- *If suspension is unavoidable, send the student to in-school suspension instead of out-of-school suspension. As suggested in Summary 67, use time spent in suspension (OS-Organized Study) to teach pro-social skills as described in the Skillstreaming section.*

5. **Misbehaving and Emotional Blow-ups:** Students with attention deficits are more likely to misbehave at several specific times:

- during transitions—for example, lunch, recess breaks, after school, or on the bus ride home,
- when the schedule or class structure changes (a substitute is present),
- when there is a personal crisis (failing a class, breakup with a girlfriend/boyfriend), or
- when medication has worn off.

At these times, some students with ADD or ADHD may talk back to a teacher, refuse to obey a teacher request, yell, hit the wall or locker, cry, or fight. Teach the student to recognize when she is about to lose control and have a crisis plan to avoid potential blow-ups. As explained in Summary 75 on Anger Management, students can: 1) learn which issues seem to trigger blow-ups, 2) learn to recognize internal feelings of anger and rage, and 3) learn to seek help when these events occur.

- *If the student suspects she is about to blow up, she has permission to go to the counselor's office to talk with the counselor or just sit and cool off. (Don't ask the student to find a written pass in the heat of an emotional blow-up. Give blanket permission to go to the counselor or place the permission card in a designated spot on the teacher's desk where she can always find it.)*

- *If a student has an emotional blow-up, the regular procedures for handling disruptive behavior may be followed.*
    1. For example, the vice principal for discipline may become involved if the student is fighting.
    2. However, the final consequence imposed may be different because the student is eligible for special education or Section 504. For example, the student may be referred to in-school suspension instead of a regular three-day suspension.
    3. Ideally, the vice principal will be familiar with this student's record and have a personal relationship with her. Disciplinary action is handled more easily if it is built upon a personal relationship. For example, the vice principal is more likely to know how to handle the student without further escalation of the problem.

- *If blow-ups are serious and may result in suspension, as discussed in Summary 45, a Behavior Intervention Plan should be developed to help the student cope more effectively with conflict. Parents should ask their doctor for advice to determine if medication should be adjusted.*

- *When a substitute teacher is present and there are concerns about students with ADHD misbehaving, several things can be done:*
    - *The substitute is given a note regarding this student's difficulty with change. A couple of suggestions along with the student's seat location are also provided.*
        - *For example, the substitute may introduce herself to a couple of students, including this student.*
        - *Ask the student to assist in various ways—pass out a written worksheet or assignment to the rest of the class.*

- *In advance, the regular classroom teacher or counselor may discuss this difficulty with the student. Ask her how teachers can best help her cope with this challenge. The procedure for her to follow is discussed in advance.*
- *If possible, designate and teach the student how to help the substitute; e.g., explain the schedule, show the location of the class roll. Have the student rehearse the proper behavior for when a substitute is present.*
- *Place a classroom aide in the room for that period to assist the substitute.*
- *If the substitute is in a regular class, send the student to her former special education teacher for this one period.*

Impaired Sense of Time

6. **Being Late to Class.** Students with ADD/ADHD may frequently be late to class due to difficulty in accurately judging the passage of time or weak organizational skills. If a student is frequently late to class, analyze when and why the problem is occurring:

   1. Identify the classes where the student is arriving late.
   2. Determine why she is late. Does she go by her locker? go the long way? have trouble opening her combination lock? meet a friend to chat?
   3. Correct the problem (e.g., organize the locker as described in Summary 30, assign a locker that is closer to the student's classes, practice opening the combination lock, or skip the meetings with the friend).
      If necessary, include an objective in the IEP:
      - *Tardies will be handled by the special education teacher or an administrator* (rather than automatically punishing tardies, as some schools do, by prohibiting student participation in sports, attendance at a school dance, or other extracurricular activities, taking points off her grade, or requiring after-school detention).
      - Develop a plan to prevent tardies.

   See Summaries 32-35 for additional suggestions.

Impaired Sense of Time Plus Sleep Disturbance

7. **Being Tardy to School:** Students with attention deficits often have problems getting to school on time. Researchers tell us that over 50 percent of these students have serious sleep disturbances (problems waking up, falling asleep, and getting restful sleep). If this is a major problem, suggest that parents talk with their physician. A detailed discussion of strategies for dealing with sleep disturbances is available in *Teenagers with ADD and ADHD*. Share these suggestions with parents:

   - Buy an alarm clock for the student.
   - Connect lights, the TV, and stereo to a timer that is set to come on at a designated time.
   - Wake the teenager up earlier to allow more time.
   - Some doctors recommend waking the student 30 minutes early, giving her medication, then letting her sleep until the regularly scheduled wake-up time. This makes it easier for the student to focus on getting ready for school.
   - Get clothes and books ready the night before.
   - Don't take Ritalin or Dexedrine too late in the day.
   - Have the student record a wake-up message from a close friend or herself.
   - Get a physical examination to rule out other problems.
   - If sleep disturbances are causing major problems, talk with the doctor about medication. Sublingual melatonin (dissolves in your mouth) is one medication commonly given for sleep problem. In addition other medications such as Clonidine, Intuniv, and, less frequently, Tofrani or Trazadone serve a dual purpose, helping with sleep and also leveling off emotional mood swings or aggression.

ⓈⓊⓂⓂⒶⓇⓎ 53 Transition Planning: After High School, What Next?

Transition planning is one of the most important but neglected elements of educational planning for students who have ADD or ADHD. The Individuals with Disabilities Education Act mandates that all students 16 and older must have transition goals in their IEP to help with long-term career planning. Younger students may also have an ITP if the IEP committee recommends it. Ideally, career planning should begin in elementary school. (Transition planning is *not* mandated for students with 504 Plans, but ideally 504 Plans will include some transition services.)

IDEA regulations state that the purpose of transition planning is "to ensure that all children with disabilities have available to them a free appropriate education that emphasizes special education and related services designed to meet their unique needs and prepare them to further education, employment and independent living" [34 CFR 300.1(a)] [20 U.S.C. 1400(d)(1)(A)].

The IDEA statutes further explain that the transition plan (ITP) must offer services that:

1. are designed to be a ***results-oriented*** process, that is focused on ***improving the academic and functional achievement*** of the child with a disability ***to facilitate the child's movement from school to post-school activities,*** including postsecondary education, vocational education, integrated employment (including supported employment), continuing and adult education, adult services, independent living, or community participation;

2. are ***based on the individual child's needs,*** taking into account the child's strengths, preferences, and interests;

3. include instruction, related services, community experiences, the ***development of employment and other post-school adult living objectives,*** and, when appropriate, acquisition of daily living skills and ***functional vocational evaluation.***

Several federal initiatives such as the School-to-Work Opportunities Act of 1994 have placed great emphasis on career development planning for all students. In spite of this increased attention, some ITPs do not include very many helpful suggestions for career development. The limited development of the ITP is probably because most teachers are unfamiliar with some of the exciting opportunities that could be offered. Other schools, however, have transition specialists, who are actively involved in developing each student's ITP.

An incredible wealth of information is available regarding transition planning. Several resources are listed at the end of this summary. A brief overview is provided here of components that are often included in a comprehensive career development program.

Comprehensive Career Development Programs

Here are examples of issues that may be addressed by writing a related objective to include in the IEP, ITP, and/or Section 504 Plan.

Self-knowledge and Student Development:

- Self-determination training
- Self-advocacy
- Problem-solving skills

- Social skills
- Money management skills
- Medication awareness and management

Assessment:

- Interest inventories
- Vocational/career assessment

A vocational/career assessment can help the student increase his self-awareness and identify potential career interest areas. Two commonly used tests to help students begin to identify career interests include the Career Occupational Preference System (COPS), and for older, college-bound students, the Strong Interest Inventory.

Work Skills:

- Filling out a job application
- Searching want ads
- Writing a resume and cover letter
- Preparing for an interview
- Role playing a job interview
- Identifying potential career paths
- Potential training programs available after high school graduation

Educational and Career Exploration

Debbie Wilkes, who is a transition specialist in Richardson, Texas, wisely advises students and parents that ***"Education . . . not just college is the key."*** It is important to make it clear that great jobs that don't require a college degree do exist. But students and parents also need to know that additional education is often needed to qualify for these technical and highly skilled jobs.

Consider which, if any, vocational/career or technology classes the student should take. If a student doesn't plan to go to college upon graduation, write an objective related to deciding what job training will be appropriate.

If the student plans to attend college and will need an extended time SAT or ACT, the "extended time on tests" accommodation should be documented as part of her IEP or Section 504 Plan.

Other objectives to consider:

- Researching career options
- Volunteering as a means of career exploration
- Career planning
- Job shadowing
- Visits to job sites
- Mentors from local industry
- Supervised employment
- Academic supports
  - tutoring
  - making up missed credits to graduate on time

Transportation:

- Learning to drive
- Studying for the driver's test
- Taking and passing the test

Collaboration with Other Agencies:

Several community agencies may teach skills or provide supports that will help the student make a successful transition to the adult work world.

- Goodwill
- Vocational Rehabilitation
- Big Brother/Big Sister (especially their mentoring program)

Vocational Activities and Services at the State Level

In 2006, Congress passed and funded the Carl D. Perkins Vocational and Technical Education Act to "provide an increased focus on the academic achievement of career and technical education students, strengthen the connections between secondary and postsecondary education, and improve state and local accountability. Most states place these services within their current departments of education. Check with the department of education in your state and ask if they have any helpful career materials.

Resources
Books

Christen, C. and Bolles, R. *What Color Is Your Parachute for Teens: Discovering Yourself, Defining Your Future.* 2nd ed. Berkeley, CA: Ten Speed Press, 2010.

Feldman, Wilma. *Finding a Career that Works for You.* 2nd ed. Plantation, FL: Specialty Press, 2006.

Miller, R., Lombard, R., & Corbey, S. *Transition Assessment: Planning Transition and IEP Development for Youth with Mild to Moderate Disabilities.* Boston, MA. Allyn & Bacon, 2006.

Maitland, T.E. and Quinn, P. *Ready for Take Off: Preparing Your Teen with ADHD or LD for College.* Washington, DC: Magination Press, 2010.

Tests

- *Career Occupational Preference System (COPS).* Available from Edits, P.O. Box 7234, San Diego, CA 92167. (619-222-166; www.edits.net).
- *Strong Interest Inventory.* Developed by Stanford University Press; available from Consulting Psychologists Press, Inc. (800-624-1765; www.cpp-db.com). This test may be more appropriate for students 15 years of age or older who plan to attend college.

Websites

- Building the Legacy: IDEA 2004 (http://idea.ed.gov). Search for Transition Services. Examples of articles available are: "Person-Centered Planning: A Tool for Transition" and "IEPs for Success," by Dr. Barbara Bateman.
- Career Development and Transition, a Division of the Council for Exceptional Children (www.cec.sped.org). The Council has published a curriculum entitled *Life Centered Career Education.* Sample modules are available at their website.
- Education World (www.education-world.com). Search "vocation" and specific topics. Several helpful articles are available at this site, including an article on job shadowing, an overview of several model school-to-work programs, and *Career Counseling Resources on the Internet*—which contains links with online resources

related to: self-assessment and interest inventories; career information; writing resumes and cover letters; job interviews; job listings.

- Office of Vocational and Adult Education, Career and Technical Education (http://ed.gov/about/offices/list/ovae/index.html).
- Wrightslaw (www.wrightslaw.com). Search for Transition Services. Articles available on this site include: "Transition—Frequently Asked Questions" and "Doing Your Homework: Making the Transition to Work and Future Education."

First Steps: What to Do When a Student is Struggling in Class?

SUMMARY 54

Often, experienced teachers say that they "know" a student has an attention deficit, even though he or she has not been evaluated or labeled. In this situation, teachers may recommend that the student be screened through a pre-referral process, although they should never suggest a diagnosis of ADHD. Teachers must walk the fine line between honoring their experience and avoiding premature conclusions and labels. Rather than ask, "Does this child have ADHD?" teachers should ask first, "*Is this student struggling to learn and complete assignments?*" If the answer is "yes," the next question should be, "*What should I do now?*"

Teachers are encouraged by law to implement a Response to Intervention (RtI) plan. When a student is struggling, the teacher must identify the problem area, provide research-based interventions in a small group or, if needed, one-on-one, and assess progress. If the student does not make sufficient progress after these steps, then she should be referred for an evaluation. Typically, teachers take several steps to ensure that students are successful at school. These include:

1. **Identify challenges.** Identify areas where the student is struggling: academic, developmental, and functional.

2. **Offer Simple Interventions.** Work with the student and parents to provide a few simple supports or interventions in hopes of addressing the learning and/or behavior problems. For example, the teacher may send an extra textbook to keep at home and assign a peer to remind the student to write down her assignments. Parents may monitor homework completion and its return to school. These simple interventions could be part of a Response to Intervention (RtI) Plan or pre-referral strategies, but should be implemented prior to referring a child to a multidisciplinary team for evaluation. Specific intervention strategies are suggested throughout this book. Refer to Summary 29 for homework tips for parents.

3. **Schedule a Parent Conference.** If teachers are concerned about a student who is struggling and suspect an attention deficit, they should contact the parents to explore possible causes and solutions. Keep in mind that other conditions and disorders share some common characteristics with ADD or ADHD. For example, a "hyperactive" child or daydreaming teen may be adjusting to a new stepparent or sibling in the home, a family crisis such as divorce or financial hardship, or have a health problem such as allergies, depression, or a sleep disorder.

    Often teachers simply describe the behaviors and state facts; for example, "Your son is not completing his school work and he has a 56 average in my algebra class." Teachers are advised never to tell parents their child has ADHD, because they can't officially diagnose the condition.

4. **Monitor and Revise Plan as Needed.** Increase the intensity and frequency of interventions, as well as the progress monitoring. According to RtI guidelines, if simple interventions don't work, the more intensive interventions should be provided in a small group of students. If that still doesn't solve the problem, then one-on-one, research-based instruction and interventions must be provided. Mary Durheim reminds us that all interventions used in the RtI process must be scientifically research-based and be proven to be effective for the problem identified. Teacher and curriculum implementation must also be monitored for fidelity—in other words, to make sure the scientifically proven intervention is carefully followed.

5. **Refer to a Multidisciplinary Team for Evaluation.** If the RtI interventions do not solve the student's problems, the child should be referred to the school's multidisciplinary team for an evaluation. All schools have a team of veteran educators that can be called in when teachers need more support for

an individual child. This team may have a variety of names, but team members discuss the behaviors of concern and the child's response to previous interventions. The team may make additional suggestions and will determine whether to refer the student for a formal evaluation

6. **Determine if a disability is present.** The student will be screened for eligibility for services under either IDEA or Section 504, depending on the degree of impairment/severity of the symptoms. Typically, eligibility under 504 is considered first before IDEA. If, however, the student fails to meet IDEA criteria, teachers should ensure that she has also been evaluated for eligibility under Section 504 to determine whether her ADHD creates a "substantial limitation."

7. **Develop, implement, and monitor an IEP or 504 Plan.** Once eligibility is determined, an educational plan known as a 504 Plan or IEP will be developed in conjunction with the IEP team or 504 committee. By law, parents must be involved in IEP development, and, in best practice situations, parents and the students themselves are involved in the development of both IEPs and 504 Plans. The IEP or Section 504 Plan establishes goals aimed at helping students improve their academic performance or address other identified challenges. Several grade-level appropriate intervention strategies and accommodations are provided throughout this book to address any specific deficits identified by the team.

SUMMARY 55
So the Student Is Failing: What Should the Teacher Do Now?

Researchers tell us that **students with ADD/ADHD are at greater risk of school failure**; roughly 30 percent have failed a grade. So it should come as no surprise that students with attention deficit disorders are often on the verge of failing a class, especially in middle and high school. When teachers see a student struggling to successfully complete school work and pass tests, it is best to intervene early, within the first three to four weeks of school, or as soon as possible after problems arise. Hopefully, the material in this book will add to the teacher's repertoire of skills so that he or she can more effectively help students who are failing.

These students are vulnerable during the transition years, especially the first year of middle and high school. The increased demands for organizational skills and independent work that begin in middle school overwhelm many of these students. In fact, sometimes parents say, "My child hit a brick wall when he started middle school." Many parents keep hoping that this will be the year that their teenager will suddenly mature and academics will no longer be a problem. So, they may be reluctant to tell the teacher about the diagnosis of ADD or ADHD. Often, they want to give the teenager a chance to make it on his own. Some suggested intervention strategies follow.

Problem Solve First

1. **Contact the Parents.** Call or meet with the student's parent: Start with the positives first.

   > "Sarah is a delightful student. I really enjoy teaching her. She has [extremely creative ideas for writing]. But I'm concerned she's having trouble making the transition to high school. She is not turning in her homework on a regular basis."

   Sometimes if the parent simply monitors homework completion, the student's grades improve significantly.

   By the time the student gets to middle and high school, most parents have been through at least five years of academic struggles. They already know the typical kinds of problems their teenager has experienced and can probably suggest effective intervention strategies. So, the teacher may ask, *"Has he had problems like this before? What seems to work best with him? What have other teachers done that has helped?"*

2. **Review Current Performance.** Look over the student's class work and homework. **Look for a pattern** of underachievement, uneven performance, strengths, and learning problems that seem to interfere with his ability to complete school work. Try to pinpoint the specific learning problems that seem to cause the greatest difficulties. For students with attention deficits, it may well be organizational and memory problems related to deficits in executive function.

3. **Check for Prior ADD/ADHD Diagnosis.** If a student has previously been diagnosed, some parents may mention it to the teacher at the first PTA meeting or early in the semester. In addition, a letter from their physician may be on file in the office confirming the diagnosis of ADD or ADHD, documenting any problems, stating known learning problems, and making some recommendations.

4. **Provide Accommodations.** Identify learning problems and give accommodations. See Summaries 16-A-E, 46, 51, and 52 to help the student succeed in class.

Seek Help from Others

If these initial strategies aren't enough, then the next steps may include:

5. ***Schedule a Parent Conference.*** Set a time for a more in-depth discussion of the student's problems. Discuss possible accommodations, the level of supervision parents should give, a system for parents to know homework assignments, and a strategy to maintain regular home/school communication, such as through a weekly or daily report.

   If the student has ADD or ADHD, ask the parents about ***medication.*** See Summary 59 for suggestions of questions to discuss with the parent, plus Summary 60 for a checklist to help determine medication effectiveness. Blank forms are available in Appendices A9-10.

6. ***Review Records.*** Review the student's cumulative folder, such as grades, school records, achievement tests, and old psychological evaluations or IEPs. Look for: 1) teacher comments regarding behavior or learning problems, 2) effective intervention strategies, and 3) higher achievement test scores with lower than expected grades—in other words, a pattern of a student who is ***underachieving***.

7. ***Ask for Advice.*** If accommodations and/or modifications alone don't work, ask for advice from other educators, such as a veteran or district level master teacher, guidance counselor, school psychologist, the vice principal, or, if the teacher is lucky, the ADD/ADHD consultant. Ask whether this student is an appropriate referral for a teacher committee staffing.

Refer the Student to a Teacher Committee Staffing

If nothing else seems to work, the next step may be to refer the student to a committee of teachers for help. Many schools have developed committees of veteran teachers, in addition to their IEP teams, to help brainstorm solutions to help students succeed in school. These groups may have different names in different states. In Georgia, these committees are called student support teams (SST).

8. ***Refer the Student to the SST.*** The student support team (SST) may:

   ■ suggest additional accommodations or strategies to the teacher; or
   ■ decide whether to refer the student to the IEP team for a special education evaluation.

9. ***Meet with the IEP Team.*** The IEP team may request that an evaluator administer some preliminary screening instruments before the school psychologist is ever involved. For example, they may schedule a variety of tests such as: a vision and hearing examination, academic achievement tests, or visual motor tests. (See Summary 6 for a list of specific tests.) The evaluator may again review the records, looking for information that will help identify learning problems or executive function deficits. He or she may also look for test scores, teacher comments, or reports of student behaviors that are indicative of ADD/ADHD.

10. ***Screen for ADD/ADHD.*** If the IEP Team suspects ADD or ADHD, teachers and parents may complete a behavioral checklist. The local school system may have a checklist such as the Conners available or may use the criteria listed in the most current edition of the *Diagnostic and Statistical Manual of Mental Disorders (DSM)*. Teachers may wish to review Summary 5 on diagnosis of attention deficit disorder for some of the basic characteristics school psychologists are looking for in the diagnosis.

11. ***Ask for a Letter from the Doctor.*** If the student has already been diagnosed with ADD/ADHD, the SST or IEP team may ask for a letter from the doctor to confirm the diagnosis. See Summary 48 for suggested content. A sample medical letter is available in my first book, *Teenagers with ADD and ADHD*.

12. ***Consider the Psychological Evaluation.*** Based upon the accumulated information, the IEP Team may ask the school psychologist to conduct an in-depth evaluation: classroom observations, review of

records, review of preliminary screening results, and intelligence testing. A functional behavior assessment (FBA) may also be done to determine when behavioral problems occur and what tends to trigger them, and/or a behavior rating scale may be completed. Additional assessments of cognitive processing and social and emotional development may also be done. The results of this evaluation will be presented to the IEP eligibility committee to help guide their decision making and planning.

13. Be Prepared with Suggestions for Paying for Medical Treatment. Some schools have been reluctant to identify attention deficit disorders for fear that they will be stuck with the cost of a medical evaluation and treatment. However, many families have the money or insurance to pay for a doctor's visit and medication to treat the condition. When families cannot afford medication, assistance may be available from Medicaid if the student is eligible, a local service group or charity, or, in some situations, the local mental health system.

What to Expect at the IDEA Eligibility Meeting

Based upon the results of the preliminary screening process, the full IEP team may then meet to determine whether the student is eligible for special education. Usually the IDEA eligibility committee is comprised of veteran teachers, school psychologists, or administrators, as listed in Summary 43.

14. Contribute to the School's Input. At the eligibility staffing, each person will have the opportunity to provide input regarding the student's strengths, present performance, challenges, and needs.

15. Listen to the Family's Input. Make certain that parents and the teenager give their input. They will have insights from previous years and probably have suggestions regarding which intervention strategies *have* and *have not* worked in the past.

- *Inclusion of the Teenager:* Committee members and parents must decide whether to invite the teenager to all the meetings or simply the meeting where intervention strategies are planned. If the meeting is too negative and becomes a recitation of every bad behavior or learning deficit the teenager has, it is probably best if he is not present. Teachers and parents may let the student decide whether to attend the meeting. See Summary 69 for a discussion of self-advocacy.
- *Seek Student Input Regardless:* Talk with the student and ask for his input before the meeting. Consider asking him to identify his strengths and the areas in which he is struggling in school. *"Max, can you tell us what is causing you the most difficulty in school? Do you have any suggestions about what would help you solve this problem? What have teachers done to help you in the past? What helped and what didn't?"*
- *Depersonalization:* Consider using depersonalization as a tool to raise important issues. For example, *"Many students with ADD or ADHD have trouble remembering to write down their homework assignments and take home the right books. Sometimes that seems to be true for you."* (Or, *"Does that seem to be true for you sometimes?"*)
- *Respect the Student:* Avoid comments about the student's work that may seem accusatory or demeaning. Many students with attention deficits have already had a lifetime of marginal academic performance and negative feedback from teachers. Without proper medication and accommodations, their self-esteem will plummet.

The IDEA Staffing to Develop the IEP

Once the student has been declared eligible for services under IDEA, another meeting will be scheduled to develop the IEP (see Summary 51). For more information on the IEP and Section 504, refer to the resources listed at the end of Summary 43.

SECTION 5

Medication Issues

According to research from the landmark NIMH/MTA study on ADHD (Summary 11), **medication is one of the most effective interventions for treating** the vast majority of children with attention deficit disorders! However, for the best results, many experts recommend medication and behavioral interventions in combination. The NIMH study also reported that most students were on doses of medication that were too low to achieve peak academic performance. Clearly, getting the right medication and dosage is critical.

Teachers should remember that medication is not a "magic bullet" and does not solve all school problems. Even when medication is working properly, **behaviors will improve somewhat but may still be problematic.** After all, most medications are not effective all day; for example, many students attempt homework in the evening without the benefit of any medication.

A KEY POINT: Monitoring the effectiveness of a student's medication during school hours is extremely important. Consequently, **teachers are in the best position to provide the family and doctor with objective information regarding medication effectiveness.** So, the more teachers know about medications and their impact on the student's work, the more likely the student with an attention deficit will succeed in school. If a student is struggling in school, teachers should consider problems with medication effectiveness as a potential contributing factor. Obviously, teachers can't correct a problem with medication, but they can share information with parents and encourage them to talk to their physician.

Reasons for Continuing Problems with Medication Effectiveness

1. Occasionally, the student is **not on the right medication** to improve his attention. For example, a student may find that Adderall works great for him but the first medicine he tried, Ritalin, did not really help, or vice versa.

2. Sometimes the **_dose of medication is not correct._** As noted earlier, many students are on doses of medication that are too low for peak academic performance.

3. The **_medication may wear off during the day._** Most medications for attention deficits last from six to ten hours. With today's longer-acting medications, providing medication coverage for the entire school day is easier. However, check the medication list in Summary 58 to see how long the medication should last. For example, if a student took a six-hour medication at 7:00 a.m., it would wear off by 1:00 p.m. So, he is attempting afternoon classes or the bus trip home without any medication.

4. **_The timing for taking medicine may be wrong._** The longer-acting medications take about an hour to kick in. So, if a student takes his medicine right before he leaves for school at 8:00 a.m. and is sitting in class by 8:30 a.m., he will have problems concentrating.

Unfounded Fears about Substance Abuse

Some teachers and parents worry about students taking medication, possibly fearing future drug addiction. However, studies by Dr. Russell Barkley and Timothy Wilens offer reassurance that drug addiction is not a major risk. Researchers found that students with attention deficit disorder who took medication were _less_ likely to abuse drugs than students with the condition who did not take medication.

Resources for Section 5

Barkley, Russell A. *Attention-Deficit Hyperactivity Disorder: A Handbook for Diagnosis and Treatment.* 3rd ed. New York: Guilford Press, 2006.

Barkley, Russell A., K. Murphy, and M. Fischer. *ADHD in Adults: What the Science Says.* New York, NY: Guilford Press, 2008.

Barkley, Russell A. Week-long ADHD workshop. 26th Annual Cape Cod Summer Symposia. Cape Cod, MA, 2004.

Brown, Thomas E. *Attention Deficit Disorders and Comorbidities in Children, Adolescents, and Adults.* Washington, DC: American Psychiatric Press, 2000.

Dendy, Chris A. Z. *A Bird's-Eye View of Life with ADD and ADHD.* Cedar Bluff, AL: Cherish the Children, 2007.

Prince, Jefferson B. "ADHD Treatment Across the Lifespan." ADDA Conference keynote presentation. Houston, TX, 2010.

Wilens, Timothy E. *Straight Talk about Psychiatric Medications for Kids.* 3rd ed. New York, NY: Guilford Press, 2008.

SUMMARY 56 — Common Medications for Treating ADD and ADHD

The primary medications used to treat ADD and ADHD are all central nervous system stimulants. However, medications from the antidepressant class are also frequently prescribed for problems such as anxiety or depression that often accompany attention deficit disorders. When teachers know which academic and behavioral changes should occur with each type of medication, they have a better idea as to whether medications are working properly.

Frequently, a teacher may not even know which medication a student is taking. However, if a student is doing poorly in school, sometimes parents tell the teacher about medications. Teachers and parents may review Summaries 51-56 together to determine whether there are potential areas of concern that should be discussed with the doctor. A detailed description of medications sometimes prescribed for students with ADD/ADHD is provided in Chapter 6 of *Teenagers with ADD & ADHD*.

Central Nervous System Stimulants

Stimulant medications, so called because they *stimulate* activity in the central nervous system, are the medications of first choice in treating attention deficits. According to results of Positron Emission Tomography (PET) Scans, these medications actually increase activity and blood flow in the front part of the brain. This area of the brain is known to control memory, speech, and thought.

Impact on Behavior: These medications are the most effective for:
1. increasing attention and concentration,
2. enhancing the speed of learning information, and
3. improving school work and behavior.

For a more detailed discussion of the impact of stimulant medication, see Summary 57. These medications affect the levels of the neurotransmitters dopamine and norepinephrine, which, in turn, improve the student's ability to pay attention and learn.

Length of Effectiveness: The ultimate goal for stimulant medications is to provide all-day coverage for the school day, thus enhancing academic performance and improving behavior. ADHD medications are available in short- and long-acting formulations. Fortunately, newer sustained-release stimulant medications last for six to eight hours on average. In addition, three of these medicines actually last ten hours or so: Adderall XR, Concerta, and the Daytrana patch. Shorter-acting medications such as Ritalin and Dexedrine only last three to four hours and may require a second dose at school. These medications are discussed in more detail in Summary 58. Both the brand and generic medication names are given below.

Stimulant Medications

Frequently Prescribed Stimulants:
- Ritalin™, Ritalin SR™, Ritalin LA™ (methylphenidate)
- Dexedrine™, Dextrostat™, Dexedrine SR™ (dextroamphetamine)
- Adderall™, Adderall XR, Vyvance™ (dextroamphetamine & amphetamine)
- Focalin™, Focalin XR™ (methylphenidate)
- Methylin™, Methylin ER™ (methylphenidate)
- Metadate ER™, Metadate CD™ (methylphenidate)
- Concerta™ (methylphenidate)
- Daytrana™ (a methylphenidate patch)

Doctors have found that ***response to these medications varies*** from person to person. Some teenagers respond better to methylphenidate medications such as Concerta and Ritalin, while others do better on dextroamphetamine-based medicines such as Dexedrine or Adderall. Effective medication dosages also vary from student to student. Generally, teenagers require higher doses of these medications than children do. Occasionally, however, an older teenager may actually take less medication than an elementary school child. In addition, some teenagers may metabolize the medication more quickly so it doesn't last as long. As a result, medication wears off sooner than expected.

Side Effects of Medication

Of all the stimulant medications, Ritalin has been studied the most extensively over the past three or four decades. In general, stimulants are considered very "clean" medications because they are in and out of the body in four to ten hours. ***Side effects are minimal.*** Reported side effects of both regular and sustained-release stimulant medications include *loss of appetite* and problems with *sleep*. However, timing the medications so as not to interfere with meals or bedtime is usually effective in eliminating these problems. In most cases, the medication does not cause sleep problems. In reality, sleep disturbances are often present *before* the student ever begins taking stimulant medication. Research from the MTA/NIMH ADHD study has shown a modest impact on growth—children who take the medications average one-half inch shorter and eight pounds lighter than peers. However, other experts point out that this growth delay may be temporary since our children mature more slowly anyway.

How do I know if the dose is too high? If the teenager is taking too high a dose of medication, teachers may observe negative side effects that include depression, lethargy, or "losing her spark." Of course, depression and lethargy may also be caused by other problems. Teachers may share their impressions or results of the rating scale (Appendix A9) if asked by parents or during a staffing or planning conference.

Non-stimulant Medications That Improve Alertness and Attention

Strattera™ is another popular medication for ADD/ADHD, primarily because it is not a stimulant medication and prescription refills are more easily obtained. Stimulants are considered controlled substances, and thus require that parents pick up the prescription at the doctor's office. Prescriptions for stimulants cannot be called in to a pharmacy.

Strattera lasts longer hours each day than the stimulants but takes time to build up to peak effectiveness. One psychiatrist reported that 1/3 of his patients did well on Strattera alone, 1/3 did not respond well at all, and 1/3 needed a low dose of a stimulant medication in addition. In other words, for peak effectiveness, doctors may prescribe medications such as Focalin XR or Adderall XR in addition to Strattera.

- Strattera (atomoxetine)—effective for improving attention; improvements continue for several weeks
- Provigil™ (modafinil)—improves wakefulness; helps people with ADD/ADHD maintain a proper level of alertness; used to treat narcolepsy.

Secondary Conditions and Medications

Several medications are used to treat conditions that may coexist with ADD or ADHD such as depression, anxiety, irritability, or aggression. However, these medications do not significantly increase a student's ability to pay attention in class.

Antidepressants

Although medications may be known by one categorical name such as antidepressants, they are often used to treat a variety of other conditions. For example, antidepressants are sometimes prescribed to treat anxiety, which may coexist with an attention deficit. In fact, antidepressants are used more often in children to treat ADD- and ADHD-related behaviors than they are to treat depression. Increasing levels of the neurotransmitter serotonin is one of their most important functions. Higher levels of serotonin give us a sense of well-being, reduce irritability and aggression, and make it easier to get a good night's sleep.

Knowing this important information gives a teacher a better understanding of which behavior changes to expect when a teenager takes antidepressants. In addition, the teacher may help a student or her parents understand why she was prescribed an antidepressant. Otherwise, the student may refuse to take an antidepressant because she knows she is "not depressed."

Impact on Behavior: Each class of antidepressant works in a slightly different way to increase levels of serotonin in the brain. These medications are prescribed to help with several issues:

1. reducing moodiness,
2. leveling off emotional highs or lows,
3. improving frustration tolerance,
4. reducing irritability and aggression,
5. reducing impulsivity, and
6. treating depression.

When levels of serotonin drop, irritability and aggression increase. The most frequently prescribed antidepressants are known as Selective Serotonin Reuptake Inhibitors (SSRI). Tricyclics, which also improve sleep, are also effective, but are prescribed much less often, primarily because of the risk of an overdose. Anafranil™ is often prescribed for students with ADD/ADHD who may also have coexisting Tourette Syndrome and/or Obsessive Compulsive Disorder (OCD).

Length of Effectiveness: Unlike Ritalin and Dexedrine, which last only three to six hours, antidepressants build up in the bloodstream and are effective all day.

Common Antidepressant Medications

Selective Serotonin Re-uptake Inhibitors (SSRI's):
- Zoloft™ (sertraline)
- Paxil™ (paroxetine)
- Prozac™ (fluoxetine)
- Lexapro™ (excitalopram oxalate)
- Celexa™ (citalopram)

Miscellaneous Antidepressants:
In addition to increasing serotonin, some medications also increase norepinephrine, which is known to enhance attention. Consult with your physician.
- Wellbutrin™, Wellbutrin SR™, Wellbutrin XL™ (bupropion)—increases norepinephrine and serotoin; provides modest improvement in attention
- Effexor™ (venlafaxine)
- Anafranil™ (clomipramine)—reduces compulsive activity, rigidity, anxiety, irritability related to Tourette syndrome and obsessive compulsive disorder

Tricyclics:
- Tofranil™ (imipramine)—in addition, helpful with Tourette syndrome
- Norpramin™ (desipramine)
- Pamelor™ or Vivactyl™ (nortryptyline)

5

Antianxiety Medication:

- Buspar™ (buspirone)—reduces coexisting worrying, nervousness, and anxiety

Other Medications

Several medications used to treat other conditions are also effective in treating certain aspects of ADD and ADHD. Generally speaking, these medications are often used to reduce impulsivity, oppositional behavior, anger, and aggression. They are often used in combination with one of the stimulant medications such as Concerta or Adderall.

Antihypertensives:

These medications are typically prescribed to reduce blood pressure, and may also reduce hyperactivity, impulsivity, aggression, sleep problems, and tics.

- Intuniv™ (guanfacine)—a long-acting form of Tenex; ADA approved in 2009
- Tenex™ (guanfacine)
- Catapres™ (clonidine)

Mood Stabilizers:

These are typically prescribed to level off moods and may also reduce emotional blow-ups, mood swings, hyperactivity, impulsivity, and aggression. Some students feel these medications dull their ability to think clearly, and the lithium may damage teeth.

- Depakote™ (valproic acid)—also prescribed to treat seizures
- Lithionate™ (lithium carbonate)

What Improvements Should I See in Students Who Take Stimulant Medication?

Researchers tell us that *when medication is working properly, certain changes in behavior will occur. If these changes are **not** observed, then the medication is not working properly.*

Dr. James Swanson and his colleagues at the University of California (Irvine) conducted a "review of the review" of the literature that included thousands of research articles on medication treatment of attention deficit disorders. These studies provide convincing evidence that the student's *school work improves significantly* when stimulant medication is taken. Additional benefits from medication have been reported based upon outcomes of Dr. Russell Barkley's Milwaukee long-term follow-up research as children reach adulthood.

Researchers have reported that *stimulant medication is slightly less effective for students with ADD* (55 to 65 percent) when compared to ADHD (70 to 90 percent). Medication response for students with ADHD alone often seems miraculous, with grades jumping from Ds and Fs to As and Bs. However, when coexisting conditions are also present, the medication response is not as dramatic. Sometimes a second medication is needed to treat the coexisting conditions. For students who have the inattentive form of ADD, the reduced medication effectiveness may perhaps be linked to the executive function deficits that plague many students. Hopefully, researchers will begin looking for new medications that will help improve executive functions even more.

Effect of Medication

When medication is working, teachers should see the following changes:

Increased:
- attention and concentration,
- compliance,
- effort on tasks,
- amount and accuracy of school work produced.

Decreased:
- activity levels,
- impulsivity,
- negative behaviors in social interactions,
- physical and verbal hostility.

Dr. Russell Barkley found specific improvement in:
- working memory and self-talk (key executive skills),
- verbal fluency,
- ability to organize thinking,
- handwriting,
- motor coordination,
- self-esteem,
- emotional control,
- acceptance by, and interaction with, peers,
- awareness of the game in sports,
- decreased punishment from others.

5

Section 5 | Medication Issues

When students who are receiving treatment continue to struggle with inattention, impulsivity, and irritability, teachers should consider four possible causes:

1. Medication doses are too low (see Summaries 58-59).
2. The student *forgot* to take his medication (maybe the parents will bring it to school or keep extra medicine at school).
3. The student's medication doesn't kick in until well into class time; this occurs when students take medication as they are walking out the door to school (it takes a hour for long-acting medication to become fully effective).
4. The student's medication lasts only six hours and thus wears off by 1:00 pm or so.

Obviously, when medication is forgotten or wears off, these problem issues will resurface.

Even with medication, most students with ADD or ADHD occasionally will:

- lose books and papers,
- forget homework assignments, long-term projects, the weekly report, and to stay after school for a teacher conference or detention,
- be late to class or school; have difficulty estimating time required for assignments (medication has not been shown to improve their impaired sense of time),
- have difficulty planning ahead,
- have difficulty knowing how to budget time necessary to complete a long-term project.

Numerous suggestions are provided in Section 3 to address these executive function deficits.

Collecting Information Regarding Medication Effectiveness

When a student is starting a new medication or trying a different dosage, parents may ask teachers for feedback on changes they note in class. Sometimes they may have behavior rating checklists from doctors or mental health professionals; other times they may request feedback more informally. Rating scales completed by teachers provide the best evidence regarding medication effectiveness.

Simple Checklists: The checklists included as Appendices A9 and A10 are good resources for assessing medication effectiveness at school. Teacher input regarding medication effectiveness is especially critical!

A Comprehensive Rating Scale: The *Vanderbilt ADHD Rating Scale* is a more comprehensive tool that will pick up on ADHD, oppositional behavior, anxiety, depression, and school issues. The ADHD toolkit and the rating scale are available free for downloading from www.psychiatry24x7.com.

Resources

Barkley, Russell A. *Attention-deficit Hyperactivity Disorder: A Handbook for Diagnosis and Treatment.* 3rd ed. New York: Guilford Press, 2006.

MTA Cooperative Group. (1999). "A 14-month Randomized Clinical Trial of Treatment Strategies for Attention-Deficit/Hyperactivity Disorder. *Archives of General Psychiatry,* Vol. 56: 1073-86.

Swanson, J.M. et al. (1993). "Effect of Stimulant Medication on Children with Attention Deficit Disorder: A "Review of Reviews." *Exceptional Children,* Vol. 60: 154-62.

Wilens, Timothy E. *Straight Talk about Psychiatric Medications for Kids.* 3rd ed. New York, NY: Guilford Press, 2008.

Action of Stimulant Medications: Regular vs. Sustained-release (SR) Forms

SUMMARY 58

The four most commonly used stimulant medications in the U.S. are Concerta™, Adderall™, Vyvance™, and Ritalin™. Researchers tell us that all four medications are equally effective in treating ADD and ADHD. However, individual student response to each medication may vary. Medications are available in regular, sustained-release, and longer-acting forms. Today, most students take the long-acting medications that give all-day school coverage.

Sustained-Release Medications

Sustained-release medications typically last six to twelve hours, as opposed to regular tablets, which may last only three hours or so. Two of the best-known stimulants, Concerta and Adderall XR, each last roughly ten hours. Vyvance is newer and is reported to last up to twelve hours or longer.

Chart Medication Coverage

Parents or teachers are encouraged to chart the hours of effectiveness of medication coverage, especially if a student continues to struggle. Note the time medication is taken and then add one hour to determine when medication is fully effective. For example, if a student took his medicine at 8:00 a.m. on the ride to school, and is sitting in math class by 8:30 a.m., medication has not yet reached peak effectiveness. The student's struggles in math (but not in other classes) may be related to the lack of medication during first period.

Concerta, Adderall XR, or Vyvance
8-12 hrs

7:30 8 8:30 9 9:30 10 10:30 11 11:30 12 12:30 1 1:30 2 2:30 3
(a.m.) (p.m.)

Again, note the time medication is taken, then add the minimum hours of effectiveness to project the time medication will wear off. For instance, when a student takes Focalin XR (a 6-8 hour medicine) at 6:00 a.m. before an early morning bus ride, medication may wear off by 1 p.m. or so.

Focalin XR or Medate ER
6-8 hrs

6 6:30 7 7:30 8 8:30 9 9:30 10 10:30 11 11:30 12 12:30 1 1:30
(a.m.) (p.m.)

Available Forms and Dosages of Commonly Prescribed Medications:

Concerta	SR capsule: 18, 27, 36, 54 mg	max. dose per day: 54 mg
Adderall XR	SR tablet 5, 10, 15, 20, 25, 30 mg	max. dose per day: 30 mg
Focalin XR	SR capsule 5, 10, 20 mg	max. dose per day: 20 mg
Metadate ER	ER tablet 10, 20 mg	max. dose per day: 60 mg

Potential Medication Challenges

Low Medication Dose: One middle school teacher reported that a student was having trouble paying attention, even though he was taking medication. The student's concentration improved significantly after the doctor raised the dose of Adderall XR from 20 mg to 25 mg. If teachers or parents know the student's dosage for a particular medication is below the maximum dose, then they will know to talk with the doctor about the student's struggles.

Impact of Puberty: Students may be successful in school for several years while taking medication. Then suddenly during middle school, their academic performance may decline. Parents and teachers should be aware that adjustments in medication may be needed in middle school due to the student's physical growth and hormonal changes.

Medication Tolerance. Over time, a student may build up a tolerance to a long-acting medication, thereby reducing its effectiveness. The doctor may increase the dosage or change medications.

Attempting Homework without Medication. With the exception of Strattera, most medications wear off by late afternoon or early evening when it's time to begin homework. Doctors often prescribe a short-acting medication, such as Ritalin, Dexedrine, or Focalin, to provide coverage for roughly three to four hours.

Short-Acting Medications (Sometimes Helpful for Assistance at Homework Time)

As shown in the diagram below, regular tablets of both Ritalin and Dexedrine usually take 15-30 minutes to begin working. After the medication starts working, ***peak academic work time may last about 3 hours*** before the effectiveness begins to fade. For example, a teenager who takes regular Ritalin at 5:30 p.m. for homework will have medication working effectively until roughly 8:30 p.m.

Younger children are more likely to take short-acting medications. This can be problematic during the school day. Medication taken at 7:00 a.m. will wear off by around 10:00 a.m. If they don't take the next tablet until 12:00, medication will not be effective again until 12:30. Consequently, there is a one- to two-hour window with no medication. Students may be completing their work and behaving well at 9:00, but by 11:30, as medication wears off, they may be failing and misbehaving. When medication wears off, emotional blow-ups or fights are more likely to occur. ***If this medication problem is corrected, typically the student's behavior and school work will improve.***

Short-acting Tablets

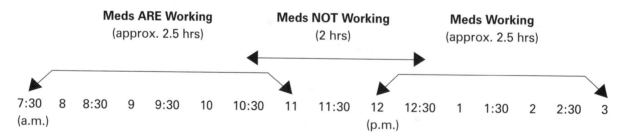

| **Meds ARE Working** | **Meds NOT Working** | **Meds Working** |
| (approx. 2.5 hrs) | (2 hrs) | (approx. 2.5 hrs) |

7:30 8 8:30 9 9:30 10 10:30 11 11:30 12 12:30 1 1:30 2 2:30 3
(a.m.)   (p.m.)

Available Forms and Dosages of Regular Stimulant Medications:

Ritalin	Tablets: 5, 10, 20 mg	max. dose per day: 60 mg
Dexedrine	Tablet: 5 mg	max. dose per day: 40 mg
Methylin	Tablets: 5, 10, 20 mg	max. dose per day: 60 mg

What Educators Need to Know about Medication: A Summary

As explained in Section 4, students who are doing poorly in school may be referred to a Student Support Team (or similar group) for a staffing to brainstorm about ways to help them succeed in school. *Since an inappropriate medication regimen may be an underlying problem, members of this team need to have a basic understanding about medication issues.* An awareness of the issues below will help team members make an educated guess about whether or not medication is a problem. Consultation from school nurses who are knowledgeable about ADHD medications will be invaluable.

Potential Medication Problems

1. When teenagers reach puberty, *hormonal and weight changes may affect medication effectiveness.* Doses may be too low and adjustments may be needed.

2. The *dosage may be too low* to obtain maximum benefit at school. (The NIMH/MTA study identified this as a major problem.)

3. Parents and teenagers often *don't know when peak medication dosages have been achieved.* Getting medication "right" is not easy, especially in complex cases of ADD/ADHD.

4. It may simply be the *wrong medication* for the teenager. Even if one stimulant does not work, a different one may work quite well.

5. Most long-acting medications typically *release equal portions of medication* in the morning and then again in the afternoon, which gives all-day medication coverage. However, *Concerta releases only 22 percent* in the morning, and some students have reported that they can't concentrate as well during morning hours. Some doctors are prescribing an additional small dose of a short-acting medication to improve attention and concentration in the morning.

6. As discussed in the preceding summary, some students develop *a tolerance to medication,* especially the sustained-release form. Not only can students develop a tolerance over a period of months, but they can also develop a tolerance during the course of the day.

7. Some students may *metabolize medication quickly,* so the effects may wear off earlier than expected.

8. In addition, the *initial morning dose of a short-acting medication may wear off* well before the second dose becomes effective, leaving a period without any medication coverage.

9. *The student may forget* to take his medication or perhaps *refuse* to take it. Sometimes teens become embarrassed about taking medication or don't want to go to the office or clinic, and problems with "medication refusal" arise.

10. *Coexisting problems may be present and untreated.* Two-thirds of teens with attention deficits have at least one coexisting problem. (See Summaries 1, 10, and 72.) Another medication may be needed in addition to Adderall or Concerta to effectively treat the student.

Getting Medication "Right"

School officials are often surprised to learn that finding the best medication for each teenager is not an exact science. In fact, a lot of trial and error is often involved. In reality, most doctors don't have the time or manpower to accurately assess medication effectiveness. Although some teenagers may luck out and get the right medication and dose on the very first visit to the doctor, this doesn't happen very often.

Typically, after a teenager takes medication, the doctor receives a general report from the family about their subjective impressions of the medication and its impact on the student's schoolwork. Rarely is any objective measurement taken from teachers to determine whether the medication is working properly. So, if the student's schoolwork improves a little even though he is still struggling, parents often think, "This must be as good as the medication gets." Parents then maintain the same ineffective medication dosages, when, in reality, there is a good chance that schoolwork could improve significantly with proper medication levels. (See Summary 11.) The fact is, when a student is struggling, it is almost impossible for a doctor to get medication right without input from teachers.

Questions to Determine Medication Effectiveness

To determine whether the student's medication is working effectively, several important questions must be answered. Teachers may tactfully lay the groundwork for discussing medication with the parent by saying something like this:

"We are trying to look at everything that may possibly interfere with your son's ability to succeed in school. His teachers have told us about his performance in class. The school psychologist has looked over his school records and will do an evaluation to look for learning problems. You have told us about his struggles with homework.

One other area we should consider is his medication and how it is working while he is at school. By asking a few questions on a checklist that both you and his other teachers answer, we should have a pretty good idea if the medication is working properly. You may not know all the answers to these questions, but you can call and tell us later."

By answering as many of the following questions as possible, teachers and parents will have a good idea whether medication is a significant problem. If physician follow-up is necessary, this information will be extremely helpful to the doctor as he considers adjustments in the medication. Summaries 56-59 on medication will also be helpful in assessing the effectiveness of a teenager's medication.

Obviously, it is not the teacher's role to suggest specific medications to parents. However, as parents review the summaries in this section, they may decide to discuss possible alternatives with their doctor.

1. **What medication is the teenager taking?**

   - Is it a central nervous system stimulant like Ritalin, Concerta, or Adderall?
   - Is it an antidepressant like Zoloft or Prozac?
   - Is it a short- or long-lasting medication?
   - What time does the medication wear off? (Chart medication coverage as explained in Summary 58.)
   - Is the medication brand name or generic? Many students have found that the generic methylphenidate doesn't work as well as Ritalin.

2. **How much medication is the teenager taking?**

   One of the most common reasons for school failure and misbehavior is that the student is not getting enough medication throughout the day for it to work effectively. In fact, as explained in Summary 11, researchers tell us that most students are taking doses that fall below the peak effectiveness levels identified in a recent NIMH study. It is important to know the milligrams being taken per dose. Common forms and dosages are given in Summary 58. If parents don't know the answer immediately, they may have a prescription bottle at the school nurse's station or they may check at home.

3. How often does the teenager take medication?

A student may take medication one or two times a day. Some may take medication at home in the morning and not take it again all day. Unfortunately, the medication may wear off earlier than the teacher and parents expect. The diagrams in Summary 58 shows the approximate time of day when both regular and sustained-release medications typically wear off.

4. What time does the teenager take each dose of medication?

Timing of these doses is critical to give all-day coverage. Depending on the timing of the first morning dose, the medication may wear off after lunch, leaving the student without coverage for afternoon classes. If students are taking their long-acting medication in the car on the way to school, peak medication effectiveness won't be achieved until well into first period.

5. Is the medication working effectively?

Many medication checklists contain medicine-related symptoms only—for example, headaches, insomnia, and loss of appetite. Unfortunately, they do not measure whether or not the medication is helping the student do better in school—which is often the primary reason for taking medication. Teachers may find the checklist in Summary 57 more useful. This checklist assesses the most critical school issues, such as whether the student is passing the class or completing his work. A regular medication symptom checklist may be used in conjunction with this one, if needed.

Teachers may also complete the rating scale in Appendix A9 to determine whether medication is working effectively. If the changes listed in Summary 57 and Appendix A9 are not observed, then something may still be wrong with the medication. If a teenager has been doing well and then his school performance suddenly drops, several factors such as those listed earlier in this summary may be causing the problem—e.g., puberty, medication tolerance, generic medication.

Sometimes adults forget to ask the real experts, the teens themselves, how the medication works for them. Some of them are quite good at articulating how medication is helping. Others have great difficulty judging its impact. But regardless, ask the teen to complete Appendix A10.

6. If medication is not working effectively, what changes are needed?

Fine-tuning medication is critical! It will take the teenager, parent, teacher, and doctor working together to find the best medication regimen. Encourage parents to meet with the doctor and share the information regarding the medication's effectiveness collected by the team.

Medication Effectiveness at School

Student's name: _____ Date & class: _____

Completed by: _____ Time of day observed: _____

To assess the impact medication is having on a student's school work, each teacher should answer several key questions. When medication is working properly and learning problems have been identified, the student should be doing much better in school. If the teacher cannot check the "Strongly agree" and "Agree" columns, then problems may still exist in several areas: 1) the proper accommodations are not being provided for the student's learning problems, 2) executive function deficits are not being addressed, or 3) the medication regimen may not be right for the student. Please circle the answer that best describes the student's behavior.

Academic Performance:

	Strongly Agree	Agree	Neutral	Disagree	Strongly Disagree
When the student is in my class, s/he:					
1. pays attention	1	2	3	4	5
2. completes class and homework	1	2	3	4	5
3. does work correctly	1	2	3	4	5
4. complies with requests	1	2	3	4	5
5. makes passing grades	1	2	3	4	5

ADD/ADHD-Related Behaviors, Including Executive Function

If the student is on medication and is not doing well in school, what else could be causing continuing problems? Are there any ADD/ADHD-related behaviors that are interfering with the student's ability to succeed in school?

ADD/ADHD-Related Behaviors:

The student:					
6. is organized	1	2	3	4	5
7. manages time well	1	2	3	4	5
8. remembers things easily	1	2	3	4	5
9. is on time to class	1	2	3	4	5
10. is on time to school	1	2	3	4	5
11. thinks carefully before acting or speaking	1	2	3	4	5
12. is awake and alert in class	1	2	3	4	5

Ask parents about any sleep problems. According to them, the student:

13. falls asleep easily	1	2	3	4	5
14. wakes up easily	1	2	3	4	5

Comments: _____
_____
_____

If problems still exist, should a behavioral intervention plan be developed to provide additional accommodations or teach the student compensatory skills, or should teachers suggest that parents seek medical advice?
_____

Student Comments about Medication

Several teenagers and young adults featured in the two videos I co-produced with our son Alex—*Real Life ADHD!* and *Teen to Teen: the ADD Experience*— made some very insightful comments about stimulant medications. These candid comments may give teachers a better understanding of the impact medication has on students.

■ *"Medication calms me down and it helps me concentrate."* —Julie, seventh grader

■ *"If I don't take my medication, I forget the small details in language arts, like writing down the work. Because if I don't take it, I just sit there. The medicine also helps me stay awake. If I don't take it, that's one of my first signs—I'm practically falling asleep."* —Jerry, high school sophomore

■ *"It helps me some. But if I'm not 'on' that day or if I'm really out of it or I don't want to study something, it's not going to make me study anything. But it does help a lot."*
—Maresa, high school senior

■ *"Well, it definitely helps me. I used to take college classes that were back-to-back, long, three-hour classes. I would always notice that my notes would be almost perfect to begin with. But towards the end of my last class, I would end up having drawings and doodles and all kinds of stuff that would just kind of fade. You could just watch it as my medicine faded off. It definitely helps me with school work."* —Alex

■ *"I don't like the way medication makes me feel but I know I need to take it so I can do okay in school."* —Lewis, high school graduate and popular Atlanta DJ

■ *"It doesn't do me any good to study unless I've had my medication. Otherwise, I won't remember what I studied."* —Alex

■ *"It helps me to get my work done. It doesn't really affect my personality that much except maybe I don't yell out in class as much or get in trouble as much."* —Jerry

■ *"It helps me with my work. It helps me focus on what needs to be done. If I don't take my medication, I get to my job and I forget what's going on. I have to sit and think and I don't know what I'm doing. I do this and I do that and I don't get anything done. With my medication I pull myself together and I complete the job and I complete it well."* —Lewis

■ *"I've taken both Ritalin and Adderall. I think both cut down on impulsivity a lot."* —Jerry

■ *"Medication cuts down on impulsivity but it only lasts while you're on it. So you can be impulsive afterwards."* —Alex

■ *"In seventh grade I had to switch medications. I don't know if it's because I went through puberty or what. I was taking Ritalin and going along just fine. Then all of a sudden the Ritalin dropped off and really no matter how much I took, it didn't really help me that much. So I had to switch medications. We tried a couple of medications and decided Adderall worked best.."* —Jerry

■ *"It takes at least an hour for Focalin (regular) to kick in. I notice the effects fading somewhere around six to eight hours later."* —Maresa

■ *"They say I have a sleep disturbance. I'd go to bed at 9 o'clock at night and couldn't fall asleep until 1 or 2 o'clock in the morning. I'd just lay there awake. Now I take imipramine (Tofranil) to help me go to sleep. Sometimes I'll be sitting there awake and I'll know I haven't taken my medicine because I can't fall asleep."* —Jerry

- *"On my medicine, I'm real calm and straightforward and don't really care to laugh a lot. But off of it, I'm whew ... my mind is really bouncing around. That's what's great about it. It's me."* —Lewis

- *"I think the medication does have an effect on creativity. When you're not on medicine, your mind just races back and forth between so many things. You can start off on one topic and end up on some other topic way far away from there within seconds. I think that has a lot to do with creativity. When you're on Adderall, your mind doesn't race as much and you won't have as many ideas pop into your head."* —Alex

- *"I knew medication worked because one day I walked into class and I was making chicken noises. When the medication kicked in, I quit making noise and I knew it was working."* —Lewis

- *"My friends tell me not to take medication before I come to a party because I'm more fun without it."* —Travis, high school senior

- *"My main concern was that I would have side effects from the medication and that I personally wouldn't be able to detect them. I was afraid I'd have all of these horrible side effects and that I wouldn't know. That I'd be barking like a dog or something."* —Marisa

- *"Once I took the medication and learned what it was like to concentrate, it was easier to force myself back on track when my mind wandered, even if my medicine was wearing off."* —Max, college student

- *"I still have side effects. I can't eat lunch and I can't sleep if I take it too late. Sometimes I get moody when the medication wears off."* —Lewis

Resources

Real Life ADHD!: A Survival Guide for Children and Teen, a DVD filmed, produced, and edited by Alex Zeigler and Chris A. Zeigler Dendy. Cedar Bluff, AL: Chris A. Zeigler Dendy Consulting LLC, 2010. (Information is available from www.chrisdendy.com.)

Teen to Teen: the ADD Experience (VHS), produced and edited by Chris A. Zeigler Dendy. Cedar Bluff, AL: Chris A. Zeigler Dendy Consulting LLC, 1999. (Information is available from www.chrisdendy.com.).

SECTION 6

Classroom Management and Challenging Behaviors

Prevention is the best behavior management strategy! Some of the most effective ways for avoiding behavior problems from students with attention deficits include:

Ensure that the student with an attention deficit disorder is succeeding academically. That means learning problems and medication issues associated with attention deficits must be addressed. Once these problems have been addressed, these students will typically have fewer behavior problems at school. Earlier sections of this book provide suggestions for dealing with academic issues.

1. **Provide a supportive, structured classroom.**

2. **Be aware of which teaching techniques and ways of speaking to students can either increase or decrease the likelihood of misbehavior.**

4. **Be aware of the impact of ADD or ADHD and executive function deficits on a student's learning and behavior** (organization, getting started, finishing, etc.).

5. **Be aware of ADD/ADHD behaviors and how they affect a student's performance in the classroom.** For example, Dr. Sam Goldstein points out that sometimes it is hard to tell the difference between inattention and noncompliance. If a student does not do as a teacher asks, is it because she was not paying attention, or intentionally refusing to do as the teacher requested? It's easy to assume incorrectly that it's intentional misbehavior.

The summaries that follow offer additional suggestions to help teachers avoid potential problems. In addition, there are strategies for coping more effectively with students with ADD or ADHD when they do have problems. Classroom management techniques and behavioral strategies are briefly reviewed. Other school-based intervention strategies such as peer mediation are also discussed.

6

Overview of Research on the Brain and Its Impact on Attention and Classroom Behavior

Teachers are encouraged to read Summary 14 about "Brain-based Learning." This summary explains the impact the brain and movement have on learning and behavior.

Highlights include:

1. Movement increases blood flow and oxygen to the brain, thus improving attention.
2. Exercise facilitates the growth of new brain cells.
3. Students must move or fidget when completing more difficult academic tasks that require working memory.
4. Laughter (and even chewing gum) increases activity in the frontal lobe and thus improves attention.
5. Students with attention deficits have reduced working memory capacity—they remember fewer items and hold information in mind for less time than their peers.
6. Academic materials must either be high interest or novel for the ADD/ADHD brain to learn effectively.
7. Students remember information better when it is connected to past experiences.
8. A positive emotional climate in the classroom enables students to learn more easily.
9. Drinking water increases the oxygen in the bloodstream and the brain, thus improving attention.
10. Restful sleep is critical for paying attention and remembering what is learned.

Classroom Management

SUMMARY **62**

Good classroom management is critical and is often the best way to prevent potential discipline problems. To use a sports metaphor: the best defense is a good offense. In other words, teachers are more likely to avoid behavior problems by having a clearly defined classroom routine in place.

Problems Contributing to Misbehavior

First let's review some of the potential situations that researchers believe may contribute to misbehavior in the classroom. ***The two primary contributors are:***

1. work that is too difficult and
2. work that takes too long to complete.

Other problems contributing to misbehavior include:

3. lack of a positive, personal relationship between the student and teacher,
4. class rules that are not clear,
5. vague expectations from the teacher,
6. too little structure in the classroom,
7. lack of a routine and unannounced transitions from one activity to another (entering and leaving class, riding the bus, changing tasks within a class, lunch, returning from active classes like PE),
8. too little feedback from the teacher,
9. work that is not high interest or novel (is repetitive, or is perceived as boring or not meaningful),
10. seating that is too near distractions (the door, aquarium, pencil sharpener),
11. overcrowded classrooms.

Proactive Classroom Management Strategies

Keeping these potential problems in mind, teachers are encouraged to use proactive classroom management strategies such as those included in this summary to prevent misbehavior in class. The suggestions provided here come from many sources, including nationally known educators Robert Reed of the University of Nebraska, Ann Welch at the University of Virginia, and the late Clare Jones from Arizona; from veteran classroom teachers who are also parents of students with attention deficits; from my sister, Dr. Billie Abney, a classroom teacher; from school psychologists; and from my own personal experience in teaching, school psychology, and mental health.

Building Rapport

Students with attention deficits are often described as being difficult to motivate. Teachers who take the time to build a strong rapport with these teenagers will be able to work with them more effectively. For better or worse, ***the academic performance of these students often depends on whether or not they like the teacher!*** Students with attention deficits perform better for teachers who like and respect them in return. These students will pass a subject one semester and fail it the next because of personality conflicts with the new teacher. Conflicts between teachers and students are more easily resolved when a strong rapport exists.

6

1. **Make an effort to get to know students personally.** Ann Welch gives an example of a teacher who did not like a particular student but went out of her way to get to know the student better. The teacher found time for one-on-one talks by sitting with the student at lunch or talking with him during a break. Eventually, she found something she liked about the young man.

2. **Ask teenagers to fill out bio sheets about themselves.** Selena Conley, EDS, a veteran Georgia special education teacher, has her students complete a bio sheet and answer these questions about themselves.
   - Hello, my name is:
   - My talents and gifts are:
   - Sometimes I need help with:
   - I like to work in this type of environment:
   - I get distracted when:
   - I get upset when:
   - I use some tools to help me with my work. These are:

3. **Give a couple of students extra attention.** Select a couple of students who need extra attention each day for some personal and positive interaction. Some students like public praise; others are embarrassed by it and prefer a pat on the shoulder or a quiet comment.

4. **Greet students at the door by name.** Work on learning all your students' names.

5. **Make a class bulletin board of both academic and nonacademic interests or skills.** Ask students to bring pictures of themselves involved in various activities: hobbies, sports, or accomplishments. In a multi-subject teaching load, a different class could be featured each month. This makes it easier to find common interests or topics for enriching school work. For example, the student could write an essay on topics of interest to her such as photography, cars, or website design. A separate board also could be used to display some of the students' best work.

6. **Ask the teenager and parents to complete Appendix A11.** This form suggests ways of looking at ADD/ADHD behaviors in a more positive manner. Sometimes the student's behavior can actually be an asset in the adult work world. For example, hyperactivity may be viewed as high energy, bossiness as leadership, and daydreaming as a sign of imaginative thinking. Advise parents in advance that the form will be sent home so they can be thinking of their teen's positive qualities. Sometimes when parents have had a lot of conflicts with their teen, they may have trouble thinking of anything positive to say about her. Help them learn to reframe their teenager's positive qualities. When the form is completed and returned to school, teachers should take a moment to review it and add a couple of things to the list.

Classroom Emotional Climate

Creating a positive emotional climate in the classroom is critical for maximizing student learning. One expert on learning, Patricia Vail, has described emotion as the *"on-off switch"* to learning. Emotions originate in the limbic system of the brain; this system also has a profound impact on memory. ***Students cannot learn in a negative, fear-based classroom.*** According to Candy Lawson, Ph.D., at the Center for Development and Learning, the negative messages sent by the limbic system to the cortex of the brain stifle thinking and learning. The bottom line is fairly simple: a positive, encouraging atmosphere sends a message of purpose and excitement to the cortex that in turn directs the student to take action to learn. Dr. Lawson advises that "positive emotions such as joy, contentment, acceptance, trust, and satisfaction can enhance learning." It's important to remember that happiness actually has a positive effect on learning, memory, and social behavior.

Dr. John Ratey, a psychiatrist who also has ADHD, noted that, "If mild stress becomes chronic, the cascade of cortisol triggers genetic actions that begin to sever synaptic connections and cause dendrites to atrophy and cells to die; eventually, the hippocampus can end up physically shriveled, like a raisin." The hippocampus plays a key role in forming, sorting, storing, and giving memories meaning. In other words, ***negative emotions and stress often block a student's ability to learn and memorize information.*** This research clearly shows that educators must help students cope with stress and fear before they can activate the executive function system.

Classroom Structure

1. **Post a written schedule** for the day, perhaps on the board.
   - Write the activities on the board. *"Continue class reports on science experiments."*
   - Include the homework assignment on the board. *"Read pp. 119–130. Answer questions 1–10."*

2. **Prompt with specific cues** about needed materials and actions. *"Get out your algebra book and open it to page 109."*

3. **Cue when changes or transitions are about to occur.** *"You have three more minutes to finish reading this section and then we are going to discuss it."*

4. **Develop a homework routine.** See Summary 27.
   - ***Designate "row captains"*** to see that homework assignments are copied down and that homework is collected from all students.
   - ***Ask students to copy their assignments*** from the board at the same time the teacher or another student writes the homework on the board. When the teacher also writes the assignment, it slows her down, giving the student adequate time to write it down. Otherwise, teachers may not allow enough time for slow processing students to write down assignments.
   - ***Place completed work in a designated spot.*** Ask students to turn in assignments at the same time each day and put it in the same place. If work is completed early, allow them to turn it in. Do not ask them to keep it until tomorrow.
   - ***Place completed work in one folder.*** Suggest that the student place completed work for all classes in one colored folder. He may have difficulty keeping up with several different folders. Ask the student to tell you what works best for him. Although certainly not ideal, one student found that it actually worked best for her if she put her math papers in her math book when she finished them.
   - ***Maintain this daily structure and routine.*** Consistent class routine is important. These students don't handle changes or transitions well and are more likely to misbehave then.

Classroom Rules

1. **Have a few good rules (3–5 at most).**

2. **Keep rules short and simple.**

3. **State rules in positive terms.** Tell students what to do rather than what not to do. Instead of saying *"Stop talking when you enter class,"* say, *"When you come into class, check the assignment on the overhead and start working quietly."*

4. **Post rules prominently.**

5. **Teach the rules.**

6. **Reinforce compliance.** Class rules work best when students:
   - are praised by the teacher for obeying the rules, and
   - are ignored or mildly reprimanded for breaking rules.

Use of Behavioral Strategies, Both Positive and Negative

Be positive: The importance of using positive reinforcement is critical. Positive interventions should always be used first. Give positive comments more often—at a rate of five to one over negative comments. See Summary 65 for more details on use of behavioral strategies.

Transitions

Students with attention deficits may have problems with transition times such as entering and leaving class, changing activities within a class, returning from an active class such as P.E. to do seatwork, going to lunch or leaving school, and riding the bus to and from school.

1. **Allow time for transitions** such as putting away books and papers or sharpening pencils.

2. **Segue, or transition, into work:** Help students transition into work by having an activity for them to start as soon as they walk into class. Have a list of vocabulary words from an essay or questions on the overhead projector. As part of the class routine, students know to start on this assignment as soon as they sit down. Occasionally, add some variety by including a fun activity. For example, ask a trivia question or *"What would you do with a million dollars?" "If you had one wish?"* Ask a couple of students to answer.

3. **Model moving quickly** from one activity to another. *"John, thanks for getting ready so quickly. You're the first one to get your workbook out."*

4. **Reinforce compliance,** possibly through a group reward. *"Good, you all quickly got out your books and notebook paper and are ready to start. I'll add 28 points to our total class points—one for each student who did as I asked."*

5. **Group rewards:** Sometimes teachers set up a point system for the whole class to earn privileges such as extra time for free reading, time to talk quietly with classmates, having the teacher read to the class from a favorite novel, or a class pizza party. When a certain number of points are earned, students earn a group reward. See Summary 65 for more information on this topic.
   - If students take too long to get ready to work, say *"When it is time for class to start, I would like for you to quickly get ready to work. Today the class didn't do that very well. Tomorrow, please come into class ready to work. When you follow this rule for five days, I'll give the class ten minutes of free reading time [or another reward]."*
   - After unsuccessful attempts for several days, subtract time lost during transitions from group free time: *"You were too slow getting started today so I'm going to subtract late time from your free reading period."* However, try positive strategies before reluctantly turning to negatives.

Scheduling

1. **Assign with compatible teachers.** Consider assigning the student to a teacher who is more understanding of ADD/ADHD challenges, who provides a positive classroom atmosphere for learning, and is good at teaching students skills to compensate for their deficits.

2. **Schedule challenging work before enjoyable activities.** *"When you finish your vocabulary words, you may have the rest of the time (5-10 minutes) for free reading."*

3. **Develop an individualized class schedule.** When classes are scheduled prior to each semester, many students with attention deficits need individualized schedules rather than computer-assigned classes. Consideration should be given to pairing students with teachers who work well with these teens.

4. **Schedule difficult classes during morning hours.**
   - During the morning, students are fresh and teachers are assured that medication is working. Typically, schoolwork deteriorates later in the day. The IEP may contain recommendations regarding class scheduling. Otherwise, the guidance counselor (class scheduler) should review past grades and ask recent teachers which subjects are most difficult.
   - Schedule hands-on classes such as computers, PE, art, or other classes the student enjoys later in the day.
   - If a student is struggling, schedule classes with former teachers with whom she has been successful.

5. **Schedule half or partial school days.** Occasionally, if a student is in crisis and can't seem to handle whole days at school without blowing up, schedule him or her for half days. After problems are resolved and medication is stabilized, phase the student back into full-day scheduling.

Classroom Set-up

Some teachers assign seats to students because they believe it helps maintain better class discipline, makes record keeping and memorizing names easier, meets the students' academic needs, and/or allows placing students near positive role models. If teachers typically assign seats, then they may want to consider the issues below and decide which seating arrangement works best for each student.

1. **Give the student a choice.** If you don't assign seats for other students and the student with an attention deficit is doing her work, let her select her own seat. Many students with ADD or ADHD don't want to be singled out and are easily embarrassed. Obviously, most don't want to sit in the front row.

2. **Assign a front row seat? Maybe, maybe not.** Sometimes these students are seated in the front row near the teacher's desk to help them pay attention. However, the teacher's desk is often at the center of activity and may provide too many distractions for the student. Instead you may want to try one of the following options.

3. **Seat student 2-3 rows from the front near one side of the classroom.** If she becomes restless, the student may stand unobtrusively or lean against the wall.

4. **Use other students to provide visual cues.** The late Clare Jones suggested that distractible students benefit from watching and taking visual cues from others regarding the activity of the moment. For example, the student can see classmates who are: 1) working on class work, 2) getting ready to do problems on the board, 3) opening their books to page 27, or 4) raising their hands to answer questions.

5. **If other seat assignments do not work, assign her a seat near where the teacher provides instruction.** Some students may stay focused if they are seated near the teacher's podium, the overhead projector, or the area where the teacher is most often standing and teaching.

6. **Make a second seat or work station available.** This allows restless students to get up and move to a different table or desk to work on class work or projects.
    - One of the extra workstations may be a ***stand-up desk.*** The legs on some desks will extend, allowing the student to stand up and work. Plus, some have a swinging footrest. Placing a desk on blocks will also accomplish the same purpose. The cost of the stand-up desk may be problematic; the cheapest I've seen was roughly $200. However, teachers are always resourceful and may find cheaper alternatives. For example, you can buy a Speedy Stand-up Portable Desk that is placed on top of a standard desk for roughly $60 (see photo).
    - Discuss how the student should move to a different desk (carry everything with you, move quickly, keep your mouth closed.) Ask her to model the right way to move.

Speedy Stand-up Portable Desk (available from www.LampsUSA.com).

7. **Seat away from major distractions.** Avoid seating near distractions such as an open door, pencil sharpener, a loud air conditioner, or, for some students, the teacher's desk.

8. **Seating in groups:**
    - Place the student with good role models.
    - If a student misbehaves when placed with friends, work with her so they can be together. Tell her what she must do to earn the privilege of being in the same group with friends. *"When you obey the rules, talk softly so I can't hear you, and talk about the required project, then you may all remain in the same group."*
    - In group teaching sessions, especially a circle, try seating the student across from you, rather than beside you. It may be easier to maintain eye contact or send a private signal to pay attention. Consider a "U" shaped seating arrangement.

Resources

Abramowitz, A.J. and O'Leary, S. "Behavioral Interventions for the Classroom: Implications for Students with ADHD." *School Psychology Review*, 1991, Vol. 20: 220-234.

Dendy, Chris A. Zeigler. *Teenagers with ADD and ADHD.* 2nd edition. Bethesda, MD: Woodbine House, 2007.

Jones, Clare. "Strategies for School Success: Middle School through High School." CHADD Conference presentation. New York, NY, 1998.

Ratey, John. *Spark: The Revolutionary New Science of Exercise and the Brain*. New York, NY: Little, Brown and Company, 2008.

Reid, Robert. "Attention Deficit Hyperactivity Disorder: Effective Methods for the Classroom. *Focus on Exceptional Children,* December 1999, Vol. 32, No.4.

Welch, Ann. "Increasing Academic Engagement of Students with ADHD." *ADHD Report,* June 1999, Vol.7, No. 3.

Zentall, Sydney. "Theory- and Evidence-based Strategies for Children with Attentional Problems." *Psychology in the Schools*, 2005, Vol. 42, No. 8.

Teaching Strategies That Affect Behavior

How a teacher provides instruction and supervision can help the student:

1. pay attention better,
2. participate actively in class,
3. complete more schoolwork,
4. minimize behavior problems.

Drawing students into active participation in class, as well as interactions with the teacher, will also reduce misbehavior. Most teachers are already familiar with these strategies, but a brief review with an added ADD/ADHD twist may be helpful. Several of these suggestions are found in Robert Reid's review of best practice for teaching students with attention deficits. Information from Drs. Rapport, Ratey, Sousa, and Zentall were also invaluable (Summary 62).

Help Students Learn What You Are Teaching

Numerous best practice teaching strategies are presented in Summaries 16A-F. A few strategies are highlighted here.

1. Give assignments that are not too difficult or too long.
2. State your goal or main point clearly; be concise.
3. Highlight key information.
4. Use global cues or models to focus on the big picture—"it looks like."
5. Give step-by-step instructions.
6. Start with easier tasks first, then move on to the more difficult tasks.
7. Model and demonstrate new skills.
8. Pair students to problem-solve together and discuss details to avoid superficial processing.
9. Relate information to something in their personal experience.
10. Link to previous lessons.
11. Add novelty: provide music, use color, show films or videos on YouTube.com.
12. Monitor understanding.
13. Provide positive corrective feedback; teach self-monitoring.
14. Provide "brain breaks" to increase oxygen to the brain, thus improving attention.
15. Use humor. Laughter also increases blood flow and oxygen to the brain.

Get Students to Listen

1. Teach the lesson with enthusiasm.
2. Use a more focused style; be concise.
3. Avoid lengthy lectures.
4. Invite frequent active responses from students rather than just having them sit quietly. (Active response strategies such as *group response* or *response cards* are discussed in Summary 16-A.)
5. Give a cue to listen. For example, say, *"Give me five."* Then count backward so that by the time you reach one, the class is listening and ready to work.

Let Students Move

Students with ADHD need to be active in order to learn. In fact, Mark Rapport has shown that the more challenging the academic task, the more active our students must become in order to stay focused on the material. Providing opportunities for movement also gives students with attention deficits a legitimate outlet for their restless energy and refreshes their brain power, which enables them to learn more easily. Exercise also stimulates the growth of new brain cells. Try these ideas with students:

1. **Allow students to stand, kneel, or fidget.** Sandra Dendy, a veteran classroom teacher and my daughter-in-law, placed one of her active students at the end of a row. This allowed her to stand, kneel, or fidget without distracting other students.

2. **Take a brief exercise break.** Ask students to stand, hold on to their desks, stretch or jump, or march to music. Exercise breaks increase blood flow and oxygen to the brain, thus enabling our students to pay attention and learn more easily.

3. **Help the teacher.** Ask the student to pick up homework from students, hand out materials, or straighten up bookshelves.

4. **Deliver messages.** Ask the student to take messages to the office or other teachers. Ann Welch gives an example of a teacher who sent a sealed envelope with this message inside: *"This student needed a movement break. Please thank him, and send him back."*

5. **Use an exercise bike.** Dr. Billie Abney has an exercise bicycle in the rear of her anatomy classroom. She knows which students may need to take a few minutes on the bike.

Make Expectations Clear

1. **Get the student's attention** before giving directions.

2. **Keep directions short and simple.**

3. **Be specific about what you want students to do.** Say *"Get out your math book and start on the first problem"* rather than *"Your assignment is on the board. Go ahead and start."*

4. **Give clear directions.** Use simple language, give examples, or model the behavior.

5. **Give directions three times/write it on the board.** 1) Say directions. 2) Paraphrase them. 3) Give an additional cue by writing it on the board or overhead.

6. **Don't give multistep directions all at once.** Give two steps, wait for compliance, and then give the last two steps.

7. **Check for understanding.** If listening to directions seems to be a problem, ask the student to repeat them to you or show you he knows what to do. Sometimes knowing whether these students are listening is tricky. They may be doodling and appear not to be listening but, when asked, can repeat verbatim what the teacher just said.

Avoid Academic Frustration

Students with attention deficits may have difficulty completing class work on their own. Their ability to control their own behavior and direct it toward completing work is often somewhat limited. To reduce the likelihood of misbehavior, teachers should address these issues:

1. **Task Too Long:** When class or homework takes too long to finish, these students become frustrated and may misbehave. One classroom teacher was surprised to learn that the homework she assigned

was taking students twice as long as she thought it would. To determine whether assignments are too long, refer to Summary 27. Or ask the whole class to report how long it takes to complete their homework. Then:

- Shorten assignments if needed. See Summary 16-B.
- Vary activities within the assignment. *("Write definitions for 10 vocabulary words and then use each of them in a sentence.")*
- Provide breaks during the school day.

2. **Task Too Difficult:** When class work is too difficult, students become frustrated and are more likely to misbehave. Match the difficulty of assignments to the student's skills.

3. **Difficult Homework:** When homework is too difficult and too long, again, students are more likely to avoid doing the work. See Summary 27.

4. **Multi-step Tasks:** Students with ADD or ADHD often lack the organizational skills to complete work on a multistep assignment such as a book report or an essay. To help:

- Give the student a job card with directions broken down step-by-step. See Summary 16-B.
- See Summaries 16, 17, 18, 19, 20 for more suggestions on written expression and organization.

5. **"Boring Routine" Assignments:** Give choices from several interesting activities. For example, list 15 spelling review activities, each worth 10-15 points. Include activities that are fun, such as writing your spelling words in water colors on the shower door or wall, air writing the words, writing the words in colored chalk on the driveway, writing the words in three different colors of ink, one on top of the other. The student chooses 8-10 activities that total 100 points. See Summary 25 for details.

6. **Getting Stuck:** These students hate waiting and become very impatient. When they get stuck and don't know what to do next or how to do it, try one of these tips.

- Give students assistance cards to display on their desks when they are stuck. Write on one side, "Please help me" and fold it into a triangle so it stands up. On the other side, where the student can see it, write, "Please keep working." You can either make your own cards or buy them from www.reallygoodstuff.com.
- Acknowledge that the student needs help and that help is coming ASAP. Ask him to skip that problem or question and move on to the next one.
- Designate a nearby student who may be able to help the student with questions.

7. **Needing Feedback:** Students with attention deficits respond better to immediate, frequent feedback. See Summary 65 for a more detailed discussion of effective use of behavioral strategies.

- Self-correcting materials such as answer sheets, folders containing answers, or answer tapes can be helpful. This type of feedback is provided immediately, confirms correct answers, reduces failure, and can increase attention to task.
- Allow students to work together in peer tutoring situations. They can give each other feedback about their performance. See Summary 16-A.
- Have the student tutor someone who is at least a couple of years younger. Typically, the tutor learns more than the person receiving tutoring. Tutors will need training in several "how to" areas: giving clear directions, encouraging and praising their students, providing feedback on correct answers, correcting errors without being negative, and not helping the student too much or too quickly. It may help to review the suggestions in the paragraphs below with the tutor.

My Favorite Teacher-Student Communication Strategies

There are a few strategies that I have found especially effective when teaching students with attention deficits. For these strategies to work, it is important to bear in mind that successful communication will only work if you treat the student with respect. Avoid public embarrassment, sarcasm, and negative put-downs.

1. **Be positive.** Researchers tell us that three to five positive statements should be given for every negative comment. Expect the best of students. An article in *Teaching Exceptional Children* recommends that teachers use words that help build self-esteem. To many students with attention deficit, a teacher's words paint a portrait of the student's soul. ("If the teacher says I can do it or that I'm smart, then I must be.") Students will work hard to become what the teacher says they are. Here are some suggested comments:

    - *"You're working really hard." "You have the skill it takes to do this."*
    - *"You're doing a great job." "I can tell you've really got a talent for this sort of thing."*
    - *"You've put a lot of effort into this activity." "Well done!" "Now you've got it."*
    - *"You're getting better at this." "I knew you could do it."*

    If a student gives an answer that is incorrect, the teacher might say:

    - *"Can you think of another way to do (say) this?"*
    - *"Let's go over this again."*
    - *"Let's talk this through." (Talk through the steps. Sometimes hearing themselves talk helps students recognize where the error is.)*
    - *"Read it to me. Does it sound right to you?"*
    - *"Do you think something is wrong here?"*
    - *"That's close (then explain)."*

2. **Give students choices, but only two or three.** Give students a limited number of choices for assignments when possible. "You may choose between these two topics for your essay: 1) one of the major characters and how they changed, or 2) what you consider the most important theme of the novel." Remember, too many choices will be confusing and students may spend excessive time simply trying to select an essay topic. Researchers tell us that when students are given choices, several positive things happen:

    - They produce more work.
    - They are more compliant.
    - They are less aggressive.

3. **Use depersonalization.** Eliminate criticism and blame. Teach the student to cope with his ADD/ADHD behaviors. Describe the problem as one common for many students with this condition. "A lot of teenagers with ADD (ADHD) have trouble . . . [remembering homework, copying summaries]. There are a couple of things that might help you. . . [a friend could remind you; I can give your assignments in writing]. What would be most helpful to you?"

4. **Give "I" messages.** State how you feel (in private). "I am surprised that you didn't turn in your work. That is not like you. Is there a problem? What is going on?" "You" messages, as opposed to "I" messages, are often negative and blaming and may put the student on the defensive. "You aren't trying. You could do this work if you would just try." These students have experienced so many failures in school that they are very sensitive to the least bit of negative feedback. When they receive negative messages, many will withdraw and shut down emotionally. As a result, they do less schoolwork.

5. **Ask, "Is that a good choice or a bad choice?"** When a student is misbehaving, the teacher may ask "Is that a good choice or a bad choice?" The student gets the message that his behavior is inappropriate without a formal reprimand from the teacher. The student is learning to label and correct his own behavior. See Summary 64 for more information on this strategy, plus additional pro-social strategies for teaching new skills.

Resources

Dendy, Chris A. Zeigler. *Teenagers with ADD and ADHD.* 2nd ed. Bethesda, MD: Woodbine House, 2006.

Dohrn, Elizabeth and Tanis, Bryan. "Attribution Retraining: A Model Program." *Teaching Exceptional Children,* 1994, Vol. 26, No. 4: 61-63.

Rapport, Mark D. "Hyperactivity Enables Children with ADHD to Stay Alert: Teachers Urged Not to Severely Limit That Activity." *ScienceDaily,* March 11, 2009

Ratey, John. *Spark: The Revolutionary New Science of Exercise and the Brain.* New York, NY: Little, Brown and Company, 2008.

Reid, Robert. "Attention Deficit Hyperactivity Disorder: Effective Methods for the Classroom. *Focus on Exceptional Children,* December 1999, Vol. 32, No.4.

Sousa, David. *How The Brain Learns.* 3rd ed. Thousand Oaks, CA: Corwin Press, 2006.

Zentall, Sydney. "Theory- and Evidence-based Strategies for Children with Attentional Problems." *Psychology in the Schools*, 2005, Vol. 42, No. 8.

Teacher Actions That Escalate or De-escalate Problem Situations

SUMMARY 64

The way a teacher handles a problem situation often determines the outcome. Will a problem situation *escalate* into a full-blown crisis or will the situation *be diffused*? The teacher's behavior often has a *dramat*ic effect on the student's behavior. Although not by choice, when a student with an attention deficit is experiencing a crisis, the classroom teacher is often called upon to be a "crisis counselor." Obviously, teachers need to know how their actions affect students.

It's important to keep in mind that many students with ADHD or other learning problems experience developmental delays in emotional maturity and control—they often speak or act before they think. Sadly, these students would rather be viewed as "bad," rather than "dumb." So they may act out to cover their academic deficits rather than look dumb. Addressing their learning challenges and mastering strategies to diffuse emotional situations are critical.

Actions that Escalate Behavior Problems

A list of behaviors that tend to escalate problem situations is provided below. *Avoid these behaviors:*

- nagging
- lecturing
- arguing
- putting a student down
- assassinating a student's character
- sarcasm
- yelling
- punishing harshly
- getting in the student's face
- punishing ADD/ADHD behaviors
- slipping into power struggles

Parents are more likely than teachers to be driven by frustration and desperation to try to physically control their teenagers. For obvious reasons, physical confrontations between teachers and students are extremely rare at school. Teachers and parents alike should avoid these behaviors:

- physically restraining
- grabbing
- pushing
- hitting
- slapping

Actions that De-escalate or Avoid Potential Crisis Situations

1. **Avoid public embarrassment:** Deal with issues in private. Some of these students will do almost anything to avoid being embarrassed. They may create a scene or cause a confrontation to divert attention from the fact that they don't know how to do the work or don't know an answer to the question.

2. **Acknowledge the student's feelings:** Respect her feelings. *"I know you're upset. Want to talk about it?"* If time is not available then, consider referring the student to a guidance counselor or talk privately after school. If the crisis is highly emotional, the student may need to talk "now" and not be able to wait until after school.

3. **Use active listening:** When the student is upset, diffuse anger: listen, reflect feelings, be understanding. Don't be judgmental or take sides. One way to acknowledge the student's feelings is through

6

active listening. *"So, why are you angry with Sam? Well, if he went out with your girlfriend, I can understand why you are so upset. My class is waiting on me and I can't talk right now. I can talk with you after school. Can you wait until then or do you need to see the counselor now? Why don't you go talk to Ms. Manis [guidance counselor]. She'll help you figure out what to do."*

4. **Offer sympathy and understanding:** *"Something must be wrong. It's unlike you to be so angry."*

5. **Lower your voice, stay calm:** When an adult raises his voice, researchers tell us that the student's anger also tends to escalate.

6. **Make statements matter-of-factly:** Keep strong emotions out of your voice but still make your point. *"It is not okay for you to talk back."*

7. **Redirect interests:** With less intense emotional situations, teachers may be able to distract and redirect the student. Rather than ask the student to stop (talking/arguing), suggest an alternative behavior. *"I need your help. Will you carry these books for me?"*

8. **Be nonthreatening:** When a student is agitated, give her plenty of space. Don't get in her face, put your hands on her, or use force when discussing the problem.

9. **Ask the student to step out of the room or remove her classmates:** Sometimes, the teacher may ask the student to step out into the hall to talk. The student may calm down, return to class, or be sent to the guidance office. However, if a student is totally out of control and there are safety concerns, the teacher may take all her students out of the class, leaving the student behind. This action removes the student's audience and may help her calm down more quickly. The teacher may call the office or send a student to ask for assistance and take the students outside or to the library. Then the teacher or another administrator can go back into the classroom to talk more calmly with the student.

10. **Teach anger management:** Teach the student the skills she needs to cope with anger and frustration. See Summary 75. However, don't expect miracles overnight. A student with an attention deficit often knows what to do, but in the emotion of the moment may explode. If accommodations are in place at school and anger is still a continuing problem for this student, parents should talk with their doctor to see if medication may help.

11. **Develop a prearranged crisis plan:** For example, if teachers know that the student has occasional crises, give her permission in advance to go to the guidance counselor's office anytime she feels she needs to go. No questions asked. One teacher places a laminated permission card on his desk that the student can get and immediately go to the counselor's office. This action helps teach the student: 1) to recognize when she is about to blow-up emotionally, and 2) to take steps to avoid the crisis. Discuss alternative actions that the student may take if she feels a crisis brewing. The student may also request a referral to "peer mediation." Identify the issues that trigger crises and develop a list of alternatives to avoid them.

12. **Offer peer mediation:** In this program, a group of students meet to problem-solve and come up with a solution. Because of concerns regarding escalating violence, some schools have established formal peer mediation programs. Students may ask for and attend a session within the same day. Teachers may also refer students. See Summary 73 for more information on peer mediation.

13. **Prevent reoccurrence:** After the crisis, the teacher and student will develop a plan to prevent reoccurrence of the problem. Identify antecedent or "trigger" behavior and intervention strategies.

The Explosive Student

Occasionally, teachers encounter explosive students who may or may not have ADD or ADHD. In his book *The Explosive Child*, Dr. Ross Green, a child psychologist, offers insights regarding explosive, inflexible students. These students may feel a flash of anger almost before they realize what has happened. During a crisis, they are often not in a coherent frame of mind and do not think or act rationally. They need time to cool down and return to a rational state. When an (inflexible) teacher has a direct confrontation with an (inflexible) teenager in this state, it is a formula for a major blow-up. Dr. Green explains these blow-ups with this formula:

$$\textbf{INFLEXIBLE STUDENT} + \textbf{INFLEXIBLE TEACHER} = \textbf{MELTDOWN}$$

Sherry Pruitt, M.Ed., coauthor of *Taming the Tiger* and *Challenging Kids, Challenged Teachers,* coined the term "Tourette storm" to describe this neurological loss of control when it happens to students who have ADHD plus Tourette syndrome. The student's ability to access abstract knowledge is impaired so she is unable to understand the impact of her actions or the probable consequences. Pruitt explains that trying to talk with the student or touch her during this storm may lead to an even more violent outburst. Sometimes, students "awaken" from this storm with no memory of what has just happened. The student may be as surprised and bewildered as everyone else, and be horribly embarrassed to have been totally out of control.

It is so important for teachers to "know" their students and know which ones are likely to have this explosive element to their personalities. ***Direct confrontation is* not *the best strategy*** to use with these students. The strategies discussed in Summaries 65 and 67 will be more effective. The old adage of "pick and chose" your battles is critical with these students. Dr. Green classifies the severity of behaviors into three categories or "baskets." The behaviors that quality for "Basket A" are nonnegotiable and require immediate confrontation or negotiation. Behaviors related to safety or illegal activity would fall into this category.

Even treatment professionals in residential facilities for young people with serious emotional problems are taught to avoid using direct confrontation or force with explosive youngsters. In fact, the nonconfrontational conflict resolution strategies suggested under "Threatening to Fight" (Summary 67) were recommended by staff at an inpatient hospital.

Resources

Dendy, Chris A. Zeigler. *Teenagers with ADD and ADHD: A Guide for Parents and Teachers.* Bethesda, MD: Woodbine House, 2005.

Dornbush, Marilyn and Pruitt, Sheryl K. *Teaching the Tiger.* Duarte, CA: Hope Press,1996.

Dornbush, Marilyn and Pruitt, Sheryl K. *Tigers Too.* Atlanta, GA: Parkaire Press, 2009.

Green, Ross W. *The Explosive Child.* Rev. ed. New York, NY: Harper, 2010.

Packer, Leslie and Pruitt, Sheryl K. *Challenging Kids, Challenged Teachers.* Bethesda, MD: Woodbine House, 2010.

Phelan, Thomas W. *Surviving Your Adolescents*. 2nd ed. Glen Ellyn, IL: Parentmagic, 1998.

    Dr. Phelan offers practical suggestions for dealing with adolescents and guidance for picking and choosing your battles.

Behavioral Strategies for Helping Students with ADD and ADHD

Behavioral strategies are extremely important in teaching academics and in helping maintain order in the classroom. Basically, these strategies involve common-sense use of psychology. Teachers know that there are certain ways of talking with students that are usually more effective in motivating them to comply with rules and complete homework, as well as to reduce the likelihood of emotional blow-ups. To get maximum effort and compliance from challenging students with ADD or ADHD, teachers must be skilled in using behavioral strategies.

Teachers often discover what parents have known for years: *behavioral techniques do not work as effectively with students with ADD or ADHD.* Dr. Russell Barkley and other experts explain that it is much more difficult for students with attention deficit disorders to learn from the consequences of past misbehavior and change their behavior. Since these students don't always learn from punishment and rewards like other students, they may repeat the misbehavior even though they have been punished. As an educator, school psychologist, and parent, I was often puzzled and frustrated by this problem with my own sons. Often, the teenagers themselves find their own behavior puzzling. To my surprise, my son once apologized for his misbehavior by saying, "I'm sorry, Mom, but when you punish me it just doesn't seem to work."

Key Elements of Effective Behavioral Programs

The rules for using behavioral strategies are somewhat different for students with attention deficits. Dr. Russell Barkley, one of the leading international researchers on attention deficit disorders, identified two key elements of successful behavioral programs.

1. **Intervene at the "point of performance."** The point of performance refers to the point in time at which a student decides to take needed action. In other words, for a student who frequently forgets books and assignments, the point of performance is at 3:00 pm when he goes to his locker and decides which books and assignments are needed.

2. **Provide external cues, either auditory or visual.** The forgetful student needs a prompt—a visual reminder (Post-It note, text message) or auditory reminder (a friend or teacher reminds, a wrist alarm rings)—at 3:00 pm to double-check his assignments and get his books.

As explained in earlier chapters, the limited capacity of their working memory and delayed development of their ability to generate internal reminder cues (self-talk) impair their ability to remember to take home the correct assignments and books.

Examples of Strategies Involving Point of Performance and Visual Cues

My colleague Sharon Weiss, an author and noted behavioral consultant for teens, has developed a strategy to address a common ADD/ADHD challenge, getting students to start promptly on their class work. Although the strategy seems simple, *it is ingenious in that it uses both point of performance intervention and visual external cues.* For example, if a student is writing an essay, you could give him a graphic organizer like the one in Appendix A3 and draw a square in the top corner. "Alex, when you finish completing this organizer (or questions 1-3), I will give you 5 bonus points if you sign your name in the square at the top and submit it by the end of class. Then put your paper on my desk." *This strategy uses a reward—bonus points—plus an external visual reminder—the square at the top of the page—to encourage the student to get started and turn in the completed assignment.*

In addition, several hands-on teaching tools are available at www.reallygoodstuff.com that provide helpful visual cues that reduce demands on the student's working memory capacity. Here are three examples:

1. **Intermediate Desktop Helpers:** These strips offer prompts for basic facts that students use frequently during assignments (multiplication tables, fractions, rules for comma use, common misspelled words, state capitols, tips for reading fiction and nonfiction.

2. **"I Need Help" Desk Sign:** When a student gets stuck and can't finish an assignment, these small tri-fold prompts allow the student to communicate with the teacher without blurting out and disrupting class. The three color-coded flip chart says, "I'm working fine"; "I need help, but I can keep working"; "I need help and I can't continue working."

3. **Reminder Loops:** These colorful animal print, self-adhesive loops can be given to students when they have specific items or assignments they need to remember. They can be worn around the wrist or stuck on a sheet in the student's notebook. If the student wants to remember a test, he can write that on the memory strip. Or he could write down items he needs to bring to school tomorrow for his science project.

General Tips for Behavioral Strategies

Russell Barkley gives the following general tips for guiding students:

1. **Provide feedback immediately.** Feedback must be clear, specific, and occur soon after the behavior occurs.

2. **Provide feedback more often.** To be effective, positive feedback must be given more often than for students who do not have ADD or ADHD.

3. **Use strong, meaningful rewards and consequences.** Stronger reinforcers work better than just a verbal "good job." Try giving the student a pat on the back, tokens, points, food, privileges, or coupons to drop a low grade or skip a homework assignment.

4. **Provide positive feedback before negatives.** Punishment alone is not effective with these students. "Catch the teenager being good." When trying to help a student change inappropriate behavior, watch for good behavior and praise it immediately. Avoid making negative comments in hopes of stopping misbehavior. Instead of saying, "Stop talking," catch him working and say "Mark, I noticed that you came into class and started working right away."

5. **Be as consistent as possible.**

6. **Teach skills.** Barkley suggests teaching a student the specific skills he needs in the setting, or at the *point of performance,* where he actually must use the skills. For example, work on remembering to take home the right books and assignments by meeting the student after school when he must decide which books to take home. Simply telling the student to remember assignments, sending him to an organizational class, or punishing him will be ineffective.

7. **Anticipate problem situations and transitions** such as the presence of a substitute teacher or going to lunch or P.E. Develop a plan for coping with the teenager.

8. **Keep a disability perspective.** ADD or ADHD *may* be a disability for some teenagers. Sometimes it is difficult to remember that the behaviors that frustrate us as teachers and parents are often caused by the disability.

9. **Practice forgiveness.** It is important to forgive students for causing problems that are often beyond their ability to fully control. And also, to forgive *ourselves,* because as Dr. Barkley points out, teenagers with attention deficit disorders have the misfortune of sometimes bringing out the worst in us as adults.

6

Use of Prompts, Reprimands, or Consequences

Experts vary in their opinions on the effectiveness of reprimands; plus, little research has been done on their impact on teenagers with ADD or ADHD. Dr. Ross Green argues that addressing the underlying reasons causing problems is a more productive and humane approach to take than punishing students.

If you do use reprimands, guidance for correcting younger children has been provided by my colleague, Dr. Ann Abramowitz, Associate Professor and Director of the Center for Learning and Attention Deficit Disorders at Emory University. In general, reprimands should be used sparingly and when they are used they should be mild. Researchers have found that the key to effectively reprimanding children with behavior problems, specifically those with oppositional defiant disorder (ODD), is the *frequency* of the penalty or consequence. Increasing the harshness of the *punishment did not change behavior*. In other words, students will change their behavior in response to repeated mild penalties, but not to increasingly harsh punishment. Try these out and see what works best with teens:

1. **Point to the rule**, if standing nearby. If the student does not see you, say his name, point, and say nothing else.

2. **Reprimand privately** in a calm, unemotional manner.

3. **State the reprimand firmly**. A reprimand doesn't have to be a negative statement. Teachers may simply state what the student should be doing. *"Start your work now."*

4. **Be brief and to the point.**

5. **Reprimand immediately** after the rule is broken.

6. **Stand near the student** and make eye contact. If the teacher touches the student, make certain the touch is in a "safe zone" such as the shoulder or hand. Some students may be overly sensitive to touch and may withdraw from it. Sometimes simply touching his desk or standing nearby may draw his attention to you.

Of course, as I say throughout this book, having ADD or ADHD is *not* an excuse for misbehavior, but it does provide an explanation for why these teenagers sometimes act as they do. Teachers may find these students more responsive when ***consequences are instructive, not just punitive!*** Teach the student the desired skills! Don't just punish the student for his disability. See Summary 66 for general suggestions for teaching new skills.

A Few Miscellaneous Thoughts
Use Praise Carefully

Interestingly enough, praise doesn't always motivate some students with ADD or ADHD. Teenagers recognize when praise seems forced, phony, or over-inflated. Or they may feel insulted for being praised for a skill that they believe they should have already mastered. Lyndon Waugh, M.D., psychiatrist and author of *Tired of Yelling*, makes a good point: the teenager may see praise as another tool that adults use to *judge him* and decide whether or not he measures up. Teenagers also may dislike the feeling that they are being manipulated by praise. ***Praise should be brief and sincere. "Nice job."*** Sometimes a smile, a pat on the back, or a "thumbs up" sign are the most effective strategies. Get to know your students and what works best for them.

Point Systems or Token Economies

On paper, point systems sound wonderful, but in the average classroom they are a bear to manage. These systems require a lot of time and consistency to run effectively. Rewards must be changed every couple of weeks since they quickly lose their effectiveness with this group of teens. In addition,

A Review of Behavioral Strategies—*Related summaries are noted by (S-#)*	
Ignore minor misbehavior	"Catch him being good" and reward good behavior.
Use positive reinforcement	It should be immediate, consistent, and given more frequently for students with an attention deficit.
Provide more positives than negatives	Balance each negative interaction with 3-5 positives. The positives may include a smile or nod, a pat on the shoulder, or walking by his desk and writing a comment or check on his paper. See S-63 for more examples.
Use stronger rewards and consequences	They don't respond well to weak rewards. Consider material rewards such as a coupon to drop the lowest grade or skip a homework assignment, a reward provided by parents, or a class pizza party.
Praise the part of the job that is well done	If the student starts his work but is daydreaming and hasn't finished it, say, *"You completed the first ten problems. That's great! Now let's look at problem eleven."*
Make consequences instructive, not just punitive	Punishment alone is usually ineffective. Students with attention deficits don't learn from rewards and punishment as easily as other students. Consequently, they may repeat the same misbehavior. Don't just tell the student what he did wrong. Teach him what you want him to do differently. For example, if the student continually forgets assignments and books, have someone meet him at the locker to get the right materials. See S-30 and 66.
Teach desired behavior: shape behavior—start at the student's present level	Inappropriate behavior cannot be changed overnight. Reinforce each small improvement in behavior; start where the student is, teach him the desired behavior; praise improvement.
Use consequences wisely	Should be immediate, consistent, brief, and reasonable; not too harsh, not too restrictive; comment on the behavior, not the teen; avoid character assassinations. Any punishment should be reasonable and done in conjunction with an incentive program. Typically, incentive programs are set up to allow the student to earn a reward or privileges by doing the desired behavior or task.
Avoid harsh punishment	Conflict will escalate when punishment is too harsh. Students may focus on getting even rather than learning from the consequence.
Repeat consequences	Avoid escalating to harsher consequences. Repeating the same consequences is okay. Students will learn eventually.
Try grandma's rule: "The Premack Principle"	First we work and then we play. "When you finish your outline, you may draw your family coat of arms for the report cover."
Use logical consequences	Where possible, make consequences the natural result of misbehavior, not an unrelated punishment. *"You didn't finish your class work. Please finish it at home tonight (or come by after school and finish it) and turn it in tomorrow."* Avoid punishment and power struggles. If logical consequences are delayed too long, they will not be effective. See discussion in Chapter 5, *Teenagers with ADD and ADHD,* 2nd ed.
Provide more supervision	Teens with an attention deficit require more supervision than other students at a time when most educators are reducing the amount of supervision given.
Two Favorite Strategies:	
If you can't change the teen's ADD/ADHD behavior, change the environment	Even with medication, some symptoms of ADD or ADHD—disorganization, forgetfulness, and an impaired sense of time—may not improve significantly. If all else fails and the student continues to forget homework, send, fax, or e-mail assignments home in writing. Work on the most important goal first, passing his classes. Develop a plan to help the student remember assignments as described in S-66.
Identify antecedent "trigger" behavior; develop a plan	Play detective. What triggered the misbehavior? If a teen acts out when a substitute teacher is present, then teach the student to cope with this change, prepare the substitute, place him with a former special education teacher for that period, or have a classroom aide present in the room. Common "trigger" behaviors are listed in Functional Behavior Assessment form in Appendix B4.

6

researchers tell us that students with an attention deficit aren't as easily motivated by rewards and punishment as their peers. Many of these students are tired of "behavior modification" since they have been on behavioral charts much of their lives. In fact, in answering an open-ended sentence completion, one teenager said, "All my life . . . I've been on stars and charts . . . and it feels like 'kibbles and bits'."

In spite of their drawbacks, point systems can be very effective under certain conditions. For example, if teachers are fortunate enough to have adequate manpower from a university program or special grant, these programs can be incredibly effective. Dr. Bill Pelham, University of Pittsburgh, has a wonderful model summer program that includes an intensive behavior modification component. This program was expanded to a year-round day-treatment program by Dr. Jim Swanson, UCLA-Irvine, at their NIMH multi-site study of ADD or ADHD. However, for teachers who use a point system in a classroom without added support, it is easier to implement the program if they keep it simple and low maintenance. Some educators say these programs may be easier to implement in middle schools than in high schools.

Group Rewards

Group rewards involve a degree of peer pressure that may be helpful. Sometimes teachers will set up a point system for the whole class to earn privileges. When the class as a whole earns a certain number of points, all of the students earn a group reward. The teacher may place marbles in a jar when certain tasks are done well. For example, a class of twenty-four students may earn twenty-four marbles each time all students come into class and quietly start working, turn in homework, or talk quietly in the halls on the way to the computer room or media center. The program may be varied by using an "all or nothing" rule. In other words, all the students have to complete their homework or no points are earned by the class.

Allow students to generate a list of ten to twenty possible rewards. For example, group rewards may include activities such as 15 minutes listening to a radio, a popcorn break, no homework for one night, 15 minutes for free reading, talking quietly with classmates, having the teacher read to the class from a favorite novel, 15 minutes in the library, add 5 points to a daily grade, or 15 minutes free time. Individual rewards might be 15 minutes on the computer, helping in the office, choosing a new seat for one day, being the errand runner for one day, raising or lowering the flag, making school announcements over the intercom, 15 minutes in the art center, or, as a larger reward, a class pizza party. Rewards may be listed on cards and then one student can draw a "Take-A-Chance Card."

Depending on the behavior the teacher wants to improve, she might also motivate students by saying,

- "When all of you complete your assignment for today, you can have ten minutes to talk quietly."
- "If you complete tonight's math homework and make at least 90 percent on it, you will receive five bonus points on the test Friday."
- "If you make a 100 percent on three spelling tests in a row, you may skip the fourth test. "

Contracts

Teachers may use two basic types of contracts: one related to grades and academic requirements for the class and the other to identify problem behaviors to change.

Academic Contracts: Academic contracts assign points to major assignments that will be given during the grading period. If a student earns the full number of points for each activity, he can secure an A for the class. A sample academic contract developed by veteran Georgia high school science teacher, Jackie Bailey, is available in Appendix A4. (This contract may not be usable in school systems in which individual teachers don't have any leeway as to how many points any given assignment is worth, or how many points are needed to earn a particular grade.)

Behavioral Contract. An agreement may be written up between the teacher and student regarding challenging school issues. The contract should describe how the student will act differently and what he will earn in return. For example, the student might sign a contract indicating that he agrees to complete his homework, and that for each five days he does his work, he will earn a reward (points added to the grade on an assignment, if allowed by the school district, or a privilege such as computer time). See Appendix A5 for a sample contract.

However, signing a contract to change ADD/ADHD behaviors is no guarantee that the problem will stop. Other prompting strategies to help with forgetfulness and disorganization will be necessary.

Peer-Mediated Reinforcement

As we all know, some students continue to misbehave because they receive positive reinforcement from their classmates, such as laughter at their antics. Although reinforcement from the teacher is important, many students value peer approval much more. So, one way to tackle this problem is to teach the other students how to respond to misbehavior so that no one is reinforced for misbehaving.

Dr. Ann Abramowitz of Emory University is a well-known researcher on the use of behavioral strategies for students with ADD or ADHD. She explains how peer mediated reinforcement can be used for a student who causes continual disruptions in class. However, simpler strategies should be tried first. In addition, some thought should be given as to how to use the approach without humiliating the student. Remember to avoid sarcasm.

1. The teacher explains to the class that *"it is easier for some students to concentrate and do their work. Some students want to do well but it is much harder for them."*
2. *"Perhaps you've noticed that sometimes it is hard for some of your classmates to keep working on their assignments and they may start talking to students around them or do something to make us all laugh. They want to do their work and not disrupt class and we can help them."*
3. *"It is important for you to be responsible and continue your work. Let's try to ignore other students when they talk at the wrong times and don't laugh at the things they do."*
4. *"The whole class can earn a reward if you ignore students when they talk to you at the wrong time. You may tap your paper as a reminder for them to get back to work, and avoid laughing at them."*

Avoid Humiliation

The late Clare Jones, author of *ADD: Strategies for School-Age Children*, was fond of saying, **"Humiliation is not a behavior management strategy!"** So, teachers should be sensitive to whether or not the point system or peer-mediated reinforcement helps the student learn something positive. For example, if the work is too difficult and the student with ADD or ADHD can't complete it, he may prevent the whole class from getting a reward. Then other students may direct their anger and frustration at this student, further adding to his feelings of failure and frustration.

Resources

Abramowitz, A.J. and O'Leary, S. "Behavioral Interventions for the Classroom: Implications for Students with ADHD." *School Psychology Review*, 1991, Vol. 20: 220-34.

Barkley, Russell A. Adapted from "Eight Principles to Guide ADHD Children." *ADHD Reports*, April, 1993, Vol. 1, No. 2.

Dendy, Chris A. Zeigler. *Teenagers with ADD and ADHD.* 2nd ed. Bethesda, MD: Woodbine House, 2006.

Green, Ross W. *The Explosive Child*. Rev. ed. New York, NY: Harper, 2010.

Luman, M., Sergeant, J., Knol, D., and Oosterlaan, J. "Impaired Decision Making in Oppositional Defiant Disorder Related to Altered Psychophysiological Responses to Reinforcement." *Biological Psychiatry,* March 31, 2010.

"Shaping" Behavior (Successive Approximation)

Students with ADD or ADHD are more likely than their peers to arrive in middle or high school without the organizational and study skills they need to succeed in school. Teachers can sometimes use an effective behavior management technique called *successive approximation* to "shape" the behavior they would like to see. This technique involves praising effort and completion of a job that comes close to meeting expectations.

Steps in Shaping Behavior

1. **Start at the student's present level of functioning** rather than the skill level where adults think she should be! In other words, start "where the student is."
2. **Break the skills down into small steps,** usually three to five segments, leading toward the desired skill.
3. **Begin teaching the new skills.** This will not be an easy task and will require frequent repetition and great patience.
4. **Learn to recognize improvement and acknowledge** the mastery of each small step and the student's overall progress toward the final goal.

Teachers have used this strategy for years as they teach their specific subject content. For example, a language arts teacher breaks the process of writing an essay into smaller steps and begins teaching the student to brainstorm ideas and finally to write the introductory, middle, and closing paragraphs.

Teachers often apply this technique to academic content, but they may also use it to help shape classroom behaviors, such as listening in class, completing homework, organizing both work and materials, or remembering to take books home. Several intervention strategies are included in Summaries 16-A to 16-E and 26 that may help with common problems. If the behavior is not too complex, the teacher may simply pick one or several of these strategies to help change behavior.

Shaping a Relatively Simple Behavior

Here is an example of how a teacher might try to shape the behavior of a student who blurts out in class, talks to others, and doesn't listen to the teacher:

The teacher starts by counting the number of times this problem behavior occurs during one class. It's important to know how many times the student is having this problem now, so the teacher will know when the student actually improves. Next, the teacher talks with the student privately about her problems listening to the teacher. He may say something like this:

> *"Many students with ADHD have trouble listening in class. Without meaning to, they may blurt out answers or talk with other students when they should be listening to the teacher. I know these students really want to listen, but it is very hard for them. Sometimes this seems to be a problem for you too. (Or: Does this seem to be a problem for you too?) Do you have any suggestions for how I can help you listen? (Get input.) Here are some things we can try. I think you can teach yourself to do this with something called self-monitoring.*
>
> *First, we can move you closer to where I stand when I teach (and away from your talking buddy, Mary Katherine). Then we can try these things to help remind you to listen."*

The teacher may state the behavior in terms of the positive ("what I want you to do") and negative ("what I want you to stop"). Here are the expected steps for shaping the desired behavior of listening:

Level 1. Sits quietly.
(without blurting out or talking to a friend, but she may not even be listening)

Level 2. Sits quietly and looks at teacher.
(no blurting or talking)

Level 3. Sits quietly, looks at the teacher, raises her hand (waits to be called upon).
(no blurting or talking)

Level 4. Sits quietly, looks at the teacher, listens, raises hand, and answers a question.
(no blurting or talking)

The teacher or an aide may mark when and how often these behaviors occur during a one-hour class. For every five minutes the student is not blurting or talking, she earns points. When the student earns a certain number of checks or points, she can earn a privilege of her choice—for example, a visit to the library, a pass to skip one night's homework, or bonus points on her grade. Sometimes the simple process of counting the behavior and getting feedback is intriguing enough to a student that that is enough to motivate her. She may not really care about a reward.

The teacher reviews the report with the student at the end of class. To be effective, feedback must be immediate, as explained in Summary 65. As an alternative, the student may come back after school to look at her results today compared with preceding days. Graph her improvement.

"Okay, you've already mastered steps one and two; now let's move to step three. Let me show you how to rate your own behavior. Here is a chart and here is how you mark it." Eventually, the student should learn to monitor her own behavior. (See Summary 69 on self-monitoring.) Over time, the rating of behavior may be completely phased out.

Shaping a More Complex Behavior

Sometimes behaviors are more complex or involve key executive function skills such as organization and forgetfulness. These skills may show limited improvement on medication, but quickly decline when medication wears off. Students with attention deficits often need help learning to compensate and cope with these executive function deficits. These complex skills must be broken down into several steps before a student's behavior can be shaped. For example, completing homework is a fairly complex skill that, when lacking, often results in school failure for these students. An example of how to shape these critical behaviors is provided below.

Shaping Homework Completion

Goal: To complete homework assignments independently including knowing correct assignments and having the right books.

Start at the student's present level, and move from Point A to Point B by mastering one step at a time. Try to figure out which step represents the student's current level of functioning. For example, if she says she wants to write down assignments (Step 2) but often forgets, let her select one of two options. Perhaps she and the teacher can ask her friend David if she will check to see that the assignment is written down. The objective is to move the student toward accepting increased responsibility for completion of her school work. Avoid extensive monitoring and interventions unless she is struggling or in danger of failing a class. Possible strategies to help achieve the goal are bulleted on the next page:

6

I. Knowing Assignments and Having Correct Books

A. Beginning Point: *Doesn't know assignments or bring books home.*

Level 1. Forgets to write down homework assignments almost every day; when parents ask, she says no homework was given or that it was done at school.

Level 2. Says she wants to write down assignments but doesn't remember to do it.
- Teacher writes down assignments weekly.
- Another student double checks or writes assignments.
- Row captains check assignments for all students.
- Student keeps extra book(s) at home.

Level 3. Writes down assignments occasionally.
- Parents review homework assignments.
- When student forgets books or assignments, parents take or send him back to school.
- Student calls classmates to get assignments or borrow a book.

Level 4. Remembers assignments and books most of the time.
- Calls a friend from home if needed.

Level 5. Writes down assignments; brings home the right books.
- Parents don't need to monitor.

B. Target Behavior Achieved: *Student knows assignments and brings books home.*

II. Completing Homework (Tips for Parents)

A. Beginning Point: *No homework done.*

Level 1. Parents get the student started on homework by talking through the assignment; clarifying what must be done; helping select work to do first, and supervising her the whole time, perhaps by actually being in the room.
- If assignments are difficult, consider asking the student to take medication at 4 or 5 in the afternoon to help her concentrate and complete her work. See medication discussion in Summaries 56-60.

Level 2. Parents get her started, monitor, and check completed work.
- Drop in her room frequently; if needed, prompt her to refocus on her work.
- Parents reward the student when she begins completing homework more independently. *"Once I remind you to get started, if you can finish your work on your own, you can study in your room. However, if you don't finish it in a reasonable period of time, you will have to work in the kitchen."*

Level 3. Parents remind student to start; drop in and prompt only once or twice; check completed work.

Level 4. Parents set a timer; student starts by herself; parents check completed work.
- If she doesn't start on her own, parents prompt her after 15 minutes.

Level 5. Student sets a timer, starts and finishes homework by herself; parents check completed work.

Level 6. No monitoring is needed from the parents.

B. Target Behavior Achieved: *The student completes homework independently!*

In summary, both ***ADD and ADHD present a lifelong challenge.*** So it is not unusual for these students to require limited "coaching" all their lives. In truth, some of these skills may never be mastered totally. Adults with attention deficits must learn to compensate or rely on a coach (spouse, administrative assistant, or supervisor) to help them cope with similar deficits in the adult work world. See Summary 71 on coaching.

Tips for Avoiding Confrontations

Because of the inattention, impulsivity, and low frustration tolerance often associated with attention deficit disorder, teachers may sometimes find themselves in conflict with these students. ***Rehearsing alternative strategies in advance*** may help teachers handle the situation effectively and perhaps avoid an unnecessary escalation of the problem. Additional suggestions are provided in Summaries 69 and 71-75 to teach students the skills they need to handle their anger and conflicts more appropriately.

Situations That May Trigger Emotional Blow-ups

Reasons for emotional blow-ups at school can include:

1. for some, the reappearance of inattention, impulsivity, and irritability if medication wears off after lunch or the dose is too low;
2. breaking up with a girlfriend or boyfriend;
3. having an emotional blow-up at home with parents before coming to school;
4. failing a test or class;
5. not getting restful sleep the night before school (56% have sleep problems);
6. not being on the "right" medication.

Interventions for Common Classroom Behaviors

Several intervention strategies are suggested in the table on pages 279-82 for common behaviors that can be difficult to deal with in the classroom. References to other summaries are noted by (S-#).

Teachers should be cautious, however, in trying to eliminate all ADD/ADHD behaviors. Some of these behaviors may actually serve a useful purpose. Researchers are beginning to take a second look at some of their seemingly purposeless behaviors. For example, Dr. Sydney Zentall believes that fidgeting or doodling may serve a purpose to help the student learn. Dr. Mark Rapport's research has shown that physical activity seems to help the student maintain a higher level of mental alertness so that he can listen to the teacher or work on an assignment. Daydreaming may also be a time for creative thinking.

Loss of Control

If a student's anger escalates to the point that he is losing control, a major Behavioral Intervention Plan (BIP) should be developed. Functional Behavior Assessments and BIPs are discussed in Summary 68.

1. Learning problems must be identified.
2. Assignments should be adjusted so they are not too long or too hard.
3. Accommodations must be provided in the classroom.
4. In addition, parents should ask for a consultation from the teenager's counselor or physician. Since aggression often masks depression, additional medication to treat the depression and irritability may be needed.
5. According to federal IDEA guidelines (Summary 44):
   - Conduct a Functional Behavioral Assessment and identify antecedent or "trigger" events that cause the behaviors.
   - Develop a Behavior Intervention Plan.

Behavior	Intervention
Irritating behavior *(Fidgety behavior, tapping a pencil or foot; forgetful; inattentive; day-dreams; wears a hat in class)*	Provide fidget toys: a Tangle, Koosh Ball, or Wikki Stix. Discuss behavior in private. If behavior is bothersome, find an acceptable alternative. Teach quiet tapping. Allow student to play with paper clips or doodle if it helps him concentrate and he can still listen or complete the work. Wrap a wide piece of elastic or thera-band exercise strip around the legs of the chair. The student inserts his legs inside the elastic and can press them against the band. Put a piece of Velcro underneath the desk that the student can rub with his fingers. Develop a private signal to remind the student to pay attention or stop fidgeting. (Pull on your ear.) Allow the student to earn the right to daydream for 5-10 minutes by first completing his assignment. Ignore behavior or use one-word cues: *"Hats!,"* said with a smile. This one word is used as a reminder to remove hats in class.
Late to school *(Sleep disturbances and an impaired sense of time may contribute to tardiness arriving at school and to class; these students don't accurately judge the passage of time; have difficulty estimating time requirements for work completion and travel; 56% have sleep disturbances and complain of not getting restful sleep)*	Suggesting changes in routine may help: e.g., shower the night before, put books by the door, lay out clothes. Check actual driving time and then schedule backwards: arrive at 8:00 am, 20 minutes for drive, 10 minutes park, 15 minutes locker & friends, 15 minutes "oops" time. Leave no later than 7:00 am. Suggest that the family talk with their physician about the possibility of a sleep disturbance plus treatment options.
Late to class	Ignore it if only one or two minutes late and if it occurs rarely. A raised eyebrow or statement of expectations may be more effective than sending the student to the office. *"This is the first time you've been late. I expect you to be on time from now on."* Ask, *"Why are you late?"* There may be a good reason. Review the student's routine between classes. He may be going to the locker too often. Help the student develop a better routine between classes (S-32). Ask him to time himself from when the bell rings and when he arrives in class. Challenge him to reduce travel times. Send a friend/escort with him. Reward five on-time arrivals at class.
Avoiding school work *(not completing or turning in homework; homework may be too long or too hard)*	Sometimes unexpected sympathy or respect will evoke a positive response. *"Maybe you can help me understand some things. I think you really would like to do well in school. Yet, you seem to be avoiding your school work. I assume you must have a good reason. Tell me what you think the reason is. (Listen.) Here's what I think might be happening...."* Involve the teenager in the problem-solving process. *"How can we solve the problem of...?"* Identify any learning problems described in S-13. Match difficulty of assignments with skill level of student. Make classroom accommodations: e.g., reduce the amount of work, allow use of a calculator, as described in S-16 and 51-52.

6

Forgetting detention *(or staying after school)*	Place a Post-It note on his locker door. Have him set his wrist alarm. Put a reminder in the cell phone or on a computer. Ask a friend to remind him. If the student is willing, remind him, e.g., send a note to the last teacher. If the student forgets, assign a make-up time for detention and implement a plan to prevent future problems.
Not telling the truth *(speaking impulsively to deny behavior; fear of punishment or failure)*	If the student doesn't tell the truth about homework or academic issues, the work may be too difficult or too long. Adjust the amount and type of homework (S-27). Identify learning problems. Make classroom accommodations (S-46, 51, 52). Don't ask a question if you know the answer. Make a statement: *"You hit Robert first."* If a question is asked, the student may not be able to resist impulsively answering "I didn't do it," showing off, or making a smart comment.
Taking things *(acting impulsively; acting on a dare; not thinking of consequences; intrusive; failing to identify boundaries of possessions and space)*	Teach the student to ask to borrow an object rather than take it without permission. Deal with the student privately rather than publicly. Identify the type of items being taken and give the student an opportunity to earn the object. Ask parents to provide reinforcers. Structure time and the environment so he has less opportunity to take things. Monitor the student; don't let him stand at the end of the line unsupervised. If he forgets something and must return to the class, send someone with him.
Irritability *(irritable with other students; snapping at teachers, sarcastic)*	Ignore minor things. May have a coexisting condition like depression, anxiety, or learning disability. Ensure academic deficits are addressed. Complete medication effectiveness rating scale. Check medication (dosage & timing). Teachers and parents may find that the irritability is a reaction to a medication dosage that is too low or is wearing off (S-55, 58, 59). Ask parents to talk with the doctor about the timing of medication; send a copy of the medication rating; may need to take meds more frequently or switch to a sustained-release.
Arguing/talking back *(impulsively talking back without thinking of consequences)*	Ignore minor mutterings, especially if the student *is* complying with teacher request all the while he is stating his disagreement. Address academic deficits; successful students aren't frustrated and are less likely to argue or talk back. Don't argue with the student. It takes two to argue. Seldom is a teenager argued into submission. Anticipate when a student may challenge authority (a substitute teacher is present) and change the environment (train him to help the substitute, send to a former special education teacher for one period, or add a classroom aide).
Name calling *(calling a student or teacher a name)*	Consider ignoring an isolated event or muttering under his breath. State expectations: *"It is not acceptable to talk to [a teacher] that way."* Use active listening. *"You seem upset. What's wrong? Do you need to go talk with the guidance counselor?"* Refer to peer mediation to resolve disputes such as arguments, name calling, or fights between two students (S-73).

	If done in front of class, say, *"Let's step out in the hall."* Then talk privately. *"What's wrong? This is unlike you to act this way."*
	Give the student the opportunity to apologize in writing or verbally. A forced apology may not be helpful.
Easily frustrated *(blowing up, hitting locker or wall, crying)*	Keep your voice low and stay calm. If your anger escalates, the student's will also.
	Use active listening skills. Acknowledge his feelings: *"I know you're upset. Want to talk about it?"* or *"Looks like you've had a lousy day. Want to talk about it?"*
	Identify the source of frustration and intervene to prevent future reoccurrence.
	Speak with the student privately if possible.
Angry outbursts *(yelling, screaming, cursing, throwing books)*	Identify what crisis has triggered the anger: failing a test, breaking up with a girlfriend, someone calling him a name.
	Giving unexpected sympathy or respect may be effective. *"Something must be wrong. This is unlike you to be so angry. Do you want to talk about it?"*
	Isolate the student and give him time to cool off. *"Let's step outside in the hall."* Or, *"Let's walk to the guidance office together."*
	If this is common, have a prearranged crisis plan in place.
	Give the student a pass to go to the guidance office when in crisis. He may go there and talk until he has calmed down or simply sit and calm down (S-64).
	Designate a place in advance where he can sit and let off steam—e.g., the office of the guidance counselor, assistant principal, special education teacher, or coach.
	Help the student learn to recognize and cope with his own potential blow-ups.
	Work with parents to develop a strategy to help the teen cope with his anger.
	Have the student participate in anger management or peer mediation training (S-72, 73, 75).
	If angry outbursts occur frequently, suggest that parents speak with their physician.
Threatening to fight *(student is yelling at another student; problem is escalating; threatening to fight)*	Be nonthreatening. Give physical space.
	Don't touch or shake your finger at students.
	If possible, separate the students. *"Let's step out in the hall for a minute."*
	Talk matter-of-factly. Keep your voice and actions neutral, devoid of emotion.
	Move to a position that is actually below eye level with the student, so the student looks down at the teacher. This often helps de-escalate an angry situation.
	To both students, state the behavior and why it is inappropriate. *"Fighting will not be tolerated. We cannot allow you to hurt yourself or anyone else."*
	Privately urge him to stop and think. *"Don't fight with him. He 's not worth getting suspended from school."*
	Use peer mediation to prevent fights. Trained students help others resolve their differences and agree upon a compromise. *"If you break it up now, we can help you resolve your differences through peer mediation."*
	State a positive consequence: *"If you break this up now, you can go back to class or talk with the guidance counselor."*
	. . . and a negative consequence: *"However, if this continues, I will have to send you to the office."*

6

	Or in a more serious situation: *"However, if you don't put down the knife, the police will be called."* (Ultimately school policy will probably require suspension or expulsion.)
	Give the student time to make a decision and save face, for 30–60 seconds. If he complies, he goes back to class or the guidance office. Otherwise, enforce the consequence. Send the student to the office. Or if necessary, call the office for help. If a teacher has time, walking the student to the office sometimes helps diffuse the crisis.
Fighting	Make brief commands. Keep your voice calm. *"Stop now!"*
	Make a statement in private that helps "save face." *"He really isn't worth a suspension, is he?"*
	Send for help. At least two adults are needed to break up a fight.
	Keep others back until help arrives.
	If the student is suspended but agrees to participate in peer mediation, consider letting him return early from a school suspension.

Positive Behavior Supports: Functional Behavior Assessments and Behavior Intervention Plans

When a student has shown a pattern of several disruptive incidents at school, especially if these incidents place the student at-risk of a school suspension, the Student Support Team (SST) or IEP Team should meet to discuss strategies to prevent future reoccurrence. In fact, IDEA requires early intervention and use of positive behavior supports to prevent behavior problems. The reason is simple: punishment alone is ineffective.

PBIS and the National Technical Assistance Center

The Office of Special Education has established a national technical assistance center, known as PBIS or Positive Behavior Interventions and Supports, to disseminate information on effective strategies for changing behavior. Instead of a punishment- or coercion-based model of changing behavior, PBIS encourages defining, teaching, and supporting appropriate student behavior. This system is based upon the belief that there is a reason for most misbehavior and adults should work with the student in compassionate ways to correct the behavior. PBIS may be implemented for individual students or school wide (www.pbis.org).

Provide Positive Behavior Supports

Two tools for effectively identifying and addressing problem behaviors at school include:
1. functional behavior assessments, and
2. positive behavior plans.

Functional Behavior Assessment (FBA)

Since the team needs good information to develop an effective intervention strategy, a functional behavior assessment (FBA) is often done before a behavior intervention plan (BIP) is developed. An FBA is a systematic way of observing a person's behavior to try to determine what "triggers" in the environment may cause the misbehavior and why the person persists in the behavior.

When a student has ADD or ADHD, misbehavior is frequently attributed to the student's intentional ill will. However, psychologist Ross Green believes that misbehavior is often linked to deficits in basic skills that are essential to completing the required academic tasks. His motto is *"Children do well if they can."* Dr. Green encourages teachers to teach needed skills rather than rely on ineffective punishment. Furthermore, traditional wisdom tells us that there is always a reason for misbehavior. However, when a student has ADD or ADHD, simple impulsivity may sometimes be the underlying cause, since these students are known for acting without thinking of future consequences.

Generally, an FBA is carried out by a school psychologist, special educator, or another professional with specific training in the method. Most school systems have developed guidelines for this process. Key elements of an FBA include investigation into:

- behavior
- context
- antecedent or "trigger"
- contributing factors
- function of behavior
- teacher response
- student reaction
- continuation of behavior
- potential rewards
- previous interventions

6

Teachers may find it helpful for planning purposes to have a list of behaviors that commonly occur in several of these FBA categories. A list was complied from information developed by the Gwinnett County (Georgia) School System, Chicago Public Schools, Walker County (Georgia) School System, and Joan Helbing, ADD Consultant, Appleton Area Schools in Wisconsin. See Appendix B4.

Positive Behavior Plan (BIP)

When students have broken the rules, the bottom line goal is to teach them the correct behavior, not just to punish them for lack of skills. Legally, as stated earlier, the school cannot just punish students who have been found eligible under IDEA. Instead, the school must develop a strategy to prevent future problems. One way to handle that is to develop a plan that might be called a behavior intervention plan (BIP) or a behavior management plan (BMP). Typically, the BIP is based upon information obtained from a functional behavior assessment or FBA. These tools are discussed in more detail in this section.

Georgia Sugai, PH.D., PBIS Director, tells one of my favorite stories related to the value of FBAs. After one student (let's call him Perry) had misbehaved on several occasions, one of the only consistent findings was that his misbehavior occurred only on mornings when it rained. The teachers were at a loss to determine the relevance of the rain. When they checked further, they found that Perry rode with his father on rainy days. The father criticized and nagged him for the duration of the morning ride. So, by the time the boy arrived at school, he was about to explode. The BIP included having teachers meet Perry at the door on rainy days and take him aside to "soothe ruffled feathers," give him a snack, and calm him down. This intervention solved the problem. One of the lessons learned from this child is *that typically there is a reason for the misbehavior but it may not be obvious at first.*

Consider School-wide PBIS programs: These programs have shown impressive changes in student behavior: higher student grades, higher test scores, increased school attendance, fewer referrals to special education for evaluation, fewer disciplinary referrals, and decreased suspensions and expulsions. This compelling research has convinced the state of Illinois to implement PBIS statewide. Visit www.pbis.org for more detailed information on PBIS, school-wide programs, functional behavior assessments, and behavior intervention plans. You might share this information with your school officials. Perhaps they will consider implementing a school-wide PBIS program.

Project ACHIEVE: Dr. Howie Knott, a former college professor, created Project ACHIEVE over 15 years ago and it has now replicated in 1,500 schools nationwide (www.projectachieve.info). This Project has achieved similar outcomes as the PBIS programs. Project ACHIEVE offers several programs including *Stop and Think Social Skills Program* that may be of interest to teachers or school counselors.

One Student's Misbehavior

Let's look at the information that was collected and analyzed during the course of an FBA for Ryan, a ninth-grade student who got into trouble for talking back, arguing, and using profanity in class.

1. **Behavior:** *What is the behavior of concern?*
   - Talking back, arguing, and using profanity; not complying with the teacher's request to write a math problem on the board.

2. **Context:** *Where and when (class and time) did the problem occur? Who was involved?*
   - Math class; 3rd period; 11:30; Mrs. Jones.

3. **Antecedent or "trigger":** *What happened just prior to the problem that may have triggered it?* If teachers can figure out what triggered the problem, they may be able to develop an effective solution.
   - The teacher asked Ryan to write a math word problem on the board that had been assigned for homework the night before.

4. **Contributing factors:** *What is going on in the student's world that may affect his behavior?* Medication issues are often a contributing factor in behavior problems.

   - Ryan took his medication (Focalin XR) at 6:30 a.m. Potential problems:
     - By 1:00 pm or so most of his medication has worn off. The doctor may decide to prescribe another capsule at around 1:00 to cover the rest of the day or switch him to a sustained release medication.
     - Perhaps his medication dose is too low.
     - Maybe he forgot his medicine this morning.
   - He played a basketball game last night and did not complete his homework.
   - Ryan is a poor math student and has always struggled in math class.
   - He was upset when he came to school this morning. He had an argument with his mother before leaving for school because he did not clean up his room last night when she told him to do it. By confronting her son just as he was leaving for school, the mother inadvertently sent her son to school in an angry, agitated state with no safe way to resolve their conflict.

   In other words, a combination of factors contributed to Ryan's confrontation with his teacher.

5. **Function of behavior:** *What seems to be the purpose or reason for the behavior?* Inappropriate behavior often serves one of two functions: 1) to obtain something or 2) to escape something. Sometimes, however, because these students may act impulsively, they do not always have a clear reason for their behavior. It may be as simple as; *"I thought it, so I did it."*

   - Ryan did not know how to do the math problem and did not want to be embarrassed. By creating a diversion, the arguing and talking back, he was able to avoid having everyone know he could not work the problem. (Teenagers with ADD or ADHD are especially sensitive and will do almost anything to avoid being embarrassed and "losing face" in front of classmates. So, a student who doesn't understand how to do a math problem may misbehave to avoid looking dumb in front of his peers.)

6. **Teacher response and student reaction:** *What did the teacher do?* Her response serves as a consequence that will either escalate or de-escalate the situation. What did the student do after the teacher responded?

   Ryan: Initially he tried to explain that he had forgotten to do his homework, plus had a basketball game last night.

   Teacher: The teacher inadvertently escalated the problem situation by forcing the issue and using sarcasm. *"Ryan, stop making excuses. I said go to the board now and do the problem. If you're too lazy to do your homework, that's your problem."*

   Ryan: After the teacher forced the issue and used sarcasm, Ryan talked back and argued more.

   Teacher: The teacher put Ryan down and embarrassed him even further in front of his peers by saying, *"I'm not going to pamper you. Your mother may be overprotective of you. But I'm not going to do it."* (Although most teachers avoid such comments, this is an actual quote a teacher made to a student in front of the whole class.)

   Ryan: After he was put down and embarrassed, he used profanity.

   Teacher: The teacher sent him to the office for use of profanity.

7. **Continuation of behavior:** *Why is the behavior continuing to be a problem? What is maintaining it?* The behavior may be repeated because of the "contributing factors" or because the behavior is still serving an important purpose (function of the behavior). See Appendix B4.

- Ryan is in danger of failing math class.
- He doesn't understand math the way Mrs. Jones teaches it.
- Ryan has had several run-ins with Mrs. Jones. There appears to be a personality conflict.

8. **Rewards:** *What does the student view as a reward or positive reinforcement?* This information may help teachers set up a strategy that will help the student change his behavior. The student may or may not need a concrete reward. Removing the threat of a negative response may be an adequate incentive for the student to change his behavior.
   - Ryan likes playing video games, having friends over, and going to the movies on the weekend. He likes working on the student newspaper and acting in plays the drama club presents. Look at the student's strengths listed in response to Appendix A11, "Reframing ADD/ADHD behaviors."
   - If a behavioral program is developed, determine what the student considers a reward that he is willing to work toward earning.
   - No longer being embarrassed in front of the whole class is a positive reinforcer.

9. **Previous interventions:** What interventions were tried previously? What worked best?
   - After school detention.
   - In-school suspension for three days.

Obviously, these punitive strategies have not worked very well. The punishment made it clear what the student should *not* do but did not teach him what to do—in other words, new coping skills to use if the situation reoccurs. Now with the new IDEA guidelines, positive interventions must be instituted.

Ryan's Behavior Intervention Plan

The positive Behavior Intervention Plan (BIP) is ideally built around the data obtained during the functional behavior assessment. Once the teacher, psychologist, or other professional has analyzed the information gathered from the FBA, then she must develop a theory of why the misbehavior occurred. Next she will use this theory and information to develop an effective BIP.

In Ryan's case, the teacher or other IEP team members might develop a number of intervention strategies to target the issues of concern. These intervention strategies may help address future problem behaviors, as well as antecedent and contributing factors.

Sample Intervention Strategies

1. **Ryan was asked to write a math problem on the board. He refused.**
   - Talk with Ryan about this issue. Ask him to explain his reason for refusing to write the problem.
     If he is too self-conscious, don't ask him to write the problem on the board.
     If he does not mind, have another student write his work on the board.
   - Discuss the inappropriate nature of his response to the teacher. Clearly this is not acceptable behavior.
   - Explain that while he is suspended, he will have the opportunity to learn alternatives to handle conflict more appropriately.

2. **Medication had worn off.**
   - The family will talk with their doctor.
   - They will share key information with the doctor: the time medication is taken, the time the class is scheduled, and the completed medication rating scales (Appendices A9 & A10) regarding his school performance.
   - Discuss with the doctor the feasibility of taking sustained-release medication or a second dose of shorter-acting medication after lunch.

3. **Did not complete his homework.**
   - Work with the family to develop a homework schedule.
   - Parents will monitor homework completion in math.

4. **Is a poor math student.**
   - Daily completion of homework by itself may be enough to learn the material.
   - Arrange for a tutor, if needed.
   - Use a weekly report to confirm completion of class work and homework.
   - Consider moving Ryan to a less challenging math class, a classroom with more support (teacher's aide, special education co-educator), or a class with fewer students.
   - Assess student for possible learning disability.

5. **Is having conflicts with adults.**
   - Teach him skills for coping with conflict: anger management, conflict resolution, and pro-social skills. See Summaries 69, 71, and 74 for suggestions.
   - Use the time he will spend in suspension to learn self-management skills to cope with potential conflicts with adults. See Summary 69.
   - Teach the student about typical ADD/ADHD behaviors.
     - Share educational summaries from this book.
     - View videos such as *Real Life ADHD!: A Survival Guide for Children and Teens* and *Teen to Teen: the ADD Experience!*
   - Suggestions are provided for shaping desired behavior in Summary 66.

6. **Is having conflicts with his parents.**
   - Make parents aware of parent support group meetings such as CHADD and ADDA and educational classes they may offer.
   - If parents show an interest, provide them with reading materials on ADD/ADHD.

7. **Is having conflicts with Mrs. Jones.**
   - Provide the student with training on how to deal with frustration and a teacher with whom he has conflicts.
   - Suggest training for the teacher. This is a situation where the teacher would benefit from knowing how to de-escalate problem situations (Summary 59).
   - Schedule with a different math teacher next semester.

8. **Has had previous conflicts with teachers.**
   - Develop a crisis intervention plan in the event the problem reoccurs.
   - Allow the student to go, no questions asked, to the guidance counselor or a trusted teacher if he feels himself losing control.

Section 6 | Classroom Management and Challenging Behaviors

Resources

Horner, R.H. and Sugai, G. "School-wide Positive Behavior Support: An Alternative Approach to Discipline in Schools (pp. 359-90). In L. Bambara and L. Kern (Eds.), *Positive Behavior Support*. New York: Guilford Press, 2005.

Knoff, H. M. "Best Practices in Implementing Statewide Positive Behavioral Support Systems. In Thomas, A. and Grimes, J. (Eds.), *Best Practices in School Psychology-V.* Bethesda, MD: National Association of School Psychologists, 2007.

Knoff, H. M. "Inside Project ACHIEVE: A comprehensive, Research-proven Whole School Improvement Process Focused on Student Academic and Behavioral Outcomes." In Robinson, K. (Ed.), *Advances in School-Based Mental Health: Best Practices and Program Models.* Kingston, NJ: Civic Research Institute, 2004.

Lewis, T.J. and Sugai, G. "Effective Behavior Support: A Systems Approach to Proactive Schoolwide Management." *Focus on Exceptional Children,* 1999, Vol. 31, No. 6: 1-24.

Shinn, M., Walker, H., and Stoner, G. (Eds.). Behaviorally Effective School Environments (pp. 315-50). In Sugai, G., Horner, R., and Gresham, F. (Eds.), *Interventions for Academic and Behavior Problems II: Preventive and Remedial Approaches.* Bethesda, MD: National Association of School Psychologists, 2002.

Sugai, G. and Horner, R.H. "The Evolution of Discipline Practices: School-wide Positive Behavior Supports. *Child and Family Behavior Therapy,* 2002, Vol. 2: 23-50.

Self-management and Study Skills Strategies

SUMMARY 69

Self-management strategies are taught so that students will take increased responsibility for their own learning and behavior. When students learn to take charge of their own lives, their self-esteem is strengthened while demands on the teacher's time are reduced.

Self-management embraces a broad range of skills for students:

- organization and study skills,
- time management,
- self-awareness and self-control,
- problem solving,
- self-monitoring,
- self-advocacy,
- anger management,
- conflict resolution.

Teachers need to recognize that students with attention deficits are slower to learn these skills and require a great deal of practice to master them. In addition, a conscious effort must be made to teach students these critical skills.

The Teacher's Role

Particularly as students with attention deficits reach adolescence, teachers should consider expanding their behavioral strategies to *include the student as a partner in the planning and problem-solving process*. For students at this age, teachers need to go beyond simply manipulating and controlling the student's behavior. Teaching students key skills is critical.

Obviously, teachers want students to be independent and take charge of their own lives. Unfortunately, researchers tell us that students with attention deficits often experience a significant developmental delay and are *not ready* for the same level of independence and responsibility as their peers. However, with supervision and practice, they *can* learn to solve their own problems. What better time to practice problem solving than during the somewhat sheltered middle and high school years when teachers and parents can still provide needed support and supervision? It is important to remember to *provide developmentally appropriate supervision*, which often means giving more support and for a longer period than for their peers.

Executive Function Deficits and Skill Training

As discussed in Section 3, executive function deficits cause students with ADD and ADHD to experience problems with forgetfulness, organizational skills, time management, emotional control, and problem solving. Most students need help coping with these so-called "ADD/ADHD behaviors." Of course, medication helps a lot, but students also must be taught several basic skills that most of us take for granted. *The Learning Lab,* a model skills training and support program that can help with these skills, is described in the next section.

Teachers should not expect miracles from skills training classes, however. These teenagers often "know what to do," but because of their impulsivity and difficulty with self-control, "don't always do what they know." So, even if students attend these training classes, they will not always act on this knowledge! Research on younger children tells us that teaching social skills is not particularly effective.

Young students do *not* use the skills in the moment when they are needed. However, don't be afraid to teach skills. Participating in these training classes certainly can't be harmful.

A Model Program: The ADHD Learning Lab in Eden Prairie, MN

In response to the struggles of students with ADHD, Judy Bandy, a school nurse, and Holly West Jones, an ADHD coach and educator, developed an innovative program called *The Learning Lab*. This program is making a difference in students' lives: student attendance, work completion, understanding of ADHD, and self-advocacy skills have improved. In addition, teachers are now more likely to identify the link between school problems and the student's ADHD. Bandy and Jones initiated this program on their own in 2005 because they saw such a great need. The program is funded by a modest grant and financial support from the PTA and school. The program has since been replicated in three other school systems, and could be fairly easily replicated in other communities.

Program Overview: Students with attention deficits receive half an hour of tutoring in key areas in which they are struggling, before and after school, four days a week. Instruction includes both academic and related skills: organization, time management, project management, review of educational plans, goal setting, self-advocacy. *The Learning Lab* serves 40-50 middle school students a year. Each year, graduates of the program return from high school and give advice to the middle school students.

Staff Responsibilities: In addition to her duties as a school nurse, Bandy spends a minimum of four hours a week as program director, providing more in-depth training for 15 teachers.

Budget: The yearly budget is $18,000; $300-400 per student. That covers four hours' pay for the school nurse/program director, four mentors/paraprofessionals, and supplies.

Program Curriculum: Bandy has published a guide, *Tools for an ADHD Learning Lab,* and has developed a workbook that contains specific curriculum content. The book and curriculum are available to anyone who completes her training program. More information available from ADHD School Specialties (612-708-0149; judybandy@q.com).

Critical Skills to Teach
Study and Organizational Skills

These skills may be defined broadly to include all activities that a student does or all supports he uses to succeed in school. For example:

- keeping a daily planner so that he knows his assignments;
- meeting a coach after school to organize his assignments and make certain he takes home all the right books;
- establishing a set time to do homework;
- using mnemonics to remember important facts;
- learning time management strategies to complete projects by developing and implementing a plan;
- dividing a large task into manageable sections;
- learning how to take notes;
- typing on a computer to express himself more quickly and clearly;
- using tools such as mechanical pencils or clipboards to work more efficiently.

Study Strategies

Here are a couple of study tips that may be helpful to teach teenagers with ADD/ADHD:

1. **SQ3R: S**urvey, **Q**uestion, **R**ead, **R**ecite, and **R**eview, known as SQ3R, is a strategy for improving reading comprehension. Students with greater challenges in

comprehension may prefer the simpler SSR strategy (refer to the article by Carol Rzadkiewicz in the Resources).

- **Survey:** Look over the chapter.
  Read the title of the chapter.
  Read the first paragraph.
  Read the section headings.
  Look at the pictures and their captions.
  Read the last paragraph or the summary.

- **Question:** From your survey of the chapter, write down some questions.

- **Read:** Read the chapter, section by section.

- **Recite:** At the end of each section, look away from the book and summarize what you have just read.

- **Review:** After reading the whole chapter, look back over it as a review of how all the parts are related.

2. Answering Chapter Questions:
- Read the first question.
- Start at the beginning of the chapter and read until you find the answer to the question.
- Answer the question.
- Read the next question, and read until you find the next answer.
- Continue until all questions are answered.

Test-taking Tips

Some schools provide students with test-taking tips for several different types of tests, including multiple choice, fill-in-the-blank, true-false, and matching test questions. Generally the tips include the following basic advice:

- *Try "brain dumping."* Immediately when the test is received, the student should write down two or three key facts or formulas that he is concerned he might forget.

- *Skim the test.* Check to make certain no questions are written on the back of the test! Determine the point value for each section. Spend more time on questions of greatest point value.

- *Read questions carefully.*

- *Answer easy questions first.* Put a check by answers you don't know and go back to them later. (This may not work for some students with ADD or ADHD because they cannot remember to go back to finish missed questions.)

- *Look for "clue words"* such as name, outline, define, explain, describe, discuss, or compare.

- *Don't go back and change answers.* Your first choice is usually correct.

- *If there is not a penalty, always guess.*

- If you don't know the exact answer on an essay test, *write down something.* You may get partial credit.

- *Mark an "X" on the choices you know are wrong* on multiple choice tests.

- *Mark out answers that use absolute words:* Never, always, only, none, all. In T/F questions these are usually false.

- ■ *Look for clues in the questions:*
  - ● Root words that are also found in the answer. For example *audi* or *audio* (word root means hear), found in words such as auditory, audience, audible, audiovisual.
  - ● Grammatical consistency between questions and answers (for example, if deciding whether to answer "acid" or "base" and the question asks for "an ——," base would not make grammatical sense.

Time Management Skills

Time management strategies are also important to teach and are addressed in Summaries 34-37.

Self-monitoring

Self-monitoring is also an effective self-management tool for teenagers. When a new skill is taught, the student monitors his progress and assumes more control and responsibility for his academic work. Sometimes teachers use self-monitoring techniques for individual students or for a whole class.

A Self-monitoring Program Using a Taped Signal

A self-monitoring program for an individual might work like this:

- ■ The teacher and the student discuss the program and the student says he wants to try it.
- ■ They identify the behavior the student will monitor; for example, staying on-task.
- ■ The student is given a self-monitoring check sheet.
- ■ The teacher shows the student what to do and practices with him.
- ■ A cue such as a beep or tone is played at intervals on a tape recorder.
- ■ The student marks on a form whether or not he was working on-task at that particular moment. Simply knowing that a beep is coming and then being reinforced for working helps change the student's behavior so that he increases the amount of time he is on-task.
- ■ Intervals between beeps are varied but should be fairly frequent as the skill is taught. Beeps are gradually spaced further apart and ultimately phased out over time as the student become more aware of being on task.
- ■ The student may wear an earphone so that he alone can hear the beep. When he hears the beep he can ask himself, "Am I on task?" and then mark on his chart whether or not he was working.
- ■ The student may use a similar system at school and home.

Dr. Harvey Parker, author of numerous books on ADD and ADHD and co-founder of national CHADD, has developed a self-monitoring program, complete with a continuously playing signaling tape, instruction manual, and forms for school or home use.

A Self-monitoring Program Using Teacher Ratings of Behaviors

Dr. Edward Shapiro and Dr. George DuPaul of LeHigh University have developed a comprehensive training program to help teachers cope more effectively with students with attention deficits. In addition to in-service training and on-site consultation, the program includes a behavioral program for training students to monitor their own behavior. In this program, several different behaviors are tracked simultaneously.

- ■ Initially, the teacher rates the student on 4-5 behaviors of concern by giving a score of 0 to 5 at the end of class. For example, the student may be rated on whether or not he completed his class and homework, follows instructions, or comes to class on time.
- ■ Then the teacher talks with the student about the behaviors and shows him how to rate his own behavior.

- Next, the student practices so that his ratings of his behavior match those of his teacher.
- Gradually, the teacher ratings are phased out and the student is the only one rating his behavior.

This program increases the student's awareness of his behavior and teaches him the desired behavior.

Other Self-monitoring Strategies

- *Have the student check his own work and give reinforcement.* The student can get the answer sheet from a folder and grade his work. He can then place stars or stamps on a chart indicating that work is complete or perhaps even record a grade.
- *Place a mirror at the student's workstation.* Dr. Sydney Zentall reports that children who look up and see themselves in the mirror are more likely to refocus on their work.
- *Use a camera or observer to monitor work.* The student is enlisted as a partner in this process. He agrees to be filmed while doing class work. Later he reviews the tape and rates himself. Or another student observes him and checks each thirty-second interval he is on task.

Pro-Social Skills

In teaching pro-social skills, educators teach responsible decision making—which often means teaching skills students are lacking. The use of "self-talk," or internal language, is one of the key skills needed to learn pro-social behavior. As the student is learning to use self-talk, the teacher provides the student with the words or language to control his behavior and make good choices, such as the phrases listed below. Next, the student is taught to use these phrases by himself when he faces a difficult situation. It may also help to ask him to visualize himself as he would like to behave (calm and in control).

- *Stop and think.* The teacher says *"Stop and think"* to interrupt the student's misbehavior.
- *Good choice or bad choice*. After the teacher has the student's attention, the teacher asks, *"Are you making a good choice or a bad choice?"*
- *Choices or steps.* If the student recognizes that he has made a bad choice but does not seem to know how to correct the problem, the teacher may have to suggest the proper way to behave.
- *Just do it.* Once the student says what he should be doing, the teacher responds briefly and simply by saying, *"Just do it"* to help move the student into action.
- *How did I do?* The student may use self-monitoring to look at how well he handled this situation. The teacher can give the student positive feedback for handling the situation well.
- *Congratulate oneself on work completion.* The student is encouraged to reinforce himself by saying, "Good job!" "I knew I could do it."
- *Use self-questioning on academic tasks.* The student may ask "How many algebra problems have I done in the last 30 minutes? How many are right?" Or, "What is the main idea of the paragraph?"

Self-Advocacy, Self-awareness, and Self-control

Students need to learn as much as they can about attention deficit disorder, how it affects their lives, and ways to compensate or master necessary skills. This will help them to advocate for themselves and their needs. Critical times for self-advocacy include when the student attends IEP meetings, as well as during daily interactions with teachers. Encourage the student to ask for what he needs in both these situations. *"I need extended time." "There is too much activity and noise in this area. May I take my test somewhere else?"*

These behavioral skills are among the tools the student learns to use to control or compensate for the characteristics of ADD or ADHD, such as acting or speaking impulsively, and executive function deficits such as forgetfulness and time impairment:

- understanding the impact of ADD or ADHD on his life;
- appreciating his own strengths and special skills;
- understanding his own learning style so he knows how he learns best;
- knowing what accommodations he needs to be successful academically;
- learning to compensate for deficits by using classroom accommodations such as extended time on tests or a note taker;
- working with teachers and parents to use problem-solving strategies to resolve academic problems such as forgetting homework or not completing homework and failing a class;
- knowing who to go to if he needs help at school;
- letting teachers, coaches, or friends teach him to compensate and master skills;
- learning to use anger management skills to avoid emotional blow-ups;
- using peer mediation and conflict resolution to solve problems in relationships;
- taking medication to increase his attention and focus.
- reviewing publications such as NICHCY's *A Student's Guide to the IEP* (in the Resources) with the long-range goal for the student to actively lead his IEP meeting.

Problem-Solving Skills

Dr. Mario Hernandez and staff at the Florida Mental Health Institute, University of South Florida, developed a concept called *"time in."* Using this innovative procedure, teachers refer students to a "time-in" counselor who teaches them new skills to substitute for the behaviors that have been getting them into trouble. The counselor works with the students to "SOLVE" the problem and role-play their response:

S—State your problem
O—Outline your response
L—List your alternatives
V—View the consequences
E—Evaluate your results

Resources

Bandy, Judy. *Tools for an ADHD Learning Lab.* Eden Prairie, MN: ADHD School Specialties, 2010.

Batsche, G.M. and Knoff, H.M. *The Use of Classroom Based Social Skills Training to Improve Student Behavior: A Project ACHIEVE Training Manual.* Tampa, FL: University of South Florida, 1995.

Hernandez, Mario and Palmer, Jo. *Time-In Counseling.* Tampa, FL: Florida Mental Health Institute (Adolescent Project, Research and Training Center for Children's Mental Health, FMHI, 13301 Bruce B. Downs Blvd., Tampa, FL 33612).

McMullen, Jerry. "A Prosocial System for Improving Student Discipline and Responsibility." *Communiqué*, October 1996.

NICHCY. *A Student's Guide to the IEP.* 2nd ed. Washington, DC: NICHY, 2002. (www.nichcy.org).

Parker, Harvey C. *Listen, Look, and Think: A Self-Regulation Program for Children.* Plantation, FL: Specialty Press, 1992. (Available through ADD WareHouse. 800-232-9273; www.addwarehouse.com).

Rzadkiewicz, Carol. "How to Improve Reading Comprehension: A Proven Technique for Improving Reading Skills." Sept. 15, 2009. (www.suite101.com/content/how-to-improve-reading-comprehension-a14862).

Shapiro, Edward and DePaul, George. *LeHigh University Consulting Center for Adolescents with Attention Deficit Disorder: A Training Manual.* A 30-minute videotape that describes components of a model program and how a school system might establish a similar program is available. 610-758-6384.

Zentall, Sydney. "Theory- and Evidence-based Strategies for Children with Attentional Problems." *Psychology in the Schools*, 2005, Vol. 42, No. 8.

Social Skills

According to researchers, roughly 50 to 60 percent of children with attention deficits have difficulty making and keeping friends. One reason may be that these students can experience up to a 30 percent developmental delay in executive skills including organizational and social skills. Consequently, they may seem less mature. These students also have trouble reading the subtle details and cues that are so critical for successful social relationships. Some students may not recognize that they are too loud, are complaining too often, are being aggressive, bossy, insensitive, demanding, or inflexible, or have said something offensive. They may also intrude into the personal space of other students or overreact angrily when things don't go their way. Of even greater concern, these students may be totally unaware of their poor social skills.

The Importance of Mastering Social Skills

Because ADD/ADHD is an invisible disability, students who are socially unskilled may be viewed by others as rude, self-centered, irresponsible, lazy, or ill-mannered. Consequently, these students may be rejected by their peers and viewed less positively by their teachers. Students with ADD inattentive are more likely to be shy, anxious, or withdrawn and may be ignored by classmates. Any student who lacks social skills is more susceptible to bullying—most often as the victim, but also as the perpetrator. These social problems get even worse in middle school, since students are also undergoing hormonal changes and dealing with increased teacher expectations. Regrettably, problems with social skills are a lifelong challenge for many.

One key predictor of how a child with an attention deficit will do in adulthood is how well he or she gets along with other children. In the school setting, more serious social skill deficits (especially aggressive behaviors) are often linked to disciplinary problems, suspensions, school failure, dropping out of school, and, ultimately for some, delinquency. Additionally, researchers tell us that *having at least one best friend may have a protective effect on children's mental health.* Obviously, teachers and parents must help these children improve their social relationships with their peers so that they can develop one strong friendship.

What Must a Student Do to Get Along with Others?

To get along with peers and teachers, students must be attentive, responsible, and able to control their impulsivity. "Highly likeable people" are considered to have the characteristics shown in the box below. Yet these characteristics are the very ones that students with attention deficits may lack. Since students with ADHD may be considered "high maintenance" in relationships, anything adults can do to help students improve their likeability characteristics may also improve their friendships.

Likeability Characteristics		
■ sincere	■ understanding	■ truthful
■ intelligent	■ thoughtful	■ reliable
■ kind	■ happy	■ humorous
■ cheerful	■ honest	■ loyal
■ trustworthy	■ dependable	■ considerate
■ warm	■ friendly	■ unselfish
■ responsible	■ trusted	

Social Skills: Boys vs. Girls

Understanding the differences in what boys and girls view as good social skills is very important. For example, relationships between boys often revolve around activities, especially sports. Girls, on the other hand, view school as the center of their social life. Boys are much less likely than girls to talk about sensitive personal or confidential topics. Girls have their most meaningful interactions at school; boys have theirs after school and on weekends. Girls enjoy talking about the lives of other people; boys do not. Girls spend a lot of time talking about the social and academics aspects of school; boys see school as an "interruption" of their social life. Boys don't require you to be friendly, but girls do. Girls who pass each other without speaking are considered "stuck-up" or "snobs"; this is not true for boys. Girls who are clean and dress fashionably are also more popular. Being trustworthy and responsible in caring for property are highly respected by both boys and girls.

Based upon what we know about gender-related social skills, students with ADD or ADHD must be taught strategies to earn greater acceptance from their peers. For example, girls must learn to smile, make eye contact, and greet other girls in social situations. Girls can also practice good hygiene and dress more appropriately. On the other hands, boys can be taught more about sports and kept up-to-date on the current won-lost record of the favorite sports team. Computer and video games are also a great common ground for building relationships among boys. Teaching both boys and girls more about the favorite topic of the desired peer group can also be helpful.

Five Intervention Strategies to Improve Peer Relationships

Researchers suggest five forms of intervention that have been successful at improving peer relationships:
- systematic teaching of social skills;
- social problem solving;
- teaching other behavioral skills that are often considered important by children, such as sports skills and board game rules;
- decreasing undesirable and antisocial behaviors;
- developing a close friendship.

These interventions may be worked on in the classroom, small groups at school, after school programs, or summer camps. Intensive summer camps established by Dr. Bill Pelham are a nationally recognized model program. These camps use all five forms of intervention and address both academic and peer problems. Most of the day is spent participating in recreational activities such as baseball or soccer where skills, strategy, and rules are taught. Two hours are reserved for academics, including related skills such as organization.

Unfortunately, most schools do not have formal programs for teaching social skills to their students. Instead, teachers and parents need to identify the individual students who most need training in social skills, and then figure out how to provide it. Some options include:

1. **Include a goal in the IEP.** If particular social skills are listed as goals in a student's IEP, then the school has to provide services to help the student meet her annual goals. So, services might include a special education teacher who can work with the student on social skills goals such as (for girls) speaking to other students, making eye contact, or entering a group discussion, or (for boys) understanding the rules of sports games, keeping up with team won-lost standings, or improving video game skills. Or the guidance counselor might schedule a social skills group for several students who need the training.

2. **Work on social skills with suspended students.** According to an article in *Communique,* the newsletter for the National Association of School Psychologists, some schools have given their in-school suspension program a new name such as OS (Organized Study) or R&R (Respect and Responsibility). These schools take advantage of time in suspension to teach students pro-social skills through discussion groups or videos. The guidance counselor or another designated teacher may teach the class.

Social Skills Training Programs

Social skills training is effective only "when it is used with parent and school interventions and rewards and consequences to reduce disruptive and negative behaviors." Reinforcing targeted social skills both at school and at home is critical. Many social skills programs involve *instruction, modeling, role-playing, instructive feedback, reward and consequences, and practice.* The targeted skill—for example, sharing or negotiating—must be clearly defined. Labeling the praise is also important: "I like the way you shared with John. That's a great way to make friends." More advanced social skills such as *negotiating, accepting the choices of others, and complimenting* should also be taught.

Four programs for teaching social skills to adolescents in a school setting may be of interest:

1. **Project ACHIEVE's Stop and Think Social Skills Program.** Project ACHIEVE is a school-wide program that improves both academic and social skills (Summary 68).

2. **Skillstreaming the Adolescent.** Arnold Goldstein and Ellen McGinnis have developed several materials to use in building social skills. Examples of topics addressed in the program: apologizing, dealing with someone else's anger, dealing with fear, standing up for your rights, responding to teasing, avoiding trouble with others, keeping out of fights, and dealing with embarrassment.

3. **"Social Skills Autopsy."** Rick Lavoie developed social autopsies to analyze, problem solve, and then role play regarding social mistakes. See Lavoie's book, *It's So Much Work to Be Your Friend,* for more details.

4. **Creative Coaching: A Support Group for Children with ADHD.** This is a model curriculum developed by two guidance counselors for coaching students with attention deficits who are in early middle and elementary school. The program relies heavily on the "coaching" metaphor to increase interest and teach concepts. Creative Coaching targets one social skill each week, and teachers and parents reinforce that specific skill in class and at home. Each new skill that is added is then reinforced on a regular basis. Booster sessions may be necessary to review and reinforce skills learned earlier in the program. The use of good skills is reinforced in the group and classroom. See Summary 71 for more details.

Other Helpful Programs
Other types of social skills programs that can benefit all students include:

- **Bullying Prevention Programs:** Bullying prevention programs help students become more aware of their own behavior and how it affects others. See Summary 72 for more details.

- **Student-mediated Conflict Resolution Programs.** School-wide peer mediation programs teach students to resolve conflict in peaceful ways. See Summary 73 for details.

Resources

Batsche, G.M. and Knoff, H.M. *The Use of Classroom Based Social Skills Training to Improve Student Behavior: A Project ACHIEVE Training Manual.* Tampa, FL: University of South Florida, 1995.

Dendy, Chris A.Z., Ellison, Anne T., and Durheim Mary. *CHADD Educators' Manual on ADHD.* Landover, MD: CHADD 2006.

Dowd, Tom and Jeff Tierney. *Teaching Social Skills to Youth: A Curriculum for Child-Care Providers.* Boys Town, NE: Boys Town Press, 1997.

Goldstein, Arnold P. and McGinnis, Ellen. *Skillstreaming the Adolescent: New Strategies and Perspectives for Teaching Prosocial Skills.* Rev. ed. Champaign, IL: Research Press, 1997.

Hagar, K., Goldstein, S., and Brooks, R. *Seven Steps to Improve Your Child's Social Skills.* Plantation, FL: Specialty Press, 2006.

Lavoie, Richard. *It's So Much Work to Be Your Friend*. New York, New York: Touchstone, 2005.

McDougall, Nancy and Roper, Janet. *Creative Coaching: A Support Group for Children with AD/HD* (for elementary and middle school age students). Chapin, SC: Youthlight, 1998.

"Psychosocial Treatment for Children and Adolescents with AD/HD: What We Know" (fact sheet #7). Landover, MD: CHADD, 2005.

Walker, H.M. et al. "Integrated Approaches to Preventing Antisocial Behavior Patterns among School-age Children and Youth." *Journal of Emotional and Behavioral Disorders*, 1996, Vol. 4: 194-209.

Walker, H.M. *The ACCEPTS Program: The Walker Social Skills Curriculum (K-6).* Austin, TX: Pro-ED, 1983.

Section 6 | Classroom Management and Challenging Behaviors

6

Coaching Students with ADD or ADHD

Teenagers with ADD or ADHD often need *coaching* at home or school to help them succeed academically. They may need academic and organizational coaching and/or tutoring, and they definitely need help with *executive function deficits* such as disorganization, forgetfulness, memorization problems, and poor time management. Typically, parents act as a coach at home and a teacher or aide serves that function at school and provides help in two major areas:

1. as an **organizational coach** to help the student be more organized, write down homework assignments, take home the necessary books, and return completed homework to school,

2. as an **academic coach for effective learning strategies** to help the student improve skills in memorization, written expression, and complex math.

Coaching serves as a tool for modeling needed skills so that the student learns to do them for himself or learns to compensate for difficulties. The ultimate goal is independence through self-management.

How Much Help Do Students with ADD or ADHD Really Need?

When considering whether to provide organizational support to a student, both parents and teachers often express ambivalent feelings about "doing too much for the student." However, because attention deficit disorder can result in a *30 percent developmental delay*, these students' maturity and readiness to accept responsibility can lag behind their peers' by about four to five years. In addition, their disorganization and forgetfulness contribute to difficulty with seemingly simple classroom demands—for example, writing down and remembering to do their homework. These problems may improve briefly while medication is working, but benefits quickly disappear when it wears off.

If a teacher has repeatedly tried to teach a skill and the student just can't get it, repeated nagging is not going to make the problem miraculously disappear. The bottom line is that **these students need more support and supervision from teachers than their peers do.** Their skill deficits are real and are not due simply to laziness or lack of motivation.

Providing Developmentally Appropriate Supervision

To ensure completion of school work, teachers and parents need to supervise students with ADD or ADHD even in middle and high school. The alternative may be school failure for the teenager, and, ultimately, dropping out of school.

The student's executive function skill deficits place him and his family *in direct conflict* with traditional middle and high school expectations that teenagers will take more responsibility for completing their schoolwork. Some educators expect more than the student is capable of producing. Many of these students seem to "hit a brick wall" when they enter middle or high school because of the increased executive skill demands placed on them. In elementary school, fewer demands are placed on executive skills. By providing more supervision and support, teachers serve as the young child's executive skills. Middle and high school students must deal with more classes, more teachers, and increased expectations to be organized and to assume greater responsibility for their work.

This is not to say that teachers should not expect anything of students or help them improve their skills and knowledge. Rather, **develop the fine art of setting reasonable expectations that the student** *can achieve.* An additional goal is for the student to become a respected partner and master of his fate rather than just a passive victim of a disability.

Giving Parents Permission to Be Involved with Their Teenager

Teachers might consider these facts when deciding whether: 1) to provide more support to the teen, and 2) to accept and not discourage parents from being involved as coaches. Edward Hallowell, M.D., and John Ratey, M.D., coauthors of the popular book, *Driven to Distraction,* explain that **even adults with ADD or ADHD need coaches** to help them remember the more routine responsibilities of life. They point out that **disorganization and forgetfulness are lifelong problems** for many people with attention deficit disorders. In adulthood, several different people may serve as coaches, including the spouse, secretary, administrative assistant, co-worker, or a friend.

Enabling vs. "Developmentally Appropriate Support": Sometimes parents who provide their teenager with organizational and academic support are unfairly referred to as "enablers." In this context, "enable" is used very negatively. However, Webster's dictionary defines *enable* positively: "to provide an opportunity, to make possible or practical." The delay in brain maturation and relative immaturity present a true dilemma. As Russell Barkley explains, some 18-year-olds with attention deficits have executive skills comparable to those of a 12-year-old. Clearly, these children *need* more supervision and support than their peers. On the other hand, parents and teachers walk a fine line between providing needed support and teaching skills and shaping behavior so that the student assumes more responsibility over time.

Teaching Students How to Master Skills and Compensate

Teachers and parents do a tremendous service when they teach these students to master or compensate for skill deficits.

- First, **help them recognize their skill deficits** without feeling bad about them.

- Second, **teach them to compensate for the deficit.**

- Third, **show parents how to shape desired behavior and teach the student new skills or compensatory skills.** Explain the concepts behind shaping behavior: start at the teenager's present level, teach each progressive step until the skill is mastered. Discuss the examples in Summary 66.

- Next, **help parents find an organizational coach** to meet the student after school to get the right books and assignments.

- Last, **share information from summaries relevant to the student's specific needs.** For example, Summary 26 addresses six points of vulnerability for school failure, and summaries in Section 3 provide suggestions for coping with executive function deficits.

Who Are the Coaches?

The most likely candidates to serve as the teenager's organizational or academic coach are first the parents, a teacher or teacher's aide, a student in a higher grade, and, later on, a girlfriend or boyfriend. The student may also try to be his own coach, or a professional coach may be hired.

Parents as Coaches

Coaching may be difficult for parents because of the emotions involved. Obviously, when a student has forgotten his assignments and books for the four thousandth time, most parents have trouble deal-

6

ing with the situation calmly. Ideally, an outside person would be hired as a coach. In reality, though, most parents cannot find or cannot afford to hire someone else and the responsibility always falls back on the family. Here are some ways to help students make the best of the situation:

1. Suggest that parents swap out homework supervision when one becomes frazzled and angry.
2. Sometimes other relatives, friends, or a college student from the neighborhood might be willing to take on the job of coach.
3. Another parent of a student with attention deficits, who may be more patient with someone else's teenager, might be willing to trade responsibilities for teaching skills. Or the parents could let their teenagers study together and alternate nights of supervision.

The Student as Coach

Summary 69 presents a variety of self-monitoring strategies that teachers and parents can use to teach the student so that he can recognize his own difficulties, master key skills, and compensate for some of his deficits. Students with ADD and ADHD will need significant practice and prompting to master these skills.

Professional ADHD Coaches

Professional coaches may meet face to face with students or may provide coaching services by phone and e-mail on a weekly basis. Some coaches who specialize in working with students will also contact teachers and talk with them. Fees for coaching vary and may range from $100 up to $200 an hour. Better weekly or monthly rates can be negotiated—for example, $250 to $500 a month.

To find a coach, parents might contact a local or national ADD or ADHD group, such as CHADD and ADDA. These groups may be aware of local coaching resources, and some coaches advertise in their newsletters and websites.

Several coaching associations have been established over the last few years. The American Coaching Association (ACA) is a well-known national group. The ACA website contains a state-by-state listing of coaches, some of whom list their target groups (www.americoach.com). Another group, International Coach Federation (ICF), although not ADHD specific, also has lists of coaches (www.coachfederation.org). Bear in mind that many coaches who receive their training through ACA and ICF specialize in helping *adults* with attention deficits cope with the work world and may not be familiar with school issues unique to students.

The Edge Foundation is perhaps a more helpful resource, as it was established to provide coaching services and scholarships for high school and college students. Edge was established by Neil Peterson after his own two teens were diagnosed with ADHD. He wanted this service to be available to more students who struggle with ADHD regardless of their financial status. Edge also provides additional training for those who want to specialize in coaching adolescents and young adults. Jodi Sleeper-Tripplet, a well-known ADHD coach, is their director of training (www.edgecoaches.org).

As with any potential counselor, parents should screen coaches to find someone they trust who could work effectively with their family. It is also important to inquire about the coach's training and certification.

Professional Consultants, Trained Tutors, or College Students Paid to Tutor

There are private and public counseling and educational centers all across the country. Psychologists, social workers, educational consultants, and tutors are available to help parents and teenagers cope with attention deficits and other learning problems. In larger cities, you may also find coaches who specialize in working with teens and young adults who have deficits in their executive functions.

Sometimes university programs can be an excellent source of help. Some universities limit their help to only one hour a week and may not provide the daily guidance that is often needed. However, some universities will provide more intensive supervision and support if the parents pay an extra fee.

Tips for Coaching

The coaching tips below have been adapted from suggestions by Dee Doochin and Holly Hamilton, trained ADHD coaches. These suggestions may be helpful to coaches regardless of whether they are teachers, parents, or other students.

The Coach's Toolbox

1. **Listening** is the most important tool in the coach's toolbox. However, the coach needs to know what to listen for in order to coach effectively. The following is a list of things coaches always listen for:
   - *Strengths:* Teachers and parents can use strengths to teach academics and develop supportive strategies. For example, a student might have a great personality, have incredible computer skills, or be creative. See Summary 76 and Appendix A11.
   - *Dominant learning styles:* Learning styles, or the way students take in information, are discussed in Summary 15. Using the teen's dominant learning style along with his strengths greatly increases coaching successes. Sometimes the comments that students make during coaching sessions reveal their dominant learning style(s):
     Visual: *"I see"* or *"I get the picture."*
     Auditory: *"I hear what you are saying."* Or *"It sounds like..."*
     Verbal: *"So what you are saying is..."*
     Kinesthetic: *"It feels like..."*
     Tactile: *"So this touches on. . ."* or *"I finally grasp what you are saying."*
     Cognitive: *"I understand"* or *"I know it now."*
   - *Issues of concern:* Important issues may include the identified problem itself or other obstacles that are keeping the student from dealing with the issues at hand.
   - *Desires and motivators:* Coaches need to find out the student's important lifetime dreams so they can identify what the student will work for, help define the teen's goals, and provide reminders of why he is bothering to "finish his stupid homework."

2. **Using language effectively** is the second most important skill in the box. The coach needs to know what words to use and how to use them appropriately. This will help the coach communicate effectively in a nonjudgmental manner. Asking key questions is one of the most important jobs a coach has. The coach is helping the student brainstorm and come up with solutions, not just giving answers. See Summary 64 on actions that escalate or de-escalate problems and 72 on problem solving.

3. **Timing** is also critical for successful coaching. Coaches must understand how long the student can pay attention and what time of day his attention is working well. Students cannot benefit from coaching if their medication has worn off, or if their brains are tired, shut down, or spaced out. See the introduction to Section 5 and Summaries 58-59 for a discussion of peak medication times.

The Coach's Attitude

Several attitudes are necessary for a successful coaching relationship:

1. **Do not be invested in how a goal is achieved.** Students can successfully achieve a goal many different ways.

2. **Always start from where the teenager is,** not from where you think he should be. See Summary 66 for a discussion of shaping behavior.

3. **Do not take personally anything a teen says or does.** As part of growing up, all teens test limits. In addition, teens with ADD or ADHD are extremely impulsive. They may tell the coach they hate coming to coaching sessions. In this case, the coach might express concern by asking, *"How can we make it better so that you don't hate it?"*

4. **Respect who the teen is and honor him for that.** This ties in with the next statement. At the same time, coaches have to set boundaries and make them clear.

5. **Give support and unconditional acceptance.** The relationship will not work otherwise. Showing genuine acceptance may be most important. If the teenager believes that you really care about him, he will be more open to working with you. See Summary 76 for a discussion on valuing teenagers with ADD or ADHD.

Although some coaches would not agree, I believe that a coach may also have to teach skills, problem-solve, and at times be directive. When a teenager has slow processing speed and slow retrieval of information, asking him to solve a problem himself can be far too time-consuming and ultimately counterproductive. Students with ADD or ADHD must be *taught* problem solving skills.

A Couple of Model School Programs
Creative Coaching

Creative Coaching: A Support Group for Children with ADHD is a model curriculum developed by two guidance counselors for coaching students with attention deficits who are in early middle and elementary school. The program relies heavily on the "coaching" metaphor to increase interest and teach concepts. For example, a "hand signal" (touching the index finger to thumb) may be used with a student who is rambling, cueing him to shorten his explanation. The curriculum addresses several important areas:

- listening
- paying attention
- organization
- self-concept
- controlling impulsivity
- understanding ADD and ADHD
- goal setting
- handling feelings
- communication
- friendships
- learning to relax

Teachers or guidance counselors in high school may be able to adapt this curriculum for the older age group. One nice thing about the curriculum is that the authors suggest ways to practice and reinforce the new skills in the classroom and at home, or as Dr. Russell Barkley says, at the "point of performance." ***Practice at the point of performance increases the likelihood that students will master the skill being taught!***

Involving Teachers in the Game

Using the *Creative Coaching* curriculum, the group being coached is known as the "All Stars." After a student learns a specific skill such as paying attention, he or she takes a colored half-sheet of paper, called the "High 5," back to the teacher. The paper includes a preprinted list of all eleven lessons with the current one circled. The teacher is asked to comment when she notices the student using the skill. For example, privately or in front of class, she might say, *"Nick, I noticed that you paid attention and wrote down the assignment. Good job!"* Or the teacher may "coach" the student during the week by saying, *"Samantha, this might be a good time to pay attention and focus on copying the assignments off the board."* At the end of the week, the teacher writes down one or two positive comments regarding the student's use of the skills (or a skill learned earlier) and the student brings the "High 5" back to the group the following week. The comments on the card are then discussed in the group and used to reinforce the skill and to earn points for rewards.

Involving Parents in "Home Play"

The *Creative Coaching* curriculum includes "Home play" activities that involve parents in reinforcing the skills that were learned that week. Take-home sheets have activities designed to stimulate conversation between the parent and student about individual skills. Younger teens may enjoy hearing the counselor explain that this is an opportunity to get their parents to do homework. The parents do the work of writing the assignments while the student dictates the answers. On the back of the activity sheet, the skills are discussed and directions are given for parents to "catch" the student applying these skills, or "coach" him to use the skills as needed. Parents then write a positive weekly comment, which the student also returns to the group. Points are given for the activity, and the parents' comments are discussed in the group. Students may earn individual awards or the group may combine points for a group reward.

The ADHD Learning Lab

This model study skills and coaching program is described in Summary 69. The co-founders of the program, Judy Bandy and Holly West, have identified key areas where our children struggle. Students in the program receive tutoring in these areas for half an hour before and after school four days a week. Instruction from mentors includes both academic and related skills: organization, time management, project management, review of educational plans, goal setting, and self-advocacy.

Resources

Bandy, Judy. *Tools for an ADHD Learning Lab.* Eden Prairie, MN: ADHD School Specialties, 2010.
"Coaching for Adults with ADHD: What We Know (fact sheet #8). Landover, MD: CHADD. (www.help4adhd.org).
McDougall, Nancy and Roper, Janet. *Creative Coaching: A Support Group for Children with ADHD.* San Antonio, TX: Glory Publications, 1998. Available through www.youthlight.com.

Conflict Resolution

Teaching conflict resolution skills to students with ADD or ADHD is very important, since these students may be impulsive and irritable, especially when their medication has worn off or they are under stress. Learning more about problem solving, peer mediation, and anger management will help these students cope successfully with potentially volatile situations. Conflict resolution strategies serve as the foundation for implementing Peer Mediation programs such as those discussed in Summary 73.

Problem-Solving Skills

Students with an attention deficit must be taught problem-solving skills for coping with school or homework issues and sometimes with relationship or behavioral issues. Learning problem-solving skills may help students understand how to analyze and talk their way through a problem rather than resorting to verbal attacks or fighting.

Students as Partners in Problem Solving

Help students develop their own solutions for completing homework and turning it in to the teacher. Students are more likely to comply with solutions they helped develop. A subtle message of respect is also conveyed: *"I know you really want to do better. ADD (ADHD) can make remembering homework assignments [chores, being on time] difficult. What can I do to help you remember?"* This is preferable to giving the implied message, *"You don't really want to do well. The only way you will do your school work [be on time] is if I, the teacher, make you complete it."*

- Discuss the problem at hand.
- Ask for the student's input on how to solve it. Generate several options.
- Give the student adequate time to respond, especially when slow processing speed is a problem.
- Listen to her input.
- Offer options, if she has no suggestions.
- Weigh the pros and cons of the options. Discuss them or help her list them.
- Help her pick the best option.
- Write down what the action will be and when it will start.
- Monitor and evaluate results. *("Check back with me tomorrow and let me know if it worked."* If the student forgets to check with the teacher, the teacher should contact the student.)
- Change the plan if it is not working.
- Assume good intentions until proven wrong.
- Assume the student is doing her best!

Conflict Resolution and Problem-solving in Relationships

Lyndon D. Waugh, M.D., author of *Tired of Yelling,* suggests fifteen key steps in teaching children and teenagers to resolve conflicts. These steps may help students improve their relationships with other students, their teachers, or parents.

The Thinking Steps
1. Assess emotions; recognize anger—it is a sign to resolve a problem.
2. Accept anger: it's okay, but handle it and behave well.
3. Gauge the intensity of anger on a scale of 1–10.
4. Who and what are you angry about? Don't misdirect it at the wrong person.
5. Do a perspective check: are you overreacting?

The Talk/Listen Steps
6. Select a good time and place for resolution.
7. Avoid coalitions; keep the argument between the right two people.
8. Express anger appropriately.
9. Listen actively.
10. Admit fault.

The Solving Steps
11. Brainstorm solutions.
12. Discuss pros and cons of each.
13. Decide and plan.
14. Do it.
15. Review/revise.

Communication Skills in Conflict Resolution

Communication skills are an integral part of conflict resolution. Some of the important skills that need to be taught include:

- understanding body language;
- using "I" messages (not "you" messages, which tend to have an element of placing blame);
- using reflective listening—getting the facts and understanding the emotions involved (*"So, you seem angry. Tell me what's going on."*);
- checking and validating the accuracy of the information gathered.

Communication skills were successfully taught in one Georgia high school as an integral part of their peer mediation program. Their assistant principal provided roughly 16 to 20 hours of training in communication and conflict resolution skills to each peer mediator. The school used a conflict resolution program from The Community Board Program to train their peer mediators. A more detailed description of a different peer mediation program is provided in the next summary.

Resources

Crawford, D. and Bodine, R. *Conflict Resolution Education: A Guide to Implementing Programs in Schools, Youth-Serving Organizations, and Community and Juvenile Justice Settings.* Washington, DC: Office of Juvenile Justice and Delinquency Prevention (OJJDP) and Safe and Drug-free Schools Program (USDOE), 1996. (Available at www.ncjrs.gov.)

Peer Medication for Middle Schools. San Francisco, CA: The Community Board Program, 2003. (Available from www.communityboards.org.)

Peer Mediation for High Schools. San Francisco, CA: The Community Board Program, 2003. (Available from www.communityboards.org.)

Waugh, Lyndon and Sweitzer, Letitia. *Tired of Yelling: Teaching Children to Resolve Conflicts.* Marietta, GA: Longstreet Press, 1999.

Peer Mediation

Peer mediation programs teach students to resolve conflict in peaceful ways. Peer mediation is one of the most popular programs schools use to help reduce conflicts among students and to avoid potential fights or other disruptions. During mediation, a student trained in mediation techniques meets with the students who are having a conflict and helps them try to agree upon a solution to their problem. Sometimes students are referred to mediation instead of being disciplined in traditional ways such as detention or suspension.

Peer mediation programs teach students improved communication skills and specific strategies for settling disagreements and misunderstandings. Involving students with ADD or ADHD in a peer mediation program may help them reduce aggressive, uncooperative behaviors that can result in rejection by their peers. Mediation programs may be based inside the school under the supervision of the principal or a guidance counselor. Trained student mediators may even be stationed at locations where problems may erupt—for example, outside, before and after school, and in the cafeteria during lunch.

Basic Rules for Peer Mediation

1. Both students involved in the dispute or conflict must agree to peer mediation and to abide by the decision that is made.

2. Mediators are neutral and don't take sides.

3. A mediation session follows these procedures:
    - Mediators introduce themselves and ask the names of the two students.
    - Mediators state the rules—i.e., students must:
        - remain with the mediator,
        - listen without interrupting,
        - tell the truth,
        - treat each other respectfully,
        - solve the problem,
        - abide by their agreement,
        - sign the agreement (indicating they believe it "resolves the issues between them").

4. Mediators ask student 1 to tell his story, then summarize it.

5. Mediators ask student 2 to tell his story, then summarize it.

6. Mediators ask for possible solutions, then summarize them.

7. Students review the pros and cons of each solution.

8. Students choose a solution and plan how and when to implement it.

9. Mediators ask if both students are satisfied with the decision.

10. Mediators write the agreement.

11. Students sign the agreement to indicate agreement with the solution.

12. Session ends.

Key Concepts Taught in Peer Mediation

The skills below are formally taught to peer mediators so they can facilitate mediation sessions:
- understanding conflict,
- effective communication,
- listening skills,
- understanding anger,
- handling anger,
- confidentiality,
- peer mediation strategies.

Students receiving mediation also benefit by learning new skills such as:
1. strategies for avoiding angry confrontations, and
2. new coping skills that will carry over into their home and adult lives.

The next summary provides more information on violence prevention.

A Typical Peer Mediation Program

A description of a typical peer mediation program may help administrators decide whether this type of program may be helpful in their school. Originally I interviewed Ottie Manis, a now retired guidance counselor, about the peer mediation program at her school. Here are some key facts about the program:
- The high school has a population of just over a thousand students and has fifteen trained student mediators available.
- Three or four students are available each period to handle conflicts.
- Students may ask for mediation or be referred by a teacher or an administrator.
- Peer mediators participate in a minimum of fifteen hours of training.
- On average, a mediation session lasts approximately one hour.
- A mediation session is usually scheduled within fifteen minutes or so of a conflict. Occasionally, if the problem occurs at the end of the day or the student is suspended, the session will be scheduled the next day. Most are handled the same day of their referral.
- The counselor meets with the peer mediators and provides supervision twice a month during school hours for about forty-five minutes. A discussion of previous mediation sessions helps these students improve their skills and expand the range of interventions they may suggest.
- On average, four or five students a week are referred to peer mediation.
- The school uses the curriculum developed by Fred Schrumpf and others that is published by Research Press (see Resources).

Students with ADD or ADHD as Peer Mediators

Some schools make a point of recruiting and training peer mediators who have personal difficulties with conflict. This training is often very helpful to these students, who may learn helpful new skills as they teach them to others. No doubt, many students with ADD or ADHD would benefit from training as peer mediators.

Resources

Cunningham, C.E. and Cunningham, L.J. "Student–Mediated Conflict Resolution Programs." Barkley, Russell, ed., *Attention Deficit Hyperactivity Disorder.* 3rd ed. New York, New York: Guilford Press, 2006.
Schrumpf, Fred, Crawford, Donna, and Usadel, H. Chu. *Peer Mediation: Conflict Resolution in Schools.* Rev. ed. Champaign, IL: Research Press Publishers, 1997. Available materials: program guide, student manual, and a training video.

6

Violence Prevention Programs

SUMMARY 74

There is no research to suggest that students with ADD or ADHD in general are more likely to be violent than other students. However, educators across the nation are greatly concerned about growing violence among *all* students. Violence prevention programs are therefore mentioned here to give an idea of the information available on this topic, as well as the work being done to develop model programs to prevent violence.

Risk Factors for Violence in Adolescents

Although it is very difficult to identify potentially violent teenagers, the American Academy of Child and Adolescent Psychiatry lists several known risk factors:

- early involvement with drugs and alcohol,
- previous aggressive or violent behavior,
- being the victim of physical and/or sexual abuse,
- genetic factors (family heredity),
- easy access to weapons, especially handguns,
- association with antisocial groups,
- pervasive exposure to violence in the media,
- stressful family socioeconomic factors (poverty, marital breakups, unemployment)
- brain damage from a head injury,
- first arrest occurring prior to age ten,
- first arrest for a serious offense,
- three or more arrests by age twelve.

Warning signs for violent behavior in children include :

- intense anger,
- frequent loss of temper or emotional blow-ups,
- extreme irritability,
- extreme impulsiveness,
- becoming easily frustrated.

Poor school performance is also known to contribute to both violence and delinquency!

Conduct Disorder and Violence

As mentioned above, there is usually no reason to assume that a student with ADD or ADHD is more prone to violence than other students. The one exception is among students with attention deficits who have also been diagnosed with a *conduct disorder*—meaning they habitually violate the rights of others and refuse to comply with rules. Fewer than one-fourth of students with ADD or ADHD eventually receive the diagnosis of conduct disorder. It is important to note, too, that even when students with conduct disorder are aggressive, they may not necessarily be violent. Conduct disorder is discussed in more detail in Summary 78.

General Observations

In writing *CHADD's Educators' Manual of ADHD*, I made several key observations regarding aggressive behavior in young children. A few children with attention deficits may have excessive rage reactions. Specific behaviors of concern include explosive temper tantrums, physical aggression, fighting, intentional destruction of property, and, in rare cases, cruelty to animals and fire setting. Early identification and intervention with children who exhibit these aggressive antisocial behaviors is critical. According to Hill Walker, Director for the Institute on Violence and Destructive Behavior at the University of Oregon, children who are identified as delinquent in middle and high school demonstrate signs of behavior problems that can be detected as early as preschool. In other words, without adequate intervention, behavior problems often remain consistent over time: children who have serious problems in preschool, left untreated, frequently have serious problems later in school and throughout their lifetime.

Dr. Walker 's research has clearly shown that early intervention can prevent serious problems in later school years. Teachers should trust their experience and instincts. Researchers explain that 80 percent of arrests in boys could be predicted by: 1) early teacher ratings of social skills, 2) total negative playground behavior, and 3) disciplinary contacts with the principal's office. Dr. Ross Green's book, *The Explosive Child*, provides insights into these explosive behaviors and offers effective, easy-to-use strategies for managing them. Similarly, Dr. Walker's *First Steps to Success* program is a highly effective nationally recognized violence prevention program for young children. Elementary schools should consider obtaining this training for at least one faculty member.

Because these children are so difficult to raise, parents also struggle. They need help mastering parenting strategies to address problem behaviors at home. Without help, many parents of these children will use ineffective, inconsistent parenting strategies. So the message is clear; intervene early, offering help to both the child and parents.

Model Violence Prevention Programs

Ten model "blueprint" programs from around the country were identified in 1996 by the Center for the Study and Prevention of Violence. The selection of model programs is reviewed and updated regularly. A series of "blueprints" were developed to describe these programs. For information on these programs, including a bullying prevention program, life skills training, and multisystemic therapy, see the website for the Center for the Study and Prevention of Violence listed in the Resources.

School-Based Mentoring

One of the original "blueprint programs"—a mentoring program—was expanded to a school-based setting by Big Brothers and Big Sisters of Abilene, Texas. Through this program, high school students are recruited and trained to provide support and encouragement to younger students. By interacting with their mentors, the younger students learn new communication skills that help build their self-confidence. They are also assigned a "lunch buddy"—an older student who sits with them during lunch and simply offers friendship and a listening ear.

A curriculum called *Character Building Traits* was developed for the program to help teach students the skills they lack. Janet Ardoyno, who was Executive Director of the program and originally trained as an ADD coach, based her curriculum upon materials developed by the Search Institute. The Institute offers materials to help students develop 40 assets that are essential for healthy development. (See www.search-institute.org for more information.)

Research has shown that this school mentoring program results in improved behavior, better grades, fewer fights, and a reduced likelihood of drug or alcohol use. Now the Big Brothers and Big Sisters organization is developing mentoring programs nationwide.

Bullying Prevention Program

Students with ADHD or ADD are more likely to be bullied by their peers. As a result, they may ultimately become bullies themselves. This makes it very important to involve students with attention deficit disorders in bullying prevention programs.

Bullying prevention programs help students become more aware of their own behavior and how it affects others. Students unknowingly give their unspoken support for bullying by silently standing by while another child is being taunted. These programs empower students to take a stand against bullying and give them the tools they need to cope with bullies. The Olweus Bullying Prevention Program (see Resources) has been endorsed by both SAMHSA (Substance Abuse and Mental Health Services Administration) and the OJJDP (Office of Juvenile Justice and Delinquency Prevention), and also is a Blueprint Model Program. Teens may also visit www.teensagainstbullying.org, an interactive program developed by PACER Center.

Resources

American Academy of Child and Adolescent Psychiatry. *Understanding Violent Behavior in Children and Adolescents,* Facts for Families series. Washington, DC: AACAP, 2001.

Center for the Study and Prevention of Violence. University of Colorado, IBS #10, Campus Box 439, Boulder, CO 80309. "Blueprints" of model programs are available (www.colorado.edu/cspv/blueprints.htm).

Green, R.W. *The Explosive Child.* Rev. ed. New York, NY: HarperCollins, 2010

Jekielek, Susan, Moore, Kristin A., and Hair, Elizabeth C. *Mentoring Programs and Youth Development: A Synthesis.* Washington, DC: Child Trends, 2002.

McGill, D.E., Mihalic, S.F., and Grotpeter, J.K. *Big Brothers Big Sisters of America: Blueprints for Violence Prevention, Book Two.* Boulder, CO: Center for the Study and Prevention of Violence, Institute of Behavioral Science, 1998.

National Center for Conflict Resolution Education, Illinois Bar Center, 424 South 2nd St., Springfield, IL 62701. (www.nccre.org).

Olweus, D., Limber, S., and Mihalic, S.F. *Bullying Prevention Program: Blueprints for Violence Prevention, Book Nine.* Boulder, CO: Center for the Study and Prevention of Violence, Institute of Behavioral Science, 1999.

Olweus Bullying Prevention Program. Clemson, SC: Institute on Family and Neighborhood Life, Clemson University, 2003. Available at www.clemson.edu/olweus.

Walker, H.M., Colvin, G, and Ramsey, E., *Antisocial Behavior in Schools: Strategies and Best Practices*. Belmont, CA: Brooks/Cole, 2000.

Walker, Hill and Gresham, Frank M. "Making Schools Safer and Violence Free." *Intervention in School and Clinic*, March 1997, Vol. 32, No. 4: 199-204.

Walker, Hill and Sylvester, Robert. "Where Is School Along the Path to Prison?" *Educational Leadership,* September, 1991.

Anger Management*

Some teenagers with ADD or ADHD have difficulty controlling their emotions when they are frustrated or upset. As a result, they may have an occasional emotional blow-up at school. Typically, teachers know which students have major problems with self-control. Any student who is struggling with emotional control (for example, screaming, yelling at other students or the teacher, or getting into fights) could benefit from anger management training.

Teachers may select a few of the strategies below to suggest to any given student. For example, the teacher may give the student a copy of the paragraphs on "Alternative Ways to Handle Anger" and discuss it with him. However, educating the student about anger management may require more time than the teacher has available. If so, ask the guidance counselor or social worker to conduct an anger management group. Or, after a blow-up occurs, find out whether training can be provided while the student is in detention or in-school suspension.

Six Key Points Teens Should Know about Anger

When teaching a teenager about anger management, there are six important points that teachers or guidance counselors may want to make initially. Ask the teen to record these points in a notebook that he can use as a reference in the future (or give him a copy from this page or book).

1. **Anger is a feeling.** In and of itself, it is not good or bad, right or wrong. It's what you do with your anger or how you express it that is important.
2. **It's okay to be angry,** but it's never okay to hurt yourself or someone else or damage property. Verbal abuse and physical violence are not okay.
3. **We learn how to express our anger by observing how others express their anger.** This can include parents, teachers, relatives, and friends, or characters on television shows, movies, or video games.
4. **We are responsible for how we express our anger.** We cannot blame others for our behavior. Even if someone does something that makes us feel angry, we still can choose *how* to respond to that person. We can respond in a way that makes things worse or we can respond in a way that makes things better.
5. **Our goal is to accept angry feelings and channel or direct them in constructive ways,** not to repress or destroy the feelings.
6. **Feeling angry is like having an elephant sitting in the living room:** You can't ignore it. It won't go away. You can't deal with anything else in your life until you have dealt with it. You must learn to cope with the anger: talk about it, take action to resolve it, or, if it is irresolvable, at least diffuse it.

Increase Awareness of Events That Trigger Anger

Sometimes students lack self-awareness and are not in touch with their own feelings. So, they can't talk easily about their anger. For these students, it's usually safer and less threatening to talk about someone else's behavior than their own. It may help to make up a few stories with at least one or two examples that are similar but not identical to this student's real-life situation. For example: *"Some students handle their anger in ways that make the situation worse. For instance, I know:*

---

* Adapted from material developed by Kathy Hubbard Weeks.

■ *One student who failed a class, yelled at his teacher, and called her an ugly name.*

■ *One student whose girlfriend broke up with him and found a new boyfriend. The three students had a confrontation in the hall and the boys got into a fight. Both students were suspended.*

I have some ideas of ways to handle your anger in a more constructive way [or words that are appropriate for the student]."

After this *safe* discussion, talk about how the student handles anger in his own life. Help the teen become aware of the kind of things that can trigger his anger. You might begin by saying something like, *"A lot of things can make people angry. Many people, not just teenagers with attention deficits, get angry to protect themselves from painful feelings, such as frustration or rejection or feeling stupid."* Then, try discussing the answers to the questions in this section.

What makes you angry?

1. frustrating school work or an irritating situation?
2. being criticized?
3. anxiety or fear about a situation over which you have no control?
4. feeling as if you are being attacked or fear that you could be?
5. feelings of dependency, sadness, or depression?

How do you use anger?

1. Do you use anger to:
   ■ avoid the situation?
   ■ gain control over it?
   ■ ward off an attack?
   ■ manipulate or have power over others?
   ■ retaliate or get revenge?
2. Does anger protect you from *painful feelings*, such as feeling incompetent, unlovable, unworthy, inadequate, or lonely?
3. When you are under stress, do you get angry more easily? What things stress you out?

Teach Students to Be Aware of Their Body's Response to Anger

Discuss the *physiological response* the human body has when we become angry.

Pay Attention to Early Physical Cues: Explain that we need to pay attention to the physical cues that our body gives us, so we can recognize when we are becoming angry. For example, a student may become tense, hold his breath, clench his fists, feel hot, or have pain or pressure in his head, chest, or stomach. Mentally, he may feel agitated, be unable to concentrate on anything else other than the problem or injustice. Next, he may want to hit or kick something, cry, scream, or begin developing a plan of revenge. In the early stages of anger we can still make good choices about what to do and how to respond. We are still thinking rationally.

To help a student think about how he responds to angry feelings, you might say:

"Think of a time when you were angry. What made you angry? Where did you feel the anger in your body? Did your muscles become tense? Did you clench your fists? Did you have pain or pressure in your head, chest, or stomach? Did you hold your breath? Did you feel hot?"

Do Not Ignore Early Warning Signals: Take action to avoid anger. If we ignore early warning signals, we are more apt to express our anger in a hurtful, ineffective, damaging way, which may result in feelings of remorse, shame, and embarrassment, and damage our self-esteem and relationships with others. Tell the student:

> *"Now that you know the types of situations that can trigger anger and how your body feels physically when you start to become angry, pay attention to these signals. Then you can stop yourself before you blow up and handle your anger better."*

Alternative Ways to Handle Anger

Brainstorm with the teenager about different ways to manage anger and express it in a positive and assertive way. Ask him to write down strategies for anger management in his notebook and tell you which ones might work for him. Some examples are:

1. **Learn how to express yourself better when you are angry.**
   - *Express your feelings:*
     - Use "I" or first person statements. "I'm angry because John tripped me in the hall." "My feelings are hurt because Mary's my friend and she was talking about me to the other girls."
     - Be respectful while communicating.
     - Share your feelings without hurting people.
     - Tell others what is bothering you by being direct, specific, and polite.
     - Be honest. Give the real reason you want what you want.

   "I'm feeling…(frustrated) because…(I had plans to go to my friend's house after school and no one told me I had to stay after school for a teacher conference). I want/would like…(for you or my parents to let me know at least a day ahead of time when I have to do something after school)."

   - *Ask for what you want or need:*
     - Be assertive by telling others what you want and need without blaming, manipulating, or attacking. ("I don't want Mary to talk about me." Or "I would like for Ms. Clark to talk to me privately when I've done something wrong—not in front of the whole class.")
     - Ask, don't demand.
     - Speak in a calm, quiet voice.
     - Avoid swearing.

   - *Listen, be tolerant of others, and be willing to compromise:*
     - Listen to what the other person is saying without interrupting.
     - Try to understand the other person's point of view.
     - Accept differences.
     - Agree to disagree.
     - Stop trying to control others.
     - Be willing to compromise.
     - Negotiate a "win-win" solution. *"Can we both get what we want from this solution?"*

2. **Take a time-out to calm down.** Take a break from the situation. When your emotions have calmed down (at least 20 minutes) come back to discuss the situation or approach the task from a different perspective.

3. **Manage your stress** through regular exercise, muscle relaxation, good nutrition, listening to music, adequate rest, planning ahead, or allowing adequate time to complete tasks.

4. **Take a deep breath and count to ten.**

6

5. **Tell yourself to relax** and don't forget to breathe deeply and slowly.

6. **Learn self-soothing behaviors** that can be called upon when you become aware of anger in your body; for example, take a hot bath, ask someone to give you a massage, or listen to soothing, calm music.

7. **Use self-talk.** *"Okay, I can remain calm. I can maintain control. I just have to take a deep breath, relax, and let it go."*

8. **Ask yourself, "How important is this to me?** *Do I really need to be angry? Is it worth getting suspended or expelled from school?"*

9. **Keep yourself safe.** *"We need to discuss this later when we are less emotional and thinking more clearly."*

10. **Reduce the amount of stimulation** in your environment; it helps to maintain calmness. Go to a quiet, calm place.

11. **Go talk to a good friend** who will listen and support you.

12. **Brainstorm solutions** for the problem at hand, after things have begun to calm down.

Role-Play Solutions

The last step is to practice managing anger with the teen by setting up role-play situations. First, the teacher demonstrates how to manage anger in a given scenario. Ask the teen for feedback about what the teacher did that was good, and what he or she could have done differently to make it better. Then let the teen demonstrate how he would manage his anger. The teen evaluates what he did well and what he would like to change. The teacher provides positive reinforcement only for the desirable responses. Ignore inappropriate answers.

Look for "Triggers" for Anger

Of course, removing the antecedent behavior or "trigger" that is causing the anger or frustration is critically important. Teachers should make certain that:
- any learning problems are identified,
- schoolwork is adjusted so that it is not too long or too difficult, and
- needed accommodations are provided.

Ultimately, medication may be necessary to help the student control his anger and impulsivity. The family should talk with their doctor about this issue.

Anger Management Programs

Two programs are listed here. Their primary drawback is their expense (ranging from $1,000 to over $5,000).

- *Mastering Anger—Resolving Conflict Curriculum* (Grades 7–12). La Luz, NM: Institute for Affective Skill Development. (Available at www.iasd.com; 800-745-0418.)

- *Resolving Conflict Creatively Program (RCCP).* This program is a model program that was funded by the Center for Disease Control and Prevention. Assistance with RCCP training and implementation is available from the Educators for Social Responsibility (www.esrnational.org/es/rccp.htm; 800-370-2515).

A Word of Caution

Remember, don't expect miracles from simply teaching these students anger management. It will take time, maturity, and practice to master this skill. The student may still have emotional blow-ups, but at least he has begun learning the skills to use when something makes him angry. He will mature with time.

Resources

Center for the Prevention of School Violence, North Carolina Department of Juvenile Justice and Delinquency Prevention. www.ncdjjdp.org/cpsv.

Office of Juvenile Justice and Delinquency Prevention (OJJDP), 810 7th St. NW, Washington, DC 20531. 202-307-5911. www.ojjdp.org. This site offers a list of model programs such as the Leadership Program's Violence Prevention Project, plus a literature review on such topics as afterschool/recreation and truancy prevention.

SelfGrowth.com: The Online Self Improvement Community. www.selfgrowth.com. (Click on "Mental Health," then "anger management" for an assortment of articles with ratings from readers.)

About Kathy Hubbard Weeks:

Kathy Hubbard Weeks, whose work provided the foundation for this summary, was formerly the ADD Consultant and Section 504 Coordinator for the Kenosha, Wisconsin Unified School District. Kathy is a pioneer in the area of school reform for students with ADD or ADHD. She was among the first to suggest enlisting other students to help children and teenagers with ADD or ADHD. She began a model program in her Kenosha school district in 1990. She also has time for a busy part-time private practice in social work, where her specialty is students with ADD or ADHD and their families. She has a unique understanding of ADD and ADHD, since she is also the mother of a young adult with ADHD.

SECTION 7

Going the Extra Mile for Students with ADD or ADHD

I recognize that there are several factors that make teaching an incredibly difficult job. For starters, teachers are expected to develop individualized teaching plans for so many students, not just those with attention deficits. Second, ADD and ADHD are challenging for parents who have only one teenager and even more so for teachers who sometimes have several students with the condition. Third, colleges don't typically offer teachers specific classes in dealing with students who are challenging. Last, because of the adverse impact that attention deficits and executive function deficits have on learning, teachers must often teach students who think and learn differently than the teacher does.

Despite these challenges, many educators are successful in teaching students with attention deficits. When teachers make a special effort to help these students, it is an extraordinary gift to parents and their teenagers. The teacher's caring attitude and positive support often make the critical difference in whether or not the student succeeds in school. In this section, I will therefore talk about the importance of teacher attitudes, beliefs, and values with regard to these students. Several common questions I often receive when I present workshops for teachers are also included.

SUMMARY 76 Valuing Students with ADD and ADHD

For many teachers, it is only natural to place the most value on teenagers who are good students and make the best grades. Students who make good grades tend to have essential learning skills such as the ability to pay attention, memorize, get started and complete homework, and do well on test scores—traits that are often lacking in many students with ADD and ADHD. So, students who have attention deficits or learning problems may not feel valued by their teachers. Their shining talents and abilities often fall outside the arena of a regular classroom. *It takes a special teacher to find the time and energy to make each student feel valued!*

My son was lucky because he had several dedicated teachers during his school years. When a teacher looked for and found the worthwhile qualities in my son, I was so deeply grateful that I was sometimes moved to tears. Students seem to have a sixth sense about which teachers really like them. For example, when my son was in first grade, he began crying when I asked to see his first report card. His plea, "Please don't read my report card; my teacher thinks I'm bad," was profoundly insightful.

These teenagers are often very sensitive to a teacher's approval or disapproval. *Students with attention deficits tend to do well in classes where the teacher likes them* and may fail the same subject with a teacher who doesn't like them. Sometimes even the slightest hint of disapproval or an embarrassing put-down in front of classmates not only dooms any future positive relationship with a teacher, but also stifles learning and memory. Remember, emotions are the "off-on" switch to learning; chemicals in the brain basically shut down and block learning when students are fearful and intimidated.

Sometimes *teachers intimidate students without intending to do so*. For instance, a teacher may roll her eyes and say, "I explained that already. Weren't you listening?" This sends an unspoken message: "I am not approachable. Do not ask me questions when you don't understand something." These students know they can't always pay attention and they miss important information. They are sometimes afraid to ask questions when they don't understand something for fear the teacher has already explained the material. If a teacher gives a negative response that embarrasses the teen, these students will forever be afraid to approach and ask for help. For teachers who find this situation frustrating, try taking a breath, don't change facial expressions, and explain the material again for the forty-seventh time. Consider also asking another student to talk it through with the teen.

Occasionally teachers make thoughtless comments based upon false assumptions. They assume the student's poor school performance is caused by laziness. For example, I cringed when I heard the story below. It's shocking that ignorant statements like this are still being made today:

> *"When my son and I went to meet his middle school teachers, the teacher greeted him with these comments: 'It's so great to see you. I've been looking over your school records and I see that you are very smart. However, you've got a lazy streak. We've just got to get that laziness out of you this year.'"*

Reframe ADD/ADHD Behaviors

Although having an attention deficit disorder is not easy, it should not be viewed as a terrible thing. Many of these teenagers grow up to be successful, happy adults. Frequently, these students will naturally gravitate toward active, hands-on careers that maximize their skills and don't penalize them for their ADD/ADHD behaviors. Unfortunately, the school years, with requirements for organization and memorization, are often the most challenging times for people with this condition. It may help a teacher to look at troubling ADD/ADHD behaviors, reframe them, and look for the positive aspects of these same behaviors. ***ADD or ADHD may be a disability in school, but it does not have to be a disability in life!***

Qualities that may not be endearing in a classroom may well be highly valued in the adult business world. A list of behaviors that could be reframed positively is contained in Summary 77 and Appendix A11. A few examples are provided here:

- These teenagers often have a wonderful ***zest for living***. Sometimes they seem to have more ***fun in life*** and are more ***creative*** than those of us who don't have ADD or ADHD.
- The pesky, talkative "class clown" may grow up to be a wonderful ***salesperson*** or bring welcome humor into many lives. Although most teachers would not want to teach a comic genius like Robin Williams, most of us greatly enjoy his humor. These ***outgoing, friendly*** types add much-needed humor to life, put us at ease, and make us feel welcome.
- Hyperactive students often have ***high energy*** as adults and work long hours once they find a career or job they like. Michael Phelps, Olympic Gold medalist swimmer, may have struggled in school, but clearly he does not struggle in a swimming pool.

Teachers can help parents and the teens themselves reframe their perception of attention deficits and look for the positives. ***Ask parents and students to complete Appendix A11.***

Identify Strengths

So often the only assessment of students who are struggling in school is a negative one. What are their deficits, problems, and shortcomings? In other words, the cup is viewed as half empty rather than half full. When teenagers are viewed only in light of their deficits, a negative self-fulfilling prophecy may be set in motion. For example, students who are told that they are bad, dumb, or lazy are more likely to act that way. Furthermore, according to one researcher, *we teachers may actually be unintentionally rationalizing the failure of our teaching efforts by describing a teenager as "unmotivated or lazy."*

Consider the Behavioral and Emotional Rating Scale (BERS)

Seldom are the strengths and outside interests of the student identified or attempts made to incorporate them into schoolwork. Yet IDEA mandates that the student's strengths be identified in the IEP. Recently, strength-based assessments have increased in popularity. These evaluations may be done informally by simply asking the student and parent to describe her strengths and to complete Appendix A11. Or a formal assessment can be done using an instrument such as the Behavioral and Emotional Rating Scale (BERS). Dr. Michael Epstein, special education professor at the University of Nebraska, developed this scale as a way to identify and focus attention on a child's strengths. The BERS evaluates five areas.

1. **Interpersonal Strengths**—the student's ability to control his or her emotions or behavior.
2. **Family Involvement**—the student's relationship with his or her family.
3. **Intrapersonal Strengths**—a student's feelings of competence and accomplishment.
4. **School Functioning**—a student's competence in school.
5. **Affective Strengths**—a student's ability to accept affection and express feelings.

Questions are also asked about the student's favorite hobbies, activities, or sports; best school subjects, best friend, favorite teacher, job responsibilities, and closest adult relationship. The scale may be completed in ten minutes by teachers, parents, counselors, or others who are knowledgeable about the student. Then a school psychologist or other trained professional may score and interpret the results. Additional information on the BERS is available at the end of this summary.

Complete a Simple Bio Sheet on Students

Teachers can identify strengths, special skills, and interests of their students that will enhance their teaching. Selena Conley, EDS, a veteran Georgia special education teacher, has her students complete a bio sheet and answer seven brief questions about themselves. The questions, listed in Summary 62, address such issues as "my gifts are…, I need help with…, and I get distracted when…."

Believe in Teenagers with ADD or ADHD

Researchers tell us that when adults with attention deficits were asked how they coped successfully, they often said, *"Someone believed in me."* That "someone" was most often their parents, but the next most-often listed person was a *teacher*. So, the impact teachers have on the lives of students with attention deficits can be profound! ***Teachers often make the difference in the success or failure of students with ADD or ADHD.***

Resources

Epstein, Michael. "The Development and Validation of a Scale to Assess the Emotional and Behavioral Strengths of Children." *Remedial and Special Education,* 1999, Vol. 20 , No. 5.

Epstein, Michael. *The Behavioral and Emotional Rating Scale (BERS).* Austin, TX: PRO-ED, 2004. A strength-based rating scale.

Reframe: Building on Strengths

Name Steven **Grade** 11 **Date** 9/26

STRENGTHS—*Home/Community/School*
1. a strong leader; not afraid to take charge
2. high-energy; works long hours
3. tenacious; doesn't give up; persuasive
4. confident public speaker
5. entertaining; always upbeat; makes others laugh
6. friendly; never meets a stranger
7. laser focused when working on an interesting project
8. independent thinker; not afraid to disagree
9. skilled in mechanical areas; works on cars and stereos
10. active in church youth group; a leader

Examples of Reframing Common ADD and ADHD Behaviors

When students are struggling, it is easy to get caught up in focusing on their problem behaviors. It is extremely important to stop and take time to identify each student's strengths and special talents. Examples of ways to reframe negative behaviors may help teachers and parents develop a list of the teenager's strengths. Remember that the desirability of specific behaviors changes over time. Characteristics that are not valued in students in school may be valued in the adult work world. Discuss the teenager's strengths with him. Ask him if he has anything to add to the list. See Appendix A11 for a blank form for listing the teenager's strengths.

Bossiness: "leadership" (albeit carried too far)

Hyperactive: "energetic"
"high energy"
"does ten projects at one time"
"works long hours"

Strong-willed:	"tenacious" "goal-oriented"
Day dreamer:	"creative" "innovative" "imaginative"
Daring:	"risk taker" "willing to try new things"
Lazy:	"laid back" / "Type B personalities live longer"
Instigator:	"initiator" "innovative"
Manipulative:	"delegates" "gets others to do the job"
Aggressive:	"assertive" "doesn't let people take advantage of him"
Questions authority:	"independent" "free thinker" "makes own decisions"
Argumentative:	"persuasive" "may be attorney material"
Poor handwriting:	"maybe he'll be a doctor one day" "good computer skills"

When Teens Continue to Struggle in School: Finding Problems Hidden Beneath the Surface

If teenagers with ADD or ADHD continue to struggle even after receiving accommodations at school and starting medication, what are the parents' options? Since complex problems may be "hidden beneath the surface," parents and teachers must work together to identify and address challenges that are interfering with the student's success. Three common reasons many students struggle are discussed in the following paragraphs. Work with parents and teens to identify which, if any, of these problems are interfering with school performance.

If parents are dissatisfied with the public school system, a second option is to consider placement in a private school. Some private schools work well for students with ADD/ADHD, but other schools that are singularly focused on college prep may not be that helpful. The key is to make certain that the private school is a good match for the teen and provides an environment where she can be successful.

Finally, homeschooling is an option that works well for some families. I am often asked about the feasibility of homeschooling students with ADHD or ADD. Unfortunately, my response is not that helpful: maybe and maybe not. It depends upon the needs of the student and the commitment level of the parents, which needs to be quite high. Another factor that comes into play regarding the homeschooling decision is that parents are often in conflict with their teenager regarding poor academic performance. So, family tensions may escalate even more if a parent becomes the primary teacher.

Many homeschooling resources are available should parents decide to take this route. Kathy Kuhl's book, *Homeschooling Your Struggling Learner*, lists numerous resources that will be helpful to families. Kuhl, a former public school teacher, homeschooled her son for grades 4–12. Her son had learning and attention problems that the public school was unable to address successfully.

Three Common Reasons Students with ADD/ADHD Struggle in School

Regardless of which educational option parents select, these three potential problems must be addressed:

1. Medication is not right;
2. Learning problems and executive function difficulties are not addressed;
3. Other coexisting problems are not treated.

1. Medication Is Not Right

- *Medication is too low:* Concern is sometimes expressed about medication being too high. But, in reality, doses that are too low are a more frequent problem, according to the 2000 NIMH study on attention deficit disorders. As teenagers go through puberty and hormones change, they may need higher doses of stimulant medications such as Concerta, Adderall, or Vyvance.

- *Medication has worn off:* Some stimulant medications such as Focalin XR, Metadate, and Methylin last roughly six or seven hours. These medicines may wear off right after lunch. For example, Focalin taken at 6:00 am will be gone by 12:00 or 1:00 pm. Short-acting medications such as a regular 10 mg tablet of Ritalin taken at 6:30 am will last only until about 9:30 or 10:00 am Concerta, Adderall, or Vyvance are longer acting and last most of the school day, although they may wear off by homework time. If so, students may be doing most of their homework without the benefit of medicine.

■ *Medication timing is wrong:* Long-acting medications take up to an hour to achieve peak effectiveness. So, if students take their medication on the way to school, they may be attempting most of their first period work without the benefit of medicine.

Talk with parents about the dosages and timing of medication. One way to know whether medication is working properly is if the student is succeeding in school—paying attention and completing work. Complete the medication checklist, Summary 60, which will show whether medication helps improve academic performance. Obviously, since teachers aren't doctors, you may feel uncomfortable talking with parents about medication. However, proper medication is critical for school success, so please don't avoid discussing it. One way to approach this issue is to review Summaries 56-61 with parents and ask whether they think this is an issue that should be *discussed with their doctor*. They can take the completed Medication Rating scale to their physician.

2. **Learning Problems and Executive Functioning Deficits Are Not Addressed**

■ *Specific Learning Disabilities (SLD):* Up to 50 percent of students with ADD or ADHD also meet criteria for a specific learning disability. According to one study, 65 percent of children with ADHD also experienced written expression deficits. See Summary 50.

■ *Executive Functioning Deficits (EF):* Many students have serious problems with executive functioning that interfere with their ability to learn and do well in school. Practically speaking, students with EF deficits have trouble in two broad areas: 1) specific academic tasks like writing essays, completing complex multistep problems, reading with comprehension, and memorizing information, and 2) essential related academic skills, such as getting started and finishing, being organized, quickly retrieving and analyzing information, organizing their thoughts, time management, and developing and following through on a plan of action to complete written school work. Although these learning problems may not meet SLD criteria, they still cause major problems and should be addressed through classroom accommodations. Sections 2 and 3 contain more detailed information.

Identify each student's unique learning problems and *make appropriate accommodations.* Most students with ADD or ADHD will benefit from one or more of the classroom accommodations listed in Summaries 46, 51, or 52.

If a student is still struggling, *refer to the SST* or *IEP Team* to determine if further evaluation is needed.

Other Coexisting Conditions Are Not Treated

As explained in Summary 1, over two-thirds of all students with ADD or ADHD have at least one other coexisting condition that complicates treatment. All these conditions are addressed in more detail in *Teenagers with ADD and ADHD* (Dendy, 2006). A brief overview of these coexisting conditions is provided below.

Neurological Disorders

This section covers the neurological disorders that are most likely to occur along with ADD or ADHD. A more detailed discussion of these disorders is contained in both the American Psychiatric Association's *Diagnostic and Statistical Manual of Mental Disorders (DSM)* and *Teenagers with ADD and ADHD, 2nd ed*. Keep in mind that this is just a brief overview and that each of these broad diagnostic categories is complex and may have several subtypes.

Anxiety Disorders

Although they may outwardly act indifferent, many teenagers with ADD or ADHD worry a lot and experience anxiety regarding their school work. About 25 percent of them have an anxiety disorder. They may feel *Generalized Anxiety* or may experience more severe anxiety disorders such as *Panic Attacks* or *Obsessive Compulsive Disorder*.

Generalized Anxiety Disorder is marked by three or more of the following characteristics:

- edginess
- muscle tension
- mind going blank
- irritability
- fatigue
- sleep disturbance

Students with attention deficits are especially fearful of being embarrassed in school. Typically, they recognize that they have problems listening. They're afraid that if the teacher calls on them, they will not have heard the question. Even when listening, they may get so flustered they may not be able to answer the question correctly. If the student also has slow processing speed, she may be so fearful of speaking in front of the class that she would rather accept a failing grade than speak.

Panic Attacks involve a period of intense fear, which starts suddenly and reaches a peak in roughly ten minutes. The student may experience four or more of the following symptoms:

- pounding heart
- shortness of breath
- feelings of being outside oneself
- chest discomfort
- dizziness
- fear of going crazy or losing control
- trembling
- nausea
- tingling sensations

Teachers may actually find it easier to deal with students with anxiety because the student is less likely to act or speak impulsively and more likely to want to complete school work.

Obsessive Compulsive Disorder (OCD) is associated with both *obsessions*—recurrent thoughts or impulses—and *compulsions*—repetitive behaviors or mental acts that the person feels driven to do (ordering, checking, counting, recopying work). This disorder has a tremendous impact on school performance. The student may have trouble being satisfied with written work and may obsess over the content and neatness of her handwriting. Obsessing over thoughts makes writing an essay especially challenging. Sherry Pruitt's books *Taming the Tiger* and *Tigers Too*, as well as her book *Challenging Kids, Challenged Teachers,* coauthored with Leslie Packer, address the academic problems unique to this group.

Tourette Syndrome (TS)

Tourette syndrome causes repeated involuntary vocal sounds and physical movements called *tics.* Vocal tics may include grunting, clearing the throat, humming, spitting, or coughing. Motor tics may include eye blinking, shoulder shrugs, mouth opening, lip licking, grimacing, sticking the tongue out, or stretching movements. Symptoms wax and wane, and stress may make them worse. Sometimes when students try to suppress their tics, an explosive build-up of tension occurs. Sherry Pruitt, coauthor of *Tiger Too,* refers to these blow-ups and loss of control as "Tourette storms." After the storm subsides, the child calms down and sometimes will have no memory of the blow-up.

Fifty to seventy percent of students with Tourette syndrome (TS) also have ADD or ADHD. Tourette syndrome is six times more common in males than in females. The average age of onset for TS is 6.5 years.

Sometimes stimulant medications taken for an attention deficit disorder will exacerbate the tic symptoms. Consequently, some doctors will stop medication immediately if a student begins to experience tics for fear that the tics may be irreversible. However, David Comings, M.D., author of *Children with Tourette Syndrome*, indicates that many students with both TS and ADD/ADHD *can* take stimulants, but medication doses should be reduced or a different medication prescribed. Sometimes a student may have ADD or ADHD, Tourette syndrome, *and* obsessive compulsive disorder, which further complicates treatment.

Asperger Syndrome

Asperger's syndrome (AS) is one of the autism spectrum disorders. Sometimes Asperger's syndrome coexists with ADD or ADHD. However, other times a child with the characteristics of this condition may be diagnosed incorrectly with an attention deficit instead of Asperger's or vice versa. Additionally, Dr. Russell Barkley reports that one in four children with autism also has ADHD.

Typically, young people with Asperger's have average to above average intelligence and don't have any language delays. However, there may be exceptions. One mother reported that her son with AS didn't speak until he was nearly four years old. Some students may also have difficulty understanding the nuances of spoken language, especially irony or humor. *Pragmatic Language Disorder* may be present. In other words, the student doesn't understand phrases when a potential double meaning is involved. For instance, when asked to select a picture of a traffic jam, the student may select a picture of a toy car stuck in a bottle of jam. In students with Asperger's syndrome may not use the usual inflections in their speech.

A classic symptom of Asperger syndrome is hyper-focusing on one or two interest areas such as dinosaurs or the makes and models of cars. Essentially, the student may become a walking encyclopedia regarding her favorite topic. These young people also have significant difficulties with social skills and may be viewed as somewhat eccentric, or lost in their own world.

According to Andrea Bilbow, executive director of ADDISS, an ADHD parent advocacy group based in the United Kingdom, teens with AS have difficulty recognizing or responding with the correct emotion and therefore seem to lack empathy. If a classmate falls, the student may laugh inappropriately without realizing his error. After Princess Diana died, one teen asked his mother if this was a sad event. He recognized that others were saddened but did not experience that emotion. They may also be vulnerable because they are very gullible. Parents worry because someone could make sexual advances and their child may not recognize that the actions were inappropriate.

Sleep Disorders

Slightly more that half of children with attention deficits (56 percent) have sleep disturbances, which is double the rate in children without attention deficits. These teens may have major problems falling asleep, waking up, or both. Researchers tell us that these children have a much more difficult time falling asleep and get fewer hours of sleep than other children do. Half also report that they feel tired when they wake up, but others appear to need less sleep. Some may have frequent night waking, nightmares, or restless sleep in which they move all around in the bed. In addition, some teens experience a delayed sleep cycle. If they could fall asleep at 4:00 am and get up at noon, they might be just fine.

Of relevance to school officials, lack of sleep often causes fatigue and impairs memory and the ability to concentrate. These teens may occasionally sleep in class.

Mood Disorders

Depression

The official diagnostic criteria for depression tend to describe adult behaviors better than those of young people. For example, depression doesn't always involve sadness in teenagers. Generally speaking, young people who are depressed may experience bad moods, lack of enjoyment in life, irritability, or aggression. So, when a teen with ADD or ADHD is often irritable or aggressive, this behavior may really be masking depression. In fact, about 25 percent of teens with attention deficits are depressed. Frequently, however, when the depression is treated, the irritability and aggression decrease significantly. Inattention may also be a symptom of depression. Occasionally, inattention related to depression may be mistaken for ADD or ADHD.

Dysthymic Disorder

A milder form of depression known as dysthymia may also occur. To meet diagnostic criteria for dysthymia, at least two of these symptoms must be present for the better part of a year:
- changes in eating habits
- changes in sleeping habits
- reduced mental energy
- reduced physical energy
- difficulty making decisions
- low self-esteem
- feelings of hopelessness

Bipolar Disorder

Bipolar disorder is one of the toughest mental health conditions to treat successfully and is even more challenging in the classroom. The classroom behavior of students with the disorder is often inappropriate and remains unchanged even when the student is repeatedly corrected by teachers. Students with the disorder often have few friends because their misbehavior is offensive to both adults and other students.

Bipolar disorder includes alternating periods of extreme high energy (mania) and low energy (depression). This disorder is extremely difficult to diagnose in young people. In fact, some mental health professionals believe that it cannot be accurately diagnosed until the mid- to late twenties. Still, researchers have recently found that approximately 12 percent of teenagers with attention deficits also have the disorder. Bipolar disorder has also been diagnosed in younger children.

Differentiating between ADD or ADHD and bipolar disorder is difficult, since they share several common characteristics:
- excessive activity
- poor judgment
- impulsive behavior
- denial of problems

Young children with bipolar disorder may have a history of horrendous, lengthy tantrums that continue even when no one is watching.

Symptoms in teens may include:
- irritability
- loud giggling

- day dreamy, floating quality
- hostility
- rejection of other people
- aggression or destructiveness

Occasionally, people with bipolar disorder may have a psychotic episode in which they lose touch with reality. In other words, they may have hallucinations or delusions (of grandeur; thinking they're rich or that they are God). In contrast, people with ADD or ADHD alone will not exhibit psychotic symptoms, unless something unusual happens. For example, psychotic symptoms can be brought on by a chemical interaction between medication (Tofranil-imipramine) and illegal drugs (marijuana).

Since bipolar disorder is often baffling to the experts, it would be unreasonable to expect teachers to recognize this disorder. My point in writing about the condition is to remind teachers that we know that some teenagers with attention deficits have bipolar disorder, but it may not be diagnosed for ten years or more. If a student is extremely difficult to handle ("mad, bad, sad, can't add"), perhaps there are hidden reasons for her school failure and misbehavior. Unfortunately, teachers may never have the benefit of knowing that the student has one of these conditions since they are usually not diagnosed until the late teen years.

Substance-Related Disorders

Treatment professionals describe substance problems in a range from less to more severe: **substance use,** then **substance abuse,** and finally **addiction**.

The two substances that teenagers with ADD or ADHD use most often are cigarettes and alcohol. Over 50 percent of these teens smoke cigarettes, which is double the rate of students who don't have ADD or ADHD. Alcohol use is at about the 40 percent level and marijuana use at 17 percent. These percentages are somewhat inflated by two subgroups of ADHD. Teens whose attention deficit coexists with conduct disorder or bipolar disorder have the worst substance abuse problems and poorest prognosis. In contrast, many teenagers with uncomplicated ADD or ADHD are no more likely than their peers to smoke, drink, or abuse illegal drugs. It is interesting to note that the actual age of onset for substance abuse is around 19, after students have graduated from high school. So the post high school years are a high-risk time for substance abuse.

Two studies, one by Tim Wilens, M.D., and the other by Russell Barkley, Ph.D, have presented some very encouraging news: **Students with ADD or ADHD who take medication are LESS likely to abuse drugs than students with ADD or ADHD who don't take medication!**

If we look at predictors of substance abuse, two or three facts are important for teachers to know. School failure, low grades, and low self-esteem are predictors of future substance abuse. Since aggression and hyperactivity are also predictors, some students with attention deficits are definitely at risk for substance abuse. Teachers can help prevent some of these problems by helping students succeed in school and building their self-esteem. Schools can also offer after-school activities and opportunities for community service, which are also thought to be good ways to prevent drug abuse.

Disruptive Behavior Disorders

Oppositional Defiant Disorder (ODD)
Unfortunately for teachers and parents, oppositional defiant disorder (ODD) is the most common coexisting condition among students with attention deficits, affecting about 67 percent of them. Generally speaking, teens with ODD are negative, disobedient, and hostile toward authority figures. As adults, we find this behavior especially irritating and difficult to cope with.

Teenagers with ODD have four or more of the following behaviors:
- loses temper
- argues with adults

- refuses to comply with adult requests
- blames others
- easily annoyed
- vindictive
- angry
- deliberately annoys people

Perhaps deficits in executive functioning skills make students with ADD or ADHD more likely to exhibit behaviors on this list. For example, difficulty controlling emotions could lead to more frequent blow-ups; working memory deficits make it difficult to recall past experiences to avoid repeating misbehavior; and speaking or acting before they think of the consequences can lead to confrontations with adults or peers. Frustration regarding their poor school performance may also contribute to these behaviors.

Conduct Disorder (CD)

About 22 percent of students with ADD or ADHD have a conduct disorder (CD). However, conduct disorder is not a permanent condition. According to the NIMH/MTA study on ADHD, when students receive proper interventions, their behavior improves to the point that they may no longer meet the criteria for CD.

Conduct disorder is characterized by behavior that violates the basic rights of others or breaks the law. Although fifteen behaviors comprise the criteria for CD, they include four broad categories. To qualify for CD, students must exhibit only three of the fifteen behaviors.

1. Aggression to people or animals
   - intimidates others
   - fights
   - uses a weapon
   - cruel to people
   - cruel to animals
   - steals while confronting a victim (mugging, armed robbery)
   - forces sex on others

2. Destruction of property
   - fire setting
   - destroys property

3. Deceitfulness or theft
   - breaking & entering
   - lies
   - steals things

4. Serious violations of rules
   - stays out at night
   - runs away
   - truant before age 13

A Closer Look at ODD and CD: Attention deficits, anxiety, depression, and bipolar disorder are all clearly neurological disorders. On the other hand, ODD and CD are often perceived as intentional misbehavior. However, some researchers have shown that many ODD and CD behaviors also have an underlying biochemical cause. Other researchers have also found differences in the brains of people with these disorders, possibly linked to subtle brain injury. Dr. Joseph Biederman, one of the leading international researchers on attention deficits, found that students with ADD or ADHD and Conduct Disorder had an average of *four additional psychiatric disorders,* such as depression, bipolar disorder, anxiety, or substance abuse. On the surface, it may look as though these young people engage in these behaviors intentionally or simply to be mean. In reality, however, many may be suffering from ***multiple biochemical disorders*** that are being untreated.

Behaviors of students with ODD are aggravating, but those with CD are much more serious and thus deeply troubling to teachers. Students with ADD or ADHD and CD seem to have the most serious problems and the poorest prognosis. For example, students with these two diagnoses are much more likely to abuse drugs, be expelled from school, and get into trouble with the law. They also have a higher rate of school suspension and dropping out when compared to students with ADD or ADHD only. Students who have an attention deficit plus ODD, on the other hand, are not at greater risk for a poor outcome in adulthood.

Handling ODD or CD in the Classroom:

- Reduce classroom frustration. Identify learning problems and make accommodations in the classroom.
- Teach students conflict resolution skills. See Summaries 72-73 for tips on resolving conflicts and peer mediation.
- Learn skills to defuse anger. Teachers who develop skills to defuse anger and handle conflict are more effective with these students. See Summaries 64-67 on actions that escalate or de-escalate conflicts, behavioral strategies, and avoiding confrontations, plus Summary 75 on anger management.

Take Home Message

My reason for writing about coexisting conditions is not to make excuses for inappropriate behavior, but rather to point out that the behavior of students with an attention deficit is often much more complicated than it appears on the surface. Treatment of these coexisting conditions is critical and may be the pivotal factor in pulling some youngsters back from the edge of life-long frustration, unhappiness, underachievement, and, for some, brushes with the law.

Resources

Atwood, Tony. *The Complete Guide to Asperger's Syndrome*. London: Jessica Kingsley Publishers, 2008.

Barkley, Russell A. *Attention-deficit Hyperactivity Disorder: A Handbook for Diagnosis and Treatment*. 3rd ed. New York, NY: Guilford Press, 2006.

Barkley, Russell A., et al. *ADHD in Adults: What the Science Says*. New York, NY: The Guilford Press. 2008

Brown, Thomas E. *Attention–Deficit Disorders and Comorbidities in Children, Adolescents, and Adults*. Washington, DC: American Psychiatric Press, 2000.

Coming, David. *Tourette Syndrome and Human Behavior*. Hope Press: Duarte, CA, 1990.

Dendy, Chris Zeigler. *Teenagers with ADD and ADHD: A Guide for Parents and Professionals*. 2nd ed. Bethesda, MD: Woodbine House, 2006.

Dornbush, Marilyn & Pruitt, Sheryl. *Tigers Two* (2nd edition of *Teaching the Tiger*). Atlanta, GA: Parkaire Associates, 2008.

This book addresses ADD/ADHD, Obsessive Compulsive Disorder, and Tourette Syndrome. One of the authors, Sherry Pruitt, directs a private learning disabilities center and is the mother of two sons with ADHD, OCD, and Tourette syndrome.

Haerle, Tracy, ed. *Children with Tourette Syndrome: A Parent's Guide*. 2nd ed. Bethesda, MD: Woodbine House, 2007.

Packer, Leslie and Pruitt, Sheryl. *Challenging Kids, Challenged Teachers: Teaching Students with Tourette's Bipolar Dysfunction, OCD, ADHD, and More*. Bethesda, MD: Woodbine House, 2010.

Papolos, Demitri and Papolos, Janice. *The Bipolar Child*. 3rd ed. New York, NY: Broadway Books, 2007.

When Parents Don't Believe It's ADD or ADHD

SUMMARY 79

Parental reactions to a diagnosis of ADD or ADHD vary considerably. Some are ***relieved*** to finally discover the root of their teenager's problems, and others are ***upset*** and may ***deny*** the possibility of an attention deficit disorder. Several factors may influence a parent's reaction to this diagnosis.

1. Unfortunately, ***negative publicity about medications*** such as Ritalin is often a major concern. My own hometown newspaper, the *Atlanta Journal Constitution*, ran a series of terribly insensitive cartoons on medication for ADD or ADHD in the spring of 2000.

2. The ***age*** of the student may influence a parent's reaction. When children are still in elementary school, parents may be reluctant to believe that their child has an attention deficit. For some teachers and parents, this reluctance continues into middle and high school. They mistakenly assume that it could not possibly be ADD or ADHD since the student is not hyperactive. However, other parents whose children have struggled through elementary or middle school may be relieved to finally have an answer for why school has always been so difficult for their teenager.

3. ***Cultural expectations*** may also influence a parent's reaction to ADD or ADHD. A researcher at the University of Florida found that some families see the behaviors associated with attention deficits as being willful misbehavior or just laziness. Other families see the same behaviors as a potential problem and refer the child or teenager for treatment. Families that rely on strict physical discipline may be less likely to accept ADD or ADHD as the underlying cause of their teenager's struggles.

4. Sometimes ***parents are divided*** on the issue. One parent believes it is an attention deficit and wants to try medication and the other parent is adamantly opposed.

5. Other times, a family may be unwilling to try medication because the ***teenager is anxious or reluctant.***

6. ***Financial constraints*** prevent some parents from pursuing medical treatment. In my rural area, many parents can't afford the medicine.

After the school evaluation has been completed and if the school psychologist believes the student has ADD or ADHD, the next step is to refer the teenager to a physician to rule out other medical disorders. At this point, some parents may be unwilling to accept a diagnosis or be adamantly opposed to medication.

Educators should be aware that ***parents often must go through a grieving process before they can accept a diagnosis of ADD or ADHD.*** Dr. Elizabeth Kubler-Ross describes the following stages of the grieving process: denial, anger, bargaining, depression, and, ultimately, acceptance. Parents will need time to come to grips with the sometimes frightening unknowns linked to this diagnosis. Later, parents may need help *reframing* their perceptions of attention deficits more positively. See Summary 77.

Given that any given parent *may* react negatively to the suggestion that his or her teenager might have ADD or ADHD, what is the best way for a teacher to approach this issue? Let's start with the typical procedure teachers follow when a student is struggling in class.

1. The student is barely passing the class. The teacher meets with the student's parents.

2. Accommodations are made in the classroom. Parents provide support at home, yet the student still struggles.

3. An SST meeting is held. Teachers suggest intervention strategies, but they are not successful.

4. Referral is made to an IEP Team. An evaluation is requested. The parent gives permission for the evaluation. The school psychologist completes the evaluation and indicates that the student meets

the criteria for attention deficit disorder. One of the recommendations includes referral to a physician for a medical evaluation to confirm the diagnosis or to rule out other problems.

5. Parents may be reluctant to accept a possible diagnosis of ADD or ADHD and may be hesitant to see a physician or may not know a physician who specializes in diagnosis and treatment of attention deficits.

6. Now what does the teacher do?

Working with Parents Who Are Apprehensive about the Diagnosis

Although there are no easy answers for working with parents who are apprehensive or are not open to accepting ADD or ADHD as a diagnosis, the following suggestions may be helpful:

1. **Sometimes the only thing a teacher, school psychologist, or principal can do is wait until the parents reach a level of readiness and receptiveness** to discuss ADD or ADHD. Express concern and willingness to help when parents are ready:

   "I am so concerned about your son and want him to succeed in school. I worry about his self-esteem being damaged. I feel that he is doing his best and he really wants to do well in school. Failing classes is a terrible thing to happen to any student."

2. **Give parents time to grieve.** Listen while they talk through their concerns and then share helpful information.

   "You really seem worried about the possibility that this might be ADD (ADHD). I also know how much you love Michael. You are his parents and you will do what is best for him. You may want to talk with Michael's doctor and share the evaluation results. You may want to talk to another parent of a teenager with an attention deficit. Let me give you a phone number for the local ADHD group. Either your physician or members of the parent group should be able to tell you which doctors specialize in treating attention deficits."

3. **Refer them to a local parent support group.** A list of national support groups is included in the resources at the end of this summary. Administrators at local schools often have phone numbers for local groups. If not, contact the district office of special education or local mental health center for phone numbers. Parents may also contact a national office to find a phone number for a local chapter.

4. **Help educate the parents about ADD or ADHD.** If they have not already reviewed the official DSM AD/HD Criteria in Summary 5, give them copies: You might say to them:

   "One of the surveys you completed for the school psychologist had these criteria in it. For your son to be diagnosed as having an attention deficit, he must meet six of these nine criteria. Did any of these characteristics sound like your son? How many of these traits does Michael have?"

   The teacher may then comment on the number and types of behaviors she observed in class. *"I've noticed some of the same things you have. He seems … (mention the ones you see) but he does really well with…."*

   Next:

   - Provide brief educational materials to read. Use the summaries in this book to educate the parents about various topics regarding attention deficits. Gradually increase the amount of information.
   - Suggest that the family watch an educational video. Several may be available through the school or local library.

- Dr. Russell Barkley and Dr. Thomas Phelan both have good videos. (See Resources.)
- Our son and I have produced a new video featuring 30 teens from across the country: *Real Life ADHD!* Teens offer advice on ADHD challenges and scientific facts regarding the disorder. This DVD is a helpful educational tool for parents, teachers, and teens. Dr. Ted Mandelkorn from Seattle, a physician specializing in treating ADHD and who has ADHD himself, also describes his personal challenges with the condition and provides guidance to teens and parents.
- *Father to Father: The ADD Experience*!, another video that my son and I produced, has also been well received by guidance counselors, teachers, and parents. The "father" video features fathers of teenagers with attention deficits talking about the challenges of parenting these youngsters. Sometimes when parents see that other parents have experienced many of the same frustrations, they feel somewhat relieved and not so alone.

5. **Help educate an anxious or reluctant teenager about ADD or ADHD.**

   - Suggest that parents provide brief educational materials for the teen to read.
     - Use the summaries in this book to educate the student about various topics regarding attention deficits. Gradually increase the amount of information.
     - Consider our *Bird's-Eye View of Life with ADD and ADHD* that was written for the teens themselves. Our son, Alex, coauthored the book with me. It is an accurate but easy and appealing book. One university also uses it as the main book for parents to read, especially busy parents who are working full time.
     - Using *Bird's-Eye View* as a model, one special education teacher in the Northeast had her students create their own book of ADHD facts and advice. The book was published in-house and copies given to the school administrators.
   - Suggest that the student talk with another teenager who also has ADD or ADHD and is taking medication.
   - Suggest that the teenager watch a video on ADD and ADHD. Several may be available through the school or local library.
     - As suggested earlier, our video, *Real Life ADHD!*, featuring 30 teens from across the country, will be of interest to teens. The teens are the experts on ADHD.
     - Many teenagers with attention deficits also have enjoyed our video, *Teen to Teen: The ADD Experience,* which features teenagers and young adults talking about the challenges of coping with ADD or ADHD. Guidance counselors, teachers, and parents have also bought the video to show special education classes and teen groups. Sometimes when teenagers see successful, positive role models and realize that other teenagers have experienced many of the same frustrations, they feel somewhat relieved and realize that they are not alone.

6. **Help parents reframe ADD or ADHD more positively.** Discuss the positive aspects of attention deficits and explain that many teenagers with ADD or ADHD are very successful. See Appendix A11 for ideas to discuss with the parents. Show parents the video, *Teen to Teen: The ADD Experience!*

7. **Ask the parents if they would like to talk to a parent of a teenager with ADD or ADHD** who is coping successfully. A member of a local parent group may be willing to answer questions for the parent. These groups may have additional materials or videos that may be helpful. Parents might also be able to connect with other parents online, through the listserv of a local or national support group for LD and/or ADHD.

8. **Consider scheduling an educational program** at a PTA meeting on teenagers with ADD or ADHD and other learning differences. This program may help parents and teens better understand ADD and ADHD, the related challenges, and learn to identify and maximize the student's strengths.

9. **Implement appropriate accommodations and teaching strategies** discussed in Summaries 16-25, 41, 46, 48, 51, and 52.

Resources
Organizations & Websites

■ ADDA-SR: Attention Deficit Disorder Association-Southern Region, 12345 Jones Rd., Suite 287, Houston, TX 77070. (281-955-3720; www.adda-sr.org).

■ CHADD: Children and Adults with Attention Deficit Disorders, 8181 Professional Place, Suite 201, Landover, MD 20785. (800-233-4050; www.chadd.org).

■ Federation of Families for Children's Mental Health, 1101 King St., Suite 420, Alexandria, VA 22314. (703-684-7710; www.ffcmh.org).

■ LDonline: "The world's leading website on learning disabilities." The site offers extensive parent forums. (www.ldonline.com).

■ Learning Disabilities Association of America, 4156 Library Rd., Pittsburgh, PA 15234 (412-341-1515; www.ldanatl.org).

■ NAMI: National Alliance for the Mentally Ill, Colonial Place Three, 2107 Wilson Blvd., Suite 300, Arlington, VA 22201. (800-950-6264; www.nami.org).

Videos

These videos may be available at your local library. Most also can be ordered from ADD WareHouse (800-233-9273; www.addwarehouse.com) or from Amazon (www.amazon.com).

■ Barkley, Russell:
- *ADHD: What Do We Know?*
- *ADHD: What Can We Do?*

These two videos provide an overview of ADHD and effective ways to manage it.

■ Dendy, Chris Zeigler and Alex Zeigler:
- *Real Life ADHD! A DVD Survival Guide for Teens and Parents* (a companion guide for our book *Bird's-Eye View of Life with ADD and ADHD)*
- *Teen to Teen: The ADD Experience*
- *Father to Father: The ADD Experience*

Both teen videos feature teens and young adults talking about their experiences coping with ADD, plus the things they do well. In the Father video, four fathers talk about their experiences parenting teens with ADD or ADHD. The VHS videos are being converted to DVD format and can be ordered from Chris Dendy at P.O. Box 189, Cedar Bluff, AL 35959 (256-779-5203; www.chrisdendy.com).

■ Phelan, Thomas:
- All about Attention Deficit Disorder
- Surviving Your Adolescents

All about Attention Deficit Disorder, a two-part video, provides basic information about ADHD and behavior management at home and at school. Dr. Phelan is also well known for "1-2-3 Magic," his popular discipline strategies for younger children. The second video provides general guidance on effective parenting strategies for teens. It is a companion guide for Phelan's book by the same name. Both DVDs are available from his website: www.parentmagicstore.com.

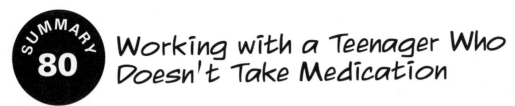

Working with a Teenager Who Doesn't Take Medication

Sometimes, for a variety of reasons, students do not take medication for their ADD or ADHD.

- Unfortunately, stimulant medications don't work for all children; however, medicines are effective for over 90 percent of students with ADHD.
- All too frequently, medication refusal is a problem with teenagers. Teenagers simply refuse to take medication because they don't want to be different from their peers or they don't like the way medication makes them feel.
- Sometimes, one or both parents may refuse to consider medication for a variety of reasons, including lack of money, concerns about medication, fear and guilt that they have been "bad" parents, worries about the long-term outcome for their teenager, or because they are in denial and grieving for their teenager's problems.

Regardless of the reason, the teacher is faced with the challenge of trying to teach a teenager who has great difficulty paying attention and may be unable to learn easily. When this happens, teachers must use strategies that are effective for students with learning problems.

All of the summaries in Sections 2, 3, and 4 contain information that will help these students be more successful in school, regardless of whether they are taking medication for an attention deficit. Some of the most important general strategies are outlined below.

1. Value the student: Summary 76.

2. Build on his or her strengths: Appendix A11.

3. Help the student understand attention deficit, its related challenges, including executive skills and her own personal strengths, and involve her as a partner in problem solving: Summaries 12, 69-71, and 77.

4. Use multisensory, high-interest teaching strategies: Section 2.

5. Modify teaching strategies:
    - Summary 16-A: Modify teaching methods and resources; use more visual cues and reminders; use active learning strategies; increase class participation; use peer tutoring.
    - Summary 16-B: Modify assignments; reduce the amount of written work; break work into smaller segments.
    - Summary 16-C: Modify testing and grading; give extended time; adjust test format.
    - Summary 16-D: Increase levels of supervision; get other students and parents to help.
    - Summary 16-E: Use technology.
    - Summary 71: Provide a coach.

6. Provide accommodations for executive function deficits: Sections 2 and 3.
    - forgetfulness: Summary 31
    - memorization problems: Summary 25
    - disorganization: Summary 30
    - written expression problems: Summaries 17-20
    - mastering math: Summaries 21-24
    - impaired sense of time: Summaries 32-35
    - organizing and completing long-term projects: Summaries 36-38.

7. Provide structure and use good classroom management strategies: Summaries 62-63.

8. Use behavioral strategies that de-escalate problem situations: Summaries 64-66.

9. Teach the student self-management skills, plus help her manage ADD/ADHD behavior. Teach skills the student is lacking:
   - conflict resolution: Summary 72
   - peer mediation: Summary 73
   - problem solving: Summary 69.
   - anger management: Summary 75
   - time management: Summaries: 32-36

10. Anticipate and avoid potential problem situations. Identify situations that students with attention deficits don't handle well—for example, transitions such as going to lunch or PE, having a substitute teacher, or breaking up with a boyfriend/girlfriend. Develop an intervention strategy to prevent the problem. Read the sections regarding use of a behavior intervention plan in an IEP (Summaries 42, 45, 52).

Teaching strategies, common learning problems, classroom accommodations, reasons for school failure, and suggested intervention strategies are discussed in more detail in Section 2 and in Chapters 13 and 14 in *Teenagers with ADD and ADHD, 2nd ed.* (Woodbine House, 2007).

Tough Questions and Comments from Teachers

As I have traveled across the country providing training on ADD and ADHD, teachers have asked me many excellent but often difficult questions. Some questions are from teachers who are eager to learn more about teaching these teenagers effectively. Other questions are most likely born of frustration. Perhaps a teacher has tried traditional teaching methods that work for most students, but they just don't work as well for these students. Consequently, he or she may think, *"Surely, this student must be lazy. He is obviously very bright. If he would only try, he could do his work."*

Some teachers who do provide needed supports worry that they are "enabling" the student to be lazy. Years ago, the term "enabling" developed a negative connotation. However, I view enabling in a positive sense—wheelchairs enable people with physical disabilities to move around; glasses enable students to see; and accommodations enable students with ADHD to succeed in school. Teachers who understand that students with ADD or ADHD have delays in brain maturation and deficits in executive skills realize that these children deserve supports.

If an educator firmly believes that ADD or ADHD is just an excuse for a lazy student, I realize that I cannot change his or her mind by arguing. All I can do is explain what I have learned about the powerful influence the brain's biochemistry has over behaviors related to deficits in attention and executive function. This knowledge comes from my forty-plus years as an educator and mental health professional, my study of the latest scientific research, and, more importantly, the profound personal experience of living with two sons, one with ADHD and the other with ADD and executive function deficits.

Having been a classroom teacher and school psychologist, I can empathize with educators: ***teaching teenagers with ADD or ADHD can be extremely challenging!*** The behavior and learning problems that these students exhibit make a teacher's job very, very difficult. Unfortunately, ADD and ADHD are often so complex that answers to questions about the disorder are seldom easy. Personally, I must confess that I have been humbled by having children with this condition. Clearly, I don't have any magic answers, but neither does anyone else. So, I will share my best thinking on these very difficult issues.

Questions and Comments from Teachers

1. "This teenager is lazy. He doesn't try hard enough. ADD and ADHD are just excuses."

Even today, this is probably the most common statement I hear from teachers. And to the casual observer, the behaviors of these teenagers may indeed look like laziness or apathy. However, as explained in Section 3, lack of "Essential Related Academic Skills" such as organizing, initiating and finishing work, managing time, and planning ahead is often judged by the uninformed as laziness. Understandably, deficits in pure academics such as writing an essay or comprehending what you read are easier for teachers to understand, accept, and accommodate. However, students with traits that are viewed as laziness often will be criticized and punished. Properly treat the ADHD and accommodate the learning problems and a different, more academically successful child will emerge.

When teens become discouraged because of teacher criticism and punishment, an "I don't care attitude" may emerge to cover up a lot of emotional pain, depression, and a sense of being overwhelmed. This attitude often really means, "I've given up!" They have been so worn down over time by continual school failure. Eventually, some teenagers who have experienced constant failure may give up in despair. One student said, "I can't wait until I get out of school so I can be successful."

In the DVD *Real Life ADHD!,* Ted Mandelkorn, a physician with ADHD who treats ADHD, made this insightful observation: "Our children do try harder. We can all do better if we try harder. But if they try hard for a long period of time, they become extremely anxious. At some point they have to 'try normal.'"

It has been my personal and professional experience that the vast majority of these teenagers want to do well in school. In fact, many of these students must try harder and actually spend more hours on their homework than their peers. Giving these students the necessary supports to succeed in school is like throwing a lifeline to a drowning person. Most of them will grab hold and try to save themselves.

 **Action Step**

Revise the educational and treatment plans to provide appropriate classroom accommodations and correct problems with medication so these teenagers ***can*** succeed in school!

This is *not* to say that these teenagers should be given permission to misbehave or not complete school work. Rather, the point is that teenagers with ADD, ADHD, or executive function deficits (EF) *may* have a disability and desperately need the teacher's understanding, support, supervision, and appropriate classroom accommodations. Having an attention deficit is not an *excuse* but rather an *explanation* for sometimes puzzling behavior.

Also remember that ADD and ADHD are no picnic for these teenagers. They did not ask to have the disorder. One younger student prayed, *"Dear God, please don't let me have ADD."* Another teenager cried, *"I feel like I am going to die of anxiety or go crazy."* As with any teenager with a disability, they may become weary, give up, and have less than perfect days at school. However, with the teacher's support and understanding, they will return another day to tackle this challenge known as attention deficit disorder!

2. **"Students with ADD or ADHD don't really need medication to help them concentrate. They could do their school work if they would just buckle down and try harder."**

As explained in Summary 11, researchers at the National Institute of Mental Health (NIMH) have shown that ***ADD or ADHD is first and foremost a neurobiological disorder for which medication is one of the most effective treatments.*** Medication helps the neurotransmitters in the brain work properly so the student can concentrate, participate in class, and complete schoolwork. Ideally, a multimodal treatment approach will include medication, academic supports and accommodations, and behavioral strategies as needed.

My current thinking about medication is 180 degrees away from where I began when I first began learning about attention deficits. As I have studied the available research on ADD, ADHD, EF, and other biochemical disorders, I have developed an increasing respect for the influence of the brain's biochemistry on the behavior of these teenagers.

As a young mother, I had very conservative views about medication. I avoided taking any medication or giving it to our sons. Initially, I didn't want my sons on any medication, but desperation led me to try it. One son was in middle school and in danger of failing most of his classes even though he was intellectually gifted. He wanted to do well in school but was unable to do so. When we finally put him on medication, his grades went from Ds and Fs to mostly Bs and Cs. With our older son, the change was even more dramatic. He first began taking medication when he started college. His grades climbed from mostly Ds to As and Bs.

Dr. Mandelkorn's personal experiences with ADHD are worth sharing. Mandelkorn, a physician who treats ADHD, also has the condition himself. His struggles in elementary school led him to say to his fifth grade teacher, "Don't tell me how smart I am unless you can tell me how to make my brain work right." Dr. Mandelkorn is the only adult featured in our DVD, *"Real Life ADHD!"*

See Section 5, especially Summaries 56-57, for a discussion of medication and its impact on the student's school performance. As explained in Summaries 59-60, determine whether medication is helping the teenager be more successful in school.

3. **"When is enough, enough?" or "What should I do now? I've tried to help him and he still won't do his work."**

One year, at an educator's conference in Illinois, a frustrated teacher asked me this question. "When is enough, enough?" The question was asked informally after the workshop was over. I really didn't have a very good answer and stumbled through a response. I can only guess that this teacher was referring to his attempts to give a student with an attention deficit extra supports that the student didn't fully utilize. Or the student may have worked well for a while and then stopped doing all his work. Obviously, this can be very frustrating for a teacher who is doing his best to help a student. Most likely, a hidden deficit has not been identified and addressed in the IEP.

The better a teacher understands attention deficits, the easier it is to set realistic expectations. Remember this: *ADD and ADHD are disabilities* for some students. Progress is not going to move along in a nice, smooth upward line. Uneven academic performance is one of the hallmarks of this disorder. The student may make good progress for a while and then begin to backslide. Expect periodic slumps in school work: it is a normal occurrence. These teenagers may go through cycles of feeling worn out and overwhelmed. Sometimes students with attention deficits become depressed, and then just "shut down." Often, no one is more frustrated than the student is. Some just get better at covering up the hurt and discouragement. When teachers offer help, the student may be too overwhelmed to accept it. The end of the school year is often especially difficult for the student, parents, and teachers. By May, these students are usually worn out emotionally and academically and may be ready to give up.

Teachers and parents can help if they *give students enough support to get them through the end of the school year.* Teachers should consider being more flexible and allowing make-up work to be turned in late or extra credit assignments to be submitted, especially if the primary goal is being met—*the teenager has in fact learned the material being taught*!

Teachers may worry that they are doing the teenager a disservice if they do not "hold him accountable." However, considering the disability and significant delay in brain maturity that is involved, these teenagers will eventually learn to handle their own affairs or will learn to compensate for their skill deficits. Research has shown that in the majority of situations, holding a student back to repeat a grade will not resolve these problems. The deficits will still be present. And, most likely, giving the student a failing grade will not change his behavior, but it may make him discouraged and depressed. Researchers tell us that students who fail classes are more likely to drop out of school. Specifically, Dr. Russell Barkley tells us that 36 percent of students with attention deficits drop out of school.

When the student struggles and experiences failure during the school year, the educational and treatment plans (IEPs and Section 504) need to be reassessed and revised. There is a major problem somewhere! The challenge is for the teacher and parent to play detective and find out what the problem is. Several potential culprits are discussed in this book:

- The student's learning problems and/or executive function deficits haven't been addressed. (See Sections 2 and 3.)
- Sleep problems have not been treated.
- Medication is wrong, medication is wearing off, teen hormonal changes make medication less effective, or tolerance to sustained-release medication has developed. (See Section 5.)

4. **"It's not fair to other students to treat this teenager differently. I don't want to lower my standards for this student."**

For teenagers with complex cases of ADD or ADHD, the disorder is often severe enough to qualify as a disability. These students need classroom accommodations to help them cope with their deficits in academics, executive function, and self-control. In this situation, *"being fair" is defined as "giving each teenager what he or she needs to succeed,"* not simply giving every student the same thing. Teenagers and parents may argue that "it isn't fair" that the teenager has ADD or ADHD.

Teachers *must* give students accommodations that are included in their IEPs. In one court ruling in West Virginia, a teacher who refused to implement accommodations in an IEP was held personally liable and fined fifteen thousand dollars.

Because many problems associated with attention deficits are invisible, it may be difficult for educators and parents alike to accept that this condition can be a disability. The complexities of ADD and ADHD and the *invisible nature* of some aspects of the disorder are displayed in the diagram of the ADD/ADHD Iceberg, Summary 4.

Teenagers with attention deficits may **have a different learning style** than their classmates. In addition, they may need to be evaluated differently to determine what they have learned. For example, let's consider a student with slow processing speed who is eligible for special education services. He is included in a general education math class but is failing it. He can do all the math problems correctly but he can't write fast enough to complete all of them on a test. The teenager is being tested on his ability to "read and write quickly" rather than his knowledge of math skills. By making accommodations for this teenager, such as an extended time on tests or reduced written work, the teacher is not lowering the standards. The teenager has mastered the math concepts being taught. Sometimes traditional testing methods create a barrier to accurately assessing a student's knowledge and should be changed by giving appropriate accommodations.

Action Step

Provide all supports and accommodations listed in the student's IEP or 504 Plan as mandated by federal education and civil rights laws.

5. **"He is old enough to take full responsibility for completing his homework. If he doesn't do his work, let him fail. Punish him. He'll learn."**

Teenagers with ADD or ADHD will eventually learn to accept responsibility for their actions, but because of their significant delay in brain maturity, they will do it later than their peers. In the interim, teachers can help by **providing accommodations, occasionally being flexible about submitting assignments on time, and "shaping" the desired behavior, e.g., timely submission of school work.**

Educators sometimes forget, or perhaps they don't know, that students with ADD or ADHD don't learn from punishment and rewards like other students. In addition, Dr. Barkley has observed, and I have learned from first-hand experience, that *"Punishment alone is ineffective."* Even younger children with attention deficits often recognize that punishment doesn't always work. Our youngest son shocked me when he was only eight by saying with regret, "I'm sorry, Mom, but when you punish me it just doesn't seem to work." Even at his tender age, he recognized what it took Dr. Barkley and me twenty years to figure out.

In some respects, ADD and ADHD are similar to diabetes, where the problem lies in an inability to regulate blood sugar levels. Teenagers with attention deficits cannot regulate the levels of neurotransmitters in their brain. As Mary Fowler points out in her book, *Maybe You Know My Child*, we often blame and punish these children because of their disability. Yet we would never dream of blaming and punishing children for their disability when they are blind, paralyzed, or diabetic. Just as punishing a child who has diabetes doesn't change glucose levels, punishing a student with ADD or ADHD doesn't change neurotransmitter levels in the brain. But educating the student and providing reminders can help change his behavior.

A typical consequence for a student who doesn't do homework is failing the class and having to attend summer school. Unfortunately, these consequences are often *not* effective in changing the behavior of these teenagers. The consequence occurs too distant in time from the behavior of concern. Typically, after attending summer school, these students will fall into the same pattern of getting zeros for not completing their schoolwork. To be effective, consequences must occur within a week after the problem behavior, plus be *instructive,* not just punitive!

Because of my graduate training at Florida State University, I thought behavioral intervention strategies, when used properly, could solve any behavior problem. Consequently, I had used behavioral strategies with my son since he was very young. However, Dr. Barkley recommends *first, get the medication right* and then use behavioral interventions to shape the remaining problem behaviors. Findings from the 1999 NIMH study on ADHD combined type have also confirmed that medication works more effectively than behavioral interventions alone. (See Summary 11.) A combination of both medicine and behavioral strategies is actually the best way to help students with attention deficits.

Based upon my personal experience, I agree 100 percent with these conclusions. As someone who is skilled in using these interventions, I have reluctantly come to the conclusion that behavioral strategies are helpful, but *limited in their effectiveness!* Teenagers with attention deficits do not respond in a typical manner to behavioral interventions. This means these strategies are much more difficult to implement with students with ADD or ADHD.

Teach the student the skill you want him to have. Using a weekly report to ensure homework completion and making weekly activities contingent upon completing the work are much more effective strategies than punishment.

If the ADD/ADHD behavior can't be changed, then change the environment. For example, if a student is late to class frequently, help him organize his locker better, change his routes between classes, reward timely arrival to class, or send another student with him (Summaries 30-33).

6. **He lies. He hides his homework and test grades from his parents."**

Students with ADD or ADHD may not always tell the truth! This is a common complaint from parents and teachers alike. Usually, it does not reflect a deep underlying moral defect in the teenager. Instead, it may be an inappropriate coping mechanism the student is using to avoid punishment or unpleasant work. And let's face it, homework is especially unpleasant for these teenagers.

Lying may occur more often during stressful periods (especially if learning problems and executive function deficits have not been identified), during transitions, or near the end of the school year. Often, impulsivity plays a major role in lying. The student says the first thing that pops into his head. Later he may regret the impulsivity, but it is done and can't be taken back. At other times, he may truly forget something as a result of his memory impairment.

Dr. Ross Green, author of *The Explosive Child,* has this to say about ADHD and lying:

"Imagine being a child who has a whole bunch of knowledge stored in your brain about appropriate ways of behaving. Also imagine being so impulsive that this store of knowledge seldom allows you to behave appropriately. In other words, you're continuously behaving in ways you 'know' are inappropriate, but you aren't gaining access to the knowledge that your behavior is inappropriate rapidly enough to keep you out of

trouble. It's like there are two of you—the 'you' who engages in inappropriate behavior and the 'you' who clearly knows better. The stage is now set for lying.

"Here's how. You behave inappropriately. Then after a brief delay, your knowledge about appropriate behavior finally kicks in, and you find yourself in the position of having to explain why you just behaved in a way you already 'know' was inappropriate. Most children with ADHD don't have the presence of mind to say, 'I know I shouldn't have done that; I just didn't access the information in time.' What many do instead is fall back on one of the most primitive defense mechanisms: denial. So what comes out of the mouths is, 'I didn't do it.'"

This is not to say that lying is okay. However, the best strategy is to **identify problem areas and make accommodations at school.** Teenagers who are happy, succeeding in school, and have strong self-esteem have less reason to lie. Drs. Sydney Zentall and Sam Goldstein, authors of *Seven Steps to Homework Success*, advise that punishment is *not* the best approach.

Correct the problem by removing the need to lie. Students who are successful in school don't need to lie. Identify any learning problems and executive function deficits and make appropriate accommodations.

Teachers should maintain close contact with parents during stressful periods. Fax or e-mail a note, or call and leave a message for parents regarding missed assignments or homework. This also removes the temptation for the student to lie to parents about whether or not homework is due.

7. **"I have other students with ADD (ADHD) and they don't have this problem."**

It is important to remember that **all teenagers with ADD or ADHD are not alike!** ADD/ADHD can be simple or complex. Furthermore, students may have an attention deficit that is mild, moderate, or severe, plus may have several coexisting problems, such as learning problems, executive function deficits, slow processing speed, memory problems, a sleep disturbance, depression, anxiety, or obsessive-compulsive disorder. The more severe the ADD or ADHD and the more coexisting problems that are present, the more challenging it is to teach and treat the teenager. The ADD/ADHD Iceberg provides a comprehensive overview of all the complexities unique to ADHD. Remember there are many potential problems hidden beneath the surface (Summary 4).

Learn more about each of these students. Identify his or her unique strengths and challenges.

8. **Sometimes parents become angry and make unreasonable demands. How am I supposed to deal with them?**

Like teachers, parents get very weary of dealing with ADD or ADHD behavior day-in and day-out. In truth, parents become very frustrated dealing with just one teenager with this condition. So, most of them understand the challenges a teacher faces in a classroom setting with twenty-five or thirty other students. When teachers encounter an angry parent, what they may really be seeing, but may not recognize, is *parental fear*—fear about the future and fear about whether or not their teenager will cope successfully with this challenging condition. In other words, **the anger parents express may actually be masking their deepest fears about their teenager's future.**

Many parents feel very much alone in this battle with ADD or ADHD, especially when it is complex. Often parents cannot find treatment professionals who seem to know how to help their teenager. In addition, parents often turn to the next group of experts—the teachers, thinking they have the magic answers needed to help their child succeed. When neither group appears to know how to deal with the ADHD, parents become frightened.

Parents come to fear the worst: potential school failure, dropping out, substance abuse, or brushes with the law. They *desperately* want your help but their fear may drive them to be less than tactful as they ask for help. Perhaps teachers can reframe their perceptions of these parents: the good news is, *"These parents care a lot about their teenager. They want to be involved. They want their child to succeed. I'll try to help them channel their concerns."*

Unfortunately, the teacher is called upon to be the "counselor" who diffuses the parent's anger and channels it positively.

Try active listening: *"I know you are deeply concerned about your son. I'm sorry school is so hard for him. Together, let's develop a plan to ensure that he succeeds in school. What do you think the problems are?…What do you think he needs?…"*

The parents may or may not be on target with suggestions for what the student needs, but usually they *know* what the problems are and what interventions have been effective in the past. As the teacher, you may come up with creative options they haven't thought of that may better address the teenager's needs, plus require less time from you. If the problems are identified first, then together you may come up with a **compromise** to meet the teenager's needs.

Sometimes parents may make **unreasonable requests at an IEP meeting.** For example, one parent went to a conference, handed the teachers my Summary 46 with the fifty classroom accommodations, and said, "I want all this for my teenager!" What do you do then? Obviously, classroom accommodations must be tailor-made to address a teenager's needs. Most teenagers with ADD or ADHD will *not* need all these accommodations. Perhaps a teacher might say,

"This information you brought us looks really good. You're exactly right—teenagers with ADD or ADHD do often need accommodations in the classroom to help them succeed in school. Usually, however, they need some, but not all, of these accommodations. Let's identify the key issues that are really difficult for your teenager and decide which classroom accommodations he needs. Typically, it is best to keep a plan simple at first and successfully implement a few strategies. Then more can be added later if needed. "

If a parent's requests are unreasonable, state what you can offer and then what your limitations are. Perhaps you can come up with a creative compromise: "I can give him extended time on tests and allow him to use a computer for written work. But I can't personally always . . . remind him to write his homework down, prompt him to start working, etc." However, I can. . . .

Seek a creative solution: Use available manpower—other students. "John and Mary sit near your son. Perhaps they could remind him of his assignment or actually write it down for him."

Involve the student in problem solving this issue. Give him a choice. *"James, students with ADD often forget to write down their assignments. One thing we can do to help you remember is to ask another student to remind you. Would you like to have either John or Mary remind you?"*

Blank Forms

APPENDIX A

The ADD/ADHD Iceberg Chart

The Tip of the Iceberg—the obvious ADD/ADHD behaviors:

HYPERACTIVITY	IMPULSIVITY	INATTENTION
_____	_____	_____
_____	_____	_____
_____	_____	_____
_____	_____	_____

"Hidden Beneath the Surface"— the not-so-obvious behaviors:

3 YEAR BRAIN MATURATION 30% DEVELOPMENTAL DELAY
Less mature
Less responsible
14 year old acts like 10

NEUROTRANSMITTER DEFICITS IMPACT BEHAVIOR
Inefficient levels of neurotransmitters (norepinephrine, dopamine, and serotonin) result in reduced brain activity on thinking tasks

COEXISTING CONDITIONS
(2/3 have at least one other condition)

_____
_____
_____
_____

WEAK EXECUTIVE FUNCTIONING

_____
_____
_____
_____

ADD/ADHD is often more complex than most people realize! Like icebergs, many problems related to ADD/ADHD are not visible. ADD/ADHD may be mild, moderate, or severe, is likely to co-exist with other conditions, and may be a disability for some students.

SERIOUS LEARNING PROBLEMS (90%)
(Specific Learning Disability; 25-50%)

_____
_____
_____
_____
_____
_____
_____

SLEEP DISTURBANCE (56%)

_____
_____
_____
_____

IMPAIRED SENSE OF TIME

_____
_____
_____
_____

NOT LEARNING EASILY FROM REWARDS AND PUNISHMENT

_____
_____
_____
_____

LOW FRUSTRATION TOLERANCE
(Difficulty Controlling Emotions)

_____
_____
_____

Essay Organizer ("Mind Map")

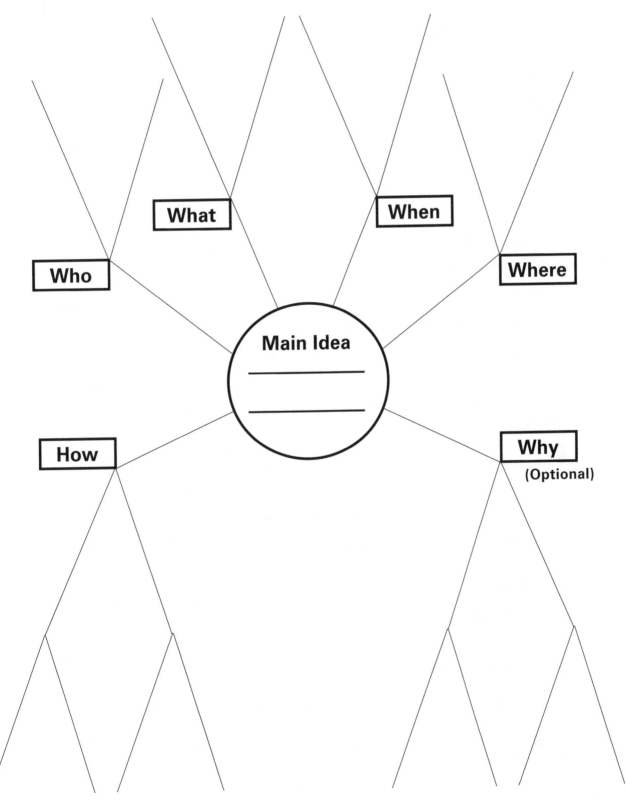

What

When

Who

Where

Main Idea

How

Why
(Optional)

Student Outline for Writing an Essay

I. Thesis Paragraph *(Topic—Mentors)*

    A. Definition _____

    B. Importance _____

    C. Three key traits   _____   _____   _____

II. First Supporting Paragraph

    A. Topic sentence (1st trait) _____

    B. Supporting examples _____

    _____

    _____

    C. Transition to next paragraph _____

III. Second Supporting Paragraph

    A. Topic sentence (2nd trait) _____

    B. Supporting examples _____

    _____

    _____

    C. Transition to next paragraph _____

IV. Third Supporting Paragraph

    A. Topic Sentence (3rd trait)_____

    B. Supporting examples _____

    _____

    _____

V. Conclusion

    A. Restate the importance of having a mentor_____

    B. Restate the three key character traits

    _____   _____   _____

    C. Explain what difference a mentor would make in your life. _____

    _____

Developed by Marcy Winograd, English Department, Paul Revere Middle School, Los Angeles, CA.

See Summary 65 for tips on adding the square to the top of a class assignment or worksheet as a visual cue and external reminder to begin working promptly.

Academic Contract

Name: _____ **Period:** _____

Biology – Contract Seven – Ecology Unit
Student Instructional Contract

Class Lectures—Required   Make sure all note-taking forms are completed.

1. (5 pts.) Bio-C7.1 Ecology and Populations PPT notes

2. (5 pts.) Bio-C7.2 Chains, Webs, Cycles, and Pollution PPT notes

3. (5 pts.) Bio-C7.3 Biome PPT notes

Assignments and Activities—Required

4. (3 pts.) Bio-C7.4 Ecology and Populations Vocabulary Matching

5. (2 pts.) Bio-C7.5 Chains, Webs, Cycles, and Pollution Vocabulary Matching

Your Choice! Choose two from the assignments below.

6. (5 pts.) Bio-C7.6 Estimating the Trends in a Deer Population

7. (2 pts.) Bio-C7.7 Graphing Human Population Growth

8. (2 pts.) Bio-C7.8   Interpreting Ecological Data

Your Choice Again! Choose two from the assignments below.

9.   (5 pts.) Bio-C7.9 Discovering the Parts of Food Chains and Food Webs

10. (3 pts.) Bio-C7.10 Using Random Sampling

11. (3 pts.) Bio-C7.11 Ecological Succession

Projects and/or Labs—Required

12. (10 pts.) Bio-C7.12   Biome Diorama (Work with a partner)

13. (5 pts) Bio-C7.13 Biogeochemical Cycles Foldable

Extra Credit (2pts)

14. Review Questions

Test—Required

15. (50 pts) Bio-C7.15 – Ecology Test

Tests are multiple choice. Hint: Study!!!!!

Developed by Jackie Bailey, Phoenix School, Dalton, GA.

APPENDIX A5 *Student Goal Setting Contract*

Date: _____

I,_____, agree to do things listed below. I will check each day I achieve my goal.

	M	T	W	TH	F
1.					
2.					
3.					
4.					
5.					

I, _____ (teacher, parent, or other), agree to provide

assistance by_____

We, _____ and _____, will meet to discuss

progress: _____(when, how often, and where).

We have read and talked about this contract and are signing it to show that we agree to these terms.

Signatures:

_____
(student)

_____
(teacher)

Options:
- The following reward/privilege will be given to the student for successfully completing the contract. _____
For example when the student earns 5 check marks, even if it takes more than a week, he gets reward/privilege provided by either the parents or teacher.
- The student will take this contract home to parents at the end of the week.

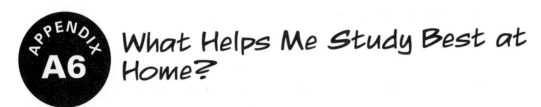

What Helps Me Study Best at Home?

Sometimes where, when, and how you study makes a big difference. Not every student likes to study the same way. What works best for you when you do your homework?

Put a ✔ next to the things that work best for you.

1. When: ____ right after school when I get home

   ____ after school, but after a break

   ____ how long a break do you need? _____

   ____ after dinner

   ____ in the morning

   ____ other _____

2. With: ____ myself only

   ____ someone in the room with me

   ____ a friend

   ____ parent

   ____ tutor

   ____ other _____

3. Where: ____ in my room   ____ in the kitchen

   ____ on the floor   ____ in the family room

   ____ on the bed   ____ in the dining room

   ____ at my desk   ____ other _____

4. Conditions: ____ sitting   ____ near a lamp

   ____ lying down   ____ in bright light

   ____ playing music   ____ walking around

   ____ in a quiet area   ____ other _____

5. How long before a break?

   ____ 15 minutes   ____ 1 hour

   ____ 30 minutes   ____ finish a certain part of the work

   (one half, one third, or one section)

6. What helps me stay organized and complete my homework?

____ use an assignment book   ____ plan what I do first

____ write down the assignments   ____ estimate how long it will take

____ call a friend for assignments   ____ put finished work in one place

____ keep an extra book at home   ____ color code folders and book covers

____ dictate assignments on a recorder

____ other _____

7. What helps me learn and remember information?

____ write things down

____ draw a picture

____ use a mind map

____ use flash cards

____ type it into a computer

____ listen to a tape recorder

____ read things out loud

____ talk about the information

____ make or build something

____ use associations; mnemonics

____ use songs or rhymes

____ other _____

*Adapted from form developed by Joan Helbing, **Focus on ADD**, the Wisconsin ADD Consortium Newsletter, February, 1998.*

Name: _____ **Class/Teacher:** _____

Project Title or Focus: _____ **Due Date:** _____

I. <u>Plan</u>: **What do you have to do? What are all the project requirements?**

(Check box when complete.)

Project Graphic Organizer

Projects may be complex and involve multiple steps. Sometimes in the rush of completing the project some key information may be overlooked. Record all requirements on this page so that no steps will be forgotten. Good Luck!

I. Plan: What are all the project requirements? What do I need?

■ Complete the Project Graphic Organizer on the facing page.

<u>Check resources needed:</u>

____ library visit

____ books

____ magazine articles

____ Internet

____ interviews

_____

_____

<u>Check products needed:</u>

____ written report

____ report cover

____ poster

____ pictures

____ bibliography

____ timelines with dates

____ model

____ maps

_____

_____

_____

_____

II. Prioritize: Do I need to set priorities? _____yes _____ no

■ Which one do I need to do first? _____

■ Which one is most complicated and will take the most time? _____

■ Do I need to allow time to order a book from the library or schedule a visit for an interview? _____

■ Number the remaining parts of the project on the organizer in the order you will do them.

III. Schedule: How long will the project take? _____ (estimate)

■ Put steps on the Weekly Project Planner (see Appendix A8).

IV. Do it: Complete all the steps on the Weekly Project Planner.

■ Check each step off on the Project Graphic Organizer when it is completed.

Weekly Project Planner

Write in the due date first. Then schedule each activity backward from there until all steps are written on the planner.

Try to schedule activities at regular intervals so that you won't end up doing too much on any given day or cramming all your work in at the last minute. Of course, you may need to change your schedule, depending on your energy level, unforeseen delays, etc. Some nights you may do four activities and the next night only one.

You may want to do all the research the first week and the written report the second. Or you may prefer to research half the topics, write half the report, and then work on the last half of the project.

Weekly Project Planner—Week 1_____ Month_____						
	Monday	**Tuesday**	**Wednesday**	**Thursday**	**Friday**	**Saturday**
7:30						
8:00						
8:30						
9:00						
9:30						
10:00						
10:30						
11:00						
11:30						
12:00						
12:30						
1:00						**Sunday**
1:30						
2:00						
2:30						
3:00						
3:30						
4:00						
4:30						
5:00						
5:30						
6:00						
6:30						
Evening						

A

Photocopy needed research, plus the publisher's name, publication date, and city. Put it all in a folder.

Some work may be completed at school during class and visits to the school library; the rest may be done via the Internet at the local library or at home.

Weekly Project Planner—Week 2					Month	
	Monday	**Tuesday**	**Wednesday**	**Thursday**	**Friday**	**Saturday**
7:30						
8:00						
8:30						
9:00						
9:30						
10:00						
10:30						
11:00						
11:30						
12:00						
12:30						
1:00						**Sunday**
1:30						
2:00						
2:30						
3:00						
3:30						
4:00						
4:30						
5:00						
5:30						
6:00						
6:30						
Evening						

Medication Effectiveness at School: Teacher Rating

APPENDIX A9

Student's name: _____ **Date & class:** _____

Completed by: _____ **Time of day observed:** _____

To assess the impact medication is having on a student's schoolwork, each teacher should answer several key questions. When medication is working properly and learning problems have been identified, the student should be doing much better in school. If the teacher cannot check the "Strongly agree" and "Agree" columns, then problems may still exist in several areas: 1) the proper accommodations are not being provided for the student's learning problems, 2) executive function deficits are not being addressed, or 3) the medication regimen may not be right for the student. Please circle the answer that best describes the student's behavior.

Academic Performance:

	Strongly Agree	Agree	Neutral	Disagree	Strongly Disagree
When the student is in my class, s/he:					
1. pays attention	1	2	3	4	5
2. completes class and homework	1	2	3	4	5
3. does work correctly	1	2	3	4	5
4. complies with requests	1	2	3	4	5
5. makes passing grades	1	2	3	4	5

ADD/ADHD-Related Behaviors, Including Executive Function

If the student is on medication and is not doing well in school, what else could be causing continuing problems? Are there any ADD/ADHD-related behaviors that are interfering with the student's ability to succeed in school?

ADD/ADHD-Essential Related Skills:

The student:					
6. organizes material/information well	1	2	3	4	5
7. gets started easily on work	1	2	3	4	5
8. manages time well	1	2	3	4	5
9. Finishes long-term projects with no problems	1	2	3	4	5
10. remembers things easily	1	2	3	4	5
11. is on time to class	1	2	3	4	5
12. is on time to school	1	2	3	4	5
13. thinks carefully before acting or speaking	1	2	3	4	5
14. is awake and alert in class	1	2	3	4	5

Ask parents about any sleep problems. According to them, the student:					
15. falls asleep easily	1	2	3	4	5
16. wakes up easily	1	2	3	4	5

Comments: _____

If problems still exist, should a behavioral intervention plan be developed to provide additional accommodations or teach the student compensatory skills, or should teachers suggest that parents seek medical advice?

Medication Effectiveness at School: Student Rating

Student's name: _____ **Date & class:** _____

Completed by: _____ **Time of day observed:** _____

Sometimes students themselves are the best judges of how well medication is working. To assess the impact medication is having on your schoolwork, please answer the questions below. When medication is working properly and learning problems have been identified, you should be doing much better in school. If you cannot check the "Strongly agree" and "Agree" columns, then problems may still exist in several areas: 1) the proper accommodations are not being provided for your learning problems, 2) executive function deficits are not being addressed, or 3) the medication regimen may not be right for you. Please circle the answer that best describes your behavior.

Academic Performance:

	Strongly Agree	Agree	Neutral	Disagree	Strongly Disagree
When I am in class, I:					
1. listen and pay attention	1	2	3	4	5
2. complete my class work	1	2	3	4	5
3. complete my homework (at home)	1	2	3	4	5
4. do my work correctly	1	2	3	4	5
5. do what the teacher tells me to do	1	2	3	4	5
6. make passing grades	1	2	3	4	5

ADD/ADHD-Related Behaviors, Including Executive Function

If you are on medication and are not doing well in school, what else could be causing continuing problems? Are there any ADD/ADHD-related behaviors that are interfering with your ability to succeed in school?

ADD/ADHD-Essential Related Behaviors:

These things describe me. I:					
7. organize materials/information well	1	2	3	4	5
8. get started easily on work	1	2	3	4	5
9. manage time well	1	2	3	4	5
10. finish long-term projects with no problems	1	2	3	4	5
11. remember things easily	1	2	3	4	5
12. am on time to class	1	2	3	4	5
am on time to school	1	2	3	4	5
13. stop and think before I do or say anything	1	2	3	4	5
14. am awake and alert in class	1	2	3	4	5
Do you have any sleep problems? I:					
15. fall asleep easily	1	2	3	4	5
16. wake up easily	1	2	3	4	5

Comments: _____

My main concern right now is: _____

Ways I am improving in this area: _____

Reframing ADD/ADHD Behaviors

Name _____ **Grade** _____ **Date** _____

STRENGTHS
Home/Community/School

Examples of Reframing Common ADD/ADHD Behaviors

When students are struggling, it is easy to get caught up in focusing on their problem behaviors. It is extremely important to stop and take time to identify each student's strengths and special talents. Examples of ways to reframe negative behaviors may help teachers and parents develop a list of the teenager's strengths. A completed form is shown in Summary 7.

Remember that the desirability of behaviors changes over time. Characteristics that are not valued in students in school may be valued in the adult work world. Discuss the teenager's strengths with him. Ask him if he has anything to add to the list.

BOSSINESS:	"leadership" (albeit carried too far)
HYPERACTIVE:	"energetic" / "high energy" / "does ten projects at one time" / "works long hours"
STRONG-WILLED:	"tenacious"
DAY DREAMER:	"creative" / "innovative" / "imaginative"
DARING:	"risk taker" / "willing to try new things"
LAZY:	"laid back" / "Type B personalities live longer"
INSTIGATOR:	"initiator" / "innovative"
MANIPULATIVE:	"delegates" / "gets others to do the job"
AGGRESSIVE:	"assertive" / "doesn't let people take advantage of him"
QUESTIONS AUTHORITY:	"independent" / "free thinker" / "makes own decisions"
ARGUMENTATIVE:	"persuasive" / "may be attorney material"
POOR HANDWRITING:	"maybe he'll be a doctor one day"

Additional Information

APPENDIX B

Writing a Three-part Essay

These basic tips may be helpful to parents who are working with their teenager as he or she writes an essay. The essay outline in Appendix A3 may also be helpful.

1. **Introduction: "Tell what you are going to tell":**

   The introduction for a high school essay may include approximately three sentences, of perhaps 40 words total. The writer is like a fisherman who is trying to hook the reader.

   - **Start with the hook.** Sometimes a question or quotation in the first sentence will hook the reader.
   - **Include the thesis statement.** The main idea that is the basis for the whole paper is stated in this first paragraph. *"When I was five years old, I experienced something very unexpected when I went on a trip with my father."*
   - **Model the desired behavior.** If the student is having trouble coming up with an introduction, the teacher or parent may write an example drawn from his or her own experience that addresses the assigned topic.
   - **Include a planning statement.** Tell the reader what is coming in the essay, but don't let the cat out of the bag. *"This trip with my father is one I'll never forget for several reasons."* Also don't explicitly tell the reader what you are going to tell him. Don't say, for example, *"I am going to tell you about a situation I experienced."*

   Example of an Introductory Paragraph:

   Have you ever known a girl who spent the night in a Young Men's Christian (YMCA) dormitory? When I was five years old, I went on an incredible trip with my dad. Several things happened on this trip that were very exciting."

2. **The Body: "Tell It."**

   The body of the essay may include from two to perhaps ten paragraphs of roughly 100 words each. It just depends on how much the writer has to say. There is nothing magic about a "five-paragraph essay."

   - **Begin the first body paragraph with a transition sentence.** The transition sentence should link the first body paragraph with the introductory paragraph in some way. For example, *"My first experience was . . ."* or *"First we drove all the way to Atlanta. It was the first time I had ever been to such a big city."* This first sentence should be a concrete statement.
   - **Write more information that is related to the opening sentence.** For example, the student may describe how he felt about the event, how he or someone else reacted, or give an example.
   - **Use transition sentences to begin other paragraphs.** For example: *"Our next adventure took us to . . ."* or *"The following day we went to the Georgia Capitol building where my dad was serving in the legislature."* Then add other related sentences.

3. **The Closing Paragraph: "Tell You What I Told You":**

The conclusion may also consist of about 40 words.

- Begin the conclusion with a word signaling you are reaching the end. For example, begin with *"Finally," "In conclusion," "In the end,"* or *"In summary."*
- Summarize. Writers don't have to repeat their thesis statement, but they may if they wish. However, don't use the same words that were in the introductory paragraph. You may also tell something you have learned.
- Try to come up with a "zinger" for the last sentence. Leave the reader thinking. The sentence may also be a personal one that describes the writer's feelings. *"I will never forget my exciting trip to Atlanta, the state capitol, and what happened when I was the only girl spending the night in the YMCA."*

Menu of Classroom Accommodations

Many school systems develop menus of possible classroom accommodations that may be helpful to students with ADD, ADHD, or other learning problems. This helpful menu was developed by the Walker County School System in LaFayette, Georgia. Do not be afraid to add other needed accommodations that may not be on the list. Numerous suggestions in this book can be effective and could be added to a student's IEP.

Name: _____   Date IEP Developed: ____/____/____
                                       Duration: _____
                                       Review Date: ____/____/____

Classroom/Program Modifications
Classroom/Program Modification Recommendations:
(To advance appropriately toward attaining goals; to be involved and progress in the general curriculum; to participate in extracurricular and non-academic activities; to be educated and participate with other non-disabled students)

A. Supplementary Aids and Services: (Access to/use of)
___Calculator
___Tape recorder (lectures and instruction)
___Reading marker
___Taped material/talking books
___Adapted furniture
___Note taker
___Visual aids to support instruction
___Modified/alternative textbooks and/or workbooks
___Feeding equipment
___Manipulative materials/study aids
___Times tables
___Augmentative/alternative communication
___Large print materials
___Computer/Word Processor
___Someone to read materials
___Preferential seating
___Study Carrel
___Other_____

B. Instructional Modifications or Supports for School Personnel:
___Secure attention before giving directions
___Have student repeat directions to check for understanding
___Material should be broken down into manageable parts
___Peer tutor/paired working arrangements
___Allow previewing of content, concepts and vocabulary
___Directions should be simplified as needed, oral, short, specific, repeated
___Oral directions should be supported with written backup
___Emphasis on major points
___Use techniques of repetition, review and summarization
___Provide frequent feedback and praise
___Check work frequently to determine level of understanding
___Other _____

Assignments:
___Written on board
___Substitute projects for written work
___Extra time for completion
___Given orally
___Provide peer assistance
___Provide printed copy of board work/notes
___Provide study guides/questions
___Provide extra review/drill and worksheets
___Assignment Notebook
___Presented and/or completed orally
___Reduce/shorten written assignments
___Reduce/shorten reading assignments
___Reduce number of spelling words
___Special projects in lieu of regular assignments
___Lower reading level of materials
___Opportunity to leave class for resource assistance
___Provide individual assistance
___Allow difficult assignments to be completed in resource room
___Other_____

C. Grading Modifications:
___Alternative/modified grading procedures (Specify) _____
___Special education grades based on IEP mastery
___Course grades will be assigned by regular education teacher
___Course grades will be assigned by regular education and special education teacher
___Regular education grading will be used in the following classes/subjects: _____
___Special education report card will be utilized
___Course grades will be assigned by special education teacher
___Interpretation of grades are designated on regular report cards
___Regular education grades based on effort, attitude and cooperation
___Grading modifications are designated on regular report cards
___Other _____

D. Testing Modifications: (Within the classroom)
___Extra time for completion of exams
___Lower readability
___Oral exam with oral response
___Short answer format
___Recognition format (multiple choice w/ two possible answers)
___Recall with cues format (fill in blank with word bank)
___Use of study sheets, notes, open book
___Include class participation in evaluation
___Fewer questions/problems on exams
___Alternative to tests (projects, reports, demonstrations, etc.)
___Individual/small group testing
___Oral exam w/written response
___Accept close approximations
___Allow tests to be taken in resource room
___Scheduling (Specify)_____
___Other _____

IEP Transition Services

This form serves as a reminder of key categories to address in a Transition Plan for teenagers. See Summary 53 for specific suggestions for possible services. This form was also developed by the Walker County (Georgia) School System.

Initial Transition Plan Date: _____   **Dates(s) Transition Plan Reviewed/Revised:** _____

Student Preferences, Needs, Interests: _____

_____

_____

Consideration of Course of Study (at age 14, or younger, if appropriate): _____

_____

_____

Needed Transition Services (at age 16, or younger, if appropriate):
(Include Interagency Responsibilities or Linkages, if any)

If needed, discuss the activities, person responsible, timelines, and anticipated outcomes of this activity.

*If the IEP Team determines that the student does not need services in one of more of these areas, include a statement to that effect and the basis upon which the determination was made.

*Instruction: _____

_____

_____

*Related Services: _____

_____

_____

*Community Experiences: _____

_____

_____

*Development of Employment and Other Post-School Adult Living Objectives: _____

_____

_____

If Appropriate, Acquisition of Daily Living Skills and Functional Vocational Evaluation: _____

_____

_____

Transfer of Rights (Required at age 17):

_____ was informed on _____ of his/her rights, if any, that will transfer at age 18.

      Student Name   *Date*

Functional Behavior Assessment (FBA): Common Behaviors

Keep in mind that misbehavior is often linked to deficits in basic skills that are essential to completing the required academic tasks. An effective behavior intervention plan will ensure the teaching of absent academic skills.

This partial list of behaviors may help teachers as they gather information and develop a Behavior Intervention Plan. The list was compiled from information developed by the Gwinnett County (Georgia) School System, Chicago Public Schools, Walker County (Georgia) School System, and Joan Helbing, ADD Consultant, Appleton Area Schools in Wisconsin. See Summary 68 for more information on Functional Behavior Assessment.

Common Misbehaviors	Context	Antecedent or Trigger	Contributing Factors
Ignoring the teacher	Class/subject	Academic deficits	Medication dose too low
Talking back and arguing	➤ gym/P.E., music, art, keyboarding, etc.	Task too difficult	Medication not fully effective; took meds on the ride to school
Yelling or cursing	➤ language arts, math, science, history, etc.	Task too long	medication has worn off
Fighting	Location	Transition: beginning or end of class, change from P.E., lunch, or between classes	Failing a class
Destroying property	➤ lunchroom		Learning problems in math or language arts
Disruptive behavior: talking to and laughing with other students inappropriately	➤ bathroom ➤ hallway ➤ outside, but on school grounds	Request from teacher	ADD/ADHD/EF behaviors: impulsivity, talking and acting without thinking; poor organizational skills; difficulty getting started and finishing; impaired sense of time
Refusing to comply with teacher requests	➤ at school function, but not on school grounds	Verbal redirection by teacher	
	➤ near school, but not on grounds	Verbal correction by teacher	
Pushing or hitting a teacher	Time of day	Told "no"	
Smoking at school		Teasing by other students	Breakup with girlfriend or boyfriend
Possession of a weapon or drugs at school		Confronted by teacher	Conflicting activities: ball game, school play, family or religious activities
Bullying other students		Asked to speak in front of class	
		Having to wait for the teacher	Conflicts with parents
		Teacher attention to others	Rejection by a friend
		Close physical proximity; teacher is "in his face"	
		Visitor to class	
		Substitute teacher	

Function of the Behavior	Consequences	Student Reaction	Intervention Strategies
For students with ADHD, simple impulsivity ➤ serves no specific function; ➤ no underlying conscious purpose; Result of academic skill or performance deficit ➤ covering up not knowing how to do the work ➤ distract the teacher so she won't know he can't do the work Escape or avoidance ➤ avoiding embarrassment ➤ avoiding a difficult task To get attention Justice or revenge Acceptance and affiliation: "I'm one of the cool guys" Power or control Expression of self Communication Access to rewards Symptoms of a disorder	Response of teacher: ➤ ignored ➤ redirected ➤ verbal warning ➤ verbal reprimand ➤ gave personal space ➤ natural consequence ➤ reflection ➤ sent to office ➤ removal of teacher's positive reinforcement ➤ halted activity; waited for student to behave ➤ physical restraint ➤ parental contact ➤ counseling ➤ isolation in class ➤ denied privileges ➤ restitution ➤ modified day (e.g., half day) ➤ sent home ➤ detention ➤ in-school suspension ➤ suspension ➤ called police ➤ administrative hearing ➤ expulsion Response of classmates: ➤ reinforced behavior by laughing	Stopped Continued Intensified; escalated Was remorseful Apologized Cried Displayed new behavior Walked away from the teacher and out of class	Ensure medications are effective Modify antecedent intervention Provide more visual, auditory prompts & supervision Teach alternative behavior Praise Special activities or privileges Points or tokens Tangible reinforcers Teach self-control skills Visit guidance counselor Parent contact Student selects reinforcing activity Peer mentor Self-management program Written contract Clarify rules & expected behavior Change seating Change schedule Counseling Reminders about expected behavior

Other Information to Gather

Continuation of Behavior: If behavior is repeated, is it due to failure to address:
1. the "contributing factors," such as forgetting medication or
2. the reason behind the behavior such as academic skill deficits?

Rewards: Talk with the student to find out what he or she thinks is a reward—what is important to him. The teacher can then give the student the opportunity to earn the reward by complying with school rules and behaving properly.

Index

About the Author

*C*hris Abney Zeigler Dendy, M.S., is an author, former educator, school psychologist, and children's mental health professional with over 40 years of experience. Perhaps more importantly, she is the mother of three grown children and four grandchildren who also have ADHD. In popular demand as a speaker, she presents nationally and internationally on ADHD, learning disabilities, and executive functions.

Chris served on the executive committee of the national CHADD Board from 2001-2005. Presently she and her husband are both members of CHADD's President's Council. They have also served on ADDA-SR's Advisory Board. In 2006 she received awards from both groups. CHADD presented Chris with the prestigious Hall of Fame Award in recognition of her outstanding contributions to the field. Earlier that year, she and her husband were awarded ADDA-SR's Eisenberg award for their efforts to educate families, educators, and other professionals about ADHD. She is the author of four highly acclaimed books and three videos. For more information about Chris, her books, and videos, visit *www.chrisdendy.com*